THE
LONGMOOR
MILITARY RAILWAY
A New History

On 4th October 1958, Dick Riley captured WD 70270 (now renumbered WD 876) in full LMR livery, with nameplates *Bari* [2] transferred from WD 70271. Note the cast running numbers on its front buffer beam. Alongside was the prototype 'WD Light Shunter', (WD 8200), possibly still officially on trials as it had not yet been given the full LMR livery. *Bari* [2] had acquired a pair of German-pattern head lamps.   *R. C. Riley*

Front Cover: The pride of the fleet of new diesel locomotives in the 1960s was WD 890 (later 610) *General Lord Robertson*, seen here shortly after arrival at Longmoor from the works of Rolls Royce/Sentinel in 1963. The covered-in walkways along the footplate, Sentinel logo incorporated into the lining and Shining Sword on the radiator grille were all Sentinel hallmarks from that era.   *WD photograph*

Rear Cover, Top: During the RCTS visit to the LMR on 30th April 1966, AD 196 hauled the first of two scheduled trains round the Hollywater Loop. Brake vans were provided to allow easier access to and from the train for photographers alighting to film the photographic 'run-pasts'.
P. J. Lynch, Kidderminster Railway Museum Photograph C/015875

Rear Cover, Middle: AD 196 started so many lineside fires during its journey around the Hollywater Loop that it was decided that the second train would have to be hauled by a diesel locomotive. AD 878 *Basra* [2] was photographed passing the platform at Woolmer, with Two Range Halt blockpost in the background.   *P. J. Lynch, Kidderminster Railway Museum Photograph C/015879*

Rear Cover, Bottom: The Ruston diesel locomotive AD 425 arrived at Longmoor painted in dark green, and retained that livery. At the Open Day on 5th July 1969 it was deployed hauling a one-coach train, despite the fact that the locomotive was not fitted with continuous brakes. It was photographed hauling coach ARMY 5310, one of the ex-British Railways Mark I suburban coaches. A number of these arrived at Longmoor still in BR maroon livery (with lining) and were eventually repainted in the LMR blue livery. The exception was ARMY 5310, which was painted in Army green when it arrived. The letters LMR were subsequently added, but more widely spaced than on the ex-BR coaches that were painted into blue.
W. Potter, Kidderminster Railway Museum Photograph C/006715

Lightmoor Press

Lightmoor Press is an imprint of Black Dwarf Lightmoor Publications Limited
144b Lydney Industrial Estate, Harbour Road
Lydney, Gloucestershire, GL15 4EJ
www.lightmoor.co.uk
Printed and bound by Berforts Information Press, Eynsham
Set in 10pt Minion Pro

Naming WD 71232 *Tobruk* (Whitcomb Bo-Bo diesel Electric, works number 60174 of 1941) at Longmoor Downs platform during the Public Day in 1948. The ceremony was performed by General (Field Marshall from January 1949) Sir William Slim. With distinguished service in both the 1914-1918 and 1939-1945 conflicts, Slim retired from the Army on 11 May 1948 to take up the role of Deputy Chairman of the newly-formed Railway Executive. He was however brought out of 'retirement' to become Chief of the Imperial General Staff on appointment to the Army Council from 1st January 1949, the first Indian Army Officer to become CIGS. The man crouching down on the left in this photograph was Waller, a local photographer who for many years took the portraits of the many groups of men who were trained at Longmoor. The locomotive was carrying the Unit Badge (see page 5) on the cab side, above the LMR lettering. The differences between the cab structure of this locomotive and that of a 'standard' Whitcomb (see illustration facing page 565) are apparent, and include a raised step up into the cab, a modified cab profile (hence the welding on the cab side), different ventilators below the cab windows and along the bonnet sides, and the fitting of handrails along the full length of the footplate. *WD photograph*

THE
LONGMOOR
MILITARY RAILWAY

A New History
Volume Three:
The Inevitable Closure,
Locomotives & Rolling Stock

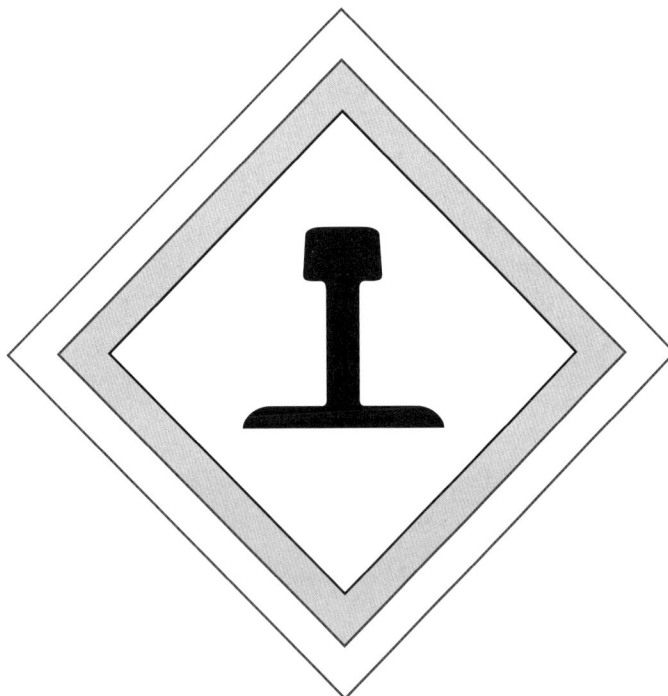

Colonel David W. Ronald
&
Mike Christensen OBE

A number of Whitcomb Bo-Bo diesel electric locomotives were prepared and tested at Longmoor without ever becoming part of the LMR's allocation of locomotives. One such was 7961, which carried that number (in USA style) in number plates at both ends of the locomotive. The locomotive was standing outside the Diesel Shop at Longmoor, in front of the Signal School building. Note the dispatch riders, with their motorcycles, in readiness beside the Signal School.

Photographer unknown

CONTENTS

16. 1965 to 1975 – The Final Era 567
17. Steam Locomotives at Longmoor 613
18. The Austerity Saddle Tank Locomotives 667
19. Other Rolling Stock: Internal Combustion Locomotives and Rail Cars 687
    Passenger, Goods & Construction Rolling Stock 710
20. Longmoor on Film 767
21. The Legacy of Longmoor 779
22. Longmoor in Colour 789
Appendices
Appendix 16. LMR Train Graph 816
Appendix 17. Summary of Establishment Steam Locomotives 818
Appendix 18. Summary of Standard Gauge Internal Combustion Locomotives 820
Appendix 19. Table of Rail Cars 821
Appendix 20. LMR Goods and Passenger Rolling Stock – 1943 to c1956 822
Appendix 21. LMR Rolling Stock – 1956 Numbering Series 827
Appendix 22. WIMR/LMR Rolling Stock Statistics 834
Appendix 23. Notes on Rolling Stock Liveries 835
Appendix 24. Where Are They Now? 837
Appendix 25. List of Commandants 839
Bibliography 840
Errata 841
Index 842

Terminology

Throughout the book, place names are rendered in the form and spelling used in contemporary sources. Where weights and measures were originally given in 'Imperial' units, these have been retained. The vocabulary (and spelling) of contemporary military documents has been used with explanations where appropriate.

Orientation

In preparing the drawings for this book, layout diagrams and maps have been prepared using the convention that 'towards Bordon' is to the left. Signalling diagrams have, however, followed the convention that the layout is shown as viewed by the blockman, so 'towards Bordon' may be to the right on a signalling diagram.

Acknowledgements

In concluding Volume One, we were able to include an acknowledgement of the great debt which this entire project owes to the late Colonel Gerry Williams. Whilst this debt remains undiminished, we are anxious to record our deep appreciation for all the additional help which has been forthcoming during the preparation of Volumes Two and Three. These volumes deal with events which are today still within living memory of those who took part in them. Whilst this brings both colour and character to our story, it also opens the door to good-natured conflict over matters of detail.

We hope that contributors to Volumes Two and Three will accept that what we have written represents a distillation of individual accounts where these vary. The opinions expressed remain those of the authors and we accept full responsibility for them. The list of contributors below is intended to be comprehensive but should anyone have been accidentally omitted, our thanks go equally to them.

For their personal contributions we would particularly like to thank:

Tony Adams, John Ailwood, Roger Bagnall, the late Hugh Ballantyne, John Bate, Alan Blackburn, Laurence Bindley, Barry Buckfield, the late David Carpenter, Roger Carpenter, Paul Chancellor (Colour Rail), Frank Collinson, Antony Coulls, Peter Coulls, Tim Edwards, Tony Edwards, Jez Fordham, Neil Howard, G. Huxley, Tony Kelly, Winston McCanna, George Moon, Iain Pardoe, John Payne, John W. Rees, Gordon Rushton, John Salmon, Chris Scott, Chris Shepheard, David Shepherd, Gordon Starling, Bryan Stone, Chris Tanous, John Teasdale, G. R. Weddell, Colin Withey, F. A. Wycherley, not forgetting the many contributors to the World War Two Railway Study Group who have added notes relevant to Longmoor and the officers and men of 17 Port and Maritime Regiment for their assistance in allowing access to equipment so that it could be photographed.

In addition we would like especially thank George Moon, John Poyntz and Laurence Bindley for their sterling work which, after many iterations, has enabled us to produce with some confidence the rolling stock lists in the Appendices to Volume Three.

Once again it is a great pleasure to acknowledge the hard work of Mark and Hannah Christensen and Clare Pope in proof reading all the text.

Time marches on – taking with it the memories of ever more of the participants in the story which we have attempted to relate. Much of the Longmoor story is already history, which we trust all the contributors will find it to be set out in a relevant and balanced way in our three volumes.

A summer's day at Longmoor, with WD 102 propelling a raft of WARFLAT wagons up from Longmoor Yard towards the platform at Longmoor Downs. By this date the Bottom Crossing had been reduced to a single line of rails, but the later road traffic lights had not yet been installed. The signal in the background marked the location where the line to Liss passed over the road at the Top Crossing.   *Bryan Stone*

CHAPTER SIXTEEN

1965 to 1975 – THE FINAL ERA

The twelve months from July 1965 were probably the most eventful in the entire history of Longmoor. As far back as 1961, the seeds of change were being sown during staff discussions at the Ministry of Defence (MOD) – into which the former War Office was incorporated at that time. The British armed forces were still deployed world-wide but with far fewer resources than had been available at the end of World War Two. Warfare was becoming much more three-dimensional with the rapidly developing use of air power. These developments now expanded into the field of logistics. New aircraft (fixed and rotary wing) were coming into service, which for the first time made possible both the strategic and tactical deployment of large forces by air. In the endless conflict between firepower and mobility, aircraft became the second major 20th century boost to the mobility of armies. In land warfare, the capabilities of surface-mobile vehicles were already being overtaken by a variety of air-mobile systems. At the same time that National Service was ending in 1961, the need for military railwaymen was shrinking dramatically. What then was to be the role of Longmoor and the LMR in support of the late 20th century army? Whilst other parts of the RE Transportation service had war tasks, Longmoor was increasingly being left behind.

Formation of the Royal Corps of Transport

The formation of the new Royal Corps of Transport (RCT) was marked on 15th July 1965 by re-badging parades wherever units of the new Corps and its constituents were to be found. Buttons, badges and most of the uniform accoutrements were changed, save for the Sappers' blue lanyard worn on the right shoulder on parade uniforms – and even this migrated to the opposite shoulder in the new Corps. All this added to an atmosphere of uncertainty at Longmoor where a completely new organisation known as the School of Transport was set up, replacing the former Transportation Centre. This brought together Longmoor's existing training commitments with those of the former RASC 'Mechanical Transport School', which remained located at Bordon. Initially it seems to have been the intention to concentrate as much post-recruit RCT training as was feasible at, or under command of, the School of Transport at Longmoor. So the future of Longmoor itself did not at this time appear to be threatened.

Re-badging Ceremonies at Longmoor

To mark the occasion, OC 8 Rly Sqn (Major Frank Carus) decided initially to hold a squadron parade on the evening of 15th July, just for the men of his unit. This quickly escalated into a regimental parade and then a full Transportation Centre parade with all former OCs of 8 Sqn invited, the salute taken by the Commandant (Brig John Woollett) and the Aldershot Band of the Royal Engineers on parade. After the parade, appropriate celebrations were laid on in the NAAFI and messes. With so many distinguished guests, the Officers' Mess dinner was a lively affair with appropriate Sapper booby traps ('matchstick mortars' and so on – harmless but noisy) for the unwary.

The less senior officers decided that the evening should be rounded off in style so an order (written by Capt Nic Carter on the back of a menu card) was delivered to the duty crew, calling out a 'blue saloon' special to meet the officers, their guests and the swing section of the RE Band at Longmoor Downs. The scratch crew then took over 100 passengers to Oakhanger and

During the 1950s and 1960s the LMR ran occasional special passenger trains, either for arranged enthusiast parties or for official guests. This view shows a train at Bordon, with the locomotive running round the train. The 6-wheeled saloon was initially only used for inspections or for VIPs. The two 'family saloons' were generally used for larger groups or courses. *Photographer unknown*

The 6-wheeled saloon was occasionally used to 'strengthen' passenger coach sets in ordinary traffic. On a summer's afternoon the guard settled down to enjoy the ride on the balcony of the saloon on a train going down to Liss – probably to collect a VIP for the journey back to Longmoor.
Bryan Stone

The saloon was commonly used for small visiting parties, though why it was stabled in the loop siding at Weavers Down on this occasion is not known. Possibly a VIP was visiting one of the regiments in camp in the adjacent Manton Lines. Hugh Ballantyne recorded that this was WD 196 passing with the 1145hrs Liss to Longmoor passenger train, but why the train was carrying the Special 2 disc is not known. 8th June 1968.
Hugh Ballantyne

With the train seen on page 566 safely over the Bottom Crossing, the flagman rode up to Longmoor Downs on the cab step.   *Bryan Stone*

back amidst much revelry, not all of which was appreciated by some of the householders living near the railway. So it fell to the Adjutant (Capt Mike Thompson) to don his best uniform and make the rounds with flowers for the complaining ladies the following day. For the staff of the LMR it was simply another case of 'business as usual'.

New Unit Titles and Responsibilities

Immediately after the formation of the RCT, the railway units at Longmoor retained their former titles, simply substituting 'RCT' for 'RE'. Very shortly afterwards however 49 Rly Trg Sqn disappeared, with its number taken by a new REME unit formed to run the LMR workshops. The remaining sappers (of the railway construction trades) formed a Construction Troop within 8 Rly Sqn where they remained until 1967 when permanent-way maintenance for MOD railways was handed over to the civilians of the newly-formed Ministry of Public Buildings and Works (MPBW). At this time, 8 Sqn lost the 'Railway' from its title, becoming a composite road transport squadron within which was to be found 411 Rly Optg Tp. This survived but with ever-diminishing manpower until January 1970 when it too was disbanded. In this environment, it was not long before postings and run-outs began to remove the former RE railway tradesmen and their accumulated skills. With no provision for technical training, particularly in railway workshop skills, the maintenance of the LMR became progressively less professional.

Formation of the School of Transport

Initially the School of Transport was organised into four wings. The School HQ and Officers' Wing were located at Longmoor along with departments responsible for Movements and Railway specialist training. The other wings: Mechanical Transport, Maritime and Air Despatch remained in their existing locations. Parts of the former RE Officers' Long Transportation Course were incorporated in a new Long Transport Course designed to train officers to fill senior appointments within the RCT. Brig Pat Claxton, who was appointed Commandant of the new school, took over in early 1966 from Brig John Woollett who was the last of the long line of Royal Engineer Commandants. A wise and diplomatic officer, Brig Pat tackled the many challenges of forming the new school in a calm but highly effective manner. Inevitably there were minor upsets and misunderstandings.

The underlying comedy of one such incident might not have been apparent at the time. One of the proudest possessions of the Officers' Mess was a trio of original paintings commissioned from Terence Cuneo by the British Transport Commission and later presented to the mess by the then BTC Chairman, General Lord Robertson. A few months into the life of the new Corps an officer, returning to the Mess after detached duty, observed the absence of all these fine pictures. When questioned, the Mess Secretary (an ex-RASC officer) remarked: "Oh, you must mean those railway posters – I've stowed them in the boot hole". A succinct explanation of their importance (and value) followed after which they were quickly re-hung in the main rooms of the mess.

The facilities at Longmoor were quickly developed so that very soon the School could host Corps Study Days and other prestigious events. To some extent this development was aided by the fact that Buller Barracks in Aldershot (the Corps HQ and 'home' of the former RASC) had to be closed for rebuilding, causing certain functions to be moved to Longmoor. Conversely, when the new Buller Barracks was opened, the pressure to move Corps activities back to Aldershot proved irresistible. For an organisation the size of the RCT it was clearly not feasible to have two major training establishments within twenty miles of each other and Longmoor suffered accordingly.

The Drewry Car [2] was delivered to the WIMR in 1936. In this wartime view (note the hooded cover on the headlight) it had been relettered LMR but was not yet carrying its running number (numbered 941 during the war and later allocated 9111). *Photographer unknown*

Although looking rather older than WD 9111, WD 9110 was delivered to Longmoor in May 1940. *Photographer unknown*

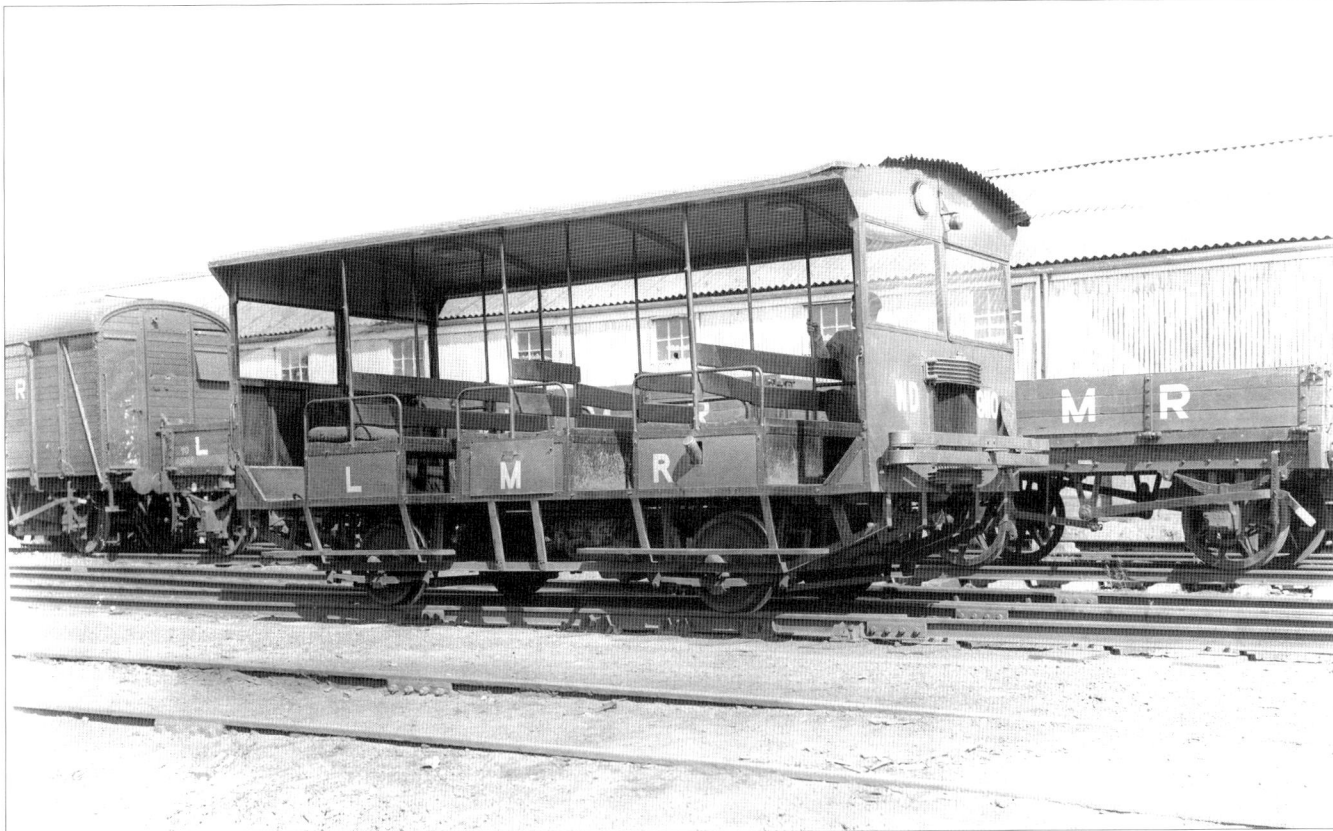

WD 9110, and its sister rail car 9109, were extremely useful for carrying small numbers of passengers and gave visiting officers a good all-round view of the railway.

WD photograph

Latterly the larger rail cars were replaced by two Wickham trollies. WD 9033 was a Type 27A Mark II rail car, delivered new to the LMR in 1954. This view shows WD 9033 leaving Oakhanger for Whitehill, while in the background WD 102 took on water.

K. Farmer

WD 9034 – seen here at Longmoor Downs – was a Type 40 Mark IIA rail car, heavier and more powerful than WD 9033. *courtesy Neil Howard*

WD 9034 – in a different style of livery and lettering – leaving Longmoor Downs in the Up direction on the Down line (Whitehill blockpost being closed) on a journey via Hollywater. The arrival of this rail car in 1960 allowed the disposal of the 1940 vehicles – 9110 in 1961 and 9109 in 1967.

Bryan Stone

By the 1950s the extensive sidings of Whitehill Sub-Depot – T.S.D. West (see page 250) – were no longer required for storage and were becoming increasingly overgrown with weeds. These sidings did however provide an ideal location for rerailing exercises, which could be undertaken clear of the main lines. On this occasion WD 102 was removing the vehicles used, after the end of an AER exercise.
Bryan Stone

The scene at Two Range Halt blockpost as WD 102 dragged its load across into Woolmer Yard – four vans, a dead locomotive and a raft of WARFLAT wagons. The double track main line towards Whitehill curved away to the right.
Bryan Stone

WD 102 drawing its train into Woolmer Yard. The first van was clearly fit only for use in rerailing exercises, in which it would be considered expendable. *Bryan Stone*

The train of vehicles used for the exercise included WD 178, now no longer in regular traffic. The reduced scale of Woolmer Yard is evident – previously sidings had filled the area in the middle distance which was now being reclaimed by forest scrub.

Bryan Stone

Wagons that had been damaged beyond economic repair during exercises were by now simply bulldozed out of the way and left. *Bryan Stone*

Having been withdrawn from traffic in 1958 WD 178 (formerly *Foligno*) was used as a rerailing engine until 1965. In the process it inevitably became increasingly battered. For this exercise the engine had simply been pushed off the end of the rails at sufficient speed for all six wheels to have sunk in the sandy heath. To make rerailing more difficult, the adjacent bogie wagon had been derailed as well. *Bryan Stone*

Impact of Changes on Trade Training

The immediate impact of the formation of the RCT fell on the individual officers and soldiers. It was not long before the effects began to be felt in the remaining railway units. It should be remembered that overall, the former Transportation and Movement Control personnel transferred from the Royal Engineers amounted to only around six per cent of the new Corps, approximately evenly divided between the two specialisations. In total the transfer amounted to 199 officers and 1,100 other ranks. 'Employability' was the cry of the day for manpower and career planners. One stumbling block to achieving wider soldier employability was the complex trade structure inherited from the former RE Transportation service. To be fair to those involved, determined efforts had been made during the previous five years to reduce this complexity. From the thirty-plus trades for which instruction had been provided at the end of World War Two, an almost fifty per cent reduction had already been made. Many of these had in any event been transferred to either REME (workshops trades) or RE (construction trades).

The most recent development in this field had been a drive to bring together port and railway trades either within the structure of the trade itself or by ensuring that the dual trades (which it was RE policy that all NCOs should hold) were taken from both port and railway skills. Thus by the time an NCO achieved senior rank, he would be expected to have both a port

and a railway trade thereby making him employable in all types of transportation unit. Some trades (e.g. Heavy Crane Operator) specifically included operation of rail, port and road-mobile equipment. In 1969, the remaining six railway operating trades recognised by the RCT were amalgamated into a single class 'A' trade of 'Railwayman'.

The Need for Military Railways – High Level Studies

Whilst all this internal and individual reorganisation was in progress, a major study was called for at the highest level into the future need for (and organisation of) the Army's railways. It was but one element of a whole range of studies then taking place throughout the Army which were to culminate in the 1967 Defence Review. The 'Future of Railways' study took place in 1966, with the final paper reaching the Army Board in the early months of 1967. The study pulled no punches. Apart from continuing war tasks in West Germany and Berlin, the study could only identify one other task which specifically called for military railwaymen on mobilisation. Even this task was small and as later events proved was to be abolished under the much larger strategic proposals contained in the main Defence Review. What then, apart from self-perpetuation, was the role of the Longmoor Military Railway? The Army Board had looked hard, could find none and therefore recommended the closure of the railway by the end of 1969. It was a stark revelation of an uncomfortable truth; with no military role, the LMR must close.

For many years the mainstay of the diesel motive power on the LMR were the 0-6-0 diesel-electric locos built at Derby in 1945. This was WD 878 (previously 70272 and later 601) – originally named *Chittagong* and later *Basra* [2]. *Photographer unknown*

WD 876 *Bari* [2] propelling coaches up from Longmoor Yard to Longmoor Downs platform. Sapper Graham Stacey was acting as crossing keeper and taking no chances – he had a red flag out as well as the road STOP signs. The Top Crossing was at the summit of the rise in the road – the flat-roofed hut built for the crossing keeper could be seen alongside the crossing. *Bryan Stone*

Above: *Bari* [2] then waited in the platform for departure time.   *Bryan Stone*

Left: The 350hp diesels were powerful engines, but the driver's view along the 'bonnet' was somewhat restricted, as this cab view over the driver's shoulder of WD 876 demonstrates.   *Bryan Stone*

A later addition to the LMR's stock of diesel locomotives was WD 890 *General Lord Robertson* (later 610), built in 1963. The locomotive was on display at an Open Day on 3rd June 1967, alongside WD 118 *Brussels* and AD 878 *Basra* [2].
G. Moon

WD 890 was not immune from the minor accidents that happened on the LMR. This was the outcome of a side-on collision.
Roger Bagnall

AD 412 (previously WD 8212) was one of the small 0-4-0 shunting diesels built by the North British Loco. Co. – seen here at Longmoor Downs on 5th July 1969.
G. Moon

WD 8205 *Matruh*, fitted with exhaust 'scrubber', photographed whilst working in support of the crane during the lifting of the boiler of WD 400.
Bryan Stone

WD 108 *Jullundur* crossing the road at the Top Crossing on arrival at Longmoor Downs from Liss Forest Road. At this date the outer home signal carried just one signal arm. *Bryan Stone*

WD 8205, not often used on trip goods workings, seen at Longmoor Downs working a Duty 'C' trip to Woolmer Yard for brakesman/shunter training. *Bryan Stone*

WD 890 – like any other LMR locomotive – was often used on trips for training purposes. This view shows WD 890 waiting in the sidings at Woolmer with a short train while WD 600 *Gordon* [2] drew towards the home signal for Woolmer blockpost with a passenger train. *Roger Bagnall*

WD 600 was a powerful locomotive and was regularly used for training trips on which heavy loads were used to test the skills of the train crew. This view shows WD 600 crossing Bridge No. 6 at the entrance to Longmoor Downs with a loaded train from the Liss direction. The signal had by now been renewed with two arms, to allow better sighting against the confused background created when the road authority installed street lighting beside the Top Crossing.

Roger Bagnall

Latterly the former diesel school in Longmoor Yard was used for the few remaining steam locomotives. WD 203 *Ahwaz* [2] was seen coming off shed, passing the old boiler (used for instructional purposes) that had also been brought over from the former running shed (and turned in the process).
Bryan Stone

WD 203, with newly painted red wheels and black side rods, standing at Longmoor Downs prior to working a special passenger train. The shine on the paintwork of the coaches was a delight to behold.
Bryan Stone

David Shepherd Comes to Longmoor

More or less at the same time as this gloomy decision was reached in London, there emerged at Longmoor a glimmer of hope from a completely unexpected source. In 1964 David Shepherd, still in the formative years of his long and successful artistic career, was creating many commissioned paintings for Army units. One such commission came from Bordon Garrison, a very different one from the artist's usual military subjects. It was to be an 8ft x 15ft portrait of Christ to be hung behind the altar of St. George's Church within the garrison and was, in the artist's own assessment, "the most challenging painting commission of my career".

At Bordon, David Shepherd was hosted by the Chief Instructor of the (then) RASC MT School (Lt-Col Charles Crew) and in due course was introduced to the military railway and in turn to the Commanding Officer of 16 Railway Training Regiment. Now the artist had just acquired his first steam locomotive (BR Standard Class 4 4-6-0 number 75029) and was coming to terms with the manifold problems of housing his new possession. Nothing official was done at this stage, but the CO at Longmoor was a pragmatist and could see a way to help.

Most of the detailed arrangements were left to the OC of 8 Rly Sqn (Major Charles Matthews). He recalls still the hospitality which he and his second-in-command received when they visited David Shepherd's farm where plans were discussed. Very quickly word spread around the railway enthusiasts' community. Even before 75029 had taken up residence at Longmoor, David Shepherd found that he was leading a group of similarly motivated amateur locomotive owners all looking for homes for their newly-purchased engines. In the end a simple but official agreement was negotiated and permission was granted for five privately-owned locomotives to be stabled at Longmoor.

The Association of Railway Preservation Societies

The complications of completing the purchase from BR of the locomotives were such that it was many months before they began to appear at Longmoor. The detail does not concern us here except that it brought into the equation a new organisation, the Association of Railway Preservation Societies (ARPS). This body was to play a significant part in the various attempts first to store and then to display privately-owned locomotives at Longmoor on a permanent 'preserved' railway. Thanks largely to the persistence of their new owner, David Shepherd's locomotives (for there were now two, 75029 having been joined by BR Standard Class 9F 2-10-0 number 92203) eventually moved from Crewe to Longmoor under their own steam, arriving on 7th April 1968. The day quickly developed into an 'event' in the best Longmoor tradition. Maj-Gen Errol Lonsdale (the Transport Officer in Chief) was there to welcome the locomotives personally and the day ended with two entirely impromptu excursions to Liss and back, hauled by 92203 and filled with enthusiastic supporters who had gathered at Longmoor to witness the event.

Restructuring of the Army Reserves – Formation of the TAVR

Whilst the saga of David Shepherd's locomotives was unfolding, a further heavy blow struck the Longmoor railway organisation. The Defence Review the previous year had proposed fundamental changes both to UK defence policy and to the deployment of the armed forces. At the spectacular end of the spectrum, these included a plan for total withdrawal of British forces from the Far East (other than Hong Kong). At a more mundane level, the Defence Review envisaged the creation of a completely new Army reserve. This single force, collectively known as the Territorial and Volunteer Reserve (TAVR) was to be formed from an amalgamation of the TA and the AER. The AER itself had only just emerged from its previous round of reductions and reorganisation. The military railway units of the AER were once more to be severely reduced, to the extent that the three remaining AER railway regiments were to be reduced to a single squadron. This was 275 Rly Sqn RCT (V), to be 'sponsored' by 79 Rly Sqn RCT in West Germany with a war task to reinforce BAOR. This unit would no longer be administered by Longmoor (although initially it continued to use the training facilities there) thus breaching the continuous tradition of reservist training at Longmoor which had existed since the first building of the camp in 1905.

Closure of the Bordon Branch and Some Special Trains

In April 1966, as part of the general network reductions begun by Dr Richard Beeching, BR closed the branch line from Bentley to Bordon to all traffic. LMR traffic from Oakhanger to Bordon ceased without ceremony at about the same time and the track from Martinique to Bordon (LMR) was disconnected. After lying derelict for some years, the Bordon station site was redeveloped as a light industrial estate. Interchange traffic between the LMR and BR(SR) was now routed via Liss. A significant portion of the traffic from the Engineer Stores Sub-Depot at Apple Pie, formerly carried on the LMR, was now being handled by road transport.

In April, having been alerted by their member Captain Roger Bagnall (then Assistant Instructor Railways at Longmoor), the RCTS arranged a tour from London to Longmoor and back whilst the BR Bordon – Bentley Branch was still available for traffic although officially closed. So popular was the tour that a second had to be run at the end of the month. Part of the attraction was the opportunity for steam haulage by AD 600 *Gordon*. Initially this had been proposed for the entire tour but there were some platform clearance problems which precluded running *Gordon* into Waterloo Station. In the end, after some effective lobbying by Major J. A. Robins, the CME of BR(SR) relented and AD 600 hauled the special train on the Woking – Liss – Longmoor – Bordon – Bentley – Woking section of the tour. As both events took place at weekends (when the LMR would normally be closed) special arrangements were made to bring in staff on a voluntary basis, both to run the LMR and to open various facilities for the RCTS members to visit during their tour. In effect, the staff laid on two more 'Open Days' in their own time. How to pay for this was apparently not covered by Army regulations at the time so in the end honour was satisfied by the RCTS making a donation to Longmoor welfare funds.

The Longmoor Museum

Under the direction of Major Robins (then CI Railways) a determined effort had been going on for several years to build and furnish a military railway museum at Longmoor. This was housed in what had originally been the camp's first electric power station and included many original items, both of Longmoor (from its earliest days) and of military railway operations overseas reaching back to the first ever British military railway

continued on page 593

AD 600 *Gordon* [2] was selected to haul the RCTS special trains on 16th and 30th April 1966 for part of the journey over BR tracks. The locomotive could not work into Waterloo, so took over the train at Woking. This was the engine waiting at Walton-on-Thames Station 'out of the way' before working forward to take over the special train at Woking.

Roger Bagnall

The RCTS special train arriving at the BR(SR) station at Liss on 30th April 1966. The connection to the LMR exchange sidings was beyond the bracket signal beside the now-disused goods shed.

Roger Bagnall

Once the RCTS special had drawn forward far enough to clear the connection to the LMR exchange sidings, another WD engine came out of the sidings on to the rear of the train, to draw it on to the LMR. The ground man was clipping the points for the facing move before the train could be signalled back.

A. E. Bennett, Transport Treasury B7155

With AD 600 now at the rear, the RCTS special was drawn into the LMR sidings.

A. E. Bennett, Transport Treasury B7156

The 0-6-0ST now heading the train drew it through the exchange sidings – AD 195 on 16th April 1966.

Roger Holmes, Photos/Fifties Ref R2381

AD 195 with the RCTS special passing the load gauge at the Liss Junction end of the exchange sidings, with the LMR main line on the right.
Roger Holmes, Photos/Fifties Ref R2423

After passing on to the LMR main line at Liss Junction, AD 600 hauled the special train into Liss (LMR) platform.
A. E. Bennett, Transport Treasury B7157

At Liss, AD 600 ran round to couple on to AD 195 for the journey to Longmoor Downs. *Photographer unknown*

Participants on the RCTS rail tour on 30th April had a choice of two departures for a trip round the Hollywater Loop. Halts for photographs were made as required. In this view, AD 196 had unloaded those who wished to take lineside photographs and was making its 'run-past'. On occasions such as this brake vans were added to the make-up of the train – it was much easier to climb down from and back up on to a brake van on open line. Note in the background the smoke from one of the fires that the locomotive had started.

P. J. Lynch, Kidderminster Railway Museum, 086564

On the first Hollywater trip of the day on 30th April, AD 196 started so many fires on the dry heathland that it was decided that the second train would have to be diesel hauled. AD 878 *Basra* [2] provided the power.   *Photographer unknown*

After the Hollywater Loop trips were complete, the RCTS special was hauled to Bordon by an 0-6-0ST, with AD 600 at the rear – in readiness for AD 600 then hauling the train in the next leg of its journey back to Waterloo on BR track.   *Roger Bagnall*

With the reopening of the through connection to BR at Liss in April 1966 came the opportunity to run a train through from British Railways to Longmoor for a major Cadet Camp that summer. The sixteen-coach train, which ran in heavy rain, was provided with an engine at each end for the climb up from Liss Forest Road.
Roger Bagnall

Bringing up the rear was AD 102 – *Caen* [2] – running without its nameplates. *Roger Bagnall*

The sixteen-coach cavalcade arriving at Longmoor Downs.
Roger Bagnall

At the end of the Camp in August 1966, the Cadets returned by special train 1O22. It was to be an eventful trip, especially for those Cadets boarding the rear coach. This time the second engine was coupled at the front of the train so there was no engineman at the rear of the train, a fact that was to have unexpected consequences.

Photographer unknown, courtesy Neil Howard

Left: With Liss Forest Road blockpost open, the Cadets train had to pass through the Down side of the passing loop. When this happened, it was customary for the points from the main line to the runaway siding to be returned to normal – set for the siding – before the trap points at the Liss end of the loop were set for the train to depart. On this day the blockman failed to remember that the train was of exceptional length such that the rear bogie of the last coach would still be on the Longmoor side of the points. When the train restarted, the last bogie of the train went up the runaway siding, the rear coach slewing sideways until the bogie finally became detached. In the foreground was the point to the runaway siding. Very unusually the bolt plunger of the facing point lock had been arranged for working by wire rather than by rod. This made it easier to work this bolt from both the blockpost (when open) or from the two-lever ground frame when the blockpost was not open.

Photographer unknown, courtesy Neil Howard

Below: The outcome of the derailment was evident for all to see, though most of the Cadets remained stoically in their seats, just wanting to get home. The long sand drag at the end of the runaway siding is evident from this view.

Photographer unknown, courtesy Neil Howard

Late into the summer afternoon, the breakdown gang were engaged in getting the hydraulic jacks under the frames of the coach bogie, prior to lifting it back on to the rails – after which would come the task of jacking the coach body up to get the bogie underneath it. The task demonstrated the flexibility of the arrangement of hydraulic jacks powered from pumps carried in one of the vans. *Photographer unknown, courtesy Neil Howard*

After rerailing the damaged coach was taken to the yard at Longmoor where it languished for many months. BR had no great shortage of coaches, so eventually the decision was taken that the coach should be broken up at Longmoor. *Photographer unknown, courtesy Neil Howard*

The rail tours, and even more so the Open Days, did not reveal the true nature of the LMR. This photograph captures more of the spirit of the railway. It shows that behind all the razzamatazz of the 'big shows' were young men running the railway, efficiently, and enjoying themselves doing it. Guard Cpl John Poyntz, driver Spr Tom Jones (who played scrum half for 16 Rly Regt).   *Bryan Stone*

continued from page 584

in the Crimea. Outside the building were two large exhibits – a World War Two German army rail-wrecking plough (recovered from Italy at the end of the war) and the part-sectioned remains of the boiler of *Mars*, the last survivor of the trio of 18-inch gauge locomotives which had begun rail operations at Longmoor in 1903. When the School of Transport closed in 1973, the greater part of the museum's contents were removed to the new Army School of Mechanical Transport at Leconfield.

Further Railway Enthusiast Activity

The daily operation of the LMR was now becoming ever more problematical. The re-roled 8 Sqn had by now been transferred to the command of 27 Transport Regiment RCT, located at Aldershot. In any event the squadron was shortly afterwards deployed to Cyprus for a tour of duty as the road transport unit in support of a United Nations' peacekeeping force. The inevitable announcement of the total closure of the LMR was greeted by a flurry of railway enthusiasts' tours, all taking a last opportunity to travel over this unique railway. Such was the demand that 1 Rly Gp RCT took the precaution of deploying to the LMR some of the ex-BR non-corridor coaches that had recently been purchased for use in various UK rail-served depots for which it was responsible. Various combinations of 'interesting' motive power were provided with both LMR and ARPS locomotives being rostered.

By 1968 the various groups that had joined David Shepherd's initiative under the overall care of the ARPS had become well-established. The owners' groups had even run their own enthusiasts' excursions (e.g. a trip sponsored by the Bulleid Pacific Preservation Society to enable members to view their locomotive *Blackmore Vale* undergoing restoration). So popular was this event that the special train from Waterloo was strengthened to fourteen coaches, clearly beyond the capacity of the LMR's only serviceable steam locomotive at that time (0-6-0ST AD 196). In the event, David Shepherd's 9F (92203) was specially prepared to haul the train from Liss. Its owner remarked that "my locomotive made a magnificent spectacle as she stormed up the bank to the delight of the crowds".

Proposals for a 'Steam Railway and Transport Centre'

The same day a further ceremony was arranged for the naming (by Maj-Gen Errol Lonsdale) of 92203 as *Black Prince*. In many ways this day in June 1968 represented the high point of the ARPS presence at Longmoor. The departure of Brig Claxton led to some changes in attitude towards the tenants, the most obvious being a total ban on the steaming of the privately-owned locomotives. This and other manifestations of change set the preservationists onto a new tack. If this was the beginning of the Army's 'Decade of the Rubber Wheel' (as it was being described in high places) then, having no further use for the

continued on page 598

Above: On top of the job and proud of it. Lcpl 'Barney' Barnes on the driver's side of the cab of WD 118 *Brussels*. *Bryan Stone*

Right: Young men, big engines. The fireman attends to the headlamp. *Photographer unknown*

Below: A group of fitters, posing alongside the veteran brake van WD 49021. *Bryan Stone*

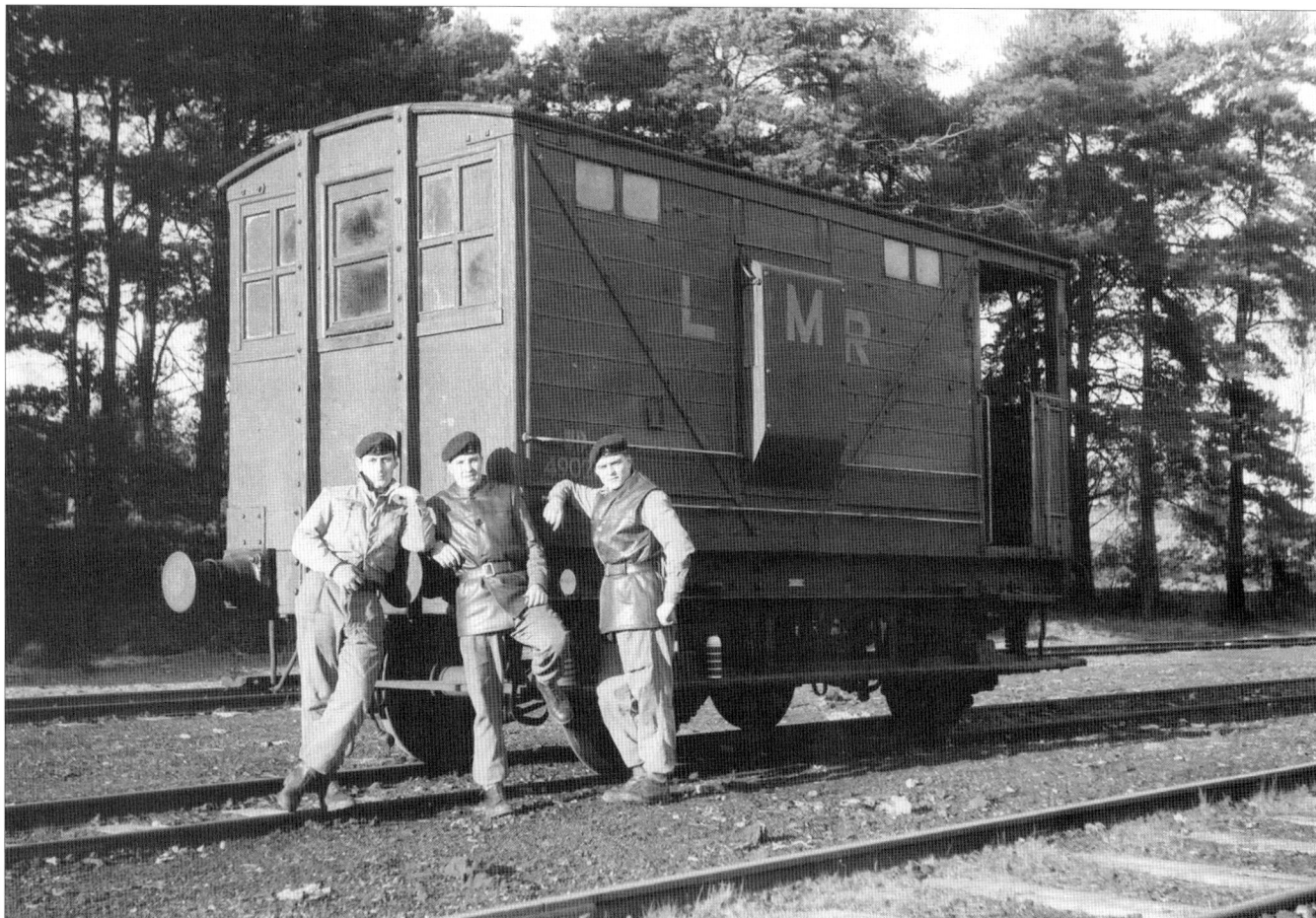

A regular part of training – be it for loco crew, shunters or guards – was to run heavy freight trains. The stock for these trains (and for shunting practice) was usually stabled in the yard at Woolmer, so the day began with working 'engine and brake' from Longmoor to Woolmer. When the exercise was over, the stock was taken back to Woolmer Yard for stabling, and the crew returned to Longmoor 'E&B'. On this occasion, the train (consisting of WARFLATs loaded with recovered track panels for added weight) was entering the yard when the locomotive derailed on the facing points.
Photographer unknown, courtesy Neil Howard

The derailment occurred almost in front of Woolmer blockpost. After the train had been drawn back to Longmoor it was revealed that the point switches were lying slightly open, though whether this was the cause of the accident or a result of damage during the accident would have to be ascertained.
Photographer unknown, courtesy Neil Howard

It would clearly take a while to rerail the engine, so the hapless fireman had the task of throwing the fire out on to safe ground to ensure that no damage happened to the firebox.

Photographer unknown, courtesy Neil Howard

It appeared at first that the derailment had blocked both running lines but, as the driver of *Hassan* demonstrated, it was possible to pass with caution.

Photographer unknown, courtesy Neil Howard

One day the Brownhoist crane derailed while entering Longmoor Downs, dragging its match wagon into derailment and doing considerable damage to the track.
Bryan Stone

The crane was truly 'derailed all wheels'.
Bryan Stone

The weight of the crane bearing down not only lifted one pair of wheels on its match wagon WD 80018 well into the air, the weight also put a considerable curve into the frame of the wagon.　*Bryan Stone*

Right: Trap points doing what they were designed to do – derail a runaway wagon at the end of the siding rather than allow it to run out on to the rest of the railway. In this instance, a WARFLAT wagon had gained some speed whilst running out of control down the gradient from XEN sidings at Brimstone towards the trap points protecting the Wood Siding adjacent to the Loop Platform at Longmoor Downs. It had sufficient speed to over-run the end of the rails by nearly a full wagon length.
Below: The WARFLAT was well embedded in the soil and bracken but it was not obstructing traffic and could be recovered at leisure as a rerailing 'exercise'.

both Bryan Stone

continued from page 593

LMR, could the Army be persuaded to part with it? The site had the potential to become a major transport preservation centre, and not just for railways. There was already a network of private roads across the adjacent training areas and there was also an operational light aircraft landing strip at Gypsy Hollow. A full feasibility study was commissioned under David Shepherd's leadership and a specific organisation (the Longmoor Trust – chaired by Maj-Gen Lonsdale) was established to develop 'The Longmoor Steam Railway and Southern Transport Centre'. Influential support was added by Sir Peter Allan (Chairman of the Transport Trust) who was at that time Chairman of Imperial Chemical Industries.

Whilst David Shepherd's efforts to 'mend fences' with the new Commandant were successful to the extent that the steaming ban was lifted, efforts by the Longmoor Trust to convince the Secretary of State for Defence of the merits of their scheme were less so. At the present time, carried along by the new-found 21st century zeal for railways, it is hard to recall how deeply unpopular and unfashionable railways had become in the UK in the late 1960s. 'Beeching's Axe', the end of steam traction and termination of the common-carrier obligation all added up in the public conscience to a widely-held feeling that railways were something the British could probably learn to live without.

Perhaps the General's comment on the 'Decade of the Rubber Wheel' was not so far-fetched after all.

Such views were certainly being expressed within the MOD and found substance in a paper submitted to the Standing Committee on Army Organisation (SCAO) regarding the future of Longmoor. There appeared to be a pressing need to retain all the training areas that surrounded Longmoor Camp. Full-bore rifle ranges in particular were at a premium in the south-east of England. The alignment of the LMR itself was seen as the basis for a new (private) road to connect the Bordon barracks complex with the training areas. This was required (it was said) to avoid the need to drive large numbers of AFV 432 vehicles (tracked armoured personnel carriers) along the busy Farnham – Petersfield main road. When all these and other factors were added together, they appeared to make a cast-iron case against the plan for the Historic Transport Centre. Accordingly at the end of 1969 the MOD advised the Longmoor Trustees that they were not prepared to release the Longmoor facilities to them.

The Final Open Day

Open Days were one of the highlights of the annual training cycle at Longmoor in the years following World War Two. A regular event since 1947 (with the exception of three years when it was

Open Days did not always run smoothly. On 3rd June 1967 AD 196 derailed all wheels at Liss while running round, offering visitors the unexpected 'bonus' of watching rerailing undertaken in earnest. *Dr I. Allen, Transport Treasury Misc332*

Although the crane came down from Longmoor with the breakdown train, it was decided that the locomotive could be rerailed using ramps (which could often be quicker than setting up the crane outriggers, especially in a location such as the platform at Liss, where a river was close by). With two axles rerailed using packing and ramps, the ramps had now been positioned to lift the third set of wheels back on to the line. *G. Moon*

With the ramps in place AD 195 then pulled the final set of wheels of AD 196 back on to the rails.

G. Moon

Another alternative to deal with derailments was the Deutschland rerailing equipment. This hydraulically-operated apparatus included substantial jacks which could be positioned as required on a stout beam laid across the rails. The Deutschland gear was especially useful where a locomotive had derailed on points so that rerailing ramps could not be positioned. Smaller hydraulic rams were available, which could be anchored over the head of a rail and used to push the errant locomotive sideways.

Bryan Stone

The final few years of the LMR saw regular Open Day events. On 3rd June 1967 a short train stood in the platform at Longmoor Downs, with AD 195 at the Woolmer end and AD 196 at the far end.   *G. Moon*

The naming of WD 196 as *Errol Lonsdale* took place on 8th January 1968 – a rather bleak winter's day. Unusually the naming ceremony took place just off the west end of the platform at Longmoor Downs. In the left background could be seen the remains of the structure gauges erected as part of the testing of the Tank Carrying Rail Wagon some months earlier.   *Photographer unknown*

On 8th June 1968 the Bulleid Pacific Preservation Society ran its 'Bulleid Commemorative Rail Tour', consisting of ten coaches. After visiting Brighton and Havant the rail tour was worked from Havant to Liss Exchange Sidings by SR loco E6108, arrival timed at 1443hrs. E6108 had recently been converted from a 'straight electric' locomotive to work as an 'electro-diesel' and so could work under diesel power on the non-electrified lines within the exchange sidings. At Liss Exchange Sidings the train was taken over by David Shepherd's 2-10-0 No. 92203. This loco was to be named (*Black Prince*) later in the day by Major-General E. H. G. Lonsdale but when this photograph was taken at Liss the nameplates were still covered over.

Photographer unknown

The rail tour train behind 92203 on the climb from Liss Forest Road was substantial – handled with ease. *Hugh Ballantyne*

cancelled due to operational priorities), the Open Day was an opportunity for all the skills and talents of the men of Longmoor to be shown to a wider public. By the summer of 1969 the end was very near and resources were becoming increasingly thinly spread. Public interest was greater than ever, steam traction having been abolished on BR the previous year. This was the challenge facing 411 Rly Optg Tp, and its commander (Lt Keith Castell) with less than thirty trained military railwaymen remaining from all the trades. 8 Sqn RCT of which the troop formed one part was now a general transport squadron, 16 Rly Trg Regt was no more, having been disbanded in late 1967 and the workshop (now under REME control) was being run down. The majority of the civilian craftsmen, many with years of railway experience, were being found new jobs within the REME organisation at Bordon.

At the beginning of July, the LMR had available only two serviceable steam locomotives and three diesels. The locomotive shed had been given over to the storage of the privately-owned preserved steam locomotives so the remaining LMR fleet was now stabled in the former Diesel Fitters' School which became the running shed. Here the remaining locomotive crews and others (often in their own time) touched up the paintwork, polished the brass and generally 'bulled-up' the two steam locomotives in traditional Longmoor style. They even added the final touches

with carefully applied 'Turtle Wax'. Cpl Tony Kelly (the driver of 196 on the day) recalls a surprise visit from the then Chief Instructor (Railways) to the shed. When Major Carter first viewed the two gleaming locomotives, and hardly believing what he saw, he could only remark: "They sparkle so brightly that they wouldn't look out of place on a Christmas tree."

A simple working timetable was devised with AD 600 *Gordon* and AD 196 *Errol Lonsdale* hauling passenger trains assisted by AD 8227 *Hassan* and AD 890 *General Lord Robertson*. The diesels would take over a train when the steam locomotives needed servicing. The final locomotive available was AD 8218 which, being too slow for passenger traffic, was 'stood-by' with the breakdown train ready for any real emergencies. Central to the timetable was the mid-day arrival of a nine-coach special train from London organised by the Bulleid Pacific Preservation Society. At Liss the train was collected by *Gordon*, in the charge of senior driver Ssgt Tom Hughes and fired by Dvr 'Willie' Williams. The day was fine and already the event was proving immensely popular with visitors so the five-coach train which *Gordon* had already brought down from Longmoor was coupled to the special. With *Gordon* in fine fettle and an enthusiastic fireman, the fourteen-coach train was lifted from the Liss Forest Road stop in fine style, watched and photographed by an almost continuous line of spectators. Willie Williams commented that the locomotive tackled the 1 in 70 gradient with consummate ease; "I never even broke into a sweat" he remarked afterwards.

A crisis occurred around midday when 196, hauling the RCT Railway Society's 'Blue Saloon Special' from Oakhanger, failed and was sent into the yard. The problem turned out to be a split blower ring, which was quickly rectified by a volunteer member of the BPPS. Their locomotives too were 'on parade' that day (but not in steam) so there was a good turnout of their members one of whom (by good fortune) happened to be a steam fitter trained by BR. A quick brazing job solved the problem and 196 was back at Longmoor Downs within the hour to take over passenger duties again from 890 (which was actually booked to substitute for 196 at this time to allow for replenishment).

One of the many features of the traditional Open Days in previous years was the demonstration of heavy lifting by the LMR's 45-ton steam breakdown crane. Various loads had been found in the past, including a small diesel locomotive, all guaranteed to entertain the crowd. At the 1966 Open Day, Dvr 'Lofty' Ailwood found himself rostered to fire the crane. This was not an arduous task until he found himself in sole charge as the driver (Cpl 'Eddie' Henderson) was called away urgently to drive the 20-ton diesel crane for a real emergency at Liss. Whilst Lofty gingerly carried out a few moves with the 'big hook', Cpl Henderson was dealing with 196 which had derailed by the water tank at Liss. It was quite a tricky task as both locomotive and crane were on the edge of the river bank, but the job was safely accomplished. Sadly by 1969, the 45-ton crane and its operator had both been posted to Marchwood where all RCT heavy crane operator training was to be concentrated.

With bigger crowds than ever before the 1969 Open Day was, by all standards, a great success. Few people, even on the staff at Longmoor, realised how slender were the resources that had made it possible. By stopping leave and calling in every available military railwayman, 411 Rly Optg Tp had been able to roster five train crews, three blockmen and two controllers. It was, as the Duke of Wellington remarked after the battle of Waterloo "a damned close run thing". Of course there were many other people available in the camp to carry out the supporting functions: front-of-house, security, catering and so on, all of which were done in good military style. In the end however it was the little band of twenty or so military railwaymen who really made the day. Retiring to the NAAFI at the end of a very long day the men of 411 Tp could with every justification feel proud of their efforts as the final curtain began to fall on over sixty years of military railways at Longmoor.

The Official Closure Ceremony

In almost complete contrast, the official closing ceremony on 31st October 1969 was a formal affair, conducted with dignity and a due sense of occasion. Longmoor had become one of the last outposts of steam operation on a passenger hauling railway in the UK not within the 'preservation' movement. The event was organised by the School of Transport with the most senior members and ex-members of the Royal Corps of Transport and its predecessors invited as official guests. The RCT Band was to take part and (as its final 'railway' duty) 8 Tpt Sqn RCT provided the Guard of Honour. Whilst all these essential military preparations were going ahead the men of 411 Rly Optg Tp were working hard to produce even better locomotives and carriages than they had

AD 600, resplendent after overhaul, working a train for Longmoor away from Liss Forest Road during the 1968 Open Day. *Bob Vice*

During the Open Day on 28th September 1968, AD 890 was used to demonstrate the haulage of heavy engineering plant. The train had arrived at Liss Forest Road, where it waited to cross a passenger train from Longmoor Downs. The short length of the passing loop at Liss Forest Road, after reconstruction, is apparent. AD 890 had drawn past the starting signal at danger, right up to the toe of the switch rails of the facing point. Even so, the rear of the train was still foul of the points at the other end of the loop and the brake van was barely clear of the road crossing.
Photographer unknown

The passenger train arrived from Longmoor Downs hauled by a Ruston diesel. This was AD 425 which was not (unlike *Hassan*) fitted with continuous brake for working passenger trains.
Photographer unknown

The last Open Day – 5th July 1969. AD 196 *Errol Lonsdale* taking on water at Oakhanger. *Photographer unknown*

Although closure was only months away, much effort had been put into ensuring that AD 196 was 'properly' turned out for the last Open Day.
Photographer unknown

At the Open Day on 5th July 1969, the Ruston diesel AD 425 hauled a short train round the Hollywater Loop line. *G. Moon*

As the run-down of the LMR continued, locomotives were sold and went away. This was AD 876 shunting 181 ready for loading. *Bryan Stone*

for the recent Open Day. Once again the 'Turtle Wax' was applied and once again a magnificent result was produced.

The programme was kept deliberately simple. Two trains were marshalled on the platform at Longmoor Downs; *Gordon* (hauling the three Blue Saloons) would convey the Representative Colonel Commandant RCT (Maj-Gen P. G. Turpin CB, OBE) and the VIP party to Oakhanger (Train 'A') whilst *Errol Lonsdale* would haul Train 'B' with the remainder of the invited guests to Liss. With the Guard of Honour formed up on the platform and the band playing suitable incidental music, all was ready. Promptly at 1435hrs, the General and his entourage arrived on the platform, the Guard of Honour and band gave the General Salute before he joined his party in the 'Webb' saloon. Equally promptly at 1445hrs, the two trains pulled out simultaneously to the strains of 'Auld Lang Syne', *Gordon*'s departure being a muted performance as the train load was insignificant on the down-hill stretch to Woolmer.

AD 196, in contrast made a stirring departure for Liss. With an unobstructed crossing of the Liphook road, fireman Williams put on an extra round or two and the result when crossing No. 6 Bridge "looked like a volcano on the move". In earlier times this would have generated a stern rebuke from the Locomotive Inspector –but this was a special day and the crew knew what the spectators wanted. Both trains made short stops at their respective termini before the very last run back

to Longmoor Downs. They arrived at 1522hrs and 1520hrs respectively and after a pause to receive well-deserved thanks and congratulations, the trains shunted into Longmoor Yard. After disposing of their locomotives, the crews cleaned up and made their way to the NAAFI for a well-deserved drink. The enthusiasts dispersed, believing that they had witnessed the very last trains to run on the LMR. As we shall see, this was not to be the case.

Military Railway Training Moves to BAOR

One of the Army Board's decisions in early 1967 had been that all future Army railway training would take place in BAOR. A very small manpower increment to undertake training duties was allocated to 79 Rly Sqn RCT and suitable rail-served accommodation was found in Mönchengladbach, co-located with a large RAOC vehicle depot. Very little of the treasure-trove of training material amassed over the previous half century at Longmoor was transferred. The chief item to go to Germany was the '0' Gauge Instructional Model Railway located in the Operating School building. This was successfully shipped and re-erected for further use. Unfortunately, its maintenance proved something of a liability and eventually it was shipped back to the Museum of Army Transport at Beverley. Despite sporadic efforts to display it, the model never appeared in public there.

On Closure Day – 31st October 1969 – the band and the Guard of Honour awaited the Colonel Commandant, due to arrive on the platform at Longmoor Downs at 1435hrs. The two last day trains were for invited guests only. There was no mass attendance by the public, though there was a small seated area out of shot in this view, behind the roped-off line. *Photographer unknown*

The distinguished guests boarded train 'A', the three Blue Saloons headed by AD 600 *Gordon*. At the far end of the Loop Line platform was a second train of three coaches, hauled by AD 196 *Errol Lonsdale*. Sharp at 1445hrs, the trains drew out – Train 'A' for Oakhanger and Train 'B' for Liss.

courtesy Soldier *magazine*

November 1969 dawned on an officially rail-less Longmoor. Still standing in the yard were the locomotives stored by the ARPS and the remaining rolling stock of the LMR itself. The latter became the responsibility of 1 Rly Gp RCT which officially took over the management of the LMR, including the remaining civilian staff. There were still consignments leaving the Engineer Stores Sub-depot so a strange twilight world prevailed over the following months with diesel-hauled freight trains operating as required on a 'one-engine-in-steam' basis to and from the exchange sidings at Liss.

An Alternative Home for the ARPS?

The Ministry of Defence had already intimated to the ARPS that it was prepared to lease the detached portion of land (purchased in the mid-1920s) that formed the extension of the LMR from Liss Forest Road to Liss. The land had specifically been purchased for the building of the railway and had no residual value for training. Within this much smaller area, the proposed Historic Transport Centre would have the use of approximately 1.3 miles of 'main line' and the area of sidings forming the LMR station and interchange at Liss. Though clearly less attractive

Train 'A' departed from Oakhanger at 1509hrs and was photographed – complete with 'Two Star' headboard – passing Woolmer blockpost on its way to Longmoor where it would arrive, as the 'Last Train', at 1522. *RCTS reference FAI 2316*

than the original scheme, the proposal did give the Historic Transport Centre access to the BR(SR) main line and the very basic facilities of a small terminal station. An initial lease of six months was proposed, commencing in April 1970, all rolling stock to have left the remainder of the LMR by the end of March.

By this time, the remaining Army rolling stock on the LMR had been assessed and divided up into two categories. Anything with a residual value that could be employed by 1 Rly Gp RCT would be transferred to one of their other depot railways. In some cases this rolling stock enjoyed a long 'second career', in one or two instances still being actively operated by the MOD today. A list of known current survivors is at Appendix Twenty-four. For the remainder, an auction sale was held at Longmoor with brisk bidding by a number of railway preservation societies. David Shepherd records his satisfaction at buying the ex-LMS ambulance coach (then numbered 3322) for £110 and the cheapest open wagon for only £4 10s (£4.50). In all he purchased about ten items which eventually found a second home on the East Somerset Railway at Cranmore.

Following the removal of the privately owned rolling stock from Longmoor, the RCT initially decided to loan AD 600 *Gordon* and the three Blue Saloons to the Longmoor Trust. The loaned coaches became a gift whilst the locomotive remained MOD property and was eventually placed on indefinite loan (and later gifted) to the Severn Valley Railway. The handover ceremony, appropriately led by Maj-Gen Pat Claxton, now the Transport Officer in Chief (Army), served to demonstrate the Army's support for the new project. David Shepherd himself always maintained an excellent relationship with the military in general and in particular with the soldier tradesmen of Longmoor.

With coaches stabled, a distinguished guest drove AD 600 on to shed. Driving was Colonel O. C. 'Ossie' Radford who was at that time the Deputy Commandant of the ASMT and the senior ex-RE(Tn) officer in the school – watched carefully by the R.E.D. (S) [Railway Engine Driver (Steam)] nominally in charge, Cpl Tony Kelly. *courtesy Soldier magazine*

The Liss Historic Transport Centre

Meanwhile, members of the Longmoor group of enthusiasts pressed ahead with plans to build a locomotive shed, workshop and carriage store at Liss (LMR). An application was submitted to Hampshire County Council for outline planning consent in the normal way. During the process of obtaining this consent (which was successful) it became apparent that despite the good support received in Liss itself there existed a nucleus of opposition in the residential area which had developed around Liss Forest. In the end this opposition grew, through a campaign which was both vitriolic and personal, to the extent that full planning consent was not granted. At this point the attitude of the Defence Lands Office (which was responsible for leasing the ground to the Trust) hardened to the extent that they intimated that in the absence of full planning consent they would revoke the lease and sell the land by auction on 28th July 1971. At the auction sale the 'Liss Forest Residents' Association' outbid the Longmoor Trust and became the owners of the line. As a result, all Trust property had to be cleared from the site by the end of the year.

The loss of the route was a fatal blow to the aspirations of the Trust. Indeed the furore surrounding the planning application had already caused divisions within the group, leaving David Shepherd battling (largely single-handedly) with the opposition from Liss Forest. Such contests are highly stressful but it is a mark of the determined character of the artist that in the last months before leaving Liss, when he was in the thick of a highly acrimonious planning dispute and under much personal stress, he found an opportunity to prepare a fine painting of *Gordon* on the LMR and then to present it to the School of Transport as a mark of his appreciation.

Filming 'The Young Winston'

At this point, with only a few weeks of tenure remaining, fate smiled upon the embattled enthusiasts at Liss. Columbia Pictures were engaged in filming the adventures of Winston Churchill during the Anglo-Boer War. 'The Young Winston', as the film was called, was directed by Richard Attenborough and required a number of key railway sequences that had to be filmed out-of-doors in appropriate locations. Longmoor, by now quite well known to film location scouts, was the best option. But how was this to be achieved with the railway closed and now even the track-bed sold (particularly as the track-bed now belonged to a dedicated anti-railway group)?

It could have been latent Churchill-mania or (more likely) an understandable wish not to generate more adverse publicity – we shall never know. However grudgingly, the LFRA agreed that the making of the film thus setting the stage for an appropriately dramatic final act in the history of the railway. During October 1971, Weavers Down again echoed to the sound of a big steam locomotive being worked hard. *Black Prince*, loosely disguised as a Victorian locomotive from South Africa – complete with a large (fibreglass) double chimney, electric headlight and a 'cowcatcher' pounded up and down the line. The main location was Liss Forest Road Station (disguised as 'Koomatipoort' – the frontier post where the young Churchill made his escape to freedom).

In the two years since the official closure of the LMR, the line had been very effectively vandalised so none of the signalling or telecommunications needed to run trains conventionally could be used. Even if the kit worked, there was no longer anyone available to operate it. The solution was for the film company to run the entire operation using portable two-way radios. Though the railway was effectively a single long siding with one engine in steam, the complications 'on the air' were many, not least because even such non-railway people as the props manager and the continuity girl all seemed to have radios. The biggest snag, revealed before any filming began, was that *Black Prince* was facing the wrong way. The only solution was to repeat the one-off adventure undertaken the previous year when both David Shepherd's locomotives were towed to Whitehill and turned on the triangle there. A year later, with nature rapidly taking over the formation, the operation took on many aspects of a voyage of discovery. To the great relief of everyone concerned *Black Prince* returned safely to Liss, the very last locomotive to travel through Longmoor Downs.

After three weeks filming, Richard Attenborough and his team left the location, well satisfied with their efforts. David Shepherd and his small crew of volunteers had triumphed over amazing odds to bring the story of the LMR to a rousing conclusion. That their valiant efforts were not rewarded by finding a permanent home at Liss will forever be a source of regret. The misfortune of Liss was the benefit of Cranmore where, after many more adventures, David Shepherd's locomotives were found a truly appropriate home on the East Somerset Railway.

The Last Rolling Stock Departs

By the end of October 1971 a new, but clearly temporary, home for the preserved locomotives and rolling stock had been obtained from BR at Eastleigh Works. Much of the rolling stock had already left for other destinations and new homes. The main train consisting of *Black Prince*, *The Green Knight*, three carriages and an assortment of goods wagons left Liss on Sunday, 24th October 1971 under tow from a diesel locomotive. The very last locomotive of all to leave was the little industrial 0-4-0ST *Lord Fisher*, which departed later in the day by road for secure storage at a location nearby in Godalming. For the first time for almost seventy years, the LMR fell silent.

Demolishing the LMR

There remained one last task, the demolition of the railway itself. This responsibility fell to the Ministry of Public Buildings and Works (MPBW) whose No. 4 District, Bournemouth Area undertook the task through its Bordon Works Depot. The District Officer of the MPBW was a retired Sapper officer (Colonel J. G. A. J. O'Ferral) who had first officially visited Longmoor on a Young Officers' Course in the late 1940s. The initial activity was the formation of a 'Closure Committee' chaired by a senior staff officer from the School of Transport. This assembled in June 1969 and set the final closure date for the railway at January 1970. Slippage to this date was caused by the problems with the Liss lease and also the arrival of the film crew. On the ground the preparatory work for setting up a demolition contract was carried out by Mr George Dance, the former civilian Permanent Way Inspector on the LMR and a TA RE officer. The railway was to be treated with respect even at this late stage so the planned demolition was to include the removal of all wayside structures, buildings etc. and the restoration of the ground for its continued use within the Army training area. Ballast was to be retained on the track bed with a view to its future use as a tank road between Bordon and

PAINTING THE GREEN KNIGHT
Contributed by Ken Nuttall

In addition to the generous voluntary help which the military community gave to David Shepherd whilst his locomotives were stabled at Longmoor, he also enjoyed the use of various facilities around the workshops when these were not being used in support of the LMR. Thus it was possible in the spring of 1968 for 75029 (not yet named *The Green Knight*) to be fully repainted in BR Brunswick green livery within the Longmoor paint shop.

When the job was done David decided to make an event of the locomotive's reappearance from the workshop. On the chosen weekend his other locomotive (92203, now named *Black Prince*) would be specially steamed to perform a ceremonial 'Towing-out' before invited guests, whilst their owner filmed the event. Cpl Ken Nuttall volunteered to drive the 2-10-0 and after preparing the locomotive drove gently to the workshop side of the yard to await instructions. As so often happens on these occasions 92203's footplate quickly filled with eager guests – so much so that Ken could not see his fireman across the crowded cab. This was clearly not the best way to go about shunting a very large locomotive in a confined space.

Ken's first, polite, request that a few people might step down had no immediate effect, and indeed it seemed to have fallen on deaf ears altogether. The guests were clearly enjoying the ride. This was, after all, a military railway and Ken was in charge on his footplate so he tried again, this time applying a more traditional Army technique: "Right then – three volunteers – you, you and you – off the footplate please!" Three guests duly stepped down and the ceremony went ahead as planned.

It was only afterwards with the guests admiring his newly-painted masterpiece and enjoying a celebratory toast, when David Shepherd quietly remarked to Ken: "Did you know that your first 'volunteer' was General Lord Robertson?" The General, who was clearly not on duty, took it all in good part and nothing more was said. There was only one casualty that day – due to an oversight David Shepherd had spent his entire day filming the event with an empty camera.

Gypsy Hollow via the former Hollywater Loop. Any items considered to be of historic interest were to be reviewed by a working party chaired by the Deputy Commandant (Colonel O. C. Radford).

As the portion south of Liss Forest Road had been sold, there was now no main line rail access to the LMR. All lifted materials would therefore have to be removed by road. At a critical point in the midst of this preparation, (December 1970) the MPBW itself was reorganised and absorbed into the new 'Department of the Environment' (DOE). Despite this change the process of letting the demolition contract continued although for the reasons mentioned above, the start date was delayed from June to October. The planned completion date was to be August 1973.

The supervision of the contractors was carried out by Mr George Randall. At the end of the contract he retired from DOE having completed no less than forty-four years service

at Longmoor. He first joined the permanent-way staff in 1928, a young member of that ubiquitous gang of civilians who appear in the background of so many inter-war photographs of construction projects on the WIMR.

The School of Transport is Closed

The camp itself fell victim to the fast moving changes that were a characteristic of service life in the 1970s. Once the rebuilt Buller Barracks opened in Aldershot, the enthusiasm for developing Longmoor rapidly waned. Furthermore, the Army was under increasing pressure to avoid the huge costs of refurbishing old barracks by taking over redundant RAF stations and moving units into them. In the case of the RCT, this led to the opening in 1974 of a new Army School of Mechanical Transport (ASMT) at Leconfield and Driffield in East Yorkshire. No further money was to be spent on Longmoor so the remaining elements of the School of Transport departed to be rehoused in Aldershot.

The first Commandant of the new ASMT in East Yorkshire was an ex- RE (Tn) officer – Brig H. R. 'Rush' Dray. He took great trouble to salvage many of the historic features of the old Longmoor Camp. The most spectacular operation was the removal and transfer of the unique stained glass windows and other memorials from St. Martin's Church to a new church in a specially converted building at Leconfield. Less spectacular but of equal interest, was the removal of the contents of the former Longmoor Museum to a new home within Normandy Barracks, Leconfield. The collection formed the nucleus of what was to grow into the Museum of Army Transport, later to be located at Beverley.

Longmoor Camp after the Railway

What remained of the Camp was then converted into training accommodation for use by the TAVR. Known now as a 'Weekend Training Centre' (WETC) the Camp provided facilities for local TAVR units to carry out field-craft, weapon training and so on, in addition to using the rifle ranges. A number of buildings found new uses, but the last of the post-Boer War huts in Kimberley Lines were finally demolished. From time to time new facilities have been added to meet new specialist training needs. Ironically, the latest of these is a detached length of permanent way (nowhere near any former LMR alignment), on which have been placed three pensioned-off items of WD rolling stock for various training uses by the reservist soldiers of the Royal Logistic Corps (successors in 1971 to the RCT).

The most recent and certainly the most dramatic change to the landscape of Longmoor arose from the construction of the long-awaited A3 Petersfield – Liphook Bypass, opened in July 1992. Over thirty years in planning, the route finally chosen bypasses Liphook to the north then follows the general line of the old Liphook – Greatham secondary road until joining the former LMR alignment at Griggs Green. In one great sweep the new road strides across the former site of Longmoor Downs Station (which has been totally obliterated). After an intersection to feed into No Road and other internal camp roads, it continues through the Apple Pie site towards Greatham where it crosses the A325 before skirting round the west side of Petersfield itself.

It would be hard to imagine today that sixty years ago this was a bustling railway centre. To all intents, the railway has vanished. Of the internal AFV road, so important in the plans of the early 1970s, there is not a trace. Despite its pressing justification at the time of the LMR closure, it was never built.

A maker's view of *Mars*, supplied in 1886 as a replacement for one of the two locomotives abandoned at Suakin. *Maker's photograph*

Mars at Longmoor c.1907, on a rebuilt section of the 18-inch gauge line. The sappers still appear to be wearing the 'peak-less' Broderick caps.
John Alsop Collection

CHAPTER SEVENTEEN

STEAM LOCOMOTIVES AT LONGMOOR

The locomotives of the Longmoor Military Railway and its predecessors in themselves form a fascinating study. To maintain a proper perspective, we have dealt in outline only with this aspect of the railway. As so many of the locomotives were obtained from other sources, information about them (or similar machines) exists elsewhere in a wide variety of formats. Indeed, of the total of over 150 locomotives that are known to have worked at Longmoor (as against merely being stored there) only three seem to have spent their entire working lives on the LMR. Surely no other railway can yield a record like this?

The locomotives have been grouped chronologically – the groups corresponding to the phases in the development of the railway – with brief biographical details. The outline dimensions and specifications of steam and internal combustion locomotives and rail cars are tabulated in Appendices Seventeen, Eighteen and Nineteen at the end of this volume. Whilst numbers were allocated to the Military Camp Railways engines from 1916, the Longmoor fleet did not carry numbers until the early years of World War Two. Thereafter the Longmoor engines were numbered within WD, Army or MOD series.

Many of the drawings prepared for this and the following chapter have been copied from originals prepared (in most cases) by trainee 'Draughtsmen (Mechanical)' as training exercises. Inevitably there were errors but, wherever possible, these have been identified by comparison with contemporary photographs and appropriate corrections made. The dimensions shown are copied from the original dimensions (which would have been recorded by the trainees at the time and are believed to be accurate). The drawings are reproduced to a consistent scale unless specifically noted otherwise.

Section I : The 18-inch narrow gauge locomotives

The three 18-inch gauge locomotives, *Mars*, *Venus* and *Flamingo*, were delivered to Longmoor from Chatham in 1905 to assist in the construction of the standard gauge railway. They had previously been used in the construction of the forts encircling Chatham Naval Dockyard and are remembered, for example, at work with convict labour gangs on the construction of Fort Darland. The rise and subsequent fall from grace of the Royal Engineers' 18-inch gauge siege tramways has been told elsewhere by Mark Smithers. The 18-inch gauge locomotive-hauled railway had failed to meet expectations when deployed to assist the construction of the Suakin forts in the abortive Sudan campaign of 1884/5. Even at that date siege warfare was not a high priority task within the Corps. Thereafter what small resources could be gathered to develop locomotive-hauled narrow gauge military railways were devoted to the 2ft 6in. gauge. This appeared to offer greater promise and was further developed both at home and in India up to the outbreak of World War One. The use of the 18-inch gauge at Chatham Dockyard and the Royal Arsenal at Woolwich was essentially an industrial rather than a siege-warfare application.

However, a small stock of 18-inch gauge equipment continued to be held at the Royal Arsenal as part of a 'Siege Park' ready for deployment in any future war. After nearly twenty years of careful storage, it was decided that this was no longer needed. Authority was given firstly to deploy part of the large stock of prefabricated track and secondly the locomotives, which were sent to Longmoor. With one exception, (*Mars*) their life at Longmoor was short and hectic. The sandy heathland of Woolmer Forest probably caused wear and tear on motion and bearings similar to that which had been earlier experienced in the Sudan campaign when such locomotives were used around Suakin Harbour. When they were in good order they were useful little engines and on the multi-gauge track from Longmoor Camp to Whitehill they were alleged to be capable of reaching a speed of 30mph. Their use after 1907 is not recorded. However, it seems possible that occasional use was made of the Weavers Down ballast pits so it is conceivable that one or more of the trio survived perhaps as late as 1919.

Mars [1]	VF/1160/1886	0-4-2T
Venus [1]	VF/1161/1886	0-4-2T

These locomotives were delivered new to Woolwich Arsenal in 1886. The order was a continuation of that for *Vulcan* (VF/989/1883) and *Mercury* (VF/1075/1884). The earlier pair had been working at Chatham until abruptly recalled in February 1885 to be included in the engineer stores to accompany Graham's ill-fated Suakin force. *Mars* and *Venus* were ordered to replace them following their abandonment at Suakin in 1886.

There are no records of *Venus* after 1907 and it is assumed that it was broken up at Longmoor. However, *Mars* survived by the fact that a boiler was needed to raise hot water for the Apple Pie Camp bath house. This project would appear to be a piece of sapper 'self help' but it operated successfully until 1924 when modernisation of the camp began. *Mars* was then honourably pensioned-off and placed on a pedestal beside the guardroom. By 1930 the locomotive had been reduced to a sectioned boiler used for instructional purposes. As a training aid (adorned with a bogus chimney) this engine survived until the final closure of Longmoor. It was then transferred to the Museum of Army Transport at Beverley where it remained on display until the closure of that establishment in 2003. It then went to the National Army Museum collection and is now loaned on display at the former Woolwich Arsenal.

Flamingo	JF/5062/1885	0-4-2T

Little is known of the early history of this locomotive. The building date suggests that it too may have been a replacement for an engine sent to Suakin. Two '6in Patent Locomotives' were supplied to the War Department by John Fowler in 1882 for a proposed light railway in Cyprus as part of a plan for building fortifications there. Two such locomotives were probably shipped to Suakin in June 1884 from Woolwich and it is reasonable to assume that *Flamingo* replaced one of these. This engine was scrapped at Longmoor in April 1919.

Venus again, hauling a train load of sappers from Bordon. The 18-inch gauge track had by this time been re-levelled and reduced to a single line. The location was Hogmoor Pond. The area in front of the train had also been levelled, in preparation for laying standard gauge track.   *J. Day*

A view showing *Venus* returning from Weavers Down ballast pits with a train of loaded side tipping wagons.   *J. Day*

Section II : Standard gauge locomotives 1905-1914

Included in this section are the standard gauge locomotives forming the permanent Peace Establishment at Longmoor between 1905 and 1914. At Longmoor none of these locomotives carried running numbers and they were identified by name only, a practice which continued until 1940. Opinions as to the final dates of disposal from Longmoor vary. There was invariably a time-lag between the decisions of the locomotive running staff to withdraw a locomotive, authority being given by the War Office to do so and the actual scrapping or sale taking place. Variations of several months have been found in the recorded dates of locomotive movements. Historically these variations are not now of great importance.

Had the WIMR been conceived a few years earlier, it might well have been supplied initially with locomotives from the apparently inexhaustible stock of the 'Suakin Dump' at Woolwich. The detail of this aspect of Victorian military history does not concern us here. Suffice it to say that, following the UK government's abrupt decision to abandon the Suakin campaign in 1885, the substantial stock of railway equipment that was at sea (in transit to or from the Sudan) was returned to the UK and placed in store at Woolwich. During the following twenty years this dump was raided from time to time to provide military railway equipment for various projects in the UK. One of these was to provide a very simple training railway for the Royal Monmouthshire RE (Militia) at Monmouth (Troy). By coincidence, this unit was one of the first to camp at Longmoor during the construction of the WIMR. Perhaps it was fortunate for the embryo railway at Longmoor that by 1905 all that seems to have remained in stock at Woolwich was track and signalling equipment.

| Bordon | AE/1505/1906 | 0-6-0ST |
| Woolmer | AE/1572/1910 | 0-6-0ST |

The first standard gauge locomotive purchased for the Bordon & Longmoor Military Tramway was *Bordon*, ordered from the Avonside Engine Co. of Bristol in 1905. This locomotive was of Avonside's Class 'B3', one of the earliest of that class to be built. The Avonside factory, located at Fishponds in Bristol, was being developed at this time but production remained relatively limited. If one accepts that construction orders followed in numerical order then their annual output at this time only amounted to sixteen or seventeen locomotives per year. The company does not appear to have developed any kind of 'niche market' with the War Department though it was responsible for the later Avonside/Parsons internal combustion locomotives developed for the WD in 1915.

In addition to the standard 'B3' specification, extra features were ordered including (as listed on the official order):

- Brick Arch to be fitted 'about one brick and a half'
- War Office boiler label (No. 2791) to be fitted to the front of the boiler
- Coupled wheel centres to be of cast steel rather than best iron
- Double sight-feed lubricator
- Vacuum brake
- Brass nameplates *Bordon*

The painting details of this locomotive are of interest as the finishing coat is specified as 'Prussian blue'. At Longmoor this did not last many years and the engine was soon turned out in the black, lined-red livery used until the late 1930s. In 1910 *Bordon*

Bordon c.1907 in lined-out blue livery as delivered. The locomotive was posed on Free Piece Curve near Bordon.   *Photographer unknown*

No longer looking pristine *Bordon*, now in a plain livery, posed between duties on the WIMR c.1910.

John Alsop Collection

This view (dated 1910) shows *Woolmer* in original condition. Though still virtually new when photographed, there are no signs of any lining-out on the cab or saddle tank. With the soldiers' flair for eccentric uniforms, the man on the right was wearing a 'Field Service' tunic but an engine drivers cap whilst the man on the footplate was wearing blue overalls with a 'Field Service' cheese-cutter cap.

John Alsop Collection

was transferred to Shoeburyness and replaced by *Woolmer*. The latter engine appears from the maker's surviving records to have been ordered and delivered as a standard class 'B3' tank engine. At an early stage it acquired vacuum brake gear and ran at Longmoor until 1919 when it was transferred to Hilsea. Later it saw service at Tidworth being withdrawn as WD 010 in August 1953.

The historic connections of *Woolmer* with the WIMR were not forgotten and it was decided that it should be restored for display outside the headquarters building at Longmoor. Before being refurbished it was occasionally pressed into use (in 'light steam') as the Longmoor shed pilot. It is particularly remembered in this role by participants in AER weekend training exercises of the period. On their arrival at Longmoor, the 'Advance Party' (as if they had been landed in a foreign country to take over part of its rail network in a war situation) would find themselves faced with a shed full of 'dead' locomotives with *Woolmer* sizzling gently in the yard outside. Their problem was to get the railway running as quickly as possible and the correct solution was to use *Woolmer* to supply steam to assist in lighting up the various oil-fired locomotives that they had discovered 'on shed'. On occasions, to add local colour to the exercise, one of the permanent staff instructors would don an Arab costume and ply the AER team with much information (some of dubious value) and all in authentic 'broken English' (as learned in the Canal Zone). It was the task of the AER officers to sift out the genuine from the misleading before they made their plans.

The work to refurbish *Woolmer* was completed by September 1954, after which it remained on display until shortly before the closure of the Army School of Transport at Longmoor, carrying a livery which had been progressively simplified down the years as suitably skilled workshops tradesmen became unobtainable. In July 1972 *Woolmer* was removed to covered accommodation in the former LMR paint shop. It remained there until its removal the following year, firstly to the new Army School of Mechanical Transport at Leconfield and later to the Museum of Army Transport at Beverley where it remained until 2003. The story of the subsequent adventures of *Woolmer* is outlined in Appendix Twenty-four, page 837.

Hampshire	AE/1520/1906	0-6-0ST

Chronologically *Hampshire* was the second locomotive to be delivered to Longmoor. Avonside treated it as a special order though it was obviously a derivative of the 'B3' class. With larger cylinders (15inch by 20inch) and a heavier boiler it was probably specified because the Longmoor authorities found *Bordon* lacking in power on the construction work then going on. Special features included:

- Angle iron ring connecting the boiler barrel to the smokebox to be double rivetted to the barrel as well as barrel to firebox shell
- Firebrick arch to be fitted, deflector plate and rivet protector to be fitted
- Regulator to be fitted with a starting valve and Roscoe's lubricator
- Copper stays in firebox water space to have $^3/_{16}$-inch hole drilled through their entire length
- Wheel centres of cast steel
- Leading and driving axleboxes to be of cast iron, trailing axleboxes to be of cast steel
- All axles and crank pins to be oil hardened
- A double sight-feed lubricator to be fitted
- Slide valves of bronze
- Valve motion made of mild steel accurately fitted and afterwards deeply case-hardened and the holes lapped out true to fit
- Vacuum brake ejector fitted

The locomotive was delivered in black 'fully lined out' in early 1906.

Hampshire remained at Longmoor throughout the busy World War One period except for a spell in 1918 and 1919 when it was loaned to the Swansea & Mumbles Railway. By the end of the war it was in a run-down state and was therefore returned to Avonside in August 1923 for general overhaul. Its boiler was shortly afterwards condemned (due to some local work

Woolmer eventually returned to Longmoor after withdrawal from service as 'WD 010' at Tidworth in 1953. After use for a period in light steam around Longmoor Yard, this locomotive was refurbished for display outside the Transportation Headquarters building. By this time the locomotive had acquired a set of conventional cast-iron wheels.
R. K. Blencowe, Negative Archive number 7577

W.I.M.R.
HAMPSHIRE

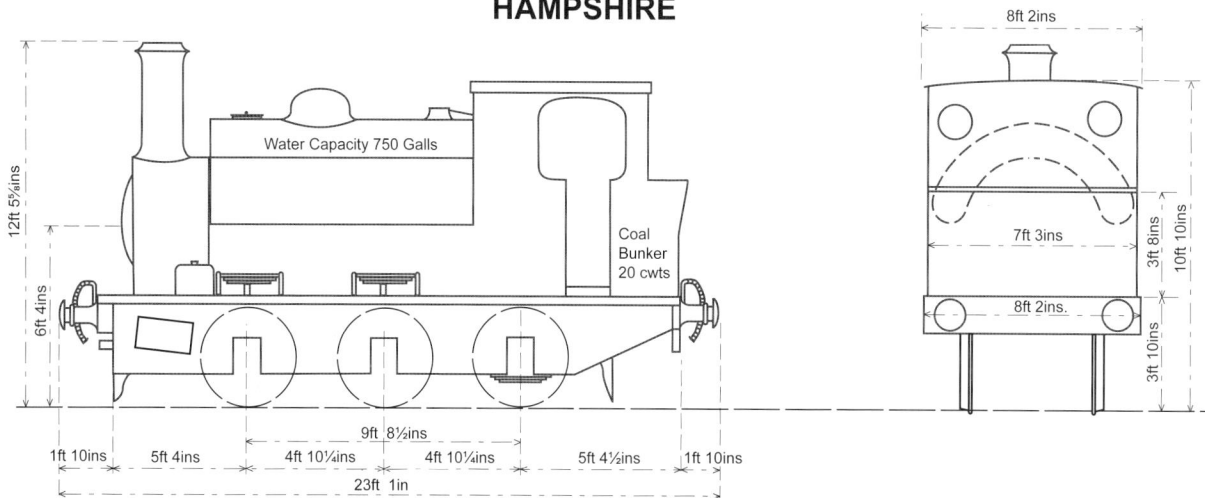

Water Capacity 750 Galls

Coal
Bunker
20 cwts

12ft 5⅝ins

6ft 4ins

9ft 8½ins

1ft 10ins | 5ft 4ins | 4ft 10¼ins | 4ft 10¼ins | 5ft 4½ins | 1ft 10ins

23ft 1in

8ft 2ins

7ft 3ins

8ft 2ins.

3ft 8ins

10ft 10ins

3ft 10ins

Based on a Weight Diagram prepared at Longmoor.

	T. C. Q.	T. C. Q.	T. C. Q.	T. C. Q.
Weight Full	10. 0. 0.	12. 0. 0.	11. 0. 0.	Total 33. 0. 0.
Weight Empty	8. 0. 0.	9. 10. 0.	8. 10. 0.	26. 0. 0.

Makers: Avonside Engine Co. Ltd, Bristol. Makers No. 1520 of 1906.
W.D. Boiler No. 2485.
Cylinders 15ins diameter x 20ins stroke.
Heating Surface 722 sq. ft. Grate Area 12.2 sq. ft.
Boiler Pressure 160 lbs per sq. inch. Tractive Effort @ 70% = 14,400 lbs.
2 Injectors.
Brakes: Combined Vacuum & Steam (Gresham & Craven).

by inexperienced RE tradesmen at Longmoor rather than any fault of Avonside). It was therefore offered for sale and bought by Charles Williams of Morriston, South Wales. Once its new owner had realised that it was not entirely the bargain he had hoped for and the boiler (or at least the firebox) had been renewed, it gave useful service until scrapped in 1932.

Hampshire, in an early view which suggests that it was also delivered from the makers in a fully lined version of the black livery adopted by the WIMR. The first vehicle in the train was one of the Leeds Forge bogie open wagons.

Photographer unknown

Another 1910 view (from a contemporary postcard) showing *Hampshire* and her crew. Relative unanimity reigned in this picture with all the crew in blue overalls. Behind can be glimpsed one of the first (ex-Midland) 10-ton covered vans. *John Alsop Collection*

Longmoor	Swindon/1179/1890	0-4-4T

The reasons for the purchase of this secondhand locomotive for the WIMR and indeed for the selection of such an unusual machine as *Longmoor* are not known. There was always quite a strong affinity with Swindon and the Great Western Railway amongst the railway-trained RE officers, many of whom had undergone technical training there. This may have influenced their choice. The locomotive in question was one of a pair of 0-4-2ST (Nos 34 and 35) built in 1890 at Swindon to the design of William Dean. The saddle tank configuration was changed in 1892 when the locomotives reappeared as 0-4-4T engines. In this form they were described and illustrated by the late J. N. Maskelyne in his book *A Further Selection of Locomotives I have Known*.

Longmoor in Longmoor Yard shortly after delivery from Swindon. The footplate crew were wearing conventional peaked caps similar to those worn at the time on the civilian railways. *John Alsop Collection*

Another photograph of *Longmoor*, dated 1910. Two of the soldiers were in the Edwardian equivalent of 'shirt-sleeve order' whilst the driver (on the right) was wearing his railway blue uniform. The carriage on the right behind the locomotive was probably an ex-Metropolitan Railway rigid 8-wheel coach. It was not retained by the WIMR after the arrival of the two K&ESR carriages in 1912. *John Alsop Collection*

No. 34 is traditionally quoted as the St. Ives Branch engine whilst No. 35 ran on the Helston line. Between 1892 and 1908 No. 34 acquired a full cab, in which form it ran at Longmoor. The details of the sale to the War Department are obscure but it had arrived at Longmoor by November 1908. At Longmoor it was used as the 'best engine' and appears on various pictures hauling passenger trains. In many respects its design was ideal for the light traffic on the steeply graded WIMR and *Longmoor* seems to have been well liked. After heavy war service it was in poor condition and was sent in 1921 to Swindon for examination prior to overhaul. The cost of a full overhaul was not thought to be justified and so *Longmoor* was scrapped at Swindon about 1921.

The official 1914 manufacturer's photograph showing *Sir John French* in 'works grey' livery. The feed-water heating system is prominent in front of the left-hand side tank. The Westinghouse brake air pump was added by Hawthorn, Leslie at a late stage in construction at the specific request of the WIMR staff, to facilitate driver training before deployment of 8 Rly Coy RE to France in August 1914.

R. & W. Hawthorn, Leslie & Co. Ltd, Newcastle-upon-Tyne

W.I.M.R.
SIR JOHN FRENCH

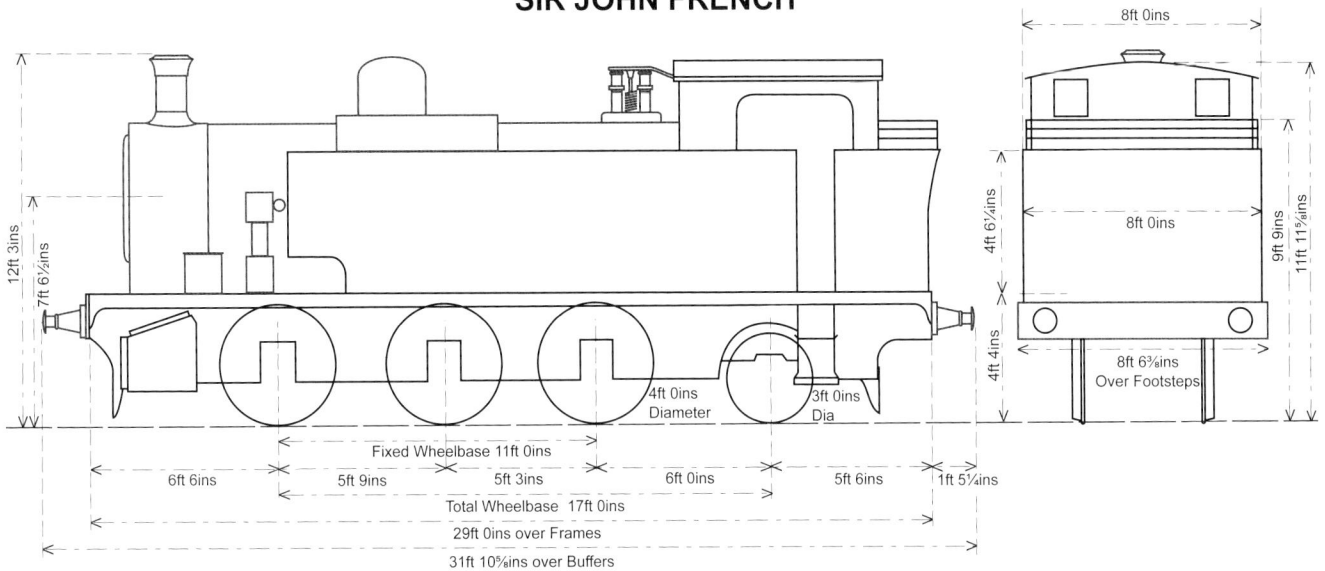

8ft 0ins

12ft 3ins

7ft 6½ins

4ft 6¼ins

8ft 0ins

9ft 9ins

11ft 11⅝ins

4ft 4ins

8ft 6⅜ins
Over Footsteps

4ft 0ins
Diameter

3ft 0ins
Dia

Fixed Wheelbase 11ft 0ins

6ft 6ins · 5ft 9ins · 5ft 3ins · 6ft 0ins · 5ft 6ins · 1ft 5¼ins

Total Wheelbase 17ft 0ins

29ft 0ins over Frames

31ft 10⅝ins over Buffers

Weight in Working Order   15t.10c.   15t.10c.   15t.10c.   12t.0c.
Total Weight in Working Order 58t.10c.

Makers: R. & W. Hawthorn, Leslie & Co. Ltd, Newcastle-Upon-Tyne.
Makers No. 3088. Date 1914.
W.D. Boiler No. 3890.

*Based on a Weight Diagram
prepared at Longmoor R.T.C. R.E.
25 March 1930.*

Dimensions & Heating Surface of Boiler
Length of Barrel 11ft 8ins.
Length of Firebox (outside) 5ft 6ins Width 4ft 0½ins
148 Steel Tubes 2inches O.D. x 12 G Thick
Heating Surface   Tubes   927.9 sq. ft
                       Firebox   88.8 sq. ft
                       Total 1,016.7 sq. ft
Grate Area 17 sq. ft
Boiler Pressure 170 lbs
Outside cylinders 16ins. dia x 24ins stroke
Tractive Effort at 85% = 18,500 lbs

Capacity of Side Tanks 1,330 Galls
Capacity of Bunker 2½ Tons

Equipment

1 Gresham & Craven No. 8 Combination Injector, on L.H.S.
1 Electric Driven Boiler Feed Pump 3½ins diameter x 4½ins stroke, on R.H.S.
1 Westinghouse Brake Pump.
1 Davis & Metcalf Vacuum Ejector.

Brakes
Westinghouse (Loco and Train).
Steam (Loco) and Vacuum (Train)
Hand Brake

Sir John French (70203)   HL/3088/1914   0-6-2T

The locomotive *Sir John French* reflected the development of the WIMR over the period immediately before the outbreak of World War One. At 58½ tons this locomotive was nearly double the weight of the original *Bordon* and the tractive effort (18,500lb at 85 per cent boiler pressure) was not exceeded until the arrival of *Kitchener* [1] in 1927. Unfortunately details of the order appear not to have survived the various amalgamations and closures in the British locomotive building industry but the specification is of interest because a number of features were included deliberately for instructional purposes. These included:

- Weir steam feed pump
- Exhaust steam feed heater
- One injector and one axle driven feed pump
- Outside Walschaerts valve gear
- Steam brake
- Vacuum ejector with combination brake valve
- Westinghouse air brake

The last item was fitted as a late afterthought to meet the need for training drivers to operate Westinghouse-fitted trains in France. It was indeed added so late that the maker's photograph was taken before it was fitted.

The detailed design of the locomotive, to meet the specification prepared by Capt Woodhouse, was based very closely on another successful recent Hawthorn, Leslie product. *Lord St. Leven* (HL 2697/1907) was one of a pair built to the order of H. F. Stephens for the Plymouth, Devonport & South Western Railway for which he was retained as engineer. Though Woodhouse never mentioned any connection with Stephens when discussing this project, it is quite likely that the PD&SWR locomotive would be known to officers from Longmoor from their visits to the West Country lines on railway planning exercises.

Whatever the design process, the end product was a great asset to Longmoor. In almost all respects, *Sir John French* was a most successful locomotive. During World War One it proved invaluable for dealing with the vastly increased traffic. It was overhauled after the war and then received a further major overhaul at Eastleigh in 1936, from which it emerged sporting a Southern Railway green livery lined-out in yellow. *Sir John French* therefore began World War Two in good condition. It was used continuously until about 1945, having acquired the number 203 and later 70203. In February 1946 it was put up for disposal and in September of the same year was sold to E. O. Edwards of Chesterfield for scrap. The locomotive was named after Field-Marshal Sir John French who was Commander-in-Chief of the British Expeditionary Force at the outbreak of war in 1914.

Sir John French in traffic. This later view from the early 1930s shows the locomotive waiting at Longmoor Downs platform. At this time it was painted in plain, unlined black livery. During an overhaul at Eastleigh works in 1936 the engine was painted in the full Southern Railway (pre-malachite) green livery. This livery was then adopted by the LMR and it had been applied to all the pre-war locomotives by 1939.

Photographer unknown

Section III : World War One and the Military Camp Railways (MCR)

In 1914 there were no plans for the expansion of Longmoor after mobilisation. The majority of the requisitioning of locomotives took place from 1916, coincidental with the opening of the various lines of the Military Camp Railways.

The locomotives listed in this section were all acquired or leased by the War Department during the war period. This list was originally compiled from old notes at Longmoor whose origin is not known. Research subsequently has proved the connections of some of these locomotives with Longmoor to be tenuous. However the original notes, based on the practical experiences of serving officers and men of the period, must have had a basis of fact. We believe that the locomotives concerned all visited Longmoor for repairs or in transit, even if they did not actually work on the WIMR for any length of time. The list is not therefore a complete catalogue of MCR locomotives. The overhaul and repair of the MCR locomotive fleet was controlled from Longmoor and whenever possible such work was carried out in the workshops there. After the war the oldest were quickly sold or scrapped, most leaving WD service by 1925. Some were retained and the last to be scrapped, *Kingsley*, survived until 1952. Even more remarkable is the fact that one of this relatively small group (*Westminster*) has survived into the preservation era and is still with us today.

424 (L&SWR)	BP/-/1882	4-4-2T

The first arrival was an 'Adams Radial' tank locomotive, initially hired from the L&SWR in October 1914. This locomotive is believed to have remained at Longmoor until mid 1916 when it was transferred to the newly opened Dinton and Fovant Military

The ex-L&SWR Adams Radial 4-4-2T retained its former main line number (424) when hired – later to be purchased – by the WD in 1914, initially for use at Longmoor. In 1916 it was redeployed to the newly opened Dinton-Fovant MCR. Though it was best remembered for service on the Catterick Military Railway after its Swindon overhaul in 1920, it was also employed for periods at Longmoor where the enhancement of an already handsome engine by adding a GWR safety-valve cover clearly caught the eye of the photographer.

W. L. (Bill) Kenning,
courtesy Adrian Vaughan

Another view of 424 at the WIMR on a passenger train (a forerunner of the 'Bullet') with hired coaches. Exactly when this service began was not recorded but the huge increase in the military population of Longmoor and Bordon from 1914 made such trains essential.

W. L. Kenning, courtesy Adrian Vaughan

This 1920 view of 424 was produced by the Swallow Studios of Richmond, Yorkshire. The original caption reads: "Man on footplate: Sgt G.Drake, NCO i/c detachment, a very intelligent loco engineer. He returned to Longmoor when the MCR was handed over to the N. E. Rly in 1923, was CQMS in charge of Loco Dept Longmoor 1925, QMSI Fieldworks Chatham 1926. Discharged 1931. Man on ground: Sapper Hall, a steeplejack by trade, enlisted as a fireman at Catterick, discharged 1924."

Railway. In June 1916 the locomotive was purchased outright. In 1920 it was overhauled by Swindon Works, acquiring in the process a GWR-pattern polished safety valve cover before returning to Longmoor again. Subsequently it was transferred to Catterick, running on the camp railway there until this was handed over to the L&NER, at which time 424 was apparently scrapped.

| 647, 655, 667, 673, 681 | LB&SCR 'Terrier' | 0-6-0T |

To cope with the problems of training military engine drivers on the Westinghouse brake, the WD arranged for the loan of a succession of 'Brighton Terrier' tank engines. The locomotives listed each spent a few months in this role between 1914 and 1918, including a second visit for 673.

| *Thisbe* (MCR 84) | HL/2878/1911 | 0-6-2T |
| *Pyramus* (MCR 85) | HL/2879/1911 | 0-6-2T |

These two locomotives were built to the specification of Holman F. Stephens for the reopening of the Shropshire & Montgomeryshire Light Railway under his guidance. Presumably they proved surplus to that line's immediate requirements and were offered to the WD when additional motive power was sought for the Military Camp Railways. The precise means by which *Pyramus* and *Thisbe* were purchased remains obscure. There is no mention of the sale in the surviving records of the S&MLR. It is quite feasible that the pair were still (in 1916) wholly or partially owned by Stephens personally. That he might therefore benefit directly from such a sale would go some way to explaining his willingness to sell

Thisbe and sister locomotive *Pyramus* had been purchased from Col H. F. Stephens for MCR use in 1916. Only *Thisbe* put in any significant service on the WIMR (from around 1918 until broken-up between 1930 and 1933). The locomotive was posed for photography in front of the original high level coaling stage in Longmoor Yard.

John Alsop Collection A15307

the S&MLR's best and newest locomotives. Both are recorded as working on the Kinmel Park Camp Railway but by the end of the war *Thisbe* had been transferred to Longmoor. There is unconfirmed evidence that this may have been a temporary exchange. One observer noted *Sir John French* on the Kinmel Park Camp Railway in 1918. *Pyramus* was sold out of WD ownership to the Nunnery Colliery Co. Ltd, being finally withdrawn by the NCB in April 1962 and scrapped by Booth of Rotherham. *Thisbe* stayed at Longmoor and was later broken up there between 1930 and 1933.

Monmouth (MCR 86)   HE/397/1886 0-6-0T

Monmouth was for many years a 'lost' engine, being wrongly credited to Hudswell, Clarke & Co. Ltd of Leeds who, it now transpires, were responsible only for overhauling it in 1915. Delivered to T. A. Walker (a contractor) at Preston Dock and later sold to Price & Wills Contractors, it was sent to the Cannock Chase MCR in 1916 and later (1919) transferred to Catterick. In 1921 it was sold out of WD service through the dealer J. F. Wake and was bought by the Carlton Main Colliery Co. Ltd for their Frickley Colliery. *Monmouth* is therefore one of the group to be counted only as a very temporary resident at Longmoor.

This view of MCR No. 86 (*Monmouth*) came from the series taken at Catterick by the Swallow Studios of Richmond in 1920. Apart from repairs, it is unlikely that this engine was ever deployed to Longmoor during World War One.

WD photograph

Kingsley was overhauled by the Yorkshire Engine Company in 1923 and continued in service at Longmoor until around 1930. This view shows the locomotive towards the end of its active life, standing in Longmoor Yard.

LPC 79428

Kingsley (MCR 51)	HC/224/1880	4-4-0T

This locomotive was delivered to the Lynn & Fakenham Railway, a constituent of the Midland and Great Northern Joint Railway (M&GNJR), in October 1880. It had a varied career, passing to the capital stock of the Midland Railway between 1906 and 1912 during which time it was fitted with auto-train control gear to work coupled to an ex-Midland Pullman car. On the M&GNJR it was known as *Norwich* (No. 10) but was un-named on arrival at Longmoor in 1917. It was rebuilt by the Yorkshire Engine Co. in 1923 and officially remained in active service until replaced by *Earl Haig* in 1930. This was not the end of its working life for it was retained as a hulk for rerailing practice. It survived in this form, albeit very battered, until 1952. Kingsley is the name of a village near Longmoor. A sister locomotive to *Kingsley* (M&GNJR No. 8) also passed into MCR service, being sold at the end of the war to Edinburgh Collieries Ltd in 1925 and continuing to work in Scotland until scrapped in 1935.

W.I.M.R.
KINGSLEY

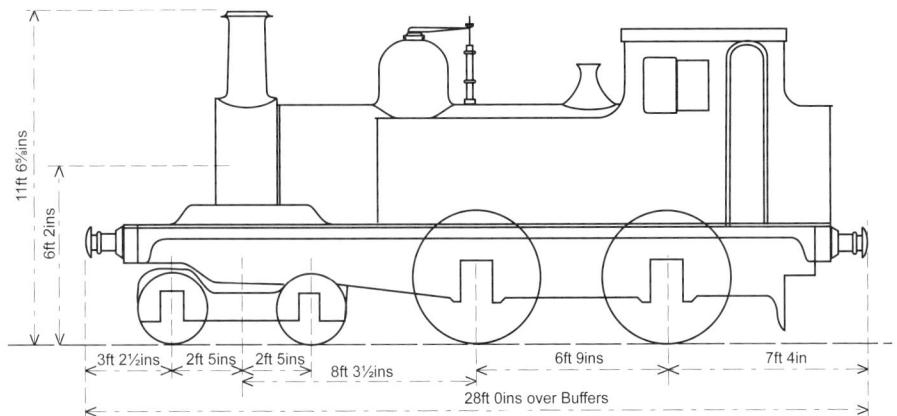

11ft 6⅝ins
6ft 2ins
3ft 2½ins 2ft 5ins 2ft 5ins
8ft 3½ins
6ft 9ins 7ft 4in
28ft 0ins over Buffers

Weight Empty	9t. 6c. 2q.	10t. 13c. 0q.	10t. 9c. 0q.
In Working Order	10t. 3c. 0q.	13t. 16c. 0q.	12t. 13c. 0q

Engine in Working Order 36 tons 12 hundredweights 0 quarters

Makers: Hudswell, Clarke & Co. Ltd
Boiler M&GN 1896. W.D. Boiler No. 4236.

Outside cylinders 15ins diameter x 20ins stroke
Wheels; Coupled Wheels 4ft 6ins diameter, Bogie Wheels 2ft 6ins diameter
Capacity of tank 690 Gallons. Coal Bunker 30 cwt.

Based on a Weight Diagram
prepared by the
Military Railway Office, Longmoor.

Heating Surface: Tubes 754.52 sq. ft
Firebox 67.25 sq. ft
Total 821.75 sq. ft
Grate Area 11.3 sq. ft
Boiler Pressure 140 lbs
Adhesive weight 11,489 lbs
Tractive 8,182 lbs

Kingsley was a well-loved and useful member of the WIMR stud throughout the 1920s. When replaced for active duties, it survived for another three decades as a hulk on which trainees could practise re-railing skills. Between exercises *Kingsley* would be stabled out of the way at the far end of Longmoor Yard or (later) by the road at Griggs Green.

Photographer unknown

| *Westminster* (MCR 13) | P/1378/1914 | 0-6-0ST |
| *Salisbury* (MCR 3) | HC/1069/1914 | 0-6-0T |

Sir John Jackson Ltd, civil engineering contractors of London, were responsible for the construction of a number of the major military camps built around Salisbury Plain in 1915 and 1916. At least two of this firm's engines were sold to the WD on completion of these contracts. *Westminster* is first recorded at Bulford Camp and then in 1917 on the Dinton and Fovant Camp Railway. About 1921 it was disposed of to Cohens who resold it to the Dunstable Portland Cement Co. In August 1970 their successors (APCM) in turn sold it to some members of the Kent & East Sussex Railway Association for restoration. This restoration never took place, but after a period in storage and later display at the former East Tisted Station, the engine was purchased by another group of enthusiasts. In 1998 they transferred their locomotive to the Northampton and Lamport Railway where it awaits restoration. It is quite remarkable that this locomotive, used for passenger traffic by the military for less than five years, still retained its vacuum brake through nearly half a century of industrial use.

Whilst *Westminster* may only have been briefly at Longmoor, the other ex-Sir John Jackson engine spent several years there after World War One. *Salisbury* was delivered new to Amesbury in 1914 for the Larkhill contract which included construction of the extensive Larkhill Military Railway. On completion of the contract, it was purchased by the WD and remained at Larkhill until early 1918. To meet the heavy demands of the Canadian timber traffic at Longmoor, *Salisbury* was transferred thence. It appears to have remained at Longmoor for about ten years, then being sold to Fountain & Burnley Ltd, North Gawber Colliery, Darton about 1928.

W.I.M.R.
WESTMINSTER

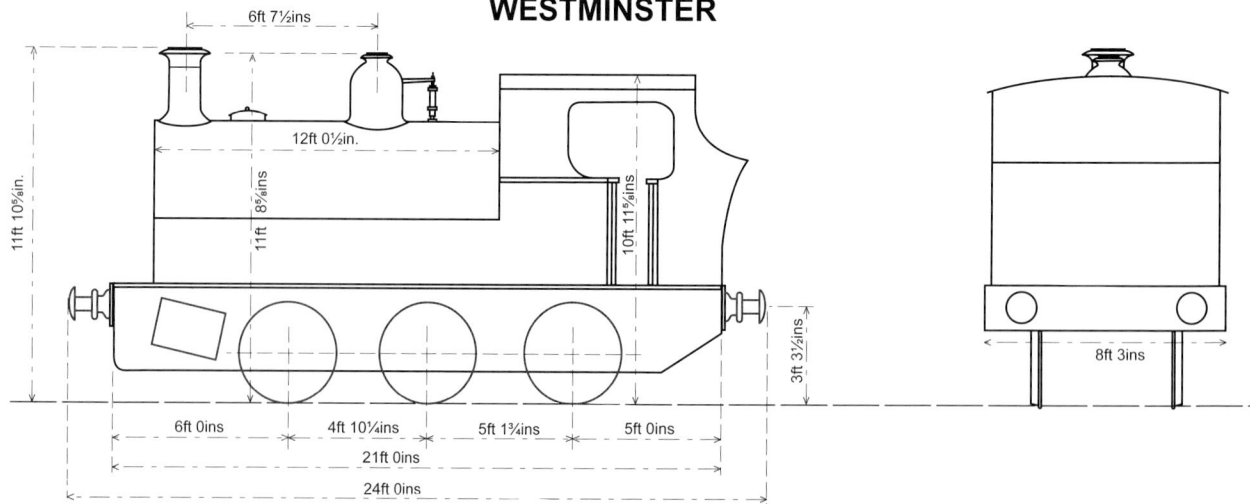

Makers: Peckett & Sons Ltd, Bistol
Makers No. 1378. Date 1914
W.D. Boiler No. 4041
Total weight Loaded 30 Tons
Capacity of Coal Bunkers 30 cwts. Capacity of Water Tanks 800 gallons
Wheels 3ft 7ins diameter
Weight on Driving Wheels 12 Tons

Boiler Pressure 160 lbs per sq. inch
Cylinders 14ins diameter x 22ins stroke
Tractive effort 12,398 lbs
Spring Balance Safety Valve
2 Injectors
Hand & Steam Brakes

Based on a Weight Diagram prepared at Longmoor.

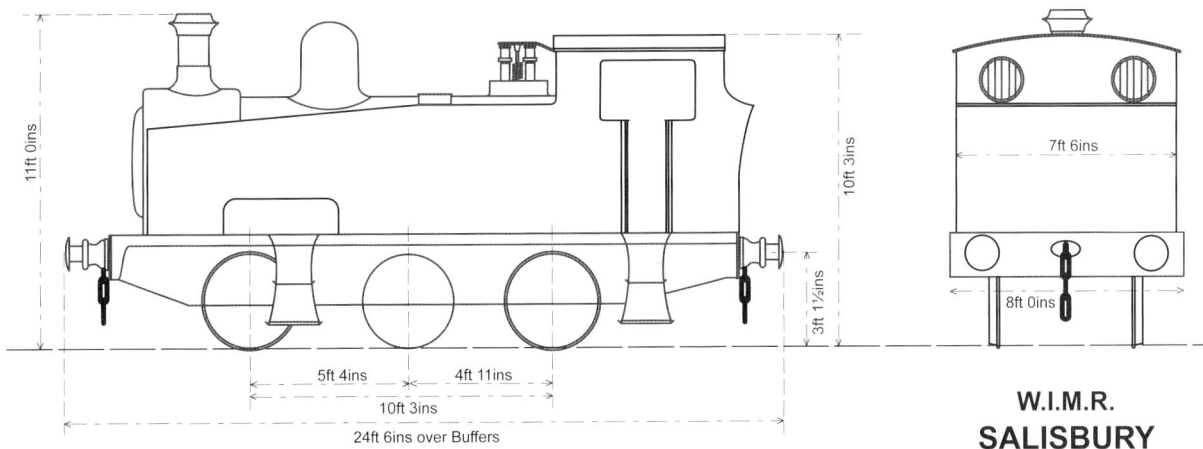

11ft 0ins

10ft 3ins

3ft 11½ins

5ft 4ins — 4ft 11ins

10ft 3ins

24ft 6ins over Buffers

7ft 6ins

8ft 0ins

W.I.M.R.
SALISBURY

Makers: Hudswell, Clarke & Co. Ltd, Leeds
Makers No. 1069. Date 1914
W.D. Boiler No. 4012
Inside Cylinder 15½ins diameter, 20ins stroke.

Boiler pressure 160 lbs per sq. inch
Tractive effort at 75% pressure 12,672 lbs
Weight Empty 27 Tons. Weight Loaded 30 Tons. Coal Bunker 30 cwt. Tank capacity 500 Gallons
Fitted with Vacuum (Dreadnought) Brake: Independent Steam Brake: Hand Brake.

| MCR 94 | BP/2365/188 | 2-4-0T |
| MCR 95 | BP/2467/188 | 2-4-0T |

In 1916, when the main line railways were running at full capacity and heavy engineering efforts were increasingly being diverted to war work, the WD had to take what it could when buying locomotives. Two typical examples of what was available were the Stratford-on-Avon & Midland Junction Railway's Nos 5 and 6. These two locomotives had been on the duplicate list of the S&MJR for sale since 1902, but were accepted after inspection by the WD at a purchase price of £1,000 each. After repairs at Stratford-on-Avon they were despatched to Catterick (No. 5) and to Longmoor (No. 6). MCR 94 (No. 5) was photographed at Catterick in 1921 though it appears to have been scrapped soon after. The Westinghouse brake was fitted to this locomotive during a general overhaul at Darlington in April 1918. A rather poor view of No. 6 at Longmoor c.1917 hauling one of the earliest passenger trains suggests that it too was Westinghouse fitted by this period. In the absence of written records, it is assumed that MCR 96 (No. 6) was taken out of service and scrapped at Longmoor by the early 1920s.

MCR No. 94 at Catterick in 1921. The pair of S&MJR 2-4-0Ts had been bought from that railway's long-term duplicate list by the WD in 1916, ending up at Catterick. Sister locomotive (MCR No. 95) spent much more time at Longmoor during World War One. The original caption of this photograph states: "Built by Bayer Peacock, Gorton, Manchester 1883. Boiler pressure 140 lbs per sq inch. Sent to N. E. Rly shops at Darlington for general overhaul and fitted with Westinghouse air-brake equipment April 1918. Total cost of repairs etc. £992. This locomotive was fitted with both aut'm (sic) brakes, Vacuum and Compressed air and used on MCR as passenger & goods. On the footplate LCpl Hayes (Catterick 1921-23)? Wksps? Discharged as LSgt J Hayes 10th Coy in 1934. On the ground Spr Finlay (fireman)." *WD photograph*

MCR No.	Rhymney Rly	Built	Works No.	
100	024		RR/2234	0-6-0ST
101	026	1872	RR/2236	0-6-0ST
102	028		RR/2238	0-6-0ST

The final trio to complete the series of MCR locomotives associated with Longmoor were the ex-Rhymney Railway saddle tanks. These were probably the oldest locomotives to appear at Longmoor. All were on the RR duplicate list by 1915. MCR 100 and 101 were sold to the WD via the Bute Works Supply Co. in November 1915 and June 1916 respectively and were sent to Catterick. 102 was sold directly to the WD in June 1916 and followed the first pair north. At the end of 1921, 101 was transferred to Longmoor where it was scrapped in 1923 whilst one of the remaining pair was sold to the Workington Iron and Steel Co., becoming their No. 52 until scrapped in 1928.

MCR 101 (nearer camera) and 102 were from the trio of elderly Rhymney Railway 0-6-0STs purchased by the WD in 1916. Built in 1872 and taken from the RR's duplicate list, they were probably past their prime when they arrived at Catterick for MCR service. 101 was transferred to Longmoor in 1921.

P. Coutanche, ref: NG4/2S

Section IV : Standard gauge 1920 - 1939

The run-down state of the WIMR and the low ebb to which its fortunes fell between 1919 and 1921 have been described already in Chapter Six. The state of the locomotives was most unsatisfactory, indeed the staff were lucky if they ever produced a locomotive to order for traffic. The first stage of recovery was to overhaul the existing engines and some examples of this have been noted in the previous section. However, as soon as funds could be obtained, a new locomotive was ordered.

Selborne (204 later 70204)   HL/3531/22   0-6-0T

R. & W. Hawthorn, Leslie & Co. Ltd obtained this order which was for a further 'instructional' locomotive. Lessons learnt in the recent war were incorporated and the engine featured Westinghouse and vacuum brakes, the latter controlled by a Davies & Metcalfe Ltd vacuum ejector with steam brake combination. An unusual feature was an overflow valve fitted to the side tanks to restrict capacity when running over lightly laid lines. The design appears to have incorporated these features on the advice of Major Woodhouse who had taken over the control of

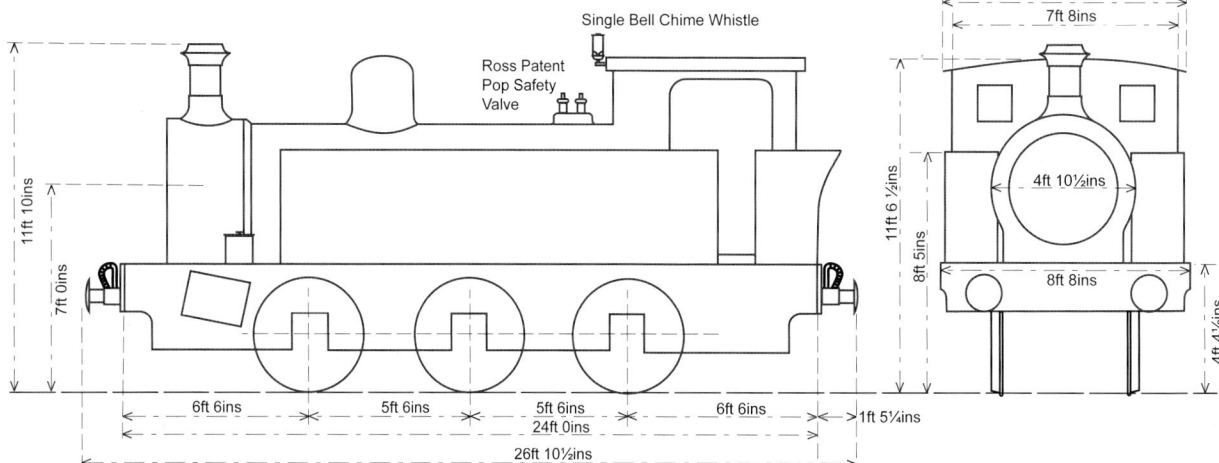

Single Bell Chime Whistle

Ross Patent Pop Safety Valve

11ft 10ins

7ft 0ins

6ft 6ins   5ft 6ins   5ft 6ins   6ft 6ins   1ft 5¼ins

24ft 0ins

26ft 10½ins

8ft 0ins

7ft 8ins

11ft 6½ins

8ft 5ins

4ft 10½ins

8ft 8ins

4ft 4¼ins

	T. C. Q.		T. C. Q.		T. C. Q.		Total T. C. Q.
Weight Empty	12. 6. 2.		10. 19. 2.		10. 3. 3.		33. 9. 3.
Weight Loaded	14. 2. 2.		14. 7. 0.		14. 4. 3.		42.14. 1.

W.I.M.R.
SELBORNE

Makers: R. & W. Hawthorn, Leslie & Co. Ltd, Newcastle-Upon-Tyne
Makers No. 3531 (1922)
W.D. Boiler No. 4660
Wheels 4ft diameter

Based on a Weight Diagram prepared at Longmoor 4 July 1933.

The arrival of *Selborne* at Longmoor in 1922 marked a turning point in the fortunes of the WIMR. A new 'instructional locomotive', built to the WIMR's specification, *Selborne* gave 25 years of good and reliable service. This view showed the locomotive at the newly-laid platform headshunt at Liss Station on 17th May 1934. Just prior to World War Two, Longmoor workshops gave this engine the 'full-works' lined-out Southern Railway livery but previously it had always carried the WIMR black livery shown here. *H. C. Casserley*

locomotive running and workshops at that time. *Selborne* had an uneventful life, remaining active until the end of World War Two. By all accounts up to the outbreak of war it met all the criteria of a 'Really Useful Engine' but was too light to meet the demands for heavier trains during the war period. Officially withdrawn in 1946, it was disposed of a year later to T. J. Thompson & Sons Ltd for scrap. The name derived from the nearby village of Selborne – part of Woolmer Forest lies within the parish of Selborne.

Selborne as best remembered by World War Two sappers, photographed on 10th March 1938. At the end of the war it was a well-used but still very useful locomotive. *R. K. Blencowe Negative Archive, number BW388*

By the end of World War Two *Selborne* had collected LMR lettering in built-up letters (and a full WD running number, 70204). It was one of only three locomotives known to have spent their entire working life at Longmoor. The ends of the buffer beams had been painted white to make them more visible in blackout conditions.

Photographer unknown

Kitchener [1] (later *Wellington*)	K/2977/1886	0-6-2T
Gordon [1] (205 later 70205)	TVR/306/1897	0-6-2T

In 1927 two powerful ex-Taff Vale Railway tank engines were bought from the GWR. *Kitchener* was built for the TVR by Kitson & Co. Ltd in 1886, designated Class 'M' and allocated running number 168. It was rebuilt at Cardiff in 1905 and on absorption by the GWR renumbered 579. As will be seen from the table of dimensions (Appendix Seventeen) the mechanical details of the two locomotives were similar, the difference in power being accounted for by the lower boiler pressure on *Kitchener* (140psi, whereas *Gordon* was 170psi).

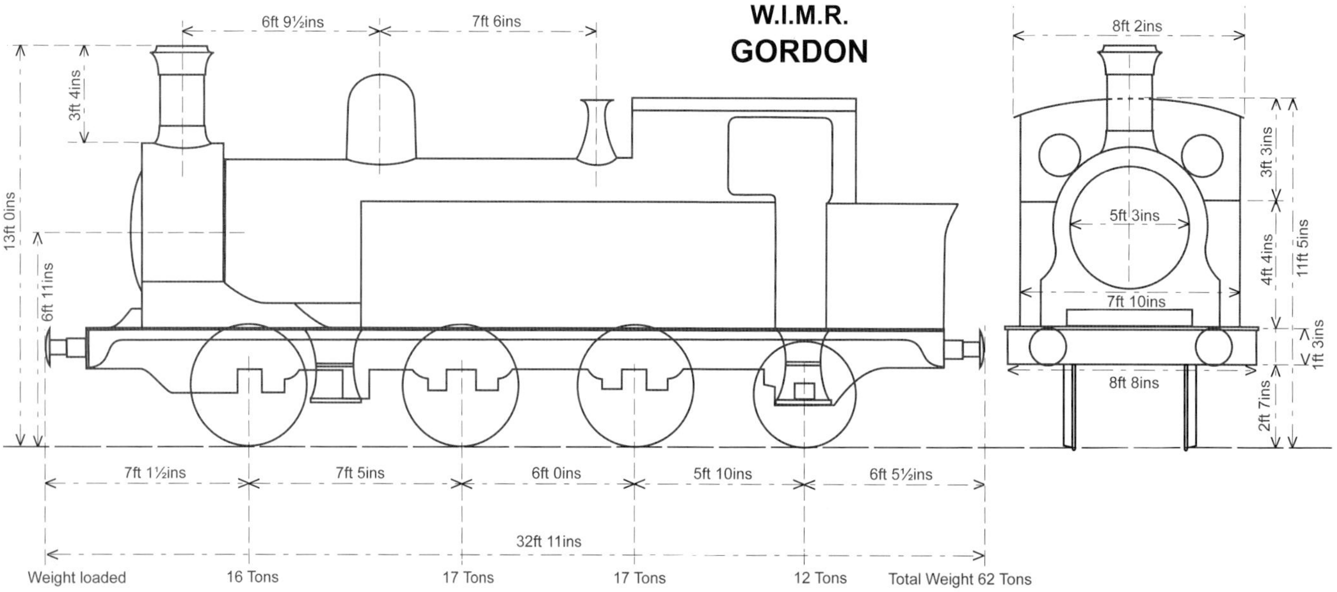

W.I.M.R.
GORDON

6ft 9½ins   7ft 6ins   8ft 2ins

3ft 4ins

13ft 0ins

6ft 11ins

3ft 3ins

5ft 3ins

4ft 4ins   11ft 5ins

7ft 10ins

1ft 3ins

8ft 8ins

2ft 7ins

7ft 1½ins   7ft 5ins   6ft 0ins   5ft 10ins   6ft 5½ins

32ft 11ins

Weight loaded   16 Tons   17 Tons   17 Tons   12 Tons   Total Weight 62 Tons

Makers: Taff Vale Railway Co. G.W.R. No. 450
W.D. Boiler No. 4736
Cylinders 17½ins x 26ins
Boiler Pressure 170 lbs per sq. Inch.

Tractive Effort 21,110 lbs
Heating Surface 1,148.5 Grate Area 19.14 sq. ft
Capacity of Bunker 3¼ Tons
Capacity of Tank 1,400 Gallons

Based on a Weight Diagram prepared at Longmoor.

Kitchener [1] was received from the GWR in 1927. At that date the WIMR needed more powerful locomotives to handle the heavy spoil trains from the Liss extension works. Though less powerful than its ex-Taff Vale sister engine, *Kitchener* [1] (seen here on 23rd August 1932) did sterling work on the WIMR. Having been renamed *Wellington* in 1938 it survived until 1940/1 when it was progressively broken up at Longmoor.

Photographer unknown

Probably taken during the 1930 press visit to the WIMR, this photograph gives a good impression of the well-used (but always well-cleaned) locomotives of that era.

John Alsop Collection

Gordon [1] in Longmoor Yard. Arriving at Longmoor only three years after receiving a new boiler, *Gordon* was probably the better bargain of the ex-Taff Vale Railway pair. Sold to a scrap dealer in 1947, *Gordon* is one of the survivors that have made it into preservation in the National Collection, being the last surviving Welsh-built main line locomotive. The two ex-TVR locomotives were distinguishable from each other. *Gordon* had a larger boiler and consequently a shorter, and 'fatter', chimney. On *Kitchener* the boiler was smaller, the chimney longer and more slender.

John Alsop Collection (L&GRP 13376)

Gordon was built at the Taff Vale Railway's works in Cardiff in 1897 being designated Class 'O1' and numbered 28. The GWR renumbered it 450 and fitted a new boiler in 1924. Of the pair it appears to have been very much the better buy and survived at Longmoor until the end of World War Two. *Kitchener* was renamed *Wellington* in 1938 when the new Bagnall locomotive received the *Kitchener* name. By this stage *Wellington* was past its prime and in the absence of an official record is assumed to have been broken up at Longmoor by 1940. It does not appear ever to have carried a WD running number.

Gordon, having worked steadily through the war, survived in a remarkable way. In 1947 it was sold to Jas. N. Connell Ltd of Coatbridge who resold it to the National Coal Board (NCB). In the hands of its new owners *Gordon* worked at South Hetton Colliery, Co. Durham until 1960 when it was withdrawn from service. At about this time its significance as the last standard

gauge locomotive built in Wales was appreciated. So in February 1962 the NCB presented it to British Railways for preservation. BR in turn passed it to the National Museum Wales who in 1967 placed *Gordon* in the care of South Wales Switchgear Ltd, which had taken over the former GWR works at Caerphilly. It is now part of the collection of the National Railway Museum and is (in 2014) in the care of the Gwili Railway and is undergoing restoration at the Llangollen Railway. *Kitchener* was named after Field-Marshal Lord Kitchener, the distinguished former Royal Engineer officer who at the time of his death in the sinking of HMS *Hampshire* in 1916 was Secretary of State for War. *Gordon* was named after Major-General Charles George Gordon, another distinguished Royal Engineer officer who achieved fame in the Chinese campaign of 1862-3 and at Khartoum, where he died defending the city in 1885.

By 1942, *Gordon* [1] had acquired the large bunker extension seen in this photograph, taken as the locomotive waited for its next turn at Longmoor Downs. A Stone's electric generator had been mounted on top of the side tank but no headlamps were fitted. This generator was used during the blackout years mainly to give additional candlepower to the carriage lighting – 'blackout' regulations effectively banned the use of headlights.

H. N. James

Earl Haig (202?)   L&NWR Crewe/3160/1891 2-4-2T
Earl Roberts [1] (205/70205) L&NWR Crewe/3165/1891 2-4-2T

The next two locomotives were bought from the LMS and were the first selected principally for passenger traffic. Why the 5ft 6in. wheeled variety was preferred to the smaller wheeled variant is not known, but the need to use their potential for the fast running cannot have entered into the case. The fact that the LMS offered them for sale at £135 each may have been a more compelling argument. *Earl Haig* (L&NWR No. 658 and later LMS No. 6613) arrived from Crewe in August 1930 and was followed by *Earl Roberts* (L&NWR No. 608 and later LMS No. 6610) the next year. They were 'on the books' at the

outbreak of war in 1939 though *Earl Haig* was out of service. Both were officially withdrawn in 1943, *Earl Roberts* surviving until 1945 before being scrapped, the boiler being retained for instructional purposes for a short period.

Earl Haig was named after Field Marshal Earl Haig, who had succeeded Sir John French as Commander-in-Chief (C-in-C) of the British Expeditionary Force in France in 1916 and commanded the British forces in France for the remainder of World War One. *Earl Roberts* was named after Field Marshal Lord Roberts of Kandahar, perhaps the greatest British military commander of the Victorian era, a hero of the Anglo-Boer War as the C-in-C British forces there from 1899 to 1900.

Above: In this 1930 view, *Earl Haig* was so newly arrived at Longmoor that the LMS smokebox door numberplate 6633 could still be seen and the WIMR workshops had not yet prepared a nameplate. The L&NWR pattern bunker coal rails were still in place. The driver was Sgt N. Tarbit.

F. Jones

Left: A much later view (from the early World War Two era) showing sister locomotive *Earl Roberts* in a version of the Southern Railway green livery adopted by the LMR in 1936. Like *Gordon*, it had also acquired a locally-made extension to the coal bunker.

H. N. James

Weight | 10t. 7c. 0. | 14t. 18c. 0.q | 14t. 0c. 0q. | 11t. 5c. 0q.
In working order

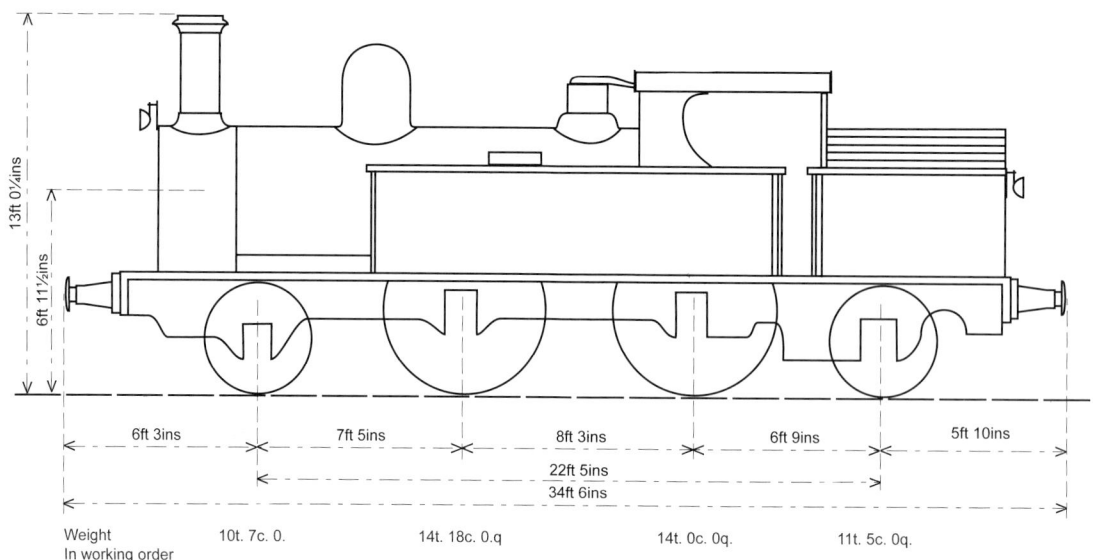

Built by: L&NWR Rly, Crewe, 1890
Cylinders 17ins x 24ins. Boiler Pressure 150 lbs per sq. inch
Driving wheels 5ft 6ins diameter. Carrying Wheels 3ft 9ins diameter
Max Tractive Force - 12,422 lbs at 80% boiler pressure; 13,198 lbs at 85% B.P.
Total Heating Surface 1,074.6 sq. ft Grate Area 17.1 sq. ft
Capacity of Bunker 2½ Tons. Capacity of Tank 1,347 Gallons
Weight Empty; 38 Tons 4 Hundredweights 0 quarters
Weight in working order 50t. 10cwt. 0q.
Similar details apply to the locomotive 'Earl Roberts'.

Based on a Weight Diagram
prepared at Longmoor on 13 August 1930,
with the addition of the headlight
fitted in 1934 .

W.I.M.R.
EARL HAIG

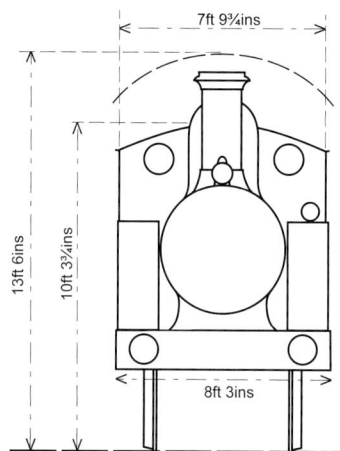

Marlborough (70207)   NSR Stoke Works/ - /1909 0-6-2T

Whether this locomotive was intended in 1936 to be a direct replacement for *Kitchener* [1] is not recorded, but at a time when the War Office budget was just being released from the constraints of 'no major war for ten years', the purchase of this locomotive from the LMS made good sense. Although similar in wheel arrangement to the two Welsh tank engines which had proved so successful at Longmoor, *Marlborough* (essentially built as a passenger locomotive) never became popular with the running staff at Longmoor. This engine had been designed for the North Staffordshire Railway's intensive regional passenger services in and around the 'Five Towns' and for the company's competitive express services to Manchester, Birmingham and Derby. The 'New L' class was therefore endowed with excellent acceleration and a good turn of speed. In this latter respect, *Marlborough* earned a small place in 'Manifold's' *North Staffordshire Railway* published in 1952:

"No. 158 of this class was called on in an emergency to work the 12.05p.m. Manchester to London express from London Road [Manchester] to Stoke. The engine reached a maximum speed of just over 53 mph on the level piece of track through Harecastle hauling a train weighing 310 tons."

At Longmoor *Marlborough* (as ex-NSR No. 158 had been named) was never a complete success, in part because it was already mechanically 'well-worn' on arrival, but also because the footplate layout was inconvenient, especially when shunting. In addition it had a reputation for leaking steam from the cab fittings. The engine gave good service in the early war years. It was set aside in 1942 and thereafter saw little use until in 1946 it was added to a batch of locomotives purchased by Jas. N. Connell Ltd of Coatbridge. Having failed to find a customer to buy it (although at least one other similar locomotive was purchased by the NCB at around this time).

Whilst at Longmoor, *Marlborough* not only retained its LMS smokebox numberplate (2253) – although renumbered 207 in the WD renumbering scheme (later 70207) – but it also gained a pair of cast brass plaques in lieu of builder's plates, fixed below the nameplates in 1940. These read:

'Designed by John H. Adams, built at Stoke Works in 1909 for the North Staffordshire Railway. Classification New L. No. 158. Taken over by LMS 1923. Purchased by War Department 1936.'

Marlborough was named after John Churchill, victor of Blenheim, who was created Duke of Marlborough by Queen Anne in 1702.

L.M.R.
MARLBOROUGH

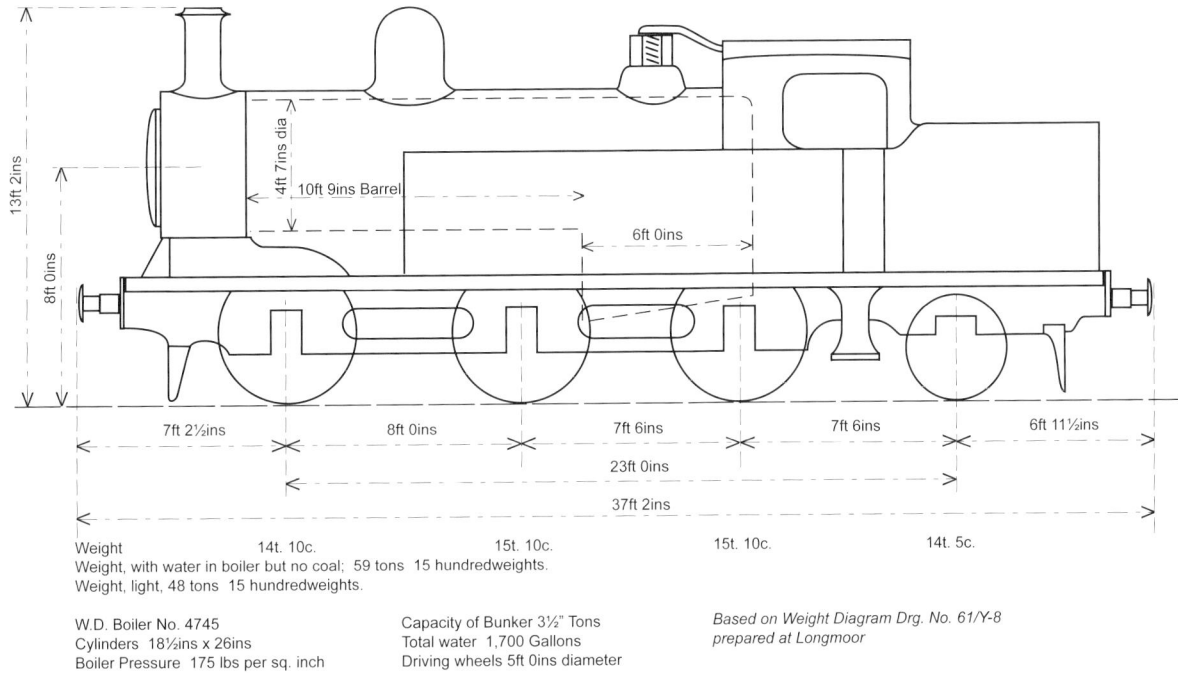

13ft 2ins
8ft 0ins
4ft 7ins dia
10ft 9ins Barrel
6ft 0ins

7ft 2½ins | 8ft 0ins | 7ft 6ins | 7ft 6ins | 6ft 11½ins

23ft 0ins

37ft 2ins

Weight   14t. 10c.   15t. 10c.   15t. 10c.   14t. 5c.
Weight, with water in boiler but no coal; 59 tons 15 hundredweights.
Weight, light, 48 tons 15 hundredweights.

W.D. Boiler No. 4745   Capacity of Bunker 3½" Tons   *Based on Weight Diagram Drg. No. 61/Y-8*
Cylinders 18½ins x 26ins   Total water 1,700 Gallons   *prepared at Longmoor*
Boiler Pressure 175 lbs per sq. inch   Driving wheels 5ft 0ins diameter

Marlborough as modified after delivery from the LMS in 1936. The livery was the post-1936 LMR version of the traditional Southern Railway green and a Stone's electric generator plus electric headlight had been fitted. The LMS smokebox numberplate remained in place throughout the locomotive's time at Longmoor. The crew posed for Spr James' camera as 'C' Passenger waited at Whitehill. The loco was carrying a pair of re-railing ramps on the front footplate – a wise precaution.

H. N. James

By 10th August 1946, *Marlborough* had joined the line of ex-LMR locomotives awaiting disposal in Longmoor Yard. Note the small cast plaque below the nameplate (in lieu of a builder's plate) made in the RE Longmoor workshops during the war. *Photographer unknown*

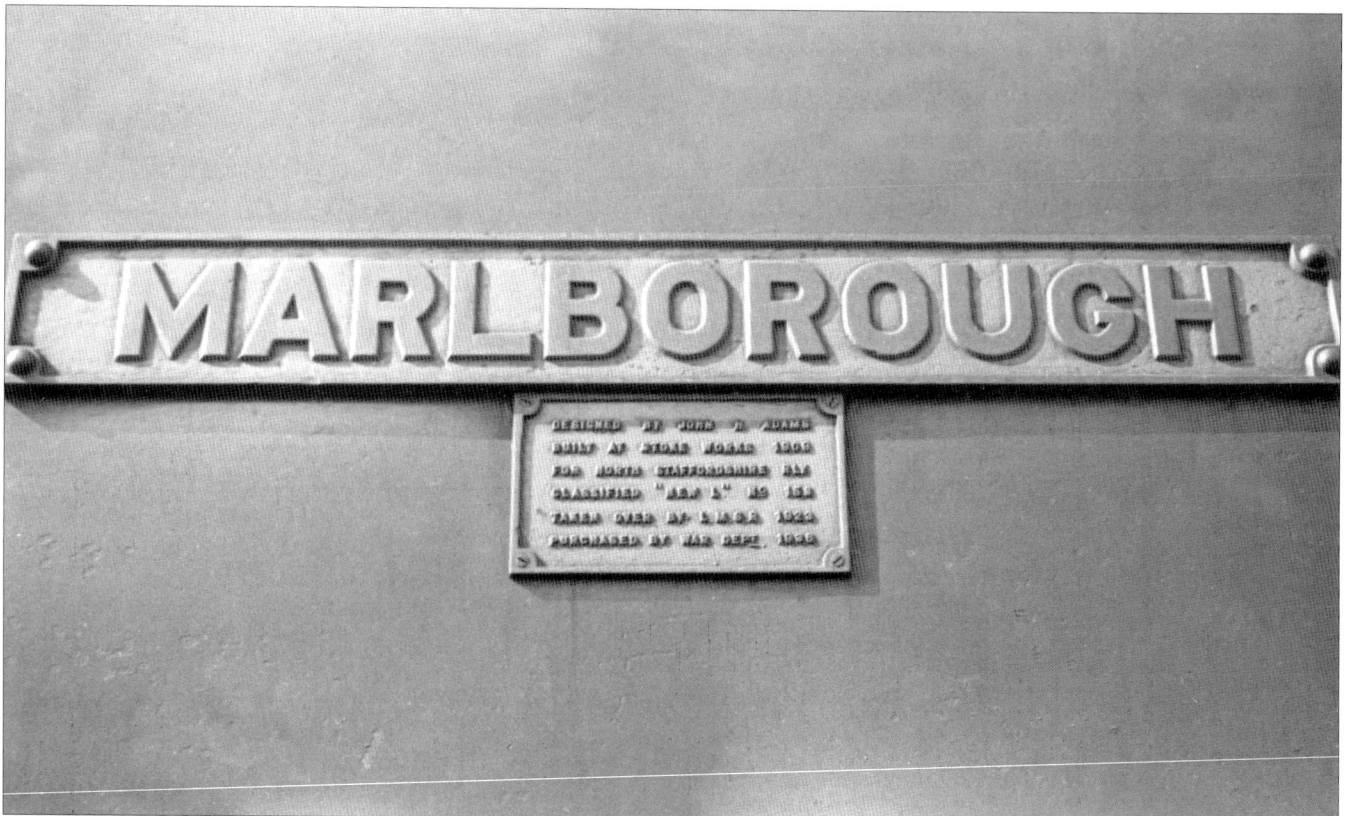

Detail of additional plate fitted by LMR Workshops. It read: 'DESIGNED BY JOHN H ADAMS BUILT AT STOKE WORKS 1909 FOR NORTH STAFFORDSHIRE RLY CLASSIFIED "NEW L." NO 158 TAKEN OVER BY L.M.S.R. 1923 PURCHASED BY WAR DEP^T. 1936'.

Photographer unknown

Kitchener [2] (70208)   WB/2587/1938   0-6-2T

By 1937 the entire political scene had changed. Retrenchment had given way to a rapid programme of rearmament in the face of threats from the Nazi government of Germany. The cost of a new 'instructional locomotive' could now be met from the War Office's enhanced rearmament budget. The official order of July 1937 was placed with W. G. Bagnall Ltd of Stafford. It would be the first new locomotive to be delivered to Longmoor for sixteen years and the last locomotive to be designed specifically for instructional use. At a time when the British locomotive builders (along with much of the country's heavy engineering industry) were recovering from the slump of the early 1930s, this was an ideal opportunity for Bagnalls to display their talents. This they did to good effect, the new locomotive being featured in a special article in the *Railway Gazette* of 8th July 1938.

This unique locomotive was designed throughout so that all working parts could be easily dismantled and replaced by trainees. Originally built for conventional coal firing, it was converted to oil-firing (for instructional purposes) in July 1942. Some of the special equipment fitted included a full array of 24volt electric lighting powered by a 550watt Stone's steam turbo-generator, Lambert's wet sanding gear, an automatic continuous blowdown valve of LMS pattern and a combined vacuum and air braking system. This used a Westinghouse No. 4 valve to operate the air brakes on the engine and train through a triple valve and double check valves. A separate quick-acting No. 9 valve mounted below the main brake valve was used to operate the air brake on the engine alone when shunting. The vacuum brake incorporated a proportional valve, automatically applying the engine air brake in proportion to the train brake when operating a vacuum braked train. The boiler was not fitted with a superheater.

Kitchener [2] was used throughout World War Two and by 1945 was in need of a heavy overhaul. It was therefore disposed of, to the Appleby Frodingham Steel Co. Ltd at Scunthorpe in 1948. In October 1949 it was sold again, passing into the ownership of the NCB. After spending some time at the Garw Colliery, it was transferred to the Duffryn Rhondda Colliery where it continued to work until scrapped in 1966. By this date the preservation movement was steaming ahead and only by a whisker did *Kitchener* miss out, having been surveyed by a group from the K&ESR who sadly went on save another locomotive instead.

The summer of 1939 marked the end of an era for the LMR. At this point it had reached a state of completion and fitness for purpose as an instructional military railway never previously achieved. It is therefore useful to summarise the motive power situation at this time. Of a total of nine steam locomotives on site, six were available for traffic and three stored 'out of use'. The three instructional locomotives (*Sir John French*, *Selborne*, and *Kitchener* [2]) were all considered to be in good running order as was *Earl Roberts* though the latter was only of use with the lightest trains. *Gordon* and *Marlborough* had been reduced to 'light duties' whilst *Kingsley*, *Earl Haig* and *Wellington* were definitely non-runners.

W. G. BAGNALL LTD., CASTLE ENGINE WORKS, STAFFORD

When W. G. Bagnall Ltd built *Kitchener* [2] they were keen to publicise their latest product to potential industrial users. This maker's official photograph was widely distributed at a time when those British locomotive manufacturers that had survived the depression years were rebuilding their markets. It showed *Kitchener* [2] as delivered in the full 'Southern Green' livery.   *Maker's photograph*

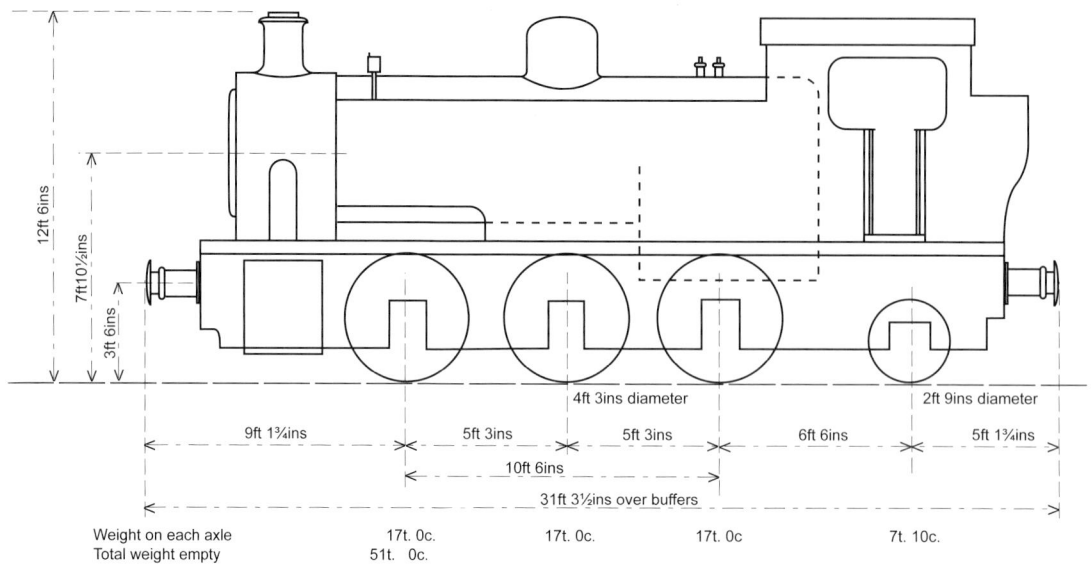

L.M.R.
KITCHENER

12ft 6ins
7ft 10½ins
3ft 6ins

4ft 3ins diameter
2ft 9ins diameter

9ft 1¾ins   5ft 3ins   5ft 3ins   6ft 6ins   5ft 1¾ins

10ft 6ins

31ft 3½ins over buffers

Weight on each axle   17t. 0c.   17t. 0c.   17t. 0c   7t. 10c.
Total weight empty   51t. 0c.

Makers: W. G. Bagnall Ltd
Makers No. 2587   Date 1938
Cylinders 18ins x 24ins

Based on a Weight Diagram prepared at Longmoor.

Left: In 1940, the late H. N. James (then a sapper under training) was able to sneak a picture of *Kitchener* [2] shunting at Woolmer. The livery was still the pre-war LMR version of 'Southern Green'. Note the SPL 1 Duty board ('target') over the buffer and the lifting eyes attached to the front buffer beam.   *H. N. James*

Below: Though well-worn by the end of its war duties on the LMR, *Kitchener* [2] still had a future when photographed on the 'awaiting disposal' line in 1946. It eventually passed to the NCB in South Wales and was not scrapped by them until 1966.   *Photographer unknown*

Section V : War Establishment loaned locomotives 1939-1945

Mobilisation and the enlargement of the Supplementary Reserve caused an immediate increase in traffic on the LMR at the end of August 1939. Additional motive power was urgently required, both to handle the increased traffic of troops and stores and to cater for the large scale training programmes that were starting. The only solution was to requisition, borrow or buy locomotives from the main line companies. The most pressing need was for additional Westinghouse braked engines to train footplate crews for operations in France.

L&NER Locomotives

The first arrivals were a group of J68/J69 Class 0-6-0T of the classes built for the London Liverpool St suburban services of the former GER. With Westinghouse brakes these simple and robust locomotives were ideal for training drivers before embarkation for France. The following table lists these locomotives. Details of their subsequent dispersal will be found in the RCTS publication *Locomotives of the LNER, Part 8A*. At Longmoor, these locomotives ran at first in L&NER livery though later some had the lettering 'LNER' or 'NE' painted out. Finally WD running numbers were painted on in large plain numerals.

L&NER Number	WD Number	At Longmoor From	At Longmoor To	Remarks
7274	78	10/39	1/42	Sent to No. 1 Mil Port (Faslane).
7272	79	10/39	1/42	Sent to No. 1 Mil Port.
7081	80	10/39	1/42	Sent to No. 2 Mil Port (Cairnryan).
7197	81	10/39	1/42	Sent to No. 2 Mil Port.
7168	82	10/39	1/42	Sent to No. 2 Mil Port.
7058	83	10/39	(1)	Sent to No. 1 Mil Port.
7388	84	10/39	(1)	Sent to ESD, Long Marston.
7041	85	10/39	3/42	Class J68; Sent to No. 1 Mil Port.
7054	86	10/39	(1)	Sent to No. 1 Mil Port.
7056	87	10/39	(1)	Sent to No. 1 Mil Port.
7344	88	10/39	(1)	Sent to No. 2 Mil Port.
7362	89	10/39	(1)	Sent to No. 2 Mil Port and scrapped there.
7167	90	5/40	(1)	Sent to No. 1 Mil Port, replaced 7271 at Longmoor.
7271	-	10/39	5/40	Defective locomotive returned to L&NER, no WD number allocated.
7088	91	10/39	(1)	Sent to No. 2 Mil Port.

Notes:

(1) After delivery to LMR probably allocated to Melbourne Military Railway and used there until January 1942. Some, but not all, may then have returned to Longmoor pending reallocation.

(2) The locomotives at Faslane were all purchased in 1946 by Metal Industries Ltd, which took over the military port for ship-breaking activities.

These ex-Great Eastern J68/J69 0-6-0Ts were amongst the first ex-L&NER locos to arrive at Longmoor after the outbreak of war in 1939. Initially they continued to carry their former main line numbers but by the time of this view (mid-1940) WD numbers had been painted on the side tanks.

H. N. James

Ex-L&NER 7056 and (behind) 7344 in Longmoor Yard, 1940. *H. N. James*

GWR Locomotives

The GWR contribution is more complicated because the locomotives concerned (all 0-6-0 Dean Goods Class) appeared on the LMR during two distinct periods. The first arrivals were those locomotives of the original WD requisition which had not been shipped to France by the time of the evacuation from Dunkirk. These were sent to Longmoor (still with all modifications for their use on French railways) whilst new tasks were found for them. The locomotives were later deployed in a variety of roles in depots and on main line duties. They were also employed supporting the super-heavy batteries of the Royal Artillery whose rail-mounted guns were deployed in south-east England to engage cross-Channel targets in Northern France. After the re-conquest of the French channel ports in the summer following D-Day there was no further need for the super-heavy batteries in England, so the locomotives attached to individual guns were returned to Longmoor. Those which were fit for service were employed to replace standard Austerity locomotives which were at that time being shipped to Europe. At the end of the war all the Dean Goods engines, except 70195, were quickly disposed of from Longmoor. 70195 was retained for rerailing practice until about 1959 when it too was broken up. In WD numerical order the locomotives with identified connections with Longmoor were:

GWR Number	WD Number	Remarks
2433	(700) 93	Purchased by WD Dec 1940 to replace Dunkirk losses. Vacuum brake fitted. Returned to Longmoor June 1944 and ran there till c1946.
2470	(700) 95	Ex-ROD 1917-1919. World War Two as for 70093 above.
2529	(70) 156	Purchased by WD Oct 1940. Part of stock requisitioned for BEF but not sent to France. At Longmoor October 1940 to March 1942 and returned 44/46.
2340	(70) 177	Ex-ROD 1917-1919. Purchased etc. as for 156. Fitted Westinghouse brake, Flaman speed recorder, pannier tanks and condensing gear. Modified for oil burning. At Longmoor October 1940 to early 1942 then to 195 Tn Coy RE Ashford and returned (less condensing gear and tanks) June 1944 to 1947.
2466	(70) 179	Requisitioned October 1939, purchased October 1940. Condensing gear and pannier tanks fitted 1940. Issued direct to 195 Tn Coy RE but returned to LMR June 1944 to 1946.
2514	(70) 180	Ex-ROD 1917-19. Detail as for 70179.
2531	(70) 195	Detail as for 70179 but retained at Longmoor until c1959 for rerailing instruction. Scrapped at Longmoor.
2576	(70) 196	Detail as for 70179. Operating unit not known.
2540	(70) 197	Detail as for 70179. Operating unit not known.
2559	(70) 198	Detail as for 70179. Operated by 195 Tn Coy RE.
2517	(70) 199	ROD 1917-19. Detail as for 70179.
2552	(70) 200	Requisitioned October 1939, purchased by WD October 1940 and at Longmoor till early 1942.

In his recent publication *WD Supporting the British Expeditionary Force* William Aves recounts in detail the movements of this class in Army service during World War Two. Their service in both World Wars earned them the affection and praise of two generations of military railwaymen.

Ex-GWR Dean Goods 0-6-0s were used in World War Two on WD service. This example (lacking any form of number) was returned to Longmoor by one of the UK-based Tn operating companies in 1944, still retaining the Westinghouse brake pump, pipes and reservoirs. Photographed outside Longmoor running shed in August 1946.
Brunel University Collection, ref: 13459

In contrast, by August 1946 GWR 2559 (WD 70198) had been through the LMR workshop, receiving a lick of paint and its full WD number in the process. Most of the ex-L&NER and ex-GWR locomotives remained at Longmoor until the latter part of 1946 when they were (with one exception) withdrawn in a second wave post-war clearance.
H. C. Casserley 47452

The sole surviving Dean Goods at Longmoor by the mid-1950s was WD 70195 which was retained until 1959 as a training aid for rerailing exercises, in which role it became increasingly battered and bent.
P. Coutanche

LMS Locomotives

The LMS contribution to the steam stock of the LMR was the least of the 'big four', but as we shall show later, this was made up for by their diesel locomotives. The two engines supplied were a pair of elderly ex-L&NWR 'Special Tanks' which are believed to have arrived at Longmoor via No. 2 Railway Training Centre at Derby in late 1941. Details are scanty:

LMS Number	Building Details	Remarks
27384	2177/1878	Arrived 1941, dismantled Sep 1942 and used for fitters' instruction on boiler and brakes.
27477	3095/1889	Arrived 1941, and broken up by early 1942. Probably never steamed at Longmoor.

Southern Railway Locomotives

As these ran at Longmoor throughout the war period, they are probably better known than the locomotives of the other companies. Nevertheless there are still a few points which, in the absence of full official records, cannot be confirmed.

| *Earl Roberts* [2] | WD(7)2400 | SRly 2013 | 4-4-2T Class 'I' (Ex LB&SCR) |
| *(Kingsley)* [2] | WD(7)2401 | SRly 2019 | 4-4-2T Class 'I' (Ex LB&SCR) |

By 1945 the two ex-LB&SCR 4-4-2Ts were completely worn out and were replaced on the 'Bullet' services by Austerity saddle tanks as the latter became available. The locomotive behind *Earl Roberts* [2] was WD 75275 (later *Matruh*), which arrived at Longmoor in March 1945 and was still in WD livery when photographed on 25th May 1946.
R. C. Riley, Transport Treasury RCR 1214

Earl Roberts [2] probably came to Longmoor first in 1941 (on loan) though the WD did not complete its purchase until April 1942. It became, to all intents, part of the LMR, collecting nameplates salvaged from its earlier namesake and being numbered 72400 as shown in this view outside the Longmoor locomotive shed.

R. K. Blencowe Negative Archive, number 32969

Not so lucky was sister engine 72401 the nameplates for which (*Kingsley*) mysteriously vanished and were never fitted. Both the ex-LB&SCR 'I' Class tanks were well worn when they arrived at Longmoor and by the end of World War Two they were only fit for scrap.

R. C. Riley, Transport Treasury RCR 1213

These locomotives were withdrawn by the SRly in January 1939 and November 1937 respectively. At the outbreak of war they were temporarily deployed as air-raid shelters at locomotive sheds, being placed above a convenient outdoor ash-pit until permanent shelters could be built. They were reinstated and overhauled at Ashford in 1941 and finally sold to the WD in April 1942. 72401 had the name *Kingsley* allocated, but it is thought that plates were never fitted. On arrival, despite their recent overhaul, these locomotives were at the end of their working lives and by 1946 they were worn out. In 1950 they were sold to Abelsons for scrap. They were generally employed on LMR passenger services.

Class 'A12' Nos 599, 618, 638, 625, (625 later exchanged for 614). All hired by WD 1940-3. Ex-L&SWR   0-4-2

It is not certain whether all five of these locomotives were at Longmoor throughout the war period. 625 had been withdrawn by SRly in January 1939, but was reinstated at the outbreak of war. Final withdrawal took place between 1946 and 1948. 625 was known affectionately as 'The Emerald Queen' having retained its Southern green livery - it was reserved for such special tasks as hauling the Commandant's saloon. At some point it was returned to the Southern in exchange for No. 614 of the same class.

Left: 'A12' Class member 618 on Duty 'D' awaiting servicing in Longmoor Yard. This locomotive appears to have been repainted in Southern unlined black livery before arriving at Longmoor.

Below: Two of the ex-L&SWR 'A12' Class transferred on loan to Longmoor by the Southern Railway during World War Two, the nearer being SR No. 638. This pair were used for basic footplate crew training whereas 625 of the same class was saved for special occasions - it had retained its Southern olive green livery.   *both H. N. James*

Ex-SE&CR Class 'O1' 1046 Hired 1940-4   0-6-0

This veteran of 1894 was usually employed on the Hollywater Loop for continuous running training for engine crews. After service at Longmoor it was returned to the SRly and survived to be withdrawn by BR in October 1948.

Ex-LB&SCR Class 'D1' 2233, 2240, 2286 Hired 1940-4 0-4-2T

The 'D1' class were used almost exclusively for camp passenger services. 2240 was fitted to work motor trains (Class 'D1/M') but the equipment was not used at Longmoor. 2233 was damaged in a collision and returned to the SRly as 'beyond economic repair'.

Between 1940 and 1944, a trio of ex-LB&SCR 'D1' Class 0-4-2Ts were hired from the Southern Railway, initially to provide extra motive power for the 'Bullet' service from Liss to Bordon. With a thirty-minute interval between trains for up to sixteen hours daily, this service required that four locomotives be rostered. Here 2233 from Duty 'B' paused at Longmoor running shed between turns.   *H. N. James*

Another of the trio of Class 'D1' locomotives was seen here at Longmoor Downs waiting to start a 'long distance run' with a trainee footplate crew. These runs created the distance by making several circuits of the Hollywater Loop. The train weight would be made up with wagons filled with ballast so that the locomotive and its crew were worked hard. For young soldiers who would soon be on active service in the Middle East this was valuable experience.

H. N. James

Ex-L&SWR Class 'O2' 213	Hired 1942-3	0-4-4T

The solitary 'O2' was hired to run the first vacuum braked passenger set acquired at the same time. Its Longmoor career came to a spectacular end in the Toronto sidings crash in November 1943. It was returned to the SRly which considered repair to be economic and so 213 became the last survivor of this group of hired locomotives, being withdrawn by BR in February 1953.

Below: Ex-L&SWR 'O2' Class 0-4-4T No. 213 was, when it arrived at Longmoor in 1942, unique in that it was the only passenger locomotive not fitted for air-braking. It was intended to operate this locomotive with the newly-acquired ex-SE&CR 'Birdcage' set to reinforce the 'Bullet' services. 213 did this most successfully until the spectacular collision at the end of Toronto sidings in November 1943. *H. N. James*

Section VI : War Establishment –
WD Standard locomotives 1941-5

To fulfil its role as a training establishment, Longmoor acquired examples of each type of WD standard locomotive as soon as these were available. Examples of the USA classes were also borrowed to assist training of British crews. Listing these locomotives in a meaningful way is complicated by the fact that Longmoor, and the area served by the LMR, had by 1944 become a vast storehouse of railway equipment. This included several hundred locomotives. Those which had seen service on the main line after their construction for the War Department were brought to Longmoor for overhaul and/ or preparation for shipping, whilst those of American origin were assembled, tested and stored. As a result, large numbers of locomotives existed on the railway, of which only a few were in continuous use. However, for testing and to overcome the occasional motive power crisis, stored locomotives would be borrowed and steamed on an 'as required' basis. The following list includes only locomotives known to have been allocated to the LMR operating stock for significant periods:

WD Number	Type	At Longmoor From	To	Remarks
(70)421	LMS 2-8-0 Stanier '8F'	2/41	10/41	BP/7001/41. Named *Wolfe* at Longmoor. Shipped to Iran (Persia) late 1941 and there numbered 41.123. In 1951 became Egyptian State Railways and withdrawn in 1962/63.
(7)7015	2-8-0 British Austerity	3/43	45	To Belgium (Muysen) 1945, returned to BR as 90113. Builder NBL (24986/43).
(7)7129		11/43	45	To France (Lille) 1945, returned to BR as 90585. Builder VF (4945/43).
(7)7168		6/43	45	To Holland (NS 4340 Roosendaal) 1945. Builder NBL (25039/43).
(7)7195		9/43	45	Experimentally armour plated on boiler before delivery to Melbourne Mil Rly. Later at Longmoor where armour plate removed before shipping in 1945 to Belgium (Muysen). Returned to BR as 90172. Builder NBL (25066/43).

One of the first of the newly-built 2-8-0 WD 'Austerity' locomotives at Longmoor was WD 7195. After delivery to the Melbourne Military Railway, it moved to Longmoor for further trials in late 1943, was later returned to normal configuration there and shipped to Belgium in 1945. The armour was designed both to disguise the profile of the engine and to give a reasonable degree of protection to the boiler and crew in an air attack. In the event, Allied air superiority in North West Europe from 1944 virtually eliminated this threat and the trials were discontinued.

Photographer unknown

Between March 1943 and early 1945, WD 7015 was allocated to Longmoor for crew training and familiarisation. When photographed in Longmoor Yard, the locomotive was in (grimy) WD livery. It was shipped to Belgium in early 1945. On return from war service it was purchased by British Railways and numbered 90113.

Photographer unknown

WD Number	Type	At Longmoor		Remarks
		From	To	
77241	2-8-0 British Austerity	11/43	45	To Belgium (Antwerp-Dam.) Returned to BR as 90205. Builder NBL (25112/43).
79250		1/45	58	Builder VF (5193/45). – See section VII.
(7)5000 (7)5002	0-6-0ST British Austerity	4/43	44	First production examples to LMR and Bicester for extended trials. To store at Longmoor (1/44) then shipped to France (1/45).
71453		6/45	9/46	Used prior to shipment to replace pre-war LMR locomotives. All shipped overseas or sold. See section VII.
75288		6/45	10/46	
75289		6/45	7/46	
2292, 2639	2-8-0 USA Austerity	7/43	6/44	Built by ALCO (Baldwin Loco Works), Philadelphia (USA). 1943. Returned to USATC after D-Day.
1255, 1286 1460 75215, 75217	0-6-0T USA Austerity	11/42	-/44	Built by Davenport Loco Works, Iowa (USA). 1255 converted to oil-firing at Longmoor. Returned to USATC after D-Day.

Unfortunately in the latter years of World War Two the record-keeping at Longmoor was patchy. Whilst proper records were certainly made at the time, it is very likely that they were subsequently destroyed after the war. The locomotives (70)421, (7)7015, (7)5000 and to a lesser extent 2292 and 1255, were used by the LMR permanent staff to prepare training material, user manuals and similar for issue to military railwaymen.

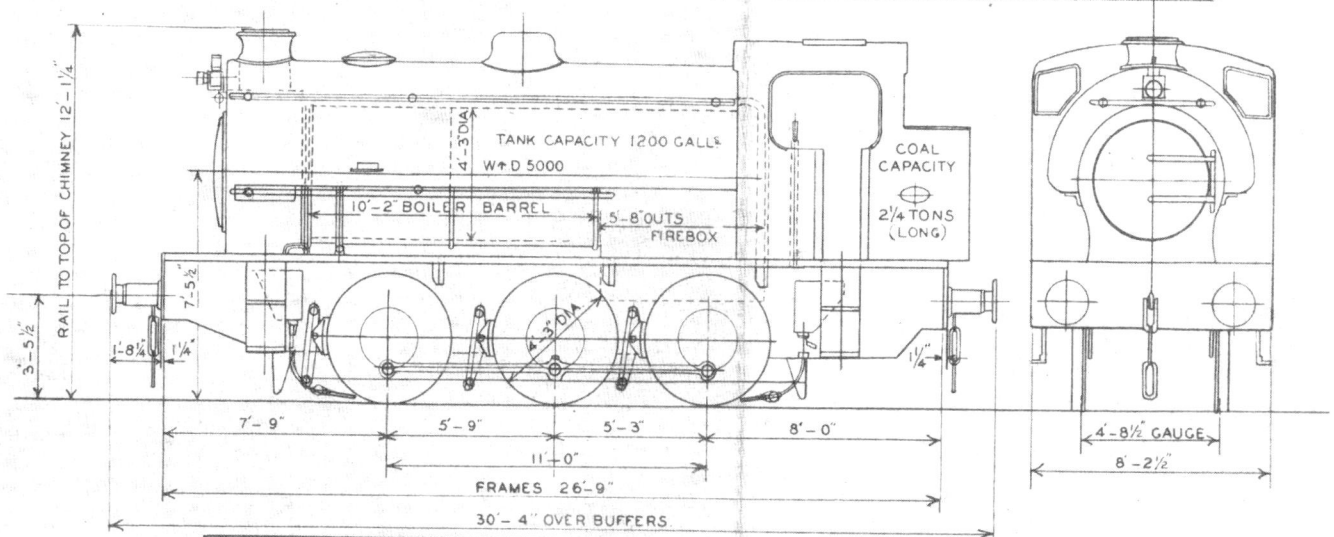

– BRITISH-060-TANK LOCOMOTIVE –

S.O.S.E.T.O.U.S.A.
OFFICE OF CHIEF OF TRANSPORTATION
MILITARY RAILWAYS.– DATE: SEPT. 1. 1943.

MINISTRY OF SUPPLY. "AUSTERITY" LOCOMOTIVE. 4' 8½" GAUGE.

CYLINDERS (2)........	19" Diam × 28" Stroke
COUPLED WHEELS........	4' 8½" Diam
TRUCK WHEELS........	3' 2" Diam
WHEEL BASE, COUPLED........	16' 3"
WHEEL BASE, TOTAL........	24' 10"
LENGTH OVER BUFFERS........	63' 6"

TANK CAPACITY........	5000 Gallons
COAL CAPACITY........	9 Tons
TENDER WHEELS........	3' 2" Diam
TENDER WHEEL BASE........	15' 9"
WHEEL BASE ENGINE AND TENDER........	53' 1½"
HEIGHT. 12' 10 9/16"	WIDTH. 8' 11"

BRAKES: STEAM ON ENGINE AND TENDER: VACUUM AND WESTINGHOUSE FOR TRAIN

HEATING SURFACE LARGE TUBES....	Sq Ft
Do do SMALL do....	Do
Do do FIREBOX....	Do
Do do TOTAL....	Do
SUPERHEATER SURFACE....	Do
GRATE AREA....	Do
TRACTIVE FORCE 85 BOILER PRESSURE	34215 lbs

BOILER MAXIMUM OUTSIDE DIAMETER........	5' 8½"
BOILER, LENGTH OF BARREL........	11' 7½"
FIREBOX LENGTH OUTSIDE........	9' 4"
LENGTH BETWEEN TUBE PLATES........	12' 0"
SUPERHEATER, 28 ELEMENTS........	1½" Diam
GRATE........ 8' 7 7/16" × 3' 3½"	
BOILER PRESSURE........	225 lbs per Sq In

WEIGHTS ENGINE, 72 Tons; TENDER, 56 Tons; ENGINE AND TENDER, 128 Tons; ADHESIVE WEIGHT, 62 Tons   ENGINE, LIGHT, 65 Tons   TENDER, LIGHT, 2½ Tons

REFERENCE No. 2808.

US-built WD 1255 was immaculately prepared as it awaited its next duty in Longmoor Yard in the summer of 1943. At Longmoor it was converted to oil firing and remained for crew training until it was returned to the USATC in late 1944. Note that UK-style lamp brackets have been fitted to the smokebox and buffer beam.

H. N. James

The second of the trio of USATC 0-6-0T 'Switchers', being usefully employed in Longmoor Yard in the summer of 1943. British-style shunting with hand-braked wagons had not been in the original design brief. Fractured buffer-beams (designed originally for use with centre couplings) became a problem with these engines, solved by some local re-design in the Longmoor workshops.

H. N. James

Ships that pass in the night. In addition to the large number of resident locomotives needed to handle the vastly increased LMR traffic during the later years of World War Two, there was a constant traffic of locomotives en route from the ports or manufacturers to military depots to await shipment overseas. Two locomotives, captured on camera in late 1944, are just one example of this kind of wartime traffic.

H. N. James

In July 1943, USATC No. 2292 was loaned to the LMR for training and familiarisation on the American-designed Austerity locomotives before they were issued to railway operating units of the Royal Engineers for the liberation of Europe. No. 2292 was returned to the USATC shortly after D-Day and sent by them to France.

F. R. M. Lawrence

WD 73651 was the first UK Austerity 2-10-0 to arrive at Longmoor, in December 1943. It was the largest locomotive to operate on the LMR, initially for crew training. As AD 600 *Gordon* [2] this engine remained at Longmoor throughout its military service, becoming the last surviving example of its kind. It was still in use at the closure of the LMR in 1969. The following year it was transferred to the Severn Valley Railway and is now (2014) on display in the Engine House at Highley.

L. Perkins

Section VII - 1945-1970

The retrenchment that followed the end of World War Two had inevitable repercussions on the LMR. These were however neither as sudden (nor as drastic) as those experienced in 1919-20. As far as locomotives are concerned there was a period of concentration during 1945-46 when various surplus assets were gathered at Longmoor prior to sale or redeployment. A motley collection of War Department stock and war-requisitioned locomotives filtered back to Longmoor as they were replaced by standard Austerity locomotives in depots and ordnance factories. Shipments to Europe continued and other locomotives were sold to the main line companies.

It is impossible to depict the activity of this period accurately as details of many of the movements went unrecorded. We therefore take up the story about 1950 when, as a result of a general stock-taking of both the equipment and the role of the LMR, a new Peace Establishment was drafted. This establishment was significantly larger than its predecessor of 1939. The steam locomotives on charge were:

Type	Arrangement	Quantity
British Austerity	2-10-0	2
British Austerity	2-8-0	2
British Austerity	0-6-0ST	11
American Austerity	2-8-0	1
American Austerity	0-6-0T	1
Miscellaneous locos		2
	TOTAL	19

Individual details of these locomotives are given below.

73651 (600)	Gordon [2]	NBL/25437/43	2-10-0
73979 (601)	Kitchener [3]	NBL/25643/45	2-10-0

Gordon [2] was the first 2-10-0 to run at Longmoor, arriving in December 1943. It had a remarkably uneventful career. This engine remained the last example of the class in service and was earmarked for preservation after the closure of the LMR. The assistance of the Transport Trust was sought and a satisfactory arrangement made with the Severn Valley Railway. *Gordon* [2] moved to Bridgnorth in September 1971 and was steamed there regularly for several years. It was used occasionally on other lines, including a time on the Great Central Railway. Eventually a firebox defect and expiry of its boiler certificate led to its withdrawal followed by a long period 'in storage'. It was chosen in 2007 as one of the non-operational SVR locomotives to be placed on exhibition in 'The Engine House' at Highley and was given a cosmetic restoration before being placed on display.

Kitchener [3] on the other hand, was one of the last batch of 2-10-0s to be delivered from Glasgow and did not enter LMR service until after the war ended. When first prepared for service there, the name *The Sapper* (allocated in the 1945 naming scheme) was carried for a short period though the better known *Kitchener* was substituted at an early stage.

In 1958 *Kitchener* [3] was selected to be modified to the WD War Standard Specification that had been prepared by the War Office Technical Design Panel. The modification work was carried out by the North British Locomotive Company in Glasgow and the locomotive subsequently carried out extended trials on the Scottish Region of BR until 1959. Oil-firing was

This view from the 1955 Open Day shows the unusual pairing of WD 600 *Gordon* [2] with an LMS pattern tender. At the time, 600's own tender was at Derby, attached to one of the newly-overhauled WD Stanier 8Fs for trials. *Photographer unknown*

There was seldom a need for more than a single large Austerity to haul even the heaviest trains on the post-war LMR. Occasionally such an impressive 'triple-header consist' might have been called for by the construction engineers to test bridge structures. On 2nd September 1950 the trio of *Kitchener* [3], *Major General Carl. R. Gray Jr.* and *Sir Guy Williams* were giving footplate rides at the Annual Open Day.

Lens of Sutton Association reference MA 32

WD 600 *Gordon* [2] at rest in Longmoor Yard on 4th October 1958, now reunited with its own tender. This locomotive always carried a single Westinghouse air pump whereas *Kitchener* received a twin pump when upgraded to the WD War Standard Specification in 1958.   *R. C. Riley*

In 1945, 73797 was delivered from the North British Locomotive Co. Ltd to Longmoor. A short time later this view showed the engine being first prepared for service. Note the curved nameplate *The Sapper* which it carried in its earliest years on the LMR. In the background was a WD 153hp diesel shunter in the livery of the Detmold Military Railway complete with a large 21st Army Group badge on the bonnet side.

Photographer unknown

WD 601 *Kitchener* [3] at Carlisle (Kingmoor) Shed during trial runs with heavy freight trains on BR(ScR) following its rebuild to the new WD War Standard Specification by the North British Locomotive Co. Ltd, and conversion to oil burning, in 1958. *Tim Edwards*

WD 601 *Kitchener* [3] at Longmoor on return from Scotland.   *Photographer unknown*

one of the options included in the specification and after its return from Carlisle (Kingmoor), *Kitchener* [3] ran as an oil-burner at Longmoor. Although the firebox sustained damage early in 1967, it was the problems relating to the removal of the green paint applied to it for the filming of 'The Great St. Trinian's Train Robbery' in the Autumn of 1965 which led directly to its being withdrawn. It remained out of service at Longmoor still with large patches of the green livery applied for filming and was later scrapped.

77337 (400) *Sir Guy Williams*	NBL/25205/43	2-8-0
79250 (401) *Major General McMullen*	VF/5193/45	2-8-0

Sir Guy Williams, running un-named as WD 77337, first appeared at Longmoor in 1944. After delivery from the makers in 1943 this locomotive had been loaned to the L&NER and was stationed at March. On 2nd June 1944 it was the engine of the munitions train which exploded catastrophically at Soham in Cambridgeshire. Though shielded from some of the

All that remained of WD 77337 after the disastrous munitions train explosion at Soham on 2nd June 1944. At the time 77337 was on loan to the L&NER from Longmoor. The direct blast, emanating from burning ammunition wagons behind the engine, totally destroyed the cab and killed the fireman – by a miracle the driver survived. Such was the force that the firebox cladding plates were embossed with the outline of the firebox rivets. The engine was later rebuilt by the makers and arrived in Europe at the end of 1944. After service in France and the Netherlands, it was returned to Longmoor in 1949. It ran as *Sir Guy Williams* until scrapped in the mid 1960s, latterly converted to oil-firing.   *Photographer unknown*

Sir Guy Williams in coal-fired configuration hauling the 'B' passenger duty in June 1953. The train was approaching Weavers Down from Liss Forest Road. The lineside hut is believed to have been used as a flagman's post for the protection of the line during firing on the adjacent mortar range (see page 494 in Volume Two). *Lens of Sutton Association reference MA 8*

Immaculately cleaned and fitted for oil-firing, WD 400 (*Sir Guy Williams*) posed at the end of Longmoor Yard before taking up a duty in 1956. The 2-8-0 and 2-10-0 locomotives suffered from rapid flange wear, mainly on the curves approaching No. 6 Bridge and on Free Piece curve at Bordon. Crews avoided taking these locomotives from Oakhanger to Bordon if at all possible. *Lens of Sutton Association*

direct effects of the blast, the locomotive was severely damaged. Subsequently it was returned to the makers for rebuilding. At the end of 1944 it was shipped to Europe. Eventually it ran as NS 4527 but en route to Holland appears to have been shedded at Lille for the shed code 'La Delivrance' was still visible on the cab when it returned to Longmoor in 1949.

Early in its career at Longmoor *Sir Guy Williams* was converted to oil-firing, but the equipment seems to have been removed in the mid-fifties. By 1965, the condition of the locomotive did not warrant a further major overhaul. It was therefore officially withdrawn but was retained for training locomotive fitters. Eventually heavy repairs could not be avoided, so the locomotive was sold to Cashmores for breaking up. General Sir Guy Williams was a divisional commander at the outbreak of World War Two, went on to be GOC-in-C Eastern Command in 1940 and ended his distinguished career as Chief Royal Engineer.

The second Austerity 2-8-0 was named after the then Director of Transportation and during its early years at Longmoor was very much a showpiece, being kept for VIP trains. When Maj-Gen Sir Donald McMullen was making a visit, 'his' locomotive would be specially prepared and, accompanied by the NCO acting as running shed foreman, would await the General's arrival at Liss. Donning the clean white boiler-suit brought by the crew he would climb to the footplate to drive the train to Longmoor Downs. As nameplates had already been cast at Longmoor for an official naming ceremony before Maj-Gen McMullen's knighthood was announced, the General agreed that they should be fitted even though they omitted his full title. Like the other 2-8-0, oil-firing was fitted during the fifties. In 1957 the engine was withdrawn pending heavy repairs, but due to the declining traffic on the LMR it was decided to scrap it instead.

93257 (700)	*Major General Carl. R. Gray Jr.*	
	ALCO/71512/44	2-8-0
94382 (300)	*Major General Frank. S. Ross*	
	Davenport/2531/43	0-6-0T

At the end of World War Two a number of equipment exchanges were made between the US and British armies. The scheme included samples of the two American standard gauge austerity designs. A British 2-8-0 (WD 79189) and an 0-6-0ST Austerity locomotive (WD 75002) were sent to America in 1947 from the Netherlands as the UK's part of the deal. The saddle tank was scrapped at Fort Eustis by 1952. Details of the fate of the 2-8-0 are not recorded but it does not appear to have survived long either.

Both American engines arrived at Longmoor in 1946 and remained in use until the major reductions of equipment during 1957-9. *Major General Carl. R. Gray Jr.* (named after the US Army Director of Railway Services in North Africa, Italy and North West Europe) was scrapped in 1957, notwithstanding a heavy overhaul the previous year by W. G. Bagnall & Co. at Stafford. Due to a driver error, all driving wheels had acquired major 'flats' from heavy braking. Lacking a suitable locomotive wheel lathe at Longmoor, this damage could only be rectified by an external contractor, at considerable cost. The locomotive was therefore withdrawn. *Major General Frank. S. Ross* was named after the Chief of Transportation North West Europe Theatre. Whilst spares for the 2-8-0 might have been hard to acquire by 1958, this problem could not have applied to the same extent to the 0-6-0T, examples of which were still in service at the time both in the UK on BR(S) and in France. Sadly, this useful little locomotive was scrapped in 1958.

On 25th May 1946, WD 79250 was being prepared for its official naming ceremony. It did not yet even carry a running number. Maj-Gen Sir Donald McMullen had been Longmoor's last pre-war Commandant and always held the place in high regard. Appropriately 79250 (Major General *McMullen*) was always earmarked for his personal use on visits. *R. C. Riley, Transport Treasury Collection RCR 1216*

WD 93257 (*Major General Carl. R. Gray Jr.*) headed the line up of Austerities preparing for the 1955 Open Day at Longmoor Downs. It had not long returned from W.G. Bagnall's works at Stafford after contract overhaul. Despite this, the engine fell victim to the economies which followed the Suez crisis and was scrapped at Longmoor in 1957, as WD 700. *D. Cull, Kidderminster Railway Museum, Ref: 028366*

WD 700 was one of the few locomotives that were cut up at Longmoor. This was the scene in the sidings at Gypsy Hollow in October 1957.
W. S. Sellar

WD 300 (formerly 94382) *Major General Frank. S. Ross.* lasted little longer, being scrapped in 1958. In the National Service era, this little engine found its niche with the team who trained Brakesmen/Shunters in practical shunting skills in Woolmer Yard. The driver (Cpl Tony Edwards) was demonstrating the seated driving position from which all the necessary controls could easily be reached.
J. D. P. Poyntz

THE LAST MAN TO DRIVE WD 300

Extract from the Diary of Cpl Tony Edwards 23491582 (then aged 21)

<u>17th September 1958</u> I signed on at 0730 hrs to work [duty] 'C' with WD 300. All the morning we worked with eight wagons and two brake vans between Longmoor and Oakhanger – five times each way – to give practical experience to brakesmen/shunters. I was relieved at 1200 hrs.

On this duty we sometimes went into Woolmer Yard to shunt wagons so that the [trainee] brakesmen/shunters could have practise in coupling and uncoupling. Loco 300 was ideal for this. There was a ledge forming the window sill. The driver could sit quite comfortably on this ledge with the ratchet regulator and the reversing lever easily to hand. You did not need to use the brake when kicking wagons off for the shunters.

<u>Monday 22nd September</u> It was a perfect day. I was booked for the week on 'C' turn. Up at 0730 hrs, book on at 0800 hrs and off shed at 0830 hrs. I had one coach on and we did Longmoor – Liss – Oakhanger seven times, covering a total of 51 miles. Finished at 1715 hrs. It was wonderful to be driving 300 again, especially as this is her last week.

<u>Friday 26th September</u> Weather fair. Last day of 300. Not much happened but in the afternoon we carried out an intentional division of the train between Woolmer box and Woolmer Yard as a shunters' exercise. When all the day's work was done (and with Control's permission) John Poyntz, 'Sooty' Lees (my fireman) and I took 300 for one last trip from Longmoor to Liss and back. We went right to the stop block at Liss and came back whistling all the way. When we came on shed, ten of the lads held their hats over their hearts while I whistled a final lament. We did not take on coal or water or drop the fire. I did not even make out a report card. So ended the career of the last original USA Austerity tank in the UK.

There appears to have been a low-key approach to the delivery of the first of this important class of WD locomotives from the designers in Leeds. Whilst no Hunslet Engine Co. Ltd official maker's photo has survived of WD 5000 or WD 5001, W. G. Bagnall Ltd took the trouble to record their contribution to the building of the WD Austerity saddle tanks. WD 75267 (Bagnall 2790/45) was delivered to Longmoor in December 1945 but remained in store until sold to the L&NER. It became No. 8055 of Class 'J94', continuing to work on British Railways until May 1963 when it was scrapped at Darlington.

Maker's Photograph

The Standard Austerity Saddle Tanks

The next class to be considered was also numerically by far the largest. The 1950 'Peace Establishment' allocated the LMR eleven of these locomotives. It is not now clear whether this total included the locomotive(s) allocated to Marchwood where the railway was run as an 'out-station' of Longmoor. This class formed the backbone of the LMR fleet. Broadly the Longmoor locomotives of this class fell into two groups. The first and larger group were collected at Longmoor at the close of the war and were gradually withdrawn as they became worn out. From 1958 these were supplemented by locomotives from a batch built by Hunslet for the War Reserve in 1953. These locomotives (WD 190 to 203) were delivered new to Longmoor for storage. When the Transportation Stores Depot was closed they were dispersed, some to storage elsewhere, others as reserve locomotives at depots where they were progressively steamed for service. Details of these engines are to be found in Chapter Eighteen.

As supplied, this class was essentially designed for shunting duties, being derived from earlier products of the Hunslet Engine Co. Ltd of Leeds who carried out the original design work. In this volume we concentrate on those examples of the class which saw service at Longmoor. Within the long-term Longmoor residents there were a number of variants. Oil-firing was fitted (and removed) at various times from at least two examples and the braking arrangements on individual locomotives were altered to meet the traffic requirements. Originally, when the post-war fleet was being set up in 1944, four engines were sent to the Southern Railway's Brighton Works for overhaul. In the process they were fitted with Westinghouse brake gear (presumably secondhand from works stock). It was not a particularly elegant modification with the brake pump vulnerably placed on a bracket mounted on the front foot-plating.

From these locomotives one stands out – WD 118 *Brussels*. This locomotive was rebuilt by Hunslet in 1958 to WD Standard Specification incorporating numerous improvements which included oil-firing, Westinghouse brakes and safety footsteps for shunters. The Westinghouse brake air pump was fitted in a more elegant way than the earlier 'Brighton' conversion by removing the front section of the saddle-tank on the right-hand side. This gave sufficient space to allow the pump to be mounted beside the smokebox. Though apparently fitted and tested at the Hunslet works, the Westinghouse pump (but not the reservoirs) were removed at or soon after its return to Longmoor. The space cut out of the front of the saddle tank to accommodate the pump was covered with plating. A vacuum brake was later substituted by the LMR workshops though there is photographic evidence of this locomotive in passenger service with neither type of continuous brake installed. In service the rebuilt WD 118 proved to be a very difficult locomotive to fire so as to maintain steam pressure. The problem was the inability of the crew to control the primary air supply to the firebox. This flowed through fixed, open-ended tubes underneath the grate. As a result, the bottom half of the firebox was constantly being cooled and efforts to raise the temperature led to greatly increased water consumption. Nonetheless in the hands of a careful crew WD 118 could do good work. On 24th October 1958 Tony Edwards, with 'Sooty' Lees as fireman, worked a test train of 300 tons on a series of trips totalling 68 miles.

No further work to rectify the deficiencies of the oil-firing system on WD 118 seems to have been done at Longmoor and *Brussels* continued to run until laid aside in the final years. In January 1969 the Brussels Preservation Society purchased it. After a spell in storage at the Hollycombe Steam Collection at Liphook, this locomotive has found a home in Yorkshire. Having been acquired by the Keighley & Worth Valley Railway, *Brussels* has joined the band of ex-LMR engines that have been preserved from the breakers torch. It is now (2014) on display as a static exhibit.

The Longmoor collection of WD Austerity 0-6-0ST engines waxed and waned down the years. The first post-war 'Peace Establishment' gave an entitlement of eleven such locomotives. This view, posed for an enthusiasts' tour on 4th October 1958, showed five 'on parade' for the visitors. They were (from left to right: 186 *Manipur Road* (no train brake but screw couplings), 118 *Brussels* (air brake but three-link couplings), 181 *Insein* (vacuum brake, screw couplings), 152 *Rennes* (no train brake, screw couplings) and 108 *Jullundur* (the last of the Brighton-fitted air brake pumps, vacuum pipes, screw couplings).
Tim Edwards

On completion of the Hunslet Engine Co. Ltd rebuild of WD 118 *Brussels* to the new WD War Standard Specification in 1958, a formal portrait was clearly in order. After this rebuild, WD 118 was fitted only for air-brake working on passenger trains. Note the recessed shunter's step and the cut-out from the saddle tank to accommodate the Westinghouse air brake pump.
Maker's photograph

This photograph taken in January 1955 shows the tender of WD 600 *Gordon* [2] coupled to WD 511 at Derby for trials, prior to delivery.

Photographer unknown

The Stanier '8F' 2-8-0s

The final group of post-war LMR steam locomotives comprised five Stanier 2-8-0 Class '8F', engines which had been used by 10 Rly Sqn RE on the military railway serving the Canal Zone base in Egypt. To meet future traffic requirements there, it was decided in 1952 to have five of the squadron's stock overhauled by BR at Derby. These were to be replaced 'temporarily' by five secondhand ex-GCR Robinson 2-8-0s, purchased from BR and duly shipped to Suez. This was the World War One ROD standard heavy main line design and the only type of WD standard locomotive never to be operated at Longmoor.

The overhaul of the five '8Fs' at Derby included the modification and retention of the oil-firing system with which they had been equipped for their previous service in the Middle East. This system was designed to burn a heavy furnace fuel oil ('mazout'), unlike the earlier British system developed by James Holden of the Great Eastern Railway which used waste oil derived from the manufacture of coal-gas. Details of the WD system as applied to the Stanier '8Fs' is at Appendix Fifteen, page 555 in Volume Two.

WD 500 as delivered to Longmoor from Derby Works. The '8F's appear to have arrived at Longmoor without tenders which were converted to carry fuel oil for working on the LMR. Behind WD 500 stood WD 108 *Jullundur*, awaiting repair. *Photographer unknown*

WD 512 and WD 508 as received at Longmoor, photographed on 3rd September 1955. Of the five ex-Middle East Land Forces Stanier '8F's, two (508 and 511) were quickly redeployed to No. 2 Military Port, Cairnryan. They worked at Cairnryan until broken up in 1959 when the War Department relinquished the port. 512 was remembered as a hard-worked locomotive during its three year working life on the LMR.

R. K. Blencowe Negative Archive number EF 448

At the 1955 Open Day, WD 501 appeared named *Lt. W. O. Lennox. V.C.* – the name which it had previously carried when deployed to 10 Rly Sqn RE in the Canal Zone. At Longmoor it had been given the full lined-out blue livery, the whitened wheels indicating its prestige status.

Photographer unknown

A photograph taken to record a derailment of a train in the Canal Zone of Egypt provides a good detailed view of the nameplate on *C/Sgt. H. McDonald. V.C.* Also visible, just below the footplate above the rear wheel, was the auxiliary oil heater fitted to the oil-burning Stanier designed 2-8-0 locomotives.

Photographer unknown

By the time the five Staniers had been overhauled political developments in Egypt had resulted in the Canal Zone base no longer having a secure future. The engines were therefore held at Longmoor until a decision was reached on their deployment. By early 1955 it had been decided to use them in the UK. 511 was sent to No. 2 Military Port Cairnryan, probably without more than trial running at Longmoor. The remainder were put to work at Longmoor until 1957-8. At this time 508 was sent to Cairnryan and the other three were sold to BR. The Arabic cab-side numbers carried in the Canal Zone still appeared when these engines entered service at Longmoor. Oil-firing was retained to train locomotive firemen on this equipment against possible operational tasks on overseas railways, except for 501 which was converted to coal firing at Longmoor.

At Longmoor WD 501 *Lt. W. O. Lennox. V.C.* received the full LMR blue livery and was very smartly turned out. Lt-Col Alexander (when previously Officer Commanding 10 Rly Sqn RE in the Canal Zone) had been originally responsible for selected '8F's being named after members of the Corps who had been awarded the Victoria Cross for exceptional gallantry. When commanding 16 Rly Trg Regt he was determined to return WD 501 to the condition in which it had run with his former squadron. 501 occupied a special place in his affection, being repainted in the full LMR blue livery, lined-out in red

with tyres picked out in white. Thereafter it was always kept immaculately 'bulled-up' by the shed staff at Longmoor. The other '8F's remained in plain black, initially with tenders lettered 'WD' and numbers in yellow on the cabside. 512 is remembered as the most hard-worked Stanier at Longmoor. The damage that this locomotive received on 13th October 1956 was repaired by BR at Eastleigh Works.

After sale to BR, the remaining trio continued their uneventful lives until 1968 when BR 48773 (formally WD 500) was selected for preservation by the Stanier 8F Locomotive Society. The choice was indeed appropriate for 48773 is one of the most widely travelled members of the class and saw service with six different railways in three continents. Today (2014) this locomotive is displayed at The Engine House at Highley on the Severn Valley Railway, in company with *Gordon* [2] making a fine display of main line military railway locomotives of World War Two. This is particularly appropriate as its present owners, the Stanier 8F Locomotive Society, decided in 1985 that this locomotive's unique war service record made it an ideal vehicle to act as a war memorial to the military railwaymen of the Corps of Royal Engineers who lost their lives on active service during World War Two. Appropriate plaques, affixed to the frames of the engine are accompanied by a Roll of Honour (listing all the soldiers thus commemorated) which is displayed beside the engine.

In contrast to the other '8F's WD 501 received the blue livery, lined-out in red. WD 501 was still looking to be in first class condition as it was readied for transfer to BR ownership – photographed on 22nd May 1957 awaiting despatch to Eastleigh from Longmoor Yard. *W. S. Sellar*

Builder	LMS Number	WD Number 1942	Later WD Number 1952	BR Number	Remarks
Crewe/37	8021	575	511	–	*Sgt. J. Smith. V.C.* (re-assumed this name when at No. 2 Military Port). LMR 12/54-55, No. 2 Mil Port 55-59. Sold to Jas N. Connell, Coatbridge and scrapped.
Crewe/37	8025	583	512	48775	LMR 1955-8. Sold to BR 1958.
NBL 24607/40	8233	307	500	48773	LMR 12/54-6/57. Sold to BR 1957. Purchased by Stanier 8F Locomotive Society 8/68, transferred to Severn Valley Rly.
NBL 24620/40	8246	320	501	48774	*Lt. W. O. Lennox. V.C.* LMR/55 to 6/57. Sold to BR. Scrapped 1965.
NBL 24716/41	–**	508	508	–	LMR 55-57, transferred to No. 2 Mil Port, Cairnryan 57-59. Sold to Jas N. Connell Ltd, Coatbridge and scrapped.

Notes:
1. All these locomotives were in service on the Iranian State Railways 1941.
2. WD 1952 renumbering implemented by 1956.
3. ** This locomotive was shipped direct from the makers for war service in Iran (Persia) in November 1941.

WD 118 *Brussels* appeared in many guises during its long service on the LMR. The changes in appearance following its rebuild in Leeds in 1958 were rapidly followed by further modifications in the workshops at Longmoor. By the early 1960s the engine had lost its air brake pump (and the unique cut-out to accommodate the pump) and had become a vacuum-fitted locomotive.
Photographer unknown

CHAPTER EIGHTEEN

THE AUSTERITY SADDLE TANK LOCOMOTIVES

Numerically the largest single group or class of locomotives to be employed at Longmoor were the WD Austerity 0-6-0 Saddle Tanks. Examples were to be found in use from the arrival of WD (7)5000 for trials in the spring of 1943 to the closure ceremony in the autumn of 1969. In this Chapter we deal with the members of this large class (almost 400 were built) which were issued to Longmoor for employment on the LMR. In the final years of World War Two a significant proportion of the newly-built locomotives of this class were delivered to Longmoor from their builders for storage prior to shipment to Europe. We have not attempted to list these here. Part 1 deals with locomotives from the original construction orders which served at Longmoor. Part 2 deals with the entire group of fourteen additional locomotives ordered from the Hunslet Engine Co. Ltd in 1952 to form part of a 'War Reserve' of RE (Tn) equipment. This equipment was to be stockpiled centrally in the knowledge that, in a national crisis, the suppliers would not be able to meet the delivery schedule which the War Department demanded to meet its mobilisation plans.

Part 1 : The 1945 Peace Establishment Locomotives

After about nine months of user trials, WD (7)5000 and WD (7)5002 were placed in store prior to shipment to France in January 1945. Subsequently WD 75000 was sold to the Dutch State Railways (NS) and scrapped in Holland in 1957. As related on page 657, WD 75002 ended its days at Fort Eustis in Virginia, following an Anglo-American equipment exchange. From contemporary notes, it is very likely that WD 71453, and WD 75288/9 were employed at Longmoor during the summer of 1945 prior to sale to civilian operators.

In 1947/8, Brian Whebell was able to record the locomotives both stored and operated on the LMR during his training there. Ten of the Austerity saddle tanks were in use at that time for traffic and training. With at least one on permanent 'detached duty' at Marchwood (where the military railway in the port area was run as an out-station of Longmoor), this satisfactorily accounts

for the establishment entitlement to eleven locomotives of this type. Of these, four (75028/41/42/79) had been sent to Brighton Works in 1944 for overhaul, during which they were fitted with (secondhand) Westinghouse brake equipment. New naming proposals (see page 677) had been partially implemented at this time. In the earliest post-war years most locomotives carried the diamond shaped Longmoor unit sign on the cab-side. When the Transportation Centre became a 'War Office Controlled Unit', such signs would have been incorrect. They gradually disappeared as locomotives were overhauled and/or repainted.

By 1950 the first post-war series of proposed names had been replaced by a new one, consisting of names derived from world-wide locations of important RE (Tn) bases, installations etc. The wider naming of the Austerities seems to have taken place as they moved through the Longmoor workshops for overhaul. 'New' locomotive names were first 'spotted' by enthusiasts in

'...in the beginning'. With a full repaint in a new blue livery and nameplates transferred from its former WIMR namesake, 75079 *Sir John French* [2] stood ready for duties outside Longmoor Shed in 1946. Whilst variants of the blue livery were to endure for the remaining life of the railway, an entire new series of locomotive names was approved by 1949, to be carried by the Longmoor members of this class. *Photographer unknown*

667

A different view of WD 75079 in 1946, showing detail of how the steam pipe was connected to the air brake pump. The locomotive behind was WD 75290, which would be named *Manipur Road*.   *Photographer unknown*

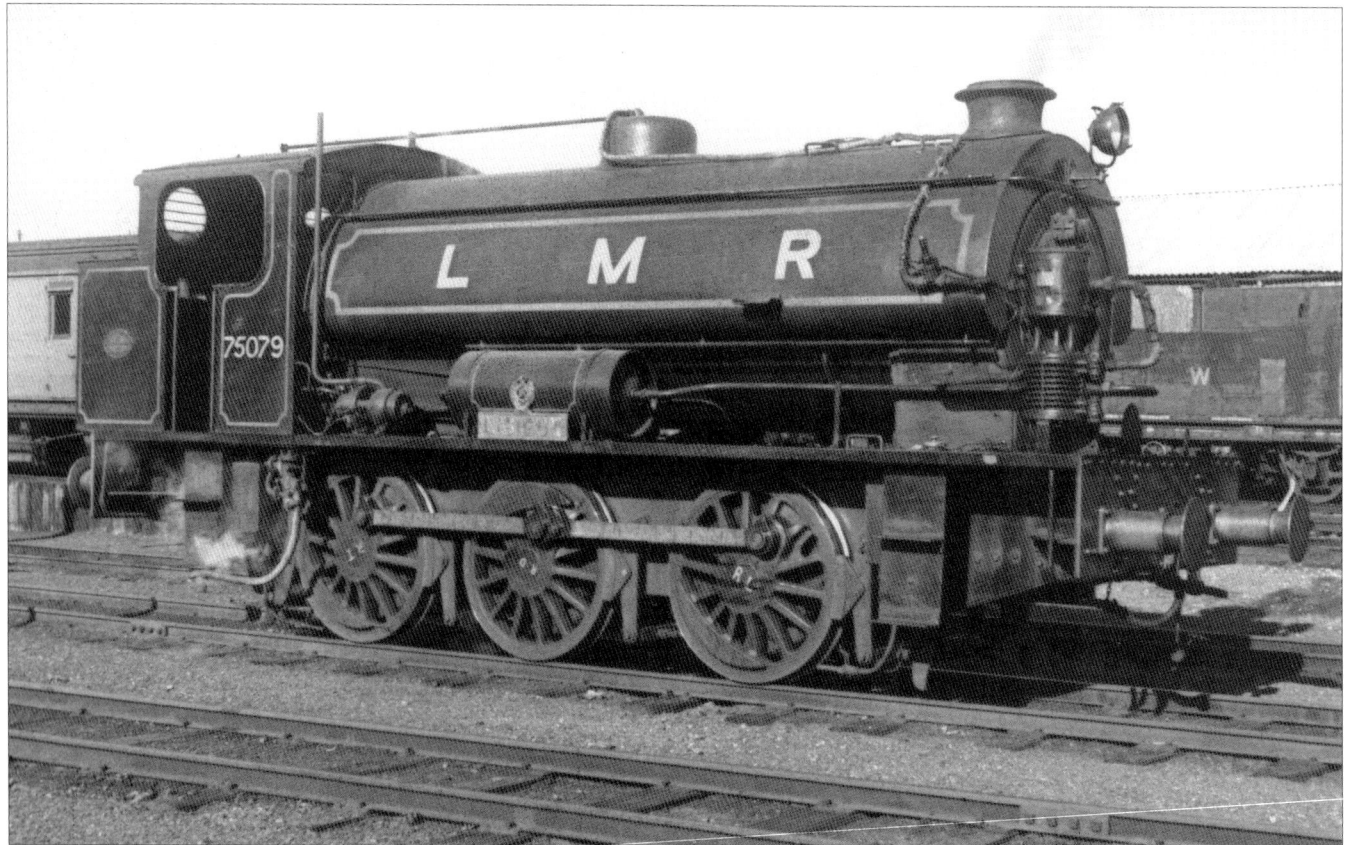

WD 75079 had lost the secondhand *Sir John French* nameplates by about 1950 and was transformed into *Lisieux*. It had also by then been fitted with a set of Stone's electric lighting equipment with a steam vent pipe vertically up the cab front. Note the bold lining with reverse corners. The Brighton Works control rod arrangements for the Westinghouse pump steam supply can be seen between the cab roof and the steam dome. A relatively early casualty, *Lisieux* was scrapped at Longmoor at the end of 1958. Photographic evidence suggests that the 'thick red lining' livery was confined to the years 1946-1953.   *Lens of Sutton Association reference PMA 950*

A few years later WD 75079, by now renumbered WD 114, was in use for one of the many passenger services operating during the annual Open Days. The ornate livery seen in the previous photograph had been replaced by a more conventional version in blue with a single thin red line with reversed corners for lining out. The Stone's electric generator with its fittings had also been removed and the routing of the steam pipe to the air brake pump tidied up, producing a very handsome and well turned out locomotive. *Photographer unknown*

1947 (75275 – *Matruh*) and as late as 1950 (71505 – *Brussels*). One of the last was 75079 (*Lisieux*) which from 1946 had been carrying the nameplates *Sir John French* originally fitted to the R & W Hawthorn, Leslie & Co. Ltd 0-6-2T by its builders when delivered in 1914. At this time (1950) only 75079 appears to have been painted in blue. This was a darker shade than that later adopted as the LMR livery, approximating more to the original 'Prussian Blue' of 1905 with lining in red, picked out in gold. The remaining saddle tanks were in the process of being repainted from war-time khaki into the post-war olive green (as used on Army road vehicles) or black.

Another exception to the collective naming policy was 71443, in 1952 named *Arnhem*. This name was retained (at Marchwood) until 1953 when the locomotive returned to Longmoor for overhaul and became *Constantine*. At various dates thereafter its nameplates were removed and refitted. This locomotive ended its service as a display item, being taken to events and shows by road low-loader.

Uniquely some of the LMR locomotives were fitted (at various dates and in various combinations) with both vacuum and air train braking systems. The four Brighton Works conversions noted above were later joined by 118

WD 75282, photographed by Henry Casserley in August 1946 at Bordon on an enthusiasts' excursion. It appears still to be painted in the unlined black WD livery of the period and carried no name. Later renumbered as WD 181 and named *Insein*, this locomotive was one of the group sold back to the Hunslet Engine Co. Ltd in 1960. It reappeared as HE 3879/62 and was sold to the NCB, serving various South Wales colliery railways. Transferred to the Caerphilly Railway Society in 1981 for preservation, it is now (2014) in the care of the Gwili Railway where it has been re-named *Haulwen*. *H. C. Casserley 47461*

WD 75028 (later *Ahwaz* [1]) was here seen in WD livery and showing clearly the details of the Westinghouse brake system as fitted to a quartet of locomotives at Brighton Works in 1944. This photograph was probably taken immediately after its arrival at Longmoor in the late summer of 1945.

R. K. Blencowe
Negative Archive number BW588

Taken on 3rd September 1949, this view shows another of the Westinghouse-fitted quartet. No running number is visible and the only evidence of ownership was the cast Unit badge on the cab side. This photograph emphasises the absence of any 'bull' in the late 1940s. These were simply workaday locomotives.

Photographer unknown

Though it carried no number, this is a photograph of WD 75290 'on shed' in the mid 1950s. Of interest as yet another livery variant was the use of the cast version of the World War Two unit sign adopted by the Railway Training Centre just before the outbreak of war.

Lens of Sutton Association

TABLE I : 0-6-0ST AUSTERITY LOCOMOTIVES EMPLOYED ON THE LONGMOOR MILITARY RAILWAY 1945 - 1970

WD Number Pre-1951	WD Number after 1951	LMR Names	Approx date of Arrival on LMR	Approx date of Dep from LMR	Builder and Date	Final Disposal	Remarks
71443	157	Constantine (in 1953)	On LMR during 47/48, then to Marchwood ex-Marchwood 1960	3/68	HE 3207/45	Scrapped by Pollock, Brown Ltd	When on detached duty at Marchwood named *Arnhem*. Employed at Longmoor for static displays and demonstrations 1962-64. Returned to traffic 1964
71438	156	Tobruk [2] (1961) McMurdo (1965)	From Bicester 12/59	3/68	HE 3202/44	ditto	Renamed on formation of RCT in July 1965
71505	118	Brussels (1950)	3/45	1/69	HC 1782/45	To K&WVR by 9/71 and currently on static display there	Rebuilt by Hunslet Engine Co. Ltd in 1958 to Revised War Standard Specification including: Oil-firing, electric generator, Westinghouse brake and shunters' refuge steps
75028	100	Ahwaz [1] (1945)	9/45	12/58	HE 2877/43	Boiler retained for instructional use, remainder scrapped on site	Westinghouse brake fitted by 1947. Name transferred to WD 203 (See Table 2)
75035	102	Caen [2] (1960-66)	From Bicester 1959	8/67	HE 2884/43	Scrapped in situ 1967	Name originally on WD 72214 (diesel), and transferred to WD 75035 after 72214 was scrapped in 1959
75040	106	Spyck (1949)	on LMR 1949, Sent to Marchwood; Returned in 1960	7/63	HE 2889/43	Withdrawn in 1960, used in Fitters' School. To Woodham Bros, Barry and scrapped	This name did not appear in the 1949 list and may first have been fitted at Marchwood
75041	107	Foggia (1949)	6/44 Ex-Brighton Works	7/60	HE 2890/43	Sold to Hunslet Engine Co. Ltd and rebuilt there as HE/3882/62 and sold to NCB	Westinghouse brake fitted by Brighton Works. Sold on from NCB service to preservation by Mid Hants Rly and rebuilt as 'Thomas' 0-6-0 *Douglas* in 2003
75042	108	Jullundur (1949)	6/44 Ex-Brighton Works	7/63	HE 2891/43	To Woodham Bros, Barry and scrapped	Westinghouse brake fitted by Brighton Works
75079	114	Sir John French [2] (1945-50) Lisieux (1950)	9/44 Ex-Brighton Works	12/58	RSH 7115/43	Scrapped at Longmoor 12/58	Westinghouse brake fitted by Brighton Works From 1945-50 this locomotive carried the plates originally cast for WD 70203 *Sir John French* [1]
75189	152	Rennes	10/46; then to Marchwood 53-56	11/60	RSH 7139/44	Sold to Hunslet Engine Co. Ltd and rebuilt as HE/3880/62.	From NCB bought for preservation and currently (2014) undergoing restoration
75275	177	Matruh [1] (1947)	3/45	8/59	RSH 7205/45	Scrapped at Longmoor	Stored out of use following accident in 1957. Possible boiler exchange with WD 100
75277	178	Foligno (1949)	ditto	7/63	RSH 7207/45	To Woodham Bros, Barry and scrapped	Withdrawn in 1958 and used for rerailing training
75282	181	Insein (1949)	6/45	2/61	VF 5272/45	Sold to Hunslet Engine Co. Ltd and rebuilt as HE/3879/61. Sold to NCB	From NCB bought for preservation when named *Haulwen* and transferred to the Caerphilly Rly Society; currently on the Gwili Rly and in service (2014)
75290	186	Manipur Road (1949)	6/45	?/60	VF 5280/45	Sold to Hunslet Engine Co. Ltd and rebuilt as HE/3878/61. Sold to NCB	Scrapped at NCB Mardy Colliery, Glamorgan in 1971

Builders Details:
HC= Hudswell, Clarke & Co. Ltd, Leeds
HE = Hunslet Engine Co. Ltd, Leeds
RSH = Robert Stephenson & Hawthorns Ltd, Newcastle-on-Tyne
VF = Vulcan Foundry Ltd, Newton-le-Willows

One of the un-fitted Austerities, WD 75275 *Matruh* was in a mix of lettering styles when photographed on 2nd September 1950. It was taken out of use following accident damage in 1957 and appears to have been scrapped at Longmoor in August 1959 bearing its later number WD 177.
J. J. Smith

which received Westinghouse equipment during its rebuild at Hunslet in 1958. Not long after returning to traffic it lost the pump and control gear although the reservoir cylinders remained in place. Vacuum brake equipment was exchanged between engines from time to time to meet the needs of traffic. In the same way, Stone's electric generator sets were installed and removed from time to time. All the 1952 batch of 'War Reserve Austerities' had vacuum brake equipment fitted during construction.

The table on the previous page summarises the locomotives which have been definitely identified as employed at Longmoor, (as against temporary storage there or transit to or from a port).

'As Issued' - WD 152 in the official War Department all-black livery shortly after return from a general overhaul by Bagnalls of Stafford. Only the nameplate *Rennes* revealed its LMR connection. Withdrawn in 1960, this was another of the quartet sold to the Hunslet Engine Co. Ltd. Emerging from the Hunslet factory as HE 3880/62, it was sold to the NCB for colliery service in South Wales. After a number of moves, it is now (2013) undergoing full restoration for the Pontypool and Blaenavon Railway.
W. S. Sellar

Part 2 : The War Reserve Hunslets of 1952

In 1952 the Hunslet Engine Co. Ltd of Leeds received an order for fourteen additional Austerity saddle tank locomotives required by the War Office to form part of its 'War Reserve'. These were delivered between 1952 and 1953 for long-term storage in No. 1 Transportation Stores Depot at Longmoor. Within a couple of years it had been decided that these locomotives should be put into traffic in UK military depots to complete the replacement of obsolete or worn out locomotives which had begun in 1945. Many of the group saw little military use and, following the decision to replace all MOD steam locomotives with diesel around 1960, were available in good condition for sale to private owners. Out of the group, 195, 196, 199 and 203 were employed at Longmoor in the final years of the LMR. No less than nine of this group have survived into preservation. Details are given below:

TABLE 2 : AUSTERITY 0-6-0ST LOCOMOTIVES OF 1952

Hunslet Builders Number	Date	WD No.	MOD No.	NAME Army in BOLD later names in Brackets	Disposal or Last Known Location	Remarks
3790	1952	190	90	(*Castle Hedingham*)	Colne Valley Railway	To Long Marston for storage: 6/55; transferred to Bicester and stored from 2/59; transferred to Shoeburyness -/67. Sold to Stour Valley Railway 1971
3791	1952	191	91	**Black Knight** (*Holman F. Stephens*)	Kent & East Sussex Railway	To Bicester for storage -/56; transferred to Long Marston 5/62; transferred to Shoeburyness 12/67. Sold to K&ESR (No. 23) in 1972 (a)
3792	1953	192	92	**Waggoner**	Isle of Wight Steam Railway	To Histon for storage 7/55; to Bicester 5/59; Stored at Long Marston 5/61; transferred to Shoeburyness 4/69; then to Marchwood 1974; returned to Shoeburyness 11/82; RCT Display Loco 82 - 84. To Museum of Army Transport Beverley 6/84. Loaned to IoWSR 6/06, gifted 5/08 (b)
3793	1953	193	93	(*Shropshire*)	Ribble Steam Railway, Preston	To Shoeburyness for storage 2/55; used on loan at other WD locations; transferred to Bicester 6/60. Sold to Severn Valley Rly 1971 and later transferred to East Lancs Rly (c)
3794	1953	194	94	(*Cumbria*)	Ribble Steam Railway, Preston	To Bicester for storage 7/59; transferred to Histon 11/55 then back to Bicester 9/59. Sold to Lakeside and Haverthwaite Railway (No. 10) in 1973
3795	1953	195	–	–	Scrapped from LMR 1968	To Bicester for storage -/55; stored to -/56; in service @ Bicester -/56 - 11/60; Transferred to LMR 11/64 and remained there until scrapped
3796	1953	196	196	**Errol Lonsdale**	Stoomcentrum Maldegem, Belgium	To Bicester for storage 6/55; returned to LMR -/64 to 11/69. Sold to K&ESR in 1970. Re-sold to Mid Hants Rly in 1976 and to South Devon Railway. Purchased and transferred to Belgium in 2010 for preservation (d)
3797	1953	197	–	**Sapper** [1] (*Northiam*)	Kent & East Sussex Railway	To Bicester for storage 10/55; in occasional use at Bicester until 1977. Loaned (1977) then sold (1979) to K&ESR (No. 25) 10/79 (e)
3798	1953	198	98	**Royal Engineer**	Isle of Wight Steam Railway	To Bicester for storage 8/55; To Lockinge 55-59; returned to Bicester -/59 to -/61; Transferred to Long Marston for storage 7/62. Transferred on loan to IoWSR 2/92 and gifted to that railway in 5/08
3799	1953	199	–	–	Scrapped at Longmoor 1968	To Bicester for storage 1955; transferred to Thatcham 7/55; returned to Bicester 7/59; transferred to LMR in 1966 (f)
3800	1953	200	95	(*William H. Austen*)	Kent & East Sussex Railway	To Bicester for storage 1955; To Bramley 2/56; returned to Bicester 5/59; Transferred to Shoeburyness 7/63. Sold to K&ESR in 1971. Became No. 24
3801	1953	201	96	–	Scrapped at Shoeburyness in 1970	To Bicester for storage 1955; Transferred to Westbury and Bramley 2/56; returned to Bicester 5/59
3802	1953	202	97	**Sapper** [2]	Scrapped at Shoeburyness in 1970	To Bicester for storage 8/55 and in service until 8/66; Transferred to Shoeburyness. Named *Sapper* at Bicester
3803	1953	203	-	**Ahwaz** [2]	Scrapped by Woodham Bros by 5/65	To LMR from store 1955; in traffic until 7/63. Name transferred from WD 100. Sold to Woodham Bros in 1963

NOTES:
(a) 191 was named **Black Knight** at Bicester taking the name from Bagnall 2773 of 1945 (WD 171) when that loco went to Kineton. Earlier the Bagnall had inherited the name from Hunslet 3150 of 1944 (WD 127).
(b) 192 was displayed at various locations. It was also exhibited while still in WD service (from Bicester) in olive green WD livery at Rushmoor Arena (Aldershot) 1959 and 1960.
(c) 193 has been hired to several preserved railways and was transferred to the Ribble Steam Railway in 1999 for overhaul.
(d) 196 repainted at one time in L&NER livery and numbered in the J94 list with the next unused number, carrying the builder's plate of 199 due to a theft just before renaming, (it now has a copy of original plates).
(e) 197 was the last steam engine to be used at Bicester.
(f) 199 was scrapped 1968 on closure at LMR having only worked for 18 months tank having been previously stored at Thatcham and Westbury. It arrived at Longmoor with all tools identified and wired with Hunslet labels and with preserving grease on all the working parts (which showed no sign of wear). By this unlikely path, it became the last new steam locomotive to be operated on the LMR.

In 1952 the War Department authorised the purchase of fourteen additional Austerity 0-6-0ST locomotives, to be placed in a War Reserve which would be deployed to UK military depots and/or military railways in the event of war. Initially these engines were delivered to Longmoor and were stored on the Transportation Stores Depot site at Woolmer. The side rods of one locomotive were damaged prior to delivery. This 1953 photograph shows a group of eight being given their periodic inspection – the nearest can be identified as WD 203. These inspections included movement on rails but not under their own power. All these locomotives were fitted with the vacuum brake. Unusually the paint finish was black enamel.

Photographer unknown

'Last in: first out'. The final member of the group of fourteen War Reserve tank locomotives was WD 203. It was removed from store at Woolmer and taken into LMR service as early as 1955. It was seen here in Longmoor Yard still in WD rather than LMR livery and awaiting the fitting of side rods. Later named *Ahwaz* [2], 203 remained in service until July 1963.

W. S. Sellar

The first War Reserve Austerity to be released to the LMR was WD 203 *Ahwaz* [2]. This locomotive spent hardly any time in store, joining the LMR in 1955. QMSI Moriarty was on the footplate during a test run. It remained in use until 1963, being sent to Woodham Brothers Ltd later that year and scrapped.

Bryan Stone

WD 102 arrived from Bicester in 1959, un-named and plain black. It was in 'as supplied' condition at this time, with no air or vacuum braking systems. So it was appropriate to see it hauling the Duty 'D' Goods through Longmoor Downs. At an early stage it gained the name *Caen* [2] when the original locomotive of this name (WD 72214) was scrapped. By 1966 it had lost its nameplates and it was scrapped the following year.

Bryan Stone

Two of War Reserve group (WD 195 and 196) came back to Longmoor in 1964 from storage at Bicester, whence they had been moved by 1 Rly Gp RE. They were employed on the LMR in its final years. Sadly 195 did not make it into preservation, being broken up at Longmoor in 1968. 196 fared better – having acquired the name *Errol Lonsdale* in January 1968, it was perhaps better known and so was sold at auction in 1970. After a number of moves, it gravitated to the South Devon Railway which in 2010 sold it to Belgian enthusiasts for long term restoration.   *R. C. Riley*

One of Longmoor's 'mystery' locomotives was WD 75291, seen here stored awaiting shipment from the sidings at Gypsy Hollow. WD 75291 was retained until September 1946 when it travelled via Ashford to Dover, whence it was shipped to France for further employment by the French equivalent of the Ministry of Transport and Public Works. A 'Hunslet type 0-6-0ST' was delivered to the port of Caronte (close to Marseilles) where it was eventually scrapped in 1957.
Lens of Sutton Association, reference 87732

Part 3 : The Locomotive Names

Two schemes to carry on the pre-war tradition of naming the locomotives of the LMR were prepared. In 1946/7 proposals were considered for naming the much enlarged locomotive fleet. One proposal was for a continuation of the pre-war custom of naming locomotives after famous commanders but this scheme had to be expanded to accommodate the larger number of locomotives stationed at Longmoor after the war. A second series of names was developed commemorating places connected with important RE (Transportation) operations in World War Two. The two are combined below:

TABLE 3 : LOCOMOTIVE NAMES, PROPOSED AND CARRIED (1945-65)

WD No.	Proposal (1947)	Selected Name (1949)	Name Carried (From 1949)	Source of Name (Campaign/Theatre)	Notes
71443	Kitchener	Constantine	Constantine	Algeria, 1943-44.	(1)
71505	Gordon	Brussels	Brussels	NW Europe campaign 1944-45.	
75028	Montgomery	Ahwaz	Ahwaz [1]	Persian LofC (supplying USSR) 1941-43.	
75041	Wavell	Foggia	Foggia	Italian (east coast) LofC 1943-44.	
75042	Lord Gort	Jullundur	Jullundur	Training base for Indian Army railway troops.	
75079	Sir John French	Lisieux	Lisieux	Normandy 1944-45.	(2)
75275	Lord Roberts	Matruh	Matruh	Western Desert Railway 1940-42.	
75277	Marlborough	Foligno	Foligno	Ancona - Rome railway 1943-44.	
75290	Alexander	Manipur Road	Manipur Road	Assam LofC 1942-45.	
75282	Earl Haig	Insein	Insein	Burma LofC 1945.	
73651	Mountbatten	Gordon	Gordon	[See Chapter 17]	
73797	Sapper	Kitchener	Kitchener	[See Chapter 17]	
70272	Eisenhower	Chittagong	-	Assam LofC 1942-45.	(3)
70271	Roosevelt	Bari	-	Southern Italy LofC 1943.	(4)
72214	Patton	Caen	Caen [1]	Normandy, NW Europe LofC 1944-45.	
72220	McArthur	Basra	Basra	Iraq 1942-44.	
71438	–	–	Tobruk (1961)	Western Desert Railway 1940-43.	(5)
75035	–	–	Caen [2] (1960)	[See above]	(6)
75040	–	–	Spyck (1949?)	River Rhine crossing 1945.	(7)
75189	–	–	Rennes (1946?)	BEF, France 1939-40.	(8)
203	–	–	Ahwaz [2] (1955)	[See above]	(9)

Notes:

(1) Between 1952 and 1954, whilst at Marchwood carried nameplate *Arnhem*.

(2) Between 1946 and 1950 carried nameplates *Sir John French* (ex-WD 70203)

(3) WD 70272 (originally allocated to LMR but not delivered) was replaced by WD 77337 *Sir Guy Williams*.

(4) WD 70271 (originally allocated to LMR but not delivered) was replaced by WD 79250 *Major General McMullen*.

(5) WD 71438 may have been issued to replace WD 75275 (written off in 1957). It was named *Tobruk* in 1961 and renamed *McMurdo* in 1965.

(6) WD 75035 was transferred from Bicester in 1959 and took the name *Caen* from WD 72214 in 1960.

(7) WD 75040 may have first been named whilst deployed to the Marchwood Military Railway.

(8) WD 75189 appears to have carried the name *Rennes* from c. 1946 but the name and number did not appear in the original or amended list of proposed names.

(9) WD 203 was the first locomotive to be released from the War Office War Reserve (in 1955), taking the name *Ahwaz* from WD 75028.

WD 157 (un-named) outside the locomotive shed at Longmoor in the late 1950s. It remained in 'as built' condition without air or vacuum braking. Its use would therefore be restricted to freight duties so it is no surprise to see the 'D' Duty board on the smokebox. Behind the buffer beam could be seen one of the Land Rover 'rail conversions' that were trialled at Longmoor.
R. K. Blencowe Negative Archive number 34737

Foggia, now renumbered WD 107, shunting in Longmoor Yard in the late 1950s and clearly revealing the vacuum brake ejector pipe on the side of the saddle tank. In addition, there was a steam pipe (laid out rather untidily and crudely lagged) from a steam manifold in the cab to the air brake pump. In July 1960 *Foggia* and three sister engines were sold to the Hunslet Engine Co. Ltd and rebuilt by them as 'new' locomotives, WD 107 becoming HE 3882/62 before being sold to the NCB. Later it was sold to the Mid Hants Railway. The latest incarnation of *Foggia* is in the form of *Douglas*, the 'Thomas the Tank Engine' character 0-6-0 tender locomotive.
R. C. Riley

A bunker view of WD 75041 *Foggia* running round at Liss in April 1950. This engine had the Westinghouse pump mounted on the right but at this date no vacuum brake had been fitted (see photograph above). *E. Meredith*

WD 100 (previously WD 75028) *Ahwaz* [1] in the late 1950s. Poor *Ahwaz* just 'faded away', being first stripped of its boiler (taken for 'instructional purposes') then the remains were cut up at Longmoor at the end of 1958 – the first of the WD Austerities at Longmoor to be scrapped.
Photographer unknown

'*Manipur* off the road - again!' WD 186 *Manipur Road* did its party piece in Longmoor Yard on 17th December 1957. Its frequent (and sometimes spectacular) derailments had no logical explanation. Unofficially it was thought that some, or all, of the tyre profiles were incorrect. This engine was the final member of the quartet sold to the Hunslet Engine Co. Ltd and the only one not to be preserved. Rebuilt as HE 3878/61, it operated at the NCB Mardy Colliery in Glamorgan where it was scrapped in 1971.   *W. S. Sellar*

WD 178 *Foligno* was another of the first series of post-war Longmoor Austerity engines, remaining 'un-fitted' throughout its working life. From around 1958 it was used for rerailing exercises and eventually went to Woodham Brothers Ltd at Barry for scrapping.   *W. S. Sellar*

In a view taken on 3rd September 1955 during the annual Open Day, WD 118 *Brussels* appeared as a conventional 'Brighton-converted', coal-fired, Westinghouse-fitted Austerity. The air-brake converted engines were intended for use on the 'Bullet' services, which were normally operated with air-braked coaches.
Photographer unknown

In 1958 *Brussels* was the subject of a major overhaul by the Hunslet Engine Co. Ltd, emerging with all the extra fittings suggested by the WD Locomotives Technical Design Panel. Electric lighting, Westinghouse air brakes, and safety shunters' steps are obvious in this photo (4th October 1958) of the newly returned locomotive. Not apparent in such a front view is the conversion to oil firing, another major modification carried out at this time. Alongside was the conventional vacuum-braked version, here represented by WD 152 *Rennes*.
R. C. Riley

"Curiouser and curiouser!" cried Alice. Even Lewis Carroll would have been puzzled by WD 118 *Brussels* in the early 1960s. This rear view showed the modifications around the bunker which formed part of the Hunslet rebuild in 1958. Note the electric headlight recessed into the back of the cab, the access ladder and the cast numbers on the buffer beam. However, there had been further modifications. The Westinghouse pump, neatly located by Hunslet by cutting away a section at the front right of the saddle tank, had been removed and the missing section of tank plated over. Further modification included substituting the vacuum brake for the former air brake. The vacuum ejector on the right of the cab was clearly visible. The continuing function of the air reservoir on the RH running plate is unclear! *Photographer unknown*

Though the Westinghouse pump (but not the reservoirs!) was removed within a couple of years of the rebuild, the oil-firing was retained, and a vacuum brake ejector fitted. Unless handled most skilfully, the array of steam driven accessories could quickly empty the boiler of steam, with dire results for the crew. *Brussels* is now preserved on the Keighley & Worth Valley Railway, currently (2014) as a static exhibit.

Photographer unknown

The elusive WD 106 *Spyck* arrived at Longmoor from Marchwood during 1949 as an un-named locomotive. The name then allocated was not included in the original 1949 proposals but is of the same genre as the main series. *Spyck* was the location of a principal British military railway crossing of the River Rhine in early 1945. This engine spent much time in service away from Longmoor, both on further detachments to Marchwood and on loan (twice) to the Port of London Authority. Returning to Longmoor in May 1960 it was used as a training aid in the Fitters' School until disposal to Woodham Brothers Ltd in 1963.

J. D. P. Poyntz

WD 106 *Spyck* at the running shed at Longmoor on 26th September 1953, in the company of WD 300. WD 106 was notably devoid of any lettering other than its number.

Leslie Freeman, Transport Treasury F1052

Spyck later received the full LMR livery, as seen in this photograph.

Bryan Stone

WD 108 *Jullundur* did not arrive at Longmoor until 1949. It seems to have remained dual-fitted until withdrawn in 1963 (note that the Westinghouse pump was mounted on the left side). It was scrapped at Barry by Woodham Bros. *Bryan Stone*

Originally WD 71443, *Constantine* was the lowest numbered Austerity to be permanently allocated to Longmoor. It spent the years 1952-54 at Marchwood where it appears to have been named *Arnhem*. For several years it represented the RCT railway trades on static display at the Aldershot Tattoo, before being scrapped in 1968. On 30th April 1966, AD 157 waited at Longmoor Downs during the second RCTS visit of that month. *Photographer unknown*

Originally the un-named WD 71438, and a replacement engine from Bicester in 1959, this locomotive acquired the name *Tobruk* in 1961 after the Whitcomb diesel-electrics were scrapped. It was again renamed in 1965, becoming *McMurdo* at the behest of the newly-formed Royal Corps of Transport. Note the Westinghouse pump fitted on the left side of the front footplate. Whilst the locomotive was fitted with both air brake pump and vacuum brake ejector, the absence of brake pipes suggests that the locomotive was not in running order and there is some doubt as to whether the air pump was ever brought into use. In 1944 Brighton Works had put the pumps on the right when converting the first Austerity 0-6-0STs for passenger services at Longmoor. (See WD 75079 page 668 and WD 75041 page 678).   *Photographer unknown*

AD 199 had the doubtful distinction of being the last new steam locomotive to be supplied to the LMR. From initial War Reserve storage it had been moved to Bicester and stored both there and at COD Thatcham until released to the LMR in 1966. It had obviously never been steamed by the Army and the neatly wrapped tools were still in their Hunslet hessian packaging on arrival. Why it was scrapped in 1969 is not clear.   *G. M. Moon*

This was AD 196 *Errol Lonsdale* on 5th July 1969 in full 'parade gloss'. Apart from having the RCT cap badge surmounting the nameplate, rather than that of the RE, nothing had changed since the locomotive was named. This view gives a good impression of the final (Oxford) blue livery with red lining.   *Photographer unknown*

The end of the line. A 1965 view of the rusting hulks of four ex-LMR Austerities awaiting their fate in a corner of Woodham Brothers Ltd scrap-yard. For the record, none were saved. Nearest was WD 106 *Spyck* followed by WD 203 *Ahwaz* [2], WD 178 *Foligno* and WD 108 *Jullundur*. The most distant locomotive is thought to have been WD 130 (not an LMR locomotive) delivered to Barry from MOD Chilwell.   *P. Davies*

As WD 70270, this locomotive left Longmoor in 1945 for service in Germany with the RE (Tn) troops of 21st Army Group, later BAOR. It was returned in early 1957 to replace WD 70271 which had been written-off following the Palmers Ball collision. On 14th January 1958, Stuart Sellar photographed it 'On Test' in Longmoor Yard, still in BAOR livery with red framing but now numbered 876. The driver was Spr B. R. Roberts ('Basil Roberts of Wem').

W. S. Sellar

CHAPTER NINETEEN

OTHER ROLLING STOCK

This chapter covers all other types of railway rolling stock used at various times on the WIMR and LMR. We begin with internal combustion locomotives. These were developed by the UK locomotive manufacturing industry working alongside the technical staff of the War Office from 1908 when the Army's first i/c engined locomotive was delivered for trials on the 2ft 6in. gauge Chattenden & Upnor Railway. At the outbreak of World War One there do not appear to have been any active plans for the use of i/c engined locomotives by the Army. This situation was to change dramatically with the development of trench warfare on the Western Front. From 1915 work went ahead rapidly to develop reliable petrol-engined locomotives for use in forward areas. The development of the equipment for what became the 'WD Light Railways' very largely took place elsewhere as that system evolved between 1915 and 1918. The contribution of Longmoor was predominantly the provision of technical training for the specialist officers and tradesmen who ran the WDLR.

The sections on other classes of rolling stock at Longmoor serve to emphasise the varied and eclectic nature of the equipment to be found there. Sapper ingenuity and an eye towards value for money resulted in a rolling stock park of the widest variety. Because the rolling stock was essentially employed for training, most of it was relatively lightly used. As a result, many vehicles survived long after their main line equivalents had been scrapped.

Internal Combustion Locomotives and Rail Cars

Section I : Internal combustion locomotives 1915-40

The first internal combustion locomotives delivered to Longmoor were some 2ft 6in. gauge 0-4-0 oil-engined locomotives. Whilst no official evidence has survived, it is most likely that these were from a batch of twelve built in 1915 by the Avonside Engine Co. Ltd for the War Department. They were 60hp locomotives (AE/1703-1714 of 1915) numbered WD 31 to 42. These were delivered from the makers for trials at Longmoor for which a mile of special track was laid. Later they were shipped to Egypt.

Also in 1915 a standard gauge petrol-engined locomotive was tested at Longmoor. The reasons behind the order and indeed the selection of the builder are not now clear. The facts are that ten 180hp locomotives were ordered in November 1914 from Manning, Wardle & Co. Ltd (MW/1867-1876 of 1915). These received numbers WD 1 to 10. WD No. 1 was completed in advance of the main order, being sent to Longmoor (ten months behind schedule) at the end of October 1915. It appears that the remainder were

held by the makers until trials were complete, when Nos 2, 3 and 4 were sent to Egypt and 5 to 10 were despatched to France. It is assumed that No. 1 (the trials locomotive) was then sent to Egypt.

Brief technical particulars of this class can be found in Appendix Eighteen. The specification refers to them as 'Armoured' and bullet-proof cab windows were fitted. A 68 gallon petrol tank supplied fuel and a 400 gallon water tank/ radiator provided cooling. The transmission was by direct mechanical drive through a flywheel-mounted clutch and a three-speed gearbox giving running speeds of 5mph, 13mph, and 26mph. In service these locomotives were not successful. Like many marine applications of this era, the engine itself was reversible so no reverse gears were provided. The engine had to be stopped and restarted for each change of direction. This was achieved by means of compressed air, the supply of which could quickly run out leaving the locomotive stranded.

From 1916 to about 1925 the 60cm gauge equipment of the Apple Pie Camp 'Scenic Railway' remained in use. These were the sole examples of internal combustion locomotives at

A group of 2ft 6in. gauge 'oil-engined' locomotives were built by Avonside for the WD in 1915, originally intended for overseas service in the Middle East. This photograph shows one at work on the Kantara - Romani Military Railway in 1916. The batch of twelve was sent to Longmoor for trials on a specially constructed track prior to shipment.
Imperial War Museum reference Q15847

Manning, Wardle & Co. Ltd does not appear to have made an official photograph of their initial batch of 'petrol tractors', built for the WD from 1915. This view shows WD (ROD) 1698 (MW 1952/18) of the second batch. The first-off production locomotive, ROD No. 1 (MW 1867/15) came from Leeds to Longmoor for trials. *WD photograph*

Longmoor at that time. Few details of the running numbers and types of motive power have survived. The 'establishment' as authorised consisted of a pair of British-Westinghouse petrol-electric locomotives, one or two Simplex tractors and probably a 'Crewe' Ford convertible tractor. This stock was moved to Longmoor Yard when the Apple Pie Camp was redeveloped in 1922-3 and seems to have been scrapped or sold about 1925. A surviving wagon diagram, probably from the early 1920s, lists the rolling stock as:

	TOTAL
Class D wagons Nos 6, 11, 14, 15	4
Class E wagons Nos 1187, 1188, 1189, 1190, 5, 9, 10	7
Holding:	11

No details were given of the motive power available at that time.

Section II : Internal combustion locomotives 1941-1955

The only internal combustion vehicles from 1920 to 1940 were the various rail cars and 'speeders' which are discussed fully in Section IV of this chapter. Indeed, instruction on the WIMR was entirely steam-orientated until just before the outbreak of World War Two, when a new trade of 'Fitter Heavy Plant' was introduced. From 1941 to closure there were examples of a variety of internal combustion locomotives continuously in service.

WD 29	Drewry/Baguley/2159/41	0-4-0DM
72220 (829)	Drewry/Baguley/2175/45	0-4-0DM
	Basra [1], *Chittagong* [2]	

WD 29 arrived at Longmoor in June 1941 for trials. It was the first production model of what was to become the standard WD 153hp light diesel shunter. During its protracted stay at Longmoor this locomotive was modified to incorporate a more reliable final drive unit, these modifications being later added to the main production batches. The power unit was originally a 153hp Gardner 6L3 diesel engine coupled to a four-speed pre-selector Wilson gearbox. The final drive was by means of a jack-shaft and side-rods. Examples were built by Barclay, Hunslet and Vulcan in addition to the prototypes built by Baguley-Drewry Ltd. After general use on yard shunting duties WD 29 was prepared for shipment in the summer of 1944 and delivered to Southampton. Unfortunately the prototype of this most successful design never returned to England, being sold to the Netherlands State Railways and scrapped as their NS 161 in Holland in 1948.

On the other hand WD 72220 had a long career at Longmoor. Early in its service life it enjoyed an unrepeatable 'Cinderella moment' when it was selected to represent the RE(Tn) railway troops in the VE-day parade in London. Highly 'bulled' and mounted on an RE heavy plant low-loader it was seen by the huge crowds that thronged the capital's streets for this event. Between delivery in 1945 and 1966 it was renumbered once (to WD 829 in 1956) and named twice (*Basra* then *Chittagong*).

L.M.R.
CHITTAGONG

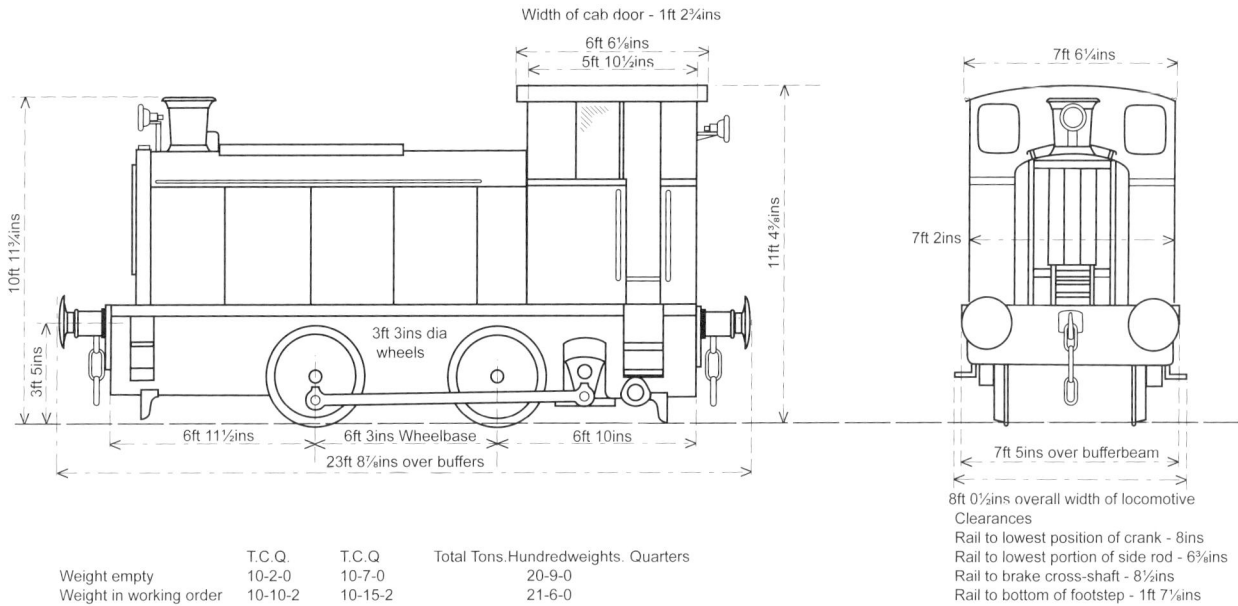

Width of cab door - 1ft 2¾ins

6ft 6⅛ins
5ft 10½ins

7ft 6¼ins

10ft 11¾ins

11ft 4⅜ins

7ft 2ins

3ft 5ins

3ft 3ins dia wheels

6ft 11½ins   6ft 3ins Wheelbase   6ft 10ins

23ft 8⅞ins over buffers

7ft 5ins over bufferbeam

8ft 0⅜ins overall width of locomotive
Clearances
Rail to lowest position of crank - 8ins
Rail to lowest portion of side rod - 6⅜ins
Rail to brake cross-shaft - 8½ins
Rail to bottom of footstep - 1ft 7⅛ins

Based on a diagram prepared at Longmoor.

	T.C.Q.	T.C.Q	Total Tons.Hundredweights. Quarters
Weight empty	10-2-0	10-7-0	20-9-0
Weight in working order	10-10-2	10-15-2	21-6-0

Locomotive No. 829 CHITTAGONG
Fuel tank capacity - 100 gallons
Cylinders - 6
153 H.P. engine
Vulcan Synclair Hyd. Coupling
Wilson 4 speed gearbox and Wilson Fwd & Reverse

Below: WD 29 was the first-off production of the successful and long-lived WD light standard gauge diesel shunter of World War Two. It was sent to Longmoor for trials and remained there, to test modifications and to train diesel loco drivers, until the summer of 1944 when it was shipped to France.   *Photographer unknown*

WD 72220 photographed taking part in the Victory Parade in London at the end of World War Two. Note that the cab-side windows had been glazed by this time. Later numbered WD 829 and named *Basra* [1], then later *Chittagong* [2], it remained at the Engineer Stores Depot at Liphook (operated as an outstation of the LMR) until 1966. *Photographer unknown*

Latterly this locomotive worked the detached depot railway at the Engineer Stores Depot, Liphook until it was transferred to Bicester in 1966. It was still going strong in 1984 when it was transferred from the Shoeburyness system to the RN Depot at Gosport.

Basra was the port of entry and main RE Transportation base for operations in Mesopotamia (Iraq) in World War Two. Chittagong was the base port on the Gulf of Bengal for the metre gauge LofC serving the campaign on India's eastern frontier from 1942 to 1945.

WD No. 2	JF/22500/38	0-4-0DM

With increasing activity in storage depots and Royal Ordnance Factories (ROF) following the onset of national rearmament in 1938, the War Department purchased a number of diesel-mechanical shunting locomotives from Fowler and Hunslet. No. 2 was one of the small (60hp) type obtained new in 1938 to work on the military railway at the Hilsea (Portsmouth) workshops and stores. It ran at Longmoor from 1941 to 1943 when it was transferred to the RA Practice Camp Sidings at Harlech. After various moves it was finally disposed of by 1 Rly Gp RE in 1960.

WD No. 2 was purchased by the War Office in 1938 as part of a scheme to equip dispersed stores depots and ordnance factories as part of the national rearmament programme. It was transferred from the Hilsea (Portsmouth) Army workshops to Longmoor in 1941 and was used for driver instruction until 1943. *Photographer unknown*

Built by Armstrong Whitworth (AW/D20/34), LMS 7058 (originally 7408) was the pioneer LMS diesel-electric shunting locomotive. This engine and a number of other contractor-built engines were initially loaned to the WD in 1941. Whereas the entire batch of later models (LMS 7059 - 7068) were eventually purchased for WD service, 7058 remained on loan at Longmoor until June 1943, when it was returned to the LMS in exchange for LMS 7098 on hire. This rare photograph shows 7058 on an LMR freight train approaching the Top Crossing at Longmoor with an instructional train bound for Liss. Characteristically the top centre engine cover had been removed to assist cooling, always a problem with this particular locomotive.

H. N. James

During the war period a number of diesel locomotives passed through Longmoor – some loaned, some new and some second-hand purchases. Full details of all of these movements are lacking. The greater part of this group comprised 0-6-0 diesel-electric locomotives developed by the LMS for continuous shunting duties in their larger freight yards. The oldest to be transferred (initially on loan) comprised ten 250hp locos supplied originally by Armstrong Whitworth & Co. Ltd of Newcastle in 1936. These were all purchased by the War Office in 1942. A further ten 300hp locomotives (built by R. & W. Hawthorn, Leslie & Co. Ltd with English-Electric equipment), also supplied to the LMS in 1936, were transferred in the opening months of the war. Many of these were lost in France in 1940. In 1945 the diesel locomotive stocks included the following in addition to WD 72220 already described.

| 70215 | Armstrong Whitworth/D57/1935 | 0-6-0DE |
| 70216 (883) | Armstrong Whitworth/D58/1935 | 0-6-0DE |

WD 70216 may have been at Longmoor as early as 1940 and certainly spent the greater part of the war there, shunting in various depots and used for instruction and testing of drivers. It was built for the LMS in 1935, numbered 7063, one of the first batch of diesel-electric shunters for that company and was noteworthy for the jack-shaft final drive. The LMS loaned the locomotive to the WD in September 1940 along with a number of other diesel shunters from this series. Around 1942 some of these were sold outright to the WD. A batch went to the Middle East where the last two (WD 70020/880 and WD 70022/881) survived to be sold to the Egyptian State Railways in 1954. The remainder of the group ended the war in Europe where four completed their

WD 70216 was later renumbered WD 883, by which time it had left Longmoor. Its service at Longmoor from September 1940 was broken by duty on both the Martin Mill Military Railway (near Dover) and with the LMR detachment at Liphook. By 1952 it had left Hampshire for Scotland, being used on the Cairnryan Military Railway until the autumn of 1955. Thereafter it was moved to Bicester where it was photographed on 3rd June 1956. In 1963 it was sold to E. L. Pitt Ltd and moved to a yard in Brackley. That was not the end of this locomotive's working life. In February 1966, WD 883 travelled under its own power from Brackley to Hams Hall (an electricity generating station east of Birmingham).

Roger Carpenter, E. J. Jones Collection (EJJ 51)

The exchanges of the LMS diesel-electric shunters loaned to (and in some cases eventually purchased by) the WD are complex. This photograph shows LMS 7098 on an LMR freight train at Oakhanger. It had arrived at Longmoor in June 1943 (in traffic on 15th June 1943) and was used for driver instruction. In November 1944 it was returned to the LMS and was allocated to Willesden. The USA tank taking water was working 'F' Duty, the Oakhanger shunting locomotive. The disc-pattern indicator in the foreground was connected to the derailer on the loop line and rotated through 90 degrees when the derailer was clear of the line. *H. N. James*

service, being transferred to the Belgian State Railways (SNCB) ownership in 1946. The LMR transferred WD 70216 to 1 (Home) Rly Gp RE who deployed it to No. 2 Military Port, Cairnryan in 1952 and again later to Bicester whence it was sold out of WD service to E. L. Pitt (Coventry) Ltd. Even then there was life in this diesel veteran for in 1966 it was sold yet again – this time to the Central Electricity Generating Board (CEGB) who used it at Hams Hall Power Station until scrapped in 1967.

70270 (876)	*Bari* [2]	English Electric/LMS	0-6-0DE
70271 (877)	*Bari* [1]	English Electric/LMS	0-6-0DE
70272 (878/601)	*Chittagong* [1] then *Basra* [2]		
		English Electric/LMS	0-6-0DE
70273 (879)		English Electric/LMS	0-6-0DE

These locomotives were delivered new from Derby Works to Longmoor in 1945. They were the last four of a group of fourteen 350hp diesel-electric shunters built for the WD by the LMS in 1944-45. By the early months of 1945 it was apparent that they would not be needed in Europe. They were therefore diverted to Longmoor whilst awaiting a decision on their post-war use. The acquisition of locomotives of this type by the WD had proceeded step by step, the first examples being taken (initially on loan) from September 1939. It is very likely that the majority would have passed through Longmoor prior to their deployment, but there is no record of their use at that time on the LMR in traffic. LMS numbers 7069 to

7078 of the 1936 construction were intended to be deployed for service with the BEF in France. Of these 7074 and 7076 do not appear to have left UK shores and spent some time at Longmoor in the winter of 1939-40 before being sent to the Martin Mill line at Dover for service with the super-heavy rail mounted guns. The others were lost in France in June 1940, six being recorded as destroyed. One of the two captured intact by the Wehrmacht (ex-7075) was recovered by the advancing Allied armies in France in 1944. Others of the class may well also have passed through Longmoor in transit for overseas duties at the same period. The Longmoor examples were built at Derby to the same design as the standard LMS 350hp diesel-electric shunter with geared final drives.

WD 70270 can only have been at Longmoor briefly in 1945 before being shipped to BAOR where it remained until 1957. The next to leave Longmoor was WD 70273, probably transferred to ROF Barby for a spell before being shipped to BAOR where it was sold out of military service in 1959. Eventually it arrived in Denmark, purchased by the state railways becoming DSB 6. It was only finally withdrawn in December 1973 and broken up a year later in Jutland. WD 70271 was written off in the Palmers Ball collision on 13th October 1956. At the time of the accident it was carrying no number though in the new series WD 877 had been allocated. As a replacement, WD 70270 (renumbered WD 876 in the 1952 WD-wide renumbering) was brought back from Germany in early 1957, probably being exchanged for

L.M.R.
BASRA

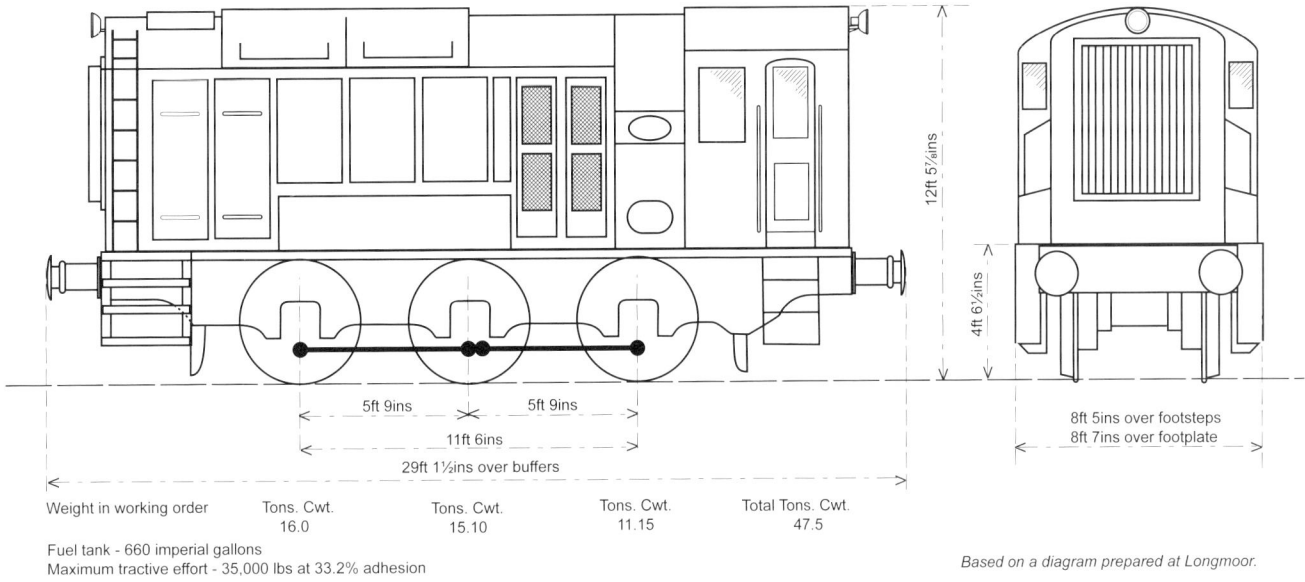

12ft 5⅜ins

4ft 6½ins

5ft 9ins   5ft 9ins

11ft 6ins

29ft 1½ins over buffers

8ft 5ins over footsteps
8ft 7ins over footplate

Weight in working order	Tons. Cwt. 16.0	Tons. Cwt. 15.10	Tons. Cwt. 11.15	Total Tons. Cwt. 47.5

Fuel tank - 660 imperial gallons
Maximum tractive effort - 35,000 lbs at 33.2% adhesion

Based on a diagram prepared at Longmoor.

WD 882 (formerly 70215) which left Longmoor at the same time. The name *Bari* was then transferred to WD 70270. This locomotive continued in use at Longmoor until 1963 when it was withdrawn due to a burnt-out main traction motor. This was alleged to be the result of excess speed between Weavers Down and Liss Forest Road. Stripped of all identity, but still in its dark blue livery, it survived for use in rerailing exercises until final closure when it was scrapped at Longmoor. As AD 876 it was finally withdrawn in 1968 and sold to Cox and Danks Ltd, Park Royal, London, for scrap in May 1969.

Between the Allied invasion of Italy in September 1943 and March 1944 (when the railways of southern Italy were handed back to the state railways [FS]), the railway facilities at the town of Bari formed the principal RE (Transportation) base for the Italian campaign.

The final member of the quartet, WD 70272, soldiered on at Longmoor. In the first post-war naming scheme *Chittagong* was allocated, but later to make some semblance of a class this name was exchanged with WD 72220 *Basra*. In 1956, WD 70272 was renumbered WD 878 and again in 1968 was changed to AD 601. As Army 601, this locomotive outlived the LMR and was transferred to Shoeburyness in April 1970. Subsequently it was sold in 1980 to the Lakeside & Haverthwaite Railway Company where it remains, used for general shunting. Recently it was noted still to be carrying its (by then 40 years old) LMR cast metal running number on the front buffer-beam.

WD 878 *Basra* [2] and WD 876 *Bari* [2] outside the shed, with WD 107 *Foggia* behind, c1959.   *Tim Edwards*

This view from the early 1950s shows *Chittagong*, un-named but renumbered as WD 878. Unfortunately the photographer did not include the whole of 72220 (the previous *Basra*) in his shot, but both locomotives seem to have been under repair. At the end of the work then in progress, WD 878 emerged as *Basra* [2] and WD 72220 as WD 829 *Chittagong*.

R. K. Blencowe Negative Archive

WD 878 *Basra* [2] resting in Longmoor Yard in the summer of 1960 in later LMR livery with plain block lettering/numerals and black frames. Note the cast numbers fitted to the buffer-beam, a single electric head-lamp and the externally mounted semi-rotary hand-pump used to fill the fuel header tank.

R. K. Blencowe Negative Archive

AD 878 outside Longmoor Shed in June 1967, looking very spruce in preparation for the Open Day. *G. Moon*

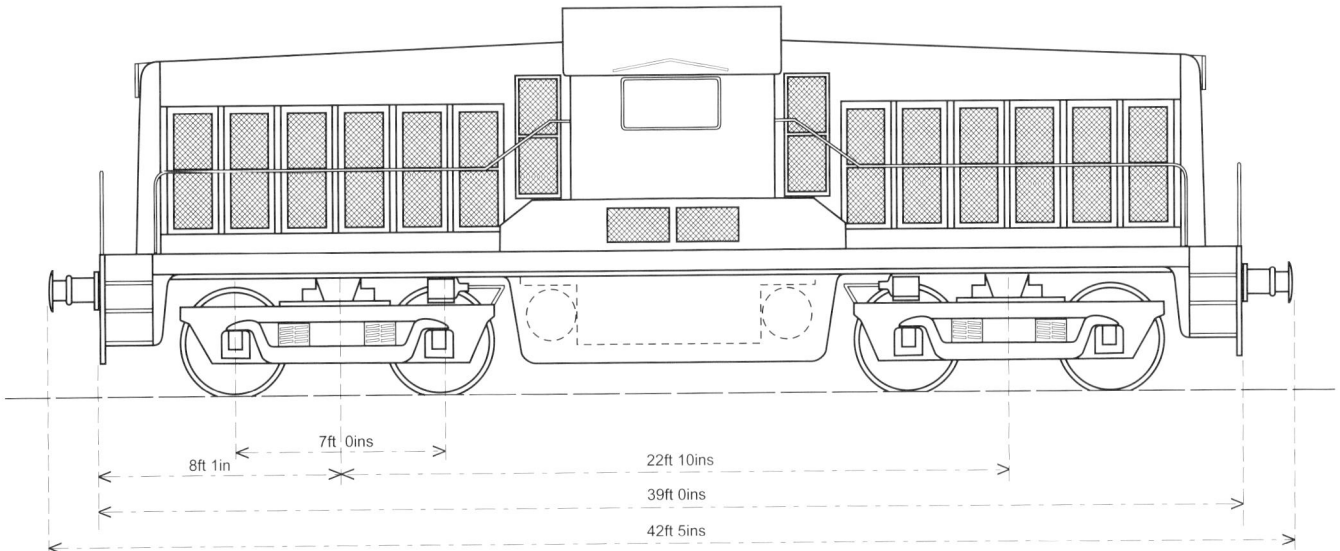

L.M.R.
650 H.P. DIESEL

8ft 1in
7ft 0ins
22ft 10ins
39ft 0ins
42ft 5ins

8ft 6ins

Particulars

Weight in working order:
Front truck - 65,000 lbs
Back truck - 65,000 lbs
Total - 130,000 lbs

Air Brakes: Westinghouse straight automatic air brakes, Schedule No. 14 E.L. or equivalent
Compressors: Two x 2 Gardner-Denver air cooled two stage air compressors with a displacement of 62 C.F.M. each

Power plant:
Engines. The Buda Coy Model 6-DHS-1879 (Supercharged, two in number). 6 cyls bored 6¾ ins. Continuous rating, 283 H.P. at 1200 rpm (each).
Traction generators: Two x Westinghouse Model 197-A-Railway Type.
Traction motors: Four x Westinghouse Model 970-A-Railway Type.
Gear Ratio: 14.72 (single reduction).

Control: Single station. Remote electric magnetic control; with two motors permanently in parallel in each power plant.

Tractive effort:
Maximum without sand (25% adhesion) 32,500 lbs
Maximum with sand (30% adhesion) 40,800 lbs

Maximum permissible speed: 46.5 Miles Per Hour.

*Based on a Diagram
prepared at S.O.S.E.T.O. - USA
Office of Chief of Transportation
Military Railways
7 October 1943.*

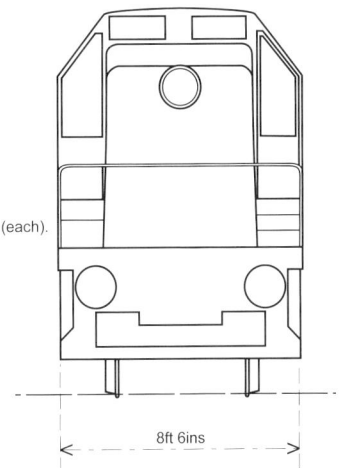

| 71232 *Tobruk* | Whitcomb/60174/41 | Bo-Bo DE |
| 71233 *Algiers* | Whitcomb/60175/41 | Bo-Bo DE |

These two locomotives were built by the Whitcomb Locomotive Co. of Rochelle (USA) for use on the British constructed Western Desert Railway to Tobruk. Though there were superficial differences in the design between these and their later US Army Transportation Corps counterparts, they were mechanically identical. The differences in appearance were accounted for by their construction to the smaller WD profile. Rated at 650hp they were the most powerful diesel locomotives to run at Longmoor and the nearest thing to a main line diesel

On 3rd September 1955, WD 890 *Tobruk* (in final form) stood outside the Diesel School (extreme right). Constructed by the Whitcomb Locomotive Co. in the USA for British use on the Western Desert Railway, this class was equipped identically to the much more numerous US Army Transportation Corps diesel-electric locomotives. How the two examples which ended up at Longmoor were repatriated is not known, although they arrived before April 1948, but they were the only true 'main line' diesels to run on the LMR.

Photographer unknown

WD 890 *Tobruk* giving locomotive rides in the early evening light in Longmoor Yard. It was in this role that the Whitcomb diesels were most often seen (and photographed) by members of the public. Availability of these engines from the mid 1950s onwards was much restricted by the lack of spares.
Photographer unknown

locomotive owned by the Army. They were capable of a 45mph top speed, with a maximum starting tractive effort of 40,800lb. 71232 was named *Tobruk* by General Sir William Slim at a formal ceremony during the annual Open Day in 1948. Both these locomotives were scrapped in 1957/58, being in need of a general overhaul which would have required the purchase of expensive non-standard spares.

Algiers (port and city) was the operational base for RE (Tn) activity in support of the Allied invasion of Algeria and Tunisia at the end of 1942. Tobruk was a vital British-held port during the North African campaigns of 1940-42. It was also important as the western terminus of the Western Desert Extension Railway, operated initially by New Zealand railway troops.

The unfortunate WD 71233 (later 891) *Algiers* appears to have been cannibalised for parts, as shown in this October 1952 view. Formally withdrawn from traffic in March 1953 it was clearly far from entire when finally sold for scrap in May 1958. Its sister *Tobruk* was sold in 1957, allegedly for scrap, though it may have later been exported to West Africa.
R. K. Blencowe Negative Archive reference EF273

72214 *Caen* [1] Ruston & Hornsby/224345/1945 4W (chain drive)

The baby of the diesel locomotive family in 1945 was WD 72214 *Caen* [1], a 48hp diesel-mechanical shunter. The biggest events in the life of this locomotive seem to have been its periodic use as a load for demonstrations by the heavy breakdown crane. In 1959 it was sold to E. L. Pitt (Coventry) Ltd who resold it the following year to Wagon Repairs Ltd who put it to work at their Wellingborough plant. The name was transferred to 0-6-0ST WD 102 which had been moved to Longmoor in the same year as 72214 was sold (see page 671). Caen was the first RE (Tn) operating base to be established in northern France following the D-Day landings of June 1944.

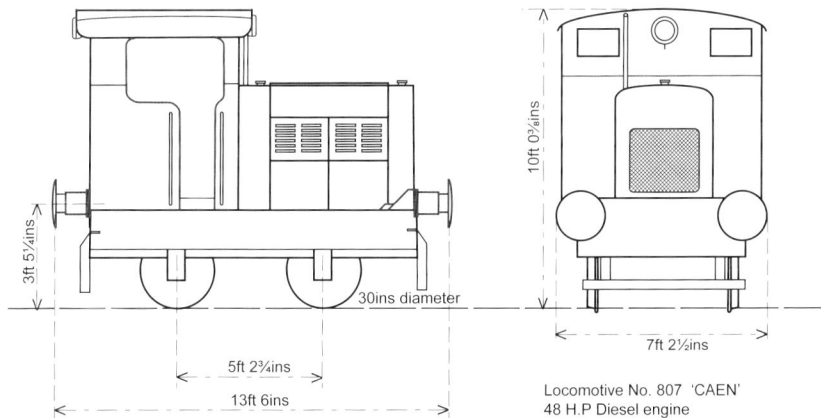

L.M.R.
CAEN

3ft 5¼ins

30ins diameter

5ft 2¾ins

13ft 6ins

Based on a diagram prepared at Longmoor.

10ft 0⅜ins

7ft 2½ins

Locomotive No. 807 'CAEN'
48 H.P Diesel engine
Cylinders Nos. 4
Fuel capacity: 7 Imperial gallons
Weight in working order: 7t. 6c. tons

Above: WD 72214 (*Caen* [1]) was definitely the baby of the Longmoor locomotive family. Seen here on 3rd September 1955 it was clearly 'open to the public'. Arriving from the maker's works in 1945 it remained in use, mostly around Longmoor Yard, until 1959 when it was sold.

R.K. Blencowe Negative Archive number EF549

Below: A comparison in sizes. WD 72214 *Caen* [1] standing alongside one of the Austerity locomotives, c1959. *Tim Edwards*

70238	JF/22976/42	0-4-0DM

A second diesel-mechanical locomotive by John Fowler & Co. (Leeds) Ltd – of their larger (150hp) variety – appears to have been in service at Longmoor during the period 1945-47. It came from ROF Rearsby and was noted in 1947 running in a khaki livery. Its primary role was as a practical subject for use by trainee diesel fitters. It was transferred to Shoeburyness in February 1949.

No. 17 was a 150hp John Fowler (22912/40) diesel-mechanical shunter that was never on the establishment of the LMR. It arrived in a BR freight train from ROF Swynnerton on 10th July 1963 with the intention that it would be used by the LMR as a long-term rebuilding project for trainee fitters. When this photograph was taken on 3rd June 1967 the project was incomplete and on closure the (still partially dismantled) locomotive was sold to the Dart Valley Railway. This view of the interior of the 1939 Diesel School revealed many other diesel locomotive components displayed for instructional purposes. Disused from 1965, the Diesel School was stripped out in the final years of the LMR to provide a secure store for 411 Railway Operating Troop to house the last operational steam locomotives of the LMR. *G. Moon*

Section III - Internal combustion locomotives 1955-1970

After 1945 followed an interval of ten years during which time no new diesel locomotives were acquired. The need for second generation diesels in military depots grew as wartime equipment wore out and the retention of steam locomotives with civilian crews became increasingly uneconomic. With many overseas railways changing to diesel traction in the mid-1950s, it was important that military locomotive crews could be trained in the latest techniques. The then-substantial network of rail-served depots in BAOR was entirely operated by diesel-hydraulic shunting locomotives, some formerly the property of the Wehrmacht and others purchased new after the war. Therefore one of the first requirements was for diesel-hydraulic locomotives for driver and fitter training. During the first post-war decade this need was met by the presence at Longmoor of the two captured 75cm gauge Gmeinder diesels. Clearly these small narrow-gauge locomotives had many limitations and were generally unsatisfactory for driver training. The need was only met fully by the delivery of the Army's prototype 275hp diesel shunter in 1955. In 1959 a Rolls-Royce engined Sentinel 'demonstrator' with hydraulic final drive appeared briefly at Longmoor, but no formal trials programme appears to have been set up for this locomotive.

In late 1945 or early 1946, Longmoor took delivery of two captured German 75cm gauge diesel-hydraulic loco-motives. This view showed the pair of Gmeinder diesel locomotives, stabled on a short length of narrow gauge track adjacent to No. 6 Bridge, shortly after arrival at Longmoor. *Photographer unknown*

In the mid-1950s the 75cm gauge line was rebuilt, becoming the Weaversdown Light Railway (see page 433, Volume Two). At this time both locomotives were overhauled and fitted with Gardner engines. In addition to new bonnet side panels a new exhaust chimney and a full repaint, they received names originally used on the first 18-inch gauge steam locomotives. This was 13.915 *Venus* preparing to haul a passenger train. *Venus* was scrapped in 1957 but 13.905 *Mars* was retired to the Diesel School and used for several years as an instructional model. *WD photograph*

Detail of the refurbished *Venus* on 21st September 1957 standing outside the shed erected to house the stock of the Weaversdown Light Railway.
W. S. Sellar

A Sentinel diesel-hydraulic shunter being demonstrated at Longmoor. It had been on trials on the Shropshire & Montgomeryshire Light Railway (then operated by the Army) early in 1959. Tony Edwards' diary noted that the engine had arrived at Longmoor by 27th April 1959 and ran trials on the LMR in May and June. Though similar in some design concepts to the later AD 890, this locomotive was not purchased by the MOD.
Tony Edwards

8200 (400)	NBL/27421/5	0-4-0DH
8205 (405) *Matruh* [2]	NBL/27426/55	0-4-0DH
(8212) 412	NBL/27647/59	0-4-0DH

WD 8200 was the prototype military light shunter. It ran at Longmoor, for trials and then for instructional purposes, from 1956 to 1960 when it was transferred to Bicester. WD 8205 (*Matruh*) was delivered to Bicester, but transferred to Longmoor in 1957, subsequently moving to Marchwood in 1962. WD 8212 (Army 412 as it had become in the 1968 scheme of renumbering) was rebuilt in 1968. It arrived at Longmoor at the end of 1969 and was retained until July 1970 to move stock following the closure. It was then transferred to Ludgershall. Matruh (also known as Mersah Matruh) was the original terminus of the Western Desert Railway, the starting point for the war time Tobruk extension line.

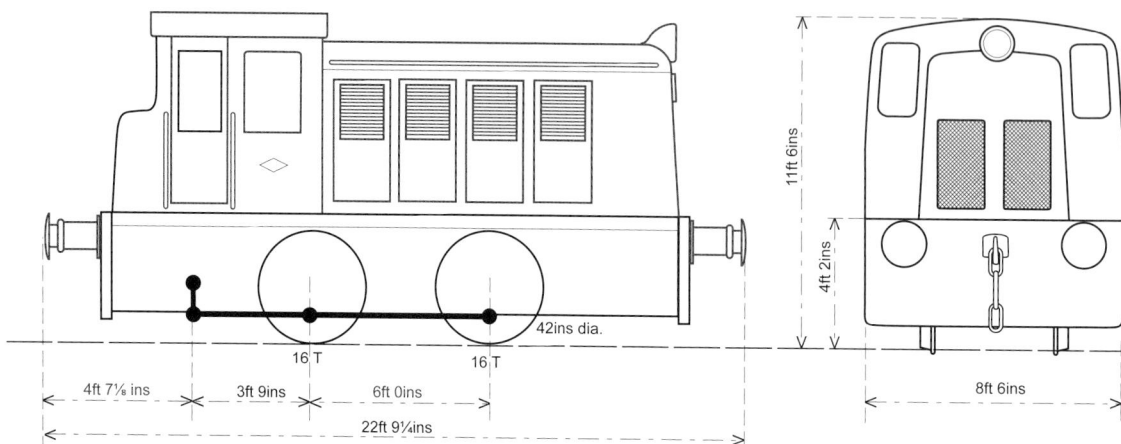

42ins dia.

16 T   16 T

4ft 7⅛ ins   3ft 9ins   6ft 0ins

22ft 9¼ins

11ft 6ins   4ft 2ins   8ft 6ins

Locomotives 8200 and 8205
Weight in working order - 32.0 tons
Fuel capacity - 15.5 imperial gallons
National engine, 5 cylinders, 275 H.P. at 1,500 R.P.M.
Voith Turbo transmission Type L24/V
Tractive effort 21,500 lbs at 30% adhesion
Maximum speed 15 M.P.H.

Based on a diagram prepared at Longmoor.

L.M.R.
275 H.P. DIESEL LOCOMOTIVE

Fresh out of the box, this view shows the brand new WD 8200 as delivered.

Tim Edwards

The first new diesel locomotive to arrive at Longmoor for a decade, WD 8200 (NB/27421/55) reflected post-war developments in both UK locomotive manufacturing and the requirements of the War Office. The Voith hydraulic transmission was similar to that installed in RE (Tn) locomotives operating in West Germany at that time. The top-mounted exhaust scrubber (an essential safety feature for locomotives operating in hazardous locations) had been fitted whilst at Longmoor as part of the on-going trials programme. This locomotive survives today in preservation in Scotland bearing the name *River Eden*.

War Office photograph

Army 412, the third of its class to be used at Longmoor, was a late arrival. By 5th July 1969 when this picture was taken, the LMR had officially been scheduled for closure. Army 412 was intended by 1 Rly Gp RCT to provide a locomotive for the collection of rolling stock after closure of the LMR.

Photographer unknown

This view taken on 11th May 1960 shows WD 8205 (now with nameplates *Matruh* [2] and exhaust scrubber) tucked away in the Diesel School. In the foreground was the trailer for rail car WD 9033.

Nick Lera Locomotion
Pictures reference 005

| 8227 (440) *Hassan* | RH/468041/62 | 0-6-0DH |
| 8219 (425) | RH/459519/61 | 0-6-0DH |

WD 8227 was delivered new in 1962 and named *Hassan* to commemorate the performance of James Elroy Flecker's play of that name with which Longmoor had won the Senior Army Dramatic Competition. As delivered 8227 had an overdrive fitted to allow a higher line speed when hauling passenger trains. Further deliveries from the makers eventually produced a group of eighteen locomotives for general shunting duties on the UK depot railways of 1 Rly Gp RE. One of these, 8219, was allocated to Longmoor in 1966 by which time the emphasis in trades training was virtually exclusively on diesel locomotives. Both these locomotives survived (in private ownership) into the 21st century.

AD 8219 (photographed on 28th September 1968) was in all respects a standard member of Class 'C3SA' (comprising seventeen locomotives) designed for general depot shunting duties. From its arrival in 1966, it was generally used for training RCT Railwaymen and for any 'real' (as against training) traffic in the final years of the LMR. It has survived into the 21st century and was last noted (2013) in commercial traffic at Shipley in Yorkshire, carrying the name *Venom*.   *G. Moon*

AD 8227, *Hassan*, was delivered new to Longmoor in 1962. Important from an operational perspective was the overdrive fitted to allow its use on passenger trains. As a result of this modification, the locomotive was given a unique Army class being designated 'C4SA' in the 1964 numbering scheme. In this view it was being used as an improvised air compressor, probably driving the Deutschland rerailing equipment.   *Photographer unknown*

890 (610) *General Lord Robertson*
Rolls-Royce/Sentinel/10143/63   0-8-0DH

This unusual machine was the final new diesel locomotive to be delivered to Longmoor. The Sentinel Works of Rolls Royce Ltd (Shrewsbury) had not previously supplied the Army, but was actively developing a new range of (Sentinel derived) diesel powered shunting locomotives whilst the main Rolls-Royce company was promoting their range of small diesel engines. This locomotive nominally replaced the Whitcomb diesel-electric *Tobruk* (WD 71232). The selection of design was partly to allow evaluation of a more powerful diesel locomotive than used previously and partly for crew training. To meet the 'main line' aspects of the specification the maximum speed was increased compared with the maker's standard design but in all other respects it remained a heavy shunter. The rigid eight-coupled wheelbase was later blamed for damage to the track, despite some fining-down of the leading flanges in the LMR workshops. Shortly after the closure of the LMR this locomotive was transferred to Shoeburyness. Army 610 remained at Shoeburyness until 1985 when it was sold to the Mid Hants Railway.

General Lord Robertson had a distinguished military career, seeing active service in both World Wars. First commissioned into the Royal Engineers in 1914, he retired from the Army in 1934 as a Major but was recalled in 1939, serving in East Africa and the Western Desert. At the German surrender in 1945 he was serving in Germany as Montgomery's chief administrative officer. He remained in Germany as Chief of Staff of the British Control Commission and in 1947 became the Military Governor of the British Occupation Zone. He then became the Commander in Chief, Middle East Land Forces (1950-53). On retirement he was appointed Chairman of the British Transport Commission and in 1961 retired as its longest serving and arguably most successful chief officer.

L.M.R.
GENERAL LORD ROBERTSON

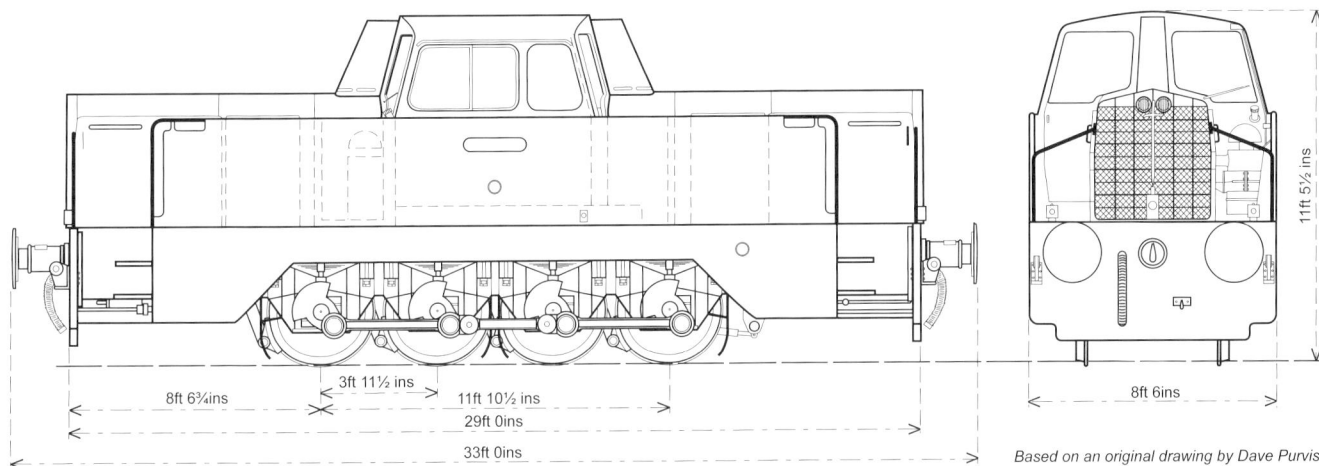

8ft 6¾ins   3ft 11½ ins   11ft 10½ ins
29ft 0ins
33ft 0ins

11ft 5½ ins

8ft 6ins

Based on an original drawing by Dave Purvis.

The final new diesel locomotive at Longmoor was WD 890 *General Lord Robertson*, completed in 1963 but not received on the LMR until 1964. It was an attempt to upgrade a heavy shunting design into a mixed-traffic locomotive capable of operating passenger trains. In this it was not totally successful, the rigid eight-coupled wheels being suspected of causing damage to the track. Later rebuilt by Thos. Hill (Rotherham) Ltd, it spent fifteen years after the closure of the LMR at Shoeburyness before being sold for preservation.   *Photographer unknown*

870	AB/509/66	0-6-0DH
871	AB/510/66	0-6-0DH
872	AB/511/66	0-6-0DH
873	AB/512/66	0-6-0DH

The final diesel locomotives to pass through Longmoor completed the cycle begun by the little 2ft 6in. gauge Avonside locomotives in 1915. In 1966 Andrew Barclay, Sons & Co. Ltd built a batch of 0-6-0 diesel-hydraulic locomotives intended for service with 79 Rly Sqn in BAOR. Being constructed to the German structure and load gauges, they could not be tested on BR tracks so were sent by the makers to Longmoor for extended trials.

Though never 'on the strength' of the LMR, four diesel-hydraulic locomotives (AD 870/3) were delivered to Longmoor in 1966 by Andrew Barclay, Sons & Co. Ltd. With air braking for use in Europe they could be employed on the Longmoor 'Bullet' – as shown here on 3rd June 1967, hauling ex-ambulance coach AD 5308 which had left Germany in 1929.   *G. Moon*

Section IV : Rail Cars 1918-1970

DREWRY CAR [1]   DC/1023/18   Four-wheel petrol

The original petrol rail car was a six-seat 10hp semi-open car built by E. E. Baguley Ltd for the Drewry Car Co. Ltd. It was ordered in the first place by the Ministry of Munitions in May 1917 for use on the Russian front and was therefore designed for both 5ft and 4ft 8½in. gauges. The order was held until the end of October 1917 when it was decided to proceed with the machine as a standard gauge product. In March 1918 the rail car was diverted to the War Department and at the end of July 1918 it was delivered to Longmoor. It was given a heavy overhaul in 1929 and the last note about it is the delivery of a replacement engine in 1940. This Drewry rail car does not feature in any of the stock lists that were kept during the war, though it is thought not to have been broken up until as late as 1946.

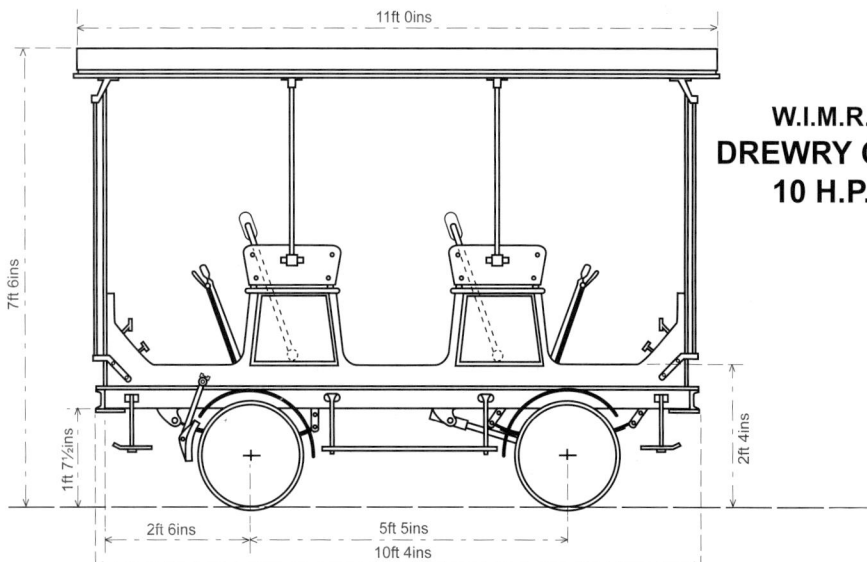

W.I.M.R.
DREWRY CAR
10 H.P.

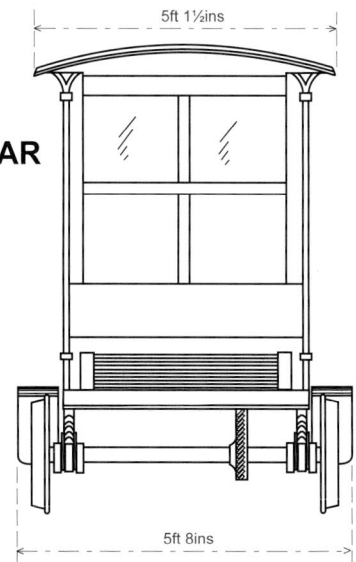

11ft 0ins

7ft 6ins

2ft 4ins

1ft 7½ins

2ft 6ins

5ft 5ins

10ft 4ins

5ft 1½ins

5ft 8ins

Seating Accommodation;
1 Driver, 5 Passengers
On reversible seats.

Note; This drawing is at twice the scale of the other rolling stock drawings in this book

Drewry 10ph C-type car
Based on W.I.M.R. Diagram No. 51
prepared at Longmoor 10 March 1933

WICKHAM CARS [1]

DW/1000/1933	Type 17a	Four-wheel petrol
DW/2204/1937	Type 17a Special	Four-wheel petrol

Neither of these rail motor gang trolleys ever appear to have been allocated numbers and as a result became mixed up during the war years. It is possible that some cannibalisation may have taken place. Both were delivered new to Bordon and at least one matching trailer was also purchased. By 1942, the stock list shows one 'No. 17 Rail car' with engine details matching DW/2204 – but the same stock list refers to it as 'bought 1934' which tallies with neither of the maker's particulars above.

DREWRY CAR [2]   DC/1820/36   2-2-0 (D)

Probably the best loved and certainly the hardest worked of the rail cars was the Drewry car delivered new in February 1936. This was a twenty seat fully-enclosed car with a Gardner 4LW 62hp diesel engine, Wilson-Drewry gearbox, Voight-Sinclair coupling and chain final drive. Apart from its obvious value in maintaining the camp passenger services, it was considered suitable for instructing drivers and fitters on some of the features of diesel locomotives. The rail car received the number 941 during the war and was allocated 9111 in the 1952 renumbering. Unfortunately by this time it was becoming worn out and was withdrawn and scrapped around 1959. It was noted as 'Painted dark green' in 1940.

Perhaps the best known of the Longmoor rail cars was this Drewry product of 1936. Solid and simple, with a reliable Gardner engine, it provided essential back-up to the 'Bullet' services throughout the war years.

WD photograph

A view of the spartan and relatively 'soldier-proof' interior of the Drewry rail car.   *WD photograph*

The gleaming Gardner 4LW diesel engine and the simple driver's controls of the Drewry rail car. The Wilson-Drewry gearbox was of a 'pre-selector' type developed from bus gearboxes of the period.

WD photograph

The originally un-numbered rail car was successively renumbered WD 941 then WD 9111 during World War Two. By 1957 when this photograph was taken it was virtually worn out and it was scrapped two years later.
W. S. Sellar

WICKHAM CARS [2]

930 (9109)	DW/2877/40	Four-wheel petrol
931 (9110)	DW/2878/40	Four-wheel petrol

A pair of thirty-seat semi-open cars was ordered from D. Wickham & Co. Ltd through the Ministry of Supply in December 1939 and delivered to Longmoor in May 1940. Power was supplied by a Ford V8 petrol engine through a Ford gearbox and shaft drive and straight air brakes were fitted. It is not known whether these two useful cars were originally destined for the LMR, but once there they proved most valuable. Both were withdrawn by the late 1950s and were scrapped in 1957 and 1961 respectively.

Delivered in May 1940, Wickham car WD 9110 was one of a pair, possibly diverted from elsewhere but once on the LMR, far too useful to let go! In 1957 there was a plan to convert sister car 9109 into a trailer but this was never done and it was scrapped ten years later. 9110 survived until 1961 when it had been replaced by WD 9034.
Photographer unknown

WICKHAM TROLLIES

WD Numbers	Maker's Numbers	
11966-11972	DW/3374 - 3380/43	Type 17a
Not known	DW/3812 - 3815/45	Fourteen seat trailers

These seven motor gang trolleys and four trailers were delivered to Longmoor during World War Two. Nothing is known of their employment at Longmoor and it is thought they were stored before shipment overseas.

9033 DW/6857/54	Type 27A Mk II Motor Trolley
DW/6858/54	Type 17 2-ton Trailer, supplied with 9033
9034 DW/7397/57	Type 40 Mk IIA Inspection Car

The well-known post-war Wickham trolleys were 9033 and 9034. 9033 was delivered new to Longmoor in 1954 and transferred to Bicester in July 1970. It was an eight seat semi-open car with canopy, fitted with a Ford 109E engine and three-speed Morris gearbox. 9034 was typical of the latest Army practice, being a heavier and more powerful car. It was transferred to Longmoor from Bicester in 1960, presumably to replace 9110. After closure it was returned to Bicester for redeployment.

WD 9033 (note the art deco numbering) was delivered in 1954, remaining on the LMR until 1970 when it was returned to Bicester for further use. The Ford 109E engine gave the workshops a valid reason to indent for a range of useful car spares. In this December 1957 view the driver was Lcpl Stuart Sellar. This rail car featured in the making of the film 'The Great St. Trianian's Train Robbery'.   *W. S. Sellar*

AD 9034 was officially a Wickham Mk IIA Inspection Car, so a trifle superior to AD 9033. *Photographer unknown*

This view shows WD 3239 in its intended role to give practical demonstrations of Walschaerts Valve Gear. It also gave the instructors a convenient and compact indoor training aid to support Lesson 1 'Describing the Parts'. It was rather hastily scrapped in 1961 when instruction on steam locomotives was giving way to diesel. Behind could be seen the boiler of the 18-inch gauge *Mars*, also used as a training aid at this time but later saved as a museum exhibit.
Bluebell Railway Museum Archive, J. J. Smith Collection

Section V : Miscellaneous locomotives

A few locomotives at Longmoor fall into no convenient category and have therefore been listed together in this section:

3239 (4530)	HE/1355/1919	4-6-0T

3239 was a narrow-gauge steam locomotive, the last 60cm gauge locomotive built by the Hunslet Engine Co. Ltd for the Ministry of Munitions to order REQ 1839 of 1919. It was used along with 3238 on the military railway at Stokes Bay, Gosport that served the WD Electric Light School. In 1934 it was transferred to Longmoor as an instructional 'model'. It survived in this role until 1961, when it was scrapped bearing the 1952-series number 4530. Its demise was not commented on at the time but there can be no doubt that had it survived until the closure of the LMR in 1969, the narrow-gauge preservation movement would have snapped it up at auction.

13.905 *Mars* [2]	Gmeinder/4117/44	0-6-0DH
13.915 *Venus* [2]	Gmeinder/4177/44	0-6-0DH

These Wehrmacht 75cm gauge diesels locomotives were painted German field grey on arrival at Longmoor but later this was changed to a sand colour used by the British Army in Egypt.Latterly they carried a scaled-down version of the 1936 LMR 'Southern-style' livery. At Longmoor they were used for instruction on diesel-hydraulic transmissions. During the early annual Open Days one was heavily disguised to form the 'Old Fashioned Railway'. In the early 1950s Gardner diesel engines were fitted to both locomotives. For a time c1953, 13.915 carried the incorrect number 13.906. By 1955 both locomotives had been given the names of two of the original 18-inch gauge steam locomotives. 13.915 was scrapped in 1957 whilst 13.905 was later (after a major engine failure) dismantled and the chassis used in the fitters' school for instruction.

No. 17	JF/22912/1940	0-4-0DM

Another standard Fowler 150hp diesel-mechanical shunter was acquired in 1963. It was the intention to rebuild the locomotive as a series of training exercises for fitters but this never came to fruition. On closure it was sold to the Dart Valley Railway.

Gazelle	A. Dodman/1893	0-4-2WT

This fascinating little engine was a centre of attention at Longmoor from 1950 when it was placed on display there. It was built in 1893 by A. Dodman & Co. of Kings Lynn for the private use of a Mr William Burkett who had been granted special running powers over sections of the GER and M&GNR. H. F. Stephens purchased it in 1911. In its original configuration it was a 2-2-2WT but, after running it for a short period on the Shropshire and Montgomeryshire Light Railway (of which

Although not in service, WD 3239 was later renumbered as WD 4530 and a plate showing its new number was duly bolted to the tank side.

Hugh Ballantyne

Below: WD 4530, photographed en route for scrapping.

Bryan Stone

Stephens was at that time the engineer), its new owner had it rebuilt by W. G. Bagnall Ltd of Stafford as an 0-4-2WT. It then ran on the S&MLR on light passenger duties, usually on the Criggion Branch coupled to a converted secondhand London horse tramcar. It was overhauled in 1937 but by World War Two was to all intents worn out. Though never transferred to WD ownership (it was only on lease) it was used – mainly as a light inspection vehicle – by the military during the war years after the Royal Engineers took over the operation of the S&MLR 'main line'. On nationalisation in 1948, the locomotive (along with the other surviving rolling stock of the S&MLR) passed into the ownership of the British Transport Commission. In 1950 the BTC agreed to present *Gazelle* to the Transportation Centre RE on indefinite loan for preservation and display. When the School of Transport at Longmoor closed in 1973, the little locomotive was transferred to the Army School of Mechanical Transport at Leconfield and stored until it could be displayed in the new Museum of Army Transport at Beverley.

By 1953, *Gazelle* had been moved to a short display track outside the main Headquarters Transportation Centre RE building. The locomotive was in a lined out livery and the cab-side lettered 'S & M R 1'. Later re-paintings became progressively simplified. *Photographer unknown*

Passenger, Goods and Construction Rolling Stock

Whilst a reasonable amount of information on almost all the locomotives has been available, relatively few details of the other rolling stock have survived. No complete primary source for a stock list before 1930 has been discovered but sufficient detail is available to present the general picture.

Fortunately, because the need for economy dictated the purchase of much secondhand equipment, the reader seeking full details of a particular vehicle will usually be able to find alternative sources detailing the history of the vehicles in the hands of their original owners. In this section the era from the opening of the line up to 1940 is treated as a single period, followed by World War Two and finally by sections on the goods and passenger stock post-1945 and on construction equipment throughout the history of the line.

This rail-mobile Land Rover conversion was just one of the many add-on accessories offered by the makers. It was trialled both at Longmoor and on the UK depot railways of 1 Railway Group RE but not adopted for general Army use. Problems with overheating while running in reverse were never satisfactorily solved, and the wheel mounting studs were not able to cope with the shocks delivered by non resilient wheels. Apart from the rail wheels, military bumper and bridge classification disc, the vehicle was a standard early Series 2 short wheelbase petrol-engined model of the 1960s. *K. Farmer*

This view, taken in 1907, shows *Hampshire* hauling a typical construction train of that era. Coincidentally it also shows most of the WIMR 'train set' at that time. Behind *Hampshire* was marshalled one of the four 30-ton bogie dropside wagons supplied new by the Leeds Forge Co. the previous year. Next was a bogie flat wagon, one of the ex-GWR MACAW vehicles, hired at this time but subsequently purchased. The remaining open wagons were some of the ex-Midland Railway low sided vehicles, of which twenty-three were purchased for the start of construction of the standard gauge route from Bordon to Longmoor. The final vehicle was also ex-MR, one of its 10-ton brake vans, also purchased in 1905. *WD photograph*

Section VI : Pre-1940 Goods and Passenger Stock

In 1905 the standard gauge railway being built from a temporary base at Bordon was initially equipped by the purchase of secondhand main line vehicles. The stock which comprised this original 'train set' consisted of two 10-ton vans, twenty-three 8-ton low sided wagons and a 10-ton brake van. It is believed that all were purchased through the agency of R. Y. Pickering & Co. Ltd from the Midland Railway. In 1906-07 four

30-ton open bogie wagons were purchased new from the Leeds Forge Co. Ltd. These wagons had detachable low sides and Fox's Patent bogies. They were used for carrying construction materials, stores and parties of troops. In general design they resembled bogie wagons supplied by the same maker to the Midland Railway at this period. The last survivor of this quartet was used for rerailing practice until the late 1950s.

Not just a charming view of an Edwardian railway picnic! This photograph by Lt J. Day shows a group of officers and their wives enjoying a trip to Whitehill. It also gives us a very good view of one of the 30-ton Leeds Forge Co. bogie wagons. The officer seated on the left was Lt Tyrrell, with Mrs Tyrell and, nearest the locomotive, Lt Maxwell. *J. Day*

35ft 6ins
35ft 0ins inside

W.I.   M.R.

3ft 4ins

Journals 9ins x 4½ins

25ft 0ins

38ft 3ins

6ft 0ins

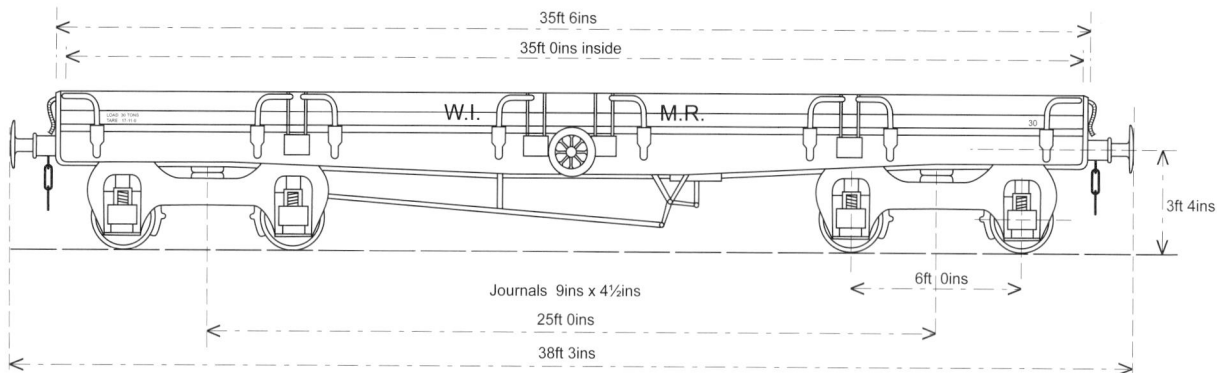

Wagons Nos. 30 - 33.
Vacuum Fitted.
Capacity 299.4 cu.ft
Load 30 Tons. Tare weight 17-11-0.

Traced from W.I.M.R. Rolling stock drawing No. 15
Signed by Mjr McMullen R.E. on 10 March 1933.

W.I.M.R.
LEEDS FORGE WAGON

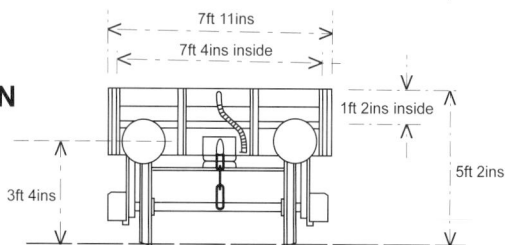

7ft 11ins
7ft 4ins inside

1ft 2ins inside

3ft 4ins

5ft 2ins

The versatile Leeds Forge Co. wagons could also be used to carry vehicle and weapon loads. In a joint operating exercise of 1938 run by 153 (LNE) and 154 (GW) Operating Coys RE (SR), gun teams from the Medium Artillery Brigade (then stationed at Longmoor) had loaded a pair of Mark IVB 18 pdr QF (Quick Firing) guns. They had already discovered what a valuable waterproof could be made from the (then newly issued) 'Capes, Anti-Gas'. The location of the photograph is Louisburg Siding with the walled and gated Bordon Garrison coal yard behind.   *WD photograph*

The bogie flat wagons built by the Leeds Forge Co. were sturdy and survived the harsh conditions of a training railway. This was WD 80011 in Longmoor Yard c1958.
Bryan Stone

There is in the Longmoor collection a photograph of 'driving the first pile' at Free Piece (see page 61). It is dated 1906 and shows one corner of a passenger coach. Unfortunately no records of this vehicle have survived but it has been suggested that it is a rigid 8-wheel ex-Metropolitan Railway carriage and probably also appears on the extreme left of the illustration on page 88. The WIMR had no need for passenger rolling stock until 1909, when the standard gauge reached Longmoor Camp, as there would have been no requirement to carry passengers other than the men engaged on building the railway.

However in 1912, once the final alignment at Whitehall had been authorised, a pair of light bogie carriages were purchased from the Kent & East Sussex Railway where they had become surplus to that company's immediate needs. They were typical Edwardian light railway carriages, built by R. Y. Pickering & Co. Ltd of Wishaw. It may seem surprising that a railway company should be selling its newest assets so soon after opening. The K&ESR always seems to have been 'strapped for cash' and it probably made better sense to sell something of value. There is indeed some doubt whether the two carriages in question were ever actually owned by the K&ESR. It is quite possible that they had been bought privately under some 'arrangement' negotiated by H. F. Stephens with the makers, or they may have reverted to R. Y. Pickering's ownership as the result of a failed hire-purchase agreement.

Whatever the reasons for their early disposal, they were a most useful addition to the WIMR. In 1923 they were rebuilt, 111 being converted into an officers' saloon with end windows. Both carriages are known to have carried royalty during official visits. The photograph of King George V visiting Longmoor in May 1928 shows the brake composite (ex-K&ESR No. 7) in this role. On the original photograph the label 'WIMR 7' appears, but no other records of stock numbering exist before 1930. About this date, the open saloon was further improved whilst the brake composite was converted into a fully equipped mobile workshop and stores van, numbered 110 in the 1934 scheme. The van was

'A' End 'B' End

11ft 3½ins

8ft 0ins over Body

8ft 6ins over Handles

L.M.R.
SALOON CARRIAGE
No. 111 Ex Kent & East Sussex Railway

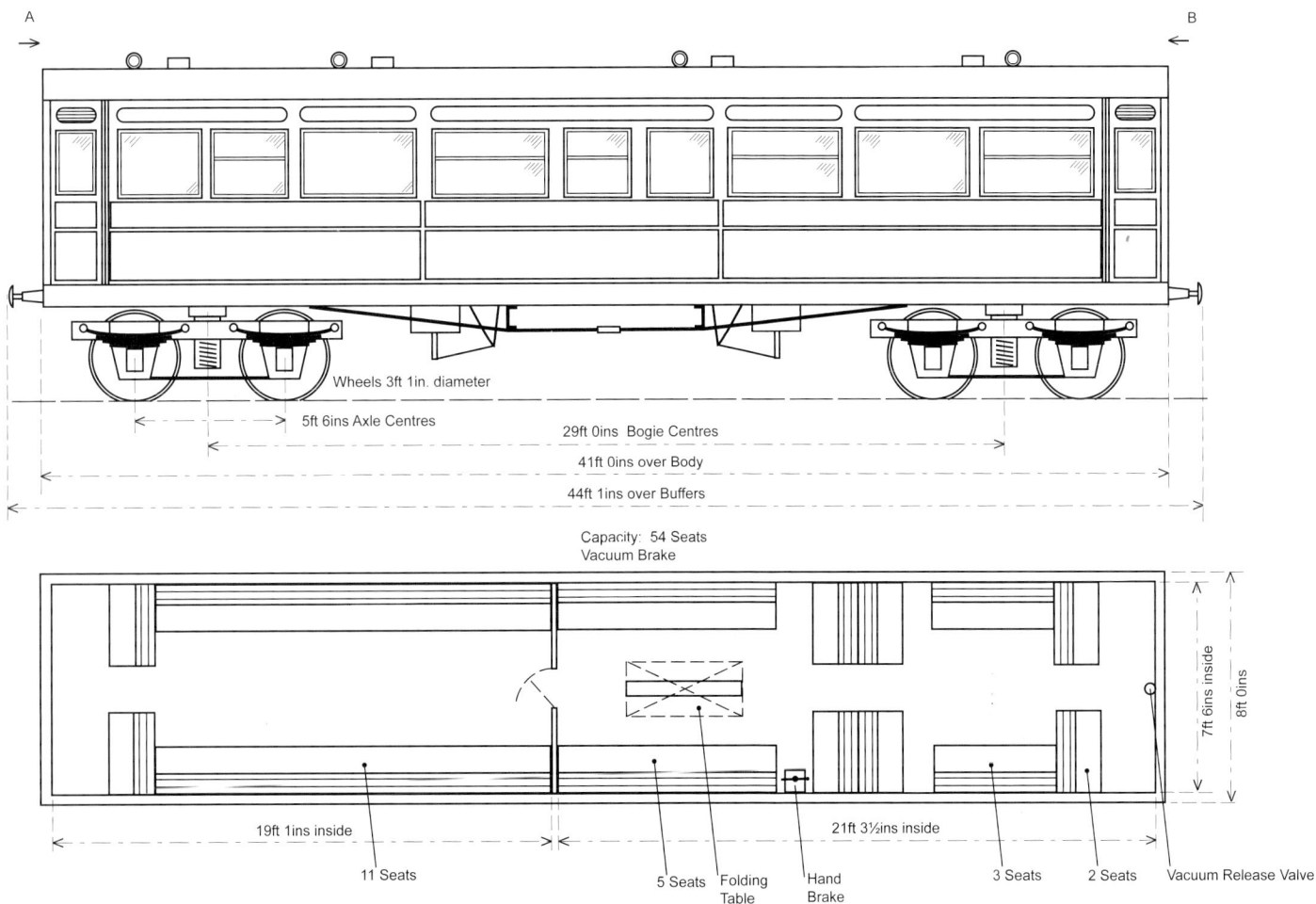

A B

Wheels 3ft 1in. diameter

5ft 6ins Axle Centres

29ft 0ins Bogie Centres

41ft 0ins over Body

44ft 1ins over Buffers

Capacity: 54 Seats
Vacuum Brake

7ft 6ins inside

8ft 0ins

19ft 1ins inside

21ft 3½ins inside

11 Seats

5 Seats Folding Table

Hand Brake

3 Seats 2 Seats

Vacuum Release Valve

A →   B ←

Wheels 3ft 1in. diameter

5ft 6ins Axle Centres

29ft 0ins Bogie Centres

41ft 0ins over Body

44ft 1in. over Buffers

f

a   b

BLACKSMITH

h

FITTERS

d   d

m

P.W.GANG

p

s

t

e

d   c   k

g

CARPENTERS

h

n

s

v

r

d

s/b

10ft 0ins inside   18ft 9ins inside   11ft 6ins inside

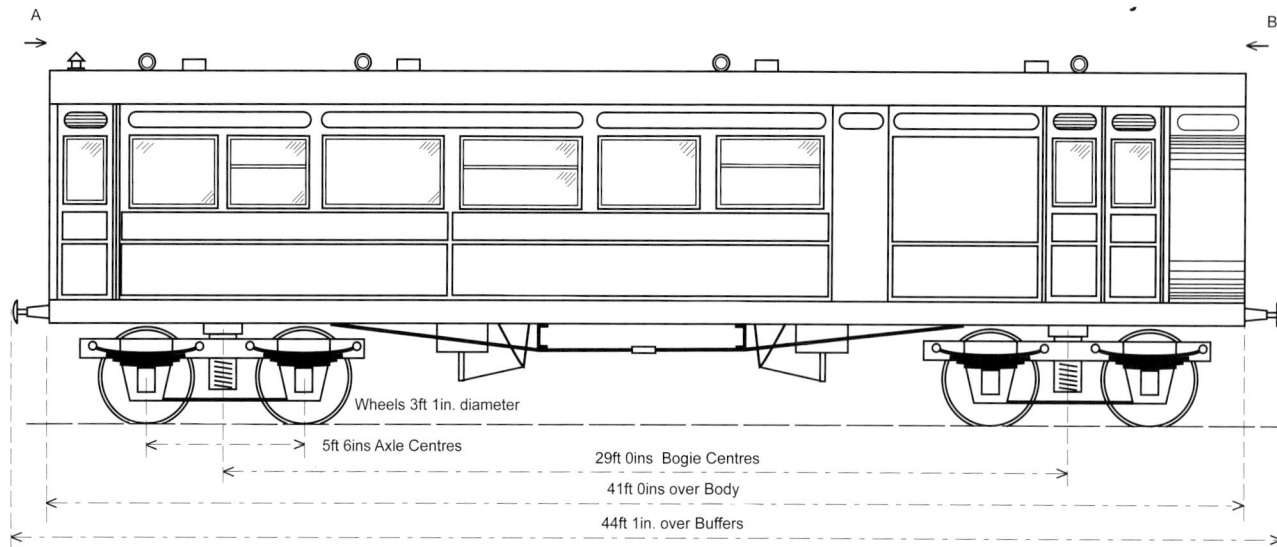

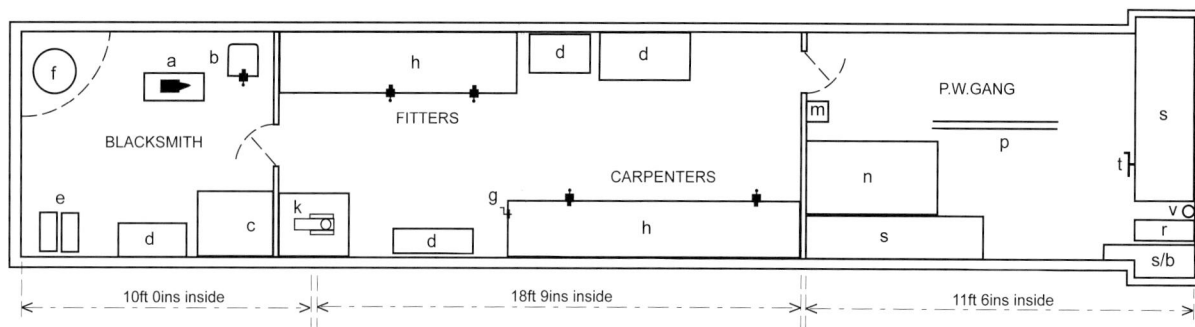

L.M.R.
TOOL VAN
No. 110 Ex Kent & East Sussex Railway

'A' End   'B' End

11ft 3½ins

8ft 0ins over Body   9ft 0¾ins

8ft 6ins over Handles

intended to support fifty men on normal construction work. It had a fitter's and carpenter's shop with tools, vices, bench drilling machinery and bench emery grinders. There was also a blacksmith's and tinsmith's shop with an anvil, field forge and vice stand (the smith's plant being portable for outdoor use). In this form it survived until destroyed by an enemy bomb in 1940. Following the delivery of the ex-Southern family saloons, 111 largely fell out of use as a VIP/Inspection vehicle. It was transferred around 1943 to the Bicester Military Railway where a vehicle for such duties was required. Later it was converted with a driving cab and a simplified form of 'push-pull' control gear to operate passenger services within the Depot. No scrapping date has been recorded for this vehicle but by the late 1950s it was superseded by one of the ex-L&SWR dining car conversions previously employed by the War Department as ambulance coaches.

The only other acquisitions in the pre-1914 period were a number of standard 10-ton open wagons from various owners. During World War One many extra vehicles were in use, but whether these were bought, hired or requisitioned is not clear. The various types of bolster wagons probably originated at this time, being essential for the Canadian Forestry Corps timber traffic. As there were no regular internal passenger services until 1916, the need for additional passenger stock does not seem to have arisen during the early years of the war. However

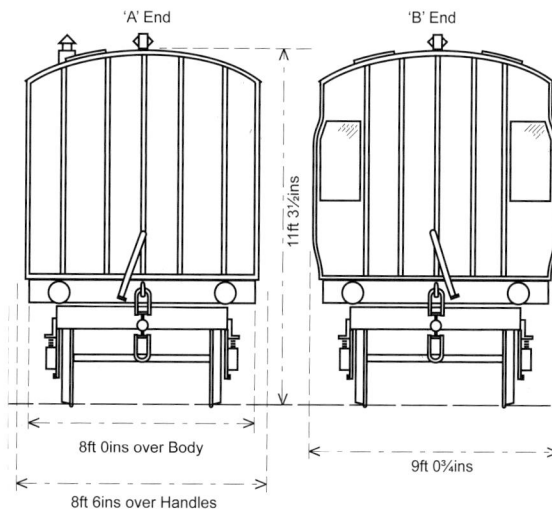

Legend
a Anvil
b Vice on Cast Iron Stand
c Bench with zinc cover
d Tool Chest
e 16 ton Traversing Jacks (2)
f Forge
g Grinder
h Bench
k Drill Press
m Rack for Crowbars
n Table with flap
p Survey Flags under roof
r Rack for Wooden levers
s Shelves
s/b Shelf with bin
t Hand Brake
v Vacuum Release Valve

Additional Equipment includes
Track Gauge
Rail Slings
Spanners
Saws
Hammers
5ft 0in. Ladder
Red and Green Flags
Pyrene Fire Extinguisher

Based on a Diagram
prepared by No. 1 R.T.C. 14 June 1940.

The ex-K&ESR bogie coach No. 111 after its conversion into an inspection saloon. This photograph was taken while the train was in motion (hence the slight camera shake) and shows a group of Longmoor officers with Lt Col Manton on an inspection of the line on 23rd March 1934.

WD photograph

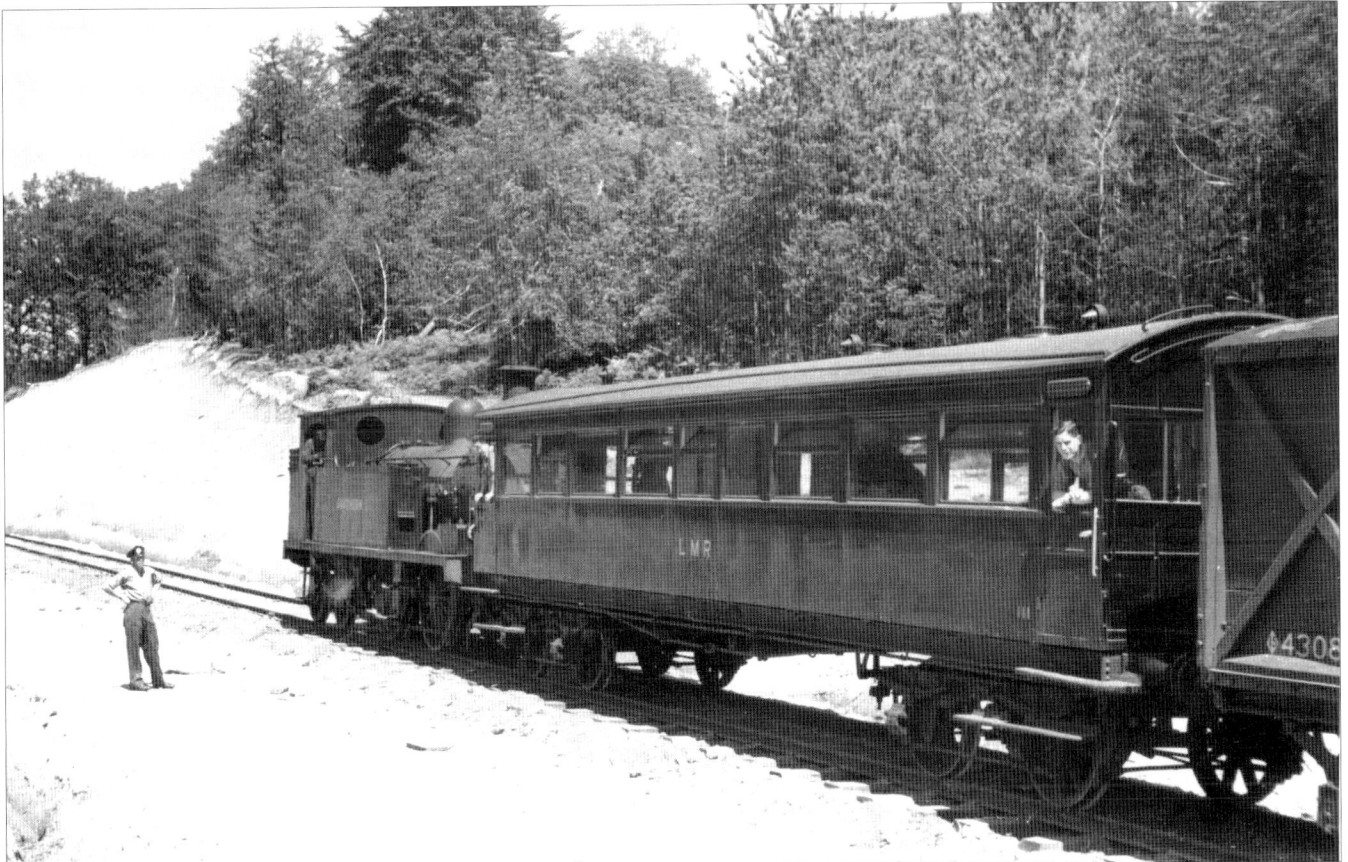

Good views of the ex-K&ESR coaches are scarce. This World War Two view shows No. 111 (Saloon) in its final form, probably on a rehearsal for the official opening of the Hollywater Loop in June 1942.

WD photograph

Timetabled passenger services on the WIMR are known to have operated from 1916. This postcard showed *Sir John French* hauling a train composed of a hired L&SWR close-coupled 'Block Set' of 6-wheeled carriages. The leading coach retained its L&SWR number 0646 indicating that it had already been removed from the company's capital stock before being transferred to Longmoor. The use of *Sir John French* on a passenger train suggests that this view dates from the very earliest days of the Longmoor passenger service. In the final year of World War One this engine was mostly employed on the timber traffic generated by the Canadian Forestry Corps. *John Alsop Collection A69478*

by 1916 a passenger service to connect with the L&SWR trains at Bordon had been initiated. It is unclear what carriages were used for the first services. Photographs of this period are very scarce and the only evidence from those so far discovered suggests that initially old coaches were borrowed from the L&SWR and the LB&SCR.

The first identified passenger rolling stock in regular use at Longmoor came from the ill-fated 'CAT 38' – the L&NWR, ex-North London Railway ambulance train (see page 87). Out

of the twenty coaches originally delivered to Longmoor in 1919/20, at least six (including two brake vans) were retained to form two passenger 'sets' (a coach each for officers, NCOs and 'general users'). The remainder were dispersed to Catterick and other Military Camp Railways which continued to operate after the Armistice. In 1922 eleven coaches were sent to the Central Ammunition Depot at Bramley near Basingstoke to provide an internal passenger service. It would be logical that these were the coaches formerly assigned to Catterick. The last survivor

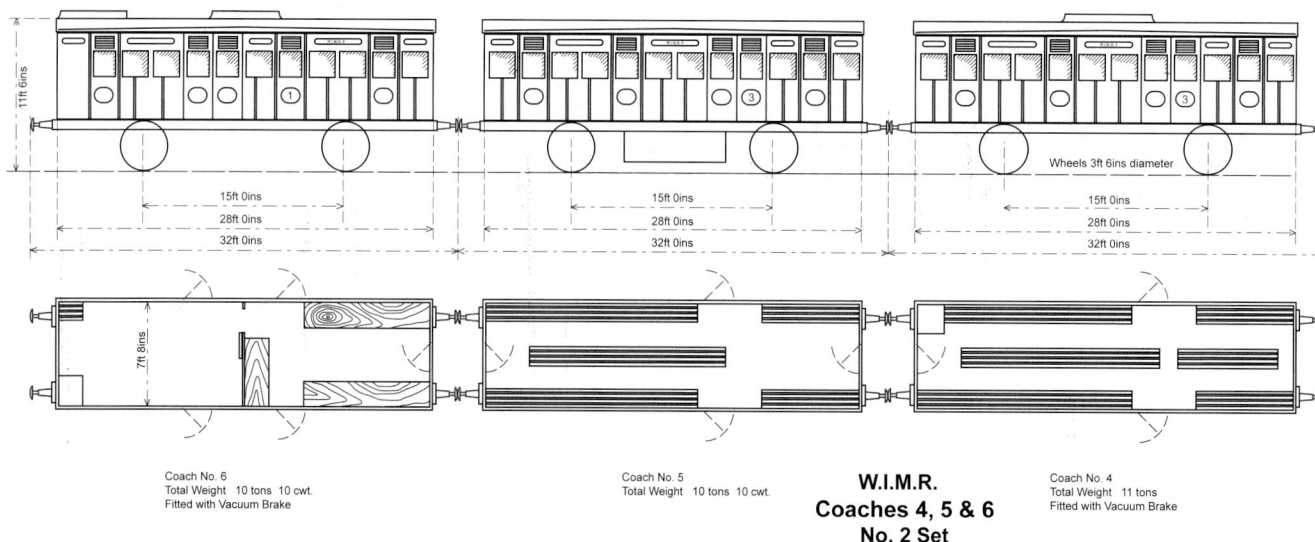

11ft 6ins

15ft 0ins
28ft 0ins
32ft 0ins

15ft 0ins
28ft 0ins
32ft 0ins

Wheels 3ft 6ins diameter

15ft 0ins
28ft 0ins
32ft 0ins

7ft 8ins

Coach No. 6
Total Weight 10 tons 10 cwt.
Fitted with Vacuum Brake

Coach No. 5
Total Weight 10 tons 10 cwt.

W.I.M.R.
Coaches 4, 5 & 6
No. 2 Set

Coach No. 4
Total Weight 11 tons
Fitted with Vacuum Brake

Makers: North London Railway

Note; due to constraints of the size of the page, this diagram is drawn to a slighty smaller scale than the other rolling stock diagrams.

Based on a Diagram prepared at Longmoor.

By 1918 coaches converted from the ex-NLR Ambulance Train (CAT 38) were in use at Longmoor. Originally there were twenty-seven 4-wheeled coaches in this train, not all of which can yet be accounted for in WD service. This photograph shows one of the three-coach sets which was deployed to the Military Camp Railway at Catterick. At least two identical sets were rebuilt for service at Longmoor. Whilst in the ambulance train configuration, the number of operable doors had been reduced to one on each side per coach. That of the nearest coach bore the inscription 'NCOs Only'. The furthest coach was probably similarly labelled 'Officers Only'. *LPC reference 79402*

at Longmoor was a grounded body in the yard which was photographed by J. A. Kay on the occasion of the first official press visit in 1930. It must be assumed that the ex-NLR coaches 'soldiered-on' at Longmoor until replaced by the ex-BAOR coaches in 1929.

The aftermath of World War One produced quantities of stock returned from overseas and awaiting disposal, in addition to surplus equipment from the Military Camp Railways. No records have survived, so we must move to 1930 when the first

article on the WIMR appeared in the *Locomotive* magazine. It is possible to deduce from the stock listed therein that a few of the items must have arrived as war surplus. Of interest, as survivors of the war, were the four ex-GWR rail-carrying wagons. These wagons had originally been requisitioned for conversion at Crewe into constituents of a pair of armoured trains intended for coastal defence in Norfolk and Fife. After the war, Longmoor converted them into rail-carrying wagons which were used in the 1920s to form the 'end-on' tracklaying machine.

Though the load (WD 3239, HE/1355/19) is of great interest to the narrow gauge enthusiast, the wagon carrying it was equally historic. WIMR No. 42 was one of four ex-GWR MACAW rail-carrying wagons which had been converted in World War One to make armoured trains for home defence. It was brought to Longmoor when these armoured trains were dismantled and was used for construction projects.
WD photograph

717

BRAKE

3

1

9ft 0ins

9ft 0ins

50ft 9ins total wheelbase

57ft 3ins over buffers

Based on a diagram drawn at Longmoor 19 July 1924.

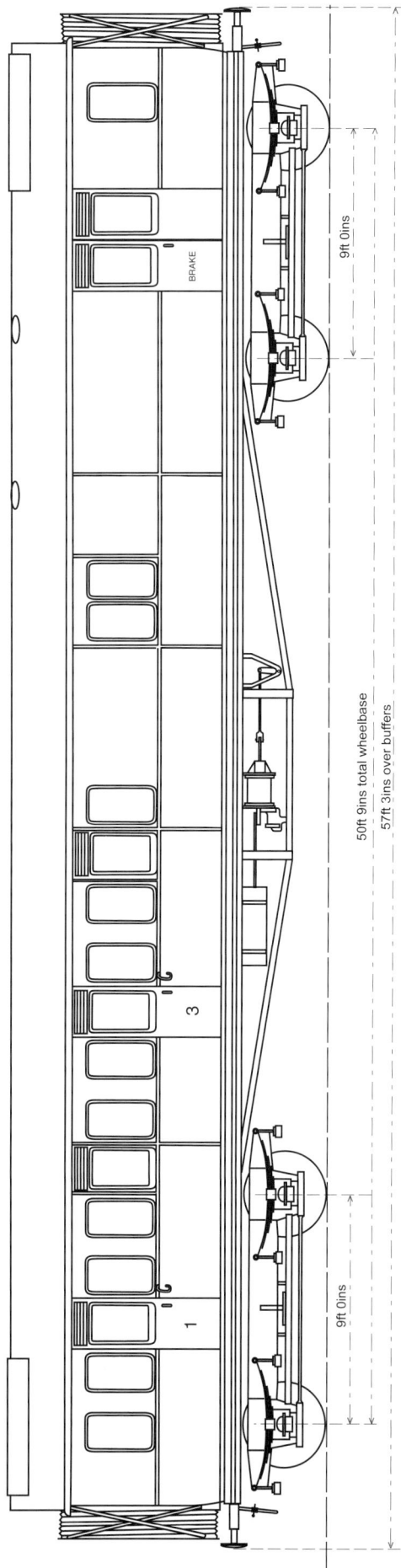

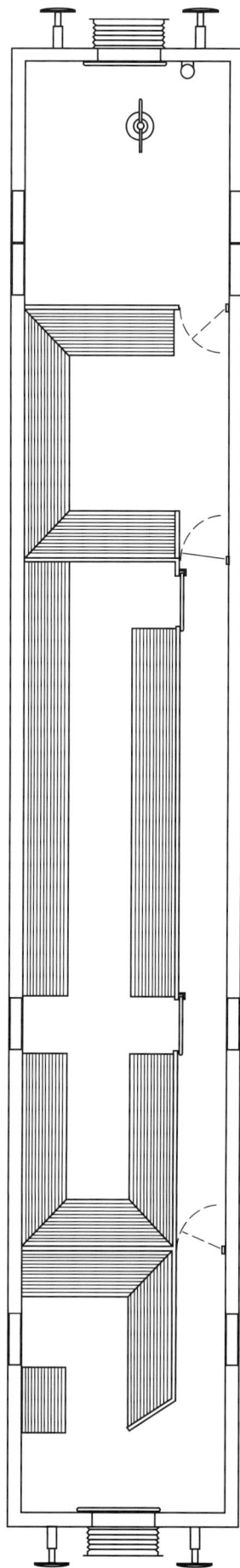

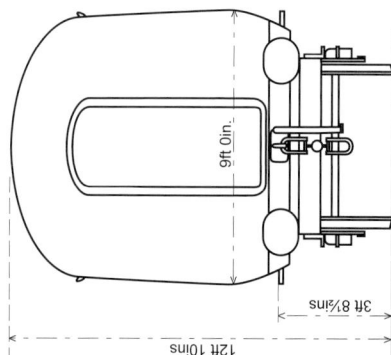

G.W.R. TYPE COACH

WIMR/LMR 117 photographed in Longmoor Yard on 2nd September 1950. When originally converted to ambulance carriages, all the ex-GWR vehicles were fitted with dual air and vacuum braking. This equipment was retained in service at Longmoor so that, until 1943, all internal passenger services were operated with Westinghouse-fitted locomotives.
Bluebell Railway Museum Archive, J. J. Smith Collection

9ft 0in.

3ft 8½ins

12ft 10ins

G.W.R. Type Coach
Received from Rhine Command July 1924
3 in Set; Tare weights
28 Tons 10 cwts.
28 Tons 2 cwts.
27 Tons 10 cwt
Brakes: Hand and Westinghouse

From 1929 until closure forty years later, the 'bread and butter' of the daily 'Bullet' passenger services at Longmoor was provided by the ex-GWR, ex-BAOR ambulance coaches. Originally nine strong, some of this group of carriages survived to the end despite the rough and tumble of forty years of military railway trades training. Here three of the newly arrived coaches were posed at Longmoor Downs in 1930 for the photographer from *Locomotive* magazine. Note the unfitted goods brake van attached to the rear of the train. *LPC 79427*

The nine former GWR bogie coaches that arrived from Germany in 1929 had originally been requisitioned to form ambulance trains for the BEF in France. They must therefore be considered to have arrived (albeit belatedly) as 'War Surplus'. They had been rebuilt from GWR 'Toplight' corridor passenger coaches, 57ft 3ins long and 9ft 0ins wide. During the conversion at Swindon, dual air and vacuum braking had been fitted and Stone's electric lighting system to enable them to operate on European railways. Details are at pages 184/5. At Longmoor the coaches replaced the two sets composed of ex-NLR pattern stock to provide the 'Bullet' internal passenger service from Longmoor (and later Liss) to Bordon.

WIMR 116, ex-GWR ambulance coach (brake third). This 1956 picture shows the 'square corner' panel mouldings applied to the lower sides by the LMR workshop. For no obvious reason, all the ex-GWR coaches retained their original WIMR '1934 series' numbers until the general renumbering of the mid 1950s. *W. S. Sellar*

Other stock which almost certainly originated with the ROD during the World War One period included a number of RECTANK 8-wheel tank carrying wagons. Of these some were dispersed to other WD railways during the 1930s. In addition there was a 20-ton goods brake van (No. 102) which was built in 1918 by the Metropolitan Railway Carriage & Wagon Co. Ltd for service in France and at the end of the war had been redeployed to Catterick. Later this van was employed in the Longmoor breakdown train. Five 12-ton insulated vans, converted by the L&SWR, came from a Ministry of Munitions order of 200 for transport of fresh meat to the troops of the BEF in France.

The WD RECTANK wagons were built in large numbers during World War One. Examples were to be found at Longmoor from 1920 until closure. A number held there before World War Two were registered with the SRly for main line running, bearing a cast iron plate 'Return Empty to Bordon W.I.M.R.'. AD 84011 was one of the last survivors of this group, here photographed on 8th June 1968. One example (AD 84003) has been preserved on the West Somerset Railway. *G. Moon*

The standard RECTANK wagon was too short to be used for carrying rails so was normally used for carrying sleepers for track laying trains whilst the ex-GWR MACAW wagons carried the rails. The location of this view was Griggs Green. The train for the visiting officers was standing on the line parallel to the Liphook road. The men of 151 (GW) Rly Constrn Coy on their summer camp in 1938 were laying the first rails at the south-eastern end of the Hollywater Loop line. *WD photograph*

During the 1920s a substantial fleet of low-sided 10-ton wagons was acquired (secondhand) from various sources. The earliest are believed to have come from the contract to convert the wartime shell factory at Chilwell into a technical stores depot. These were heavily used during the construction of the Liss extension, after which many were worn out and scrapped. A number of goods brake vans were also purchased during this period and a solitary 6-wheel locomotive tender (allegedly from the M&GNJR) which was used to carry water for the steam excavator when at work 'in the field'.

The final pre-World War Two acquisitions were two family or invalid saloons purchased from the Southern Railway. These first appeared in 1938, their initial role being the provision of temporary VIP accommodation for senior officers visiting Supplementary Reserve units in camp at Apple Pie. The first of these, ex-SRly 7913 and LMR 118 (later 3006) was built by

One of the reasons for the lack of precise rolling stock records is that much of the stock was heavily used (and abused). This photo shows WIMR 62 being unloaded, the spoil being built up to form the embankment approach to No. 6 Bridge over Longmoor Yard. The men so hard at work were the civilian permanent way gang. Construction of the Liss extension required the building of a large-span bridge across the entrance to the yard with substantial approach embankments. As a start, a lightweight timber crib was built to support track along which wagons could be pushed to the site where the spoil could be shovelled out. *WD photograph*

Although not part of the original 1905 purchases, these elderly and well-used low-sided wagons were typical of the vehicles held in large numbers by the WIMR for moving spoil from major construction projects. Henry Casserley found these two (including number 62 as seen above) in Longmoor Yard on 17th May 1934, by which date the heaviest construction work had been completed. Thereafter, these wagons were replaced by other ex-main line rolling stock. *H. C. Casserley*

5ft 6ins

19ft 0ins

33ft 0ins

*Based on a Diagram
prepared at Longmoor c1933.*

**W.I.M.R.
COMPRESSOR VAN**

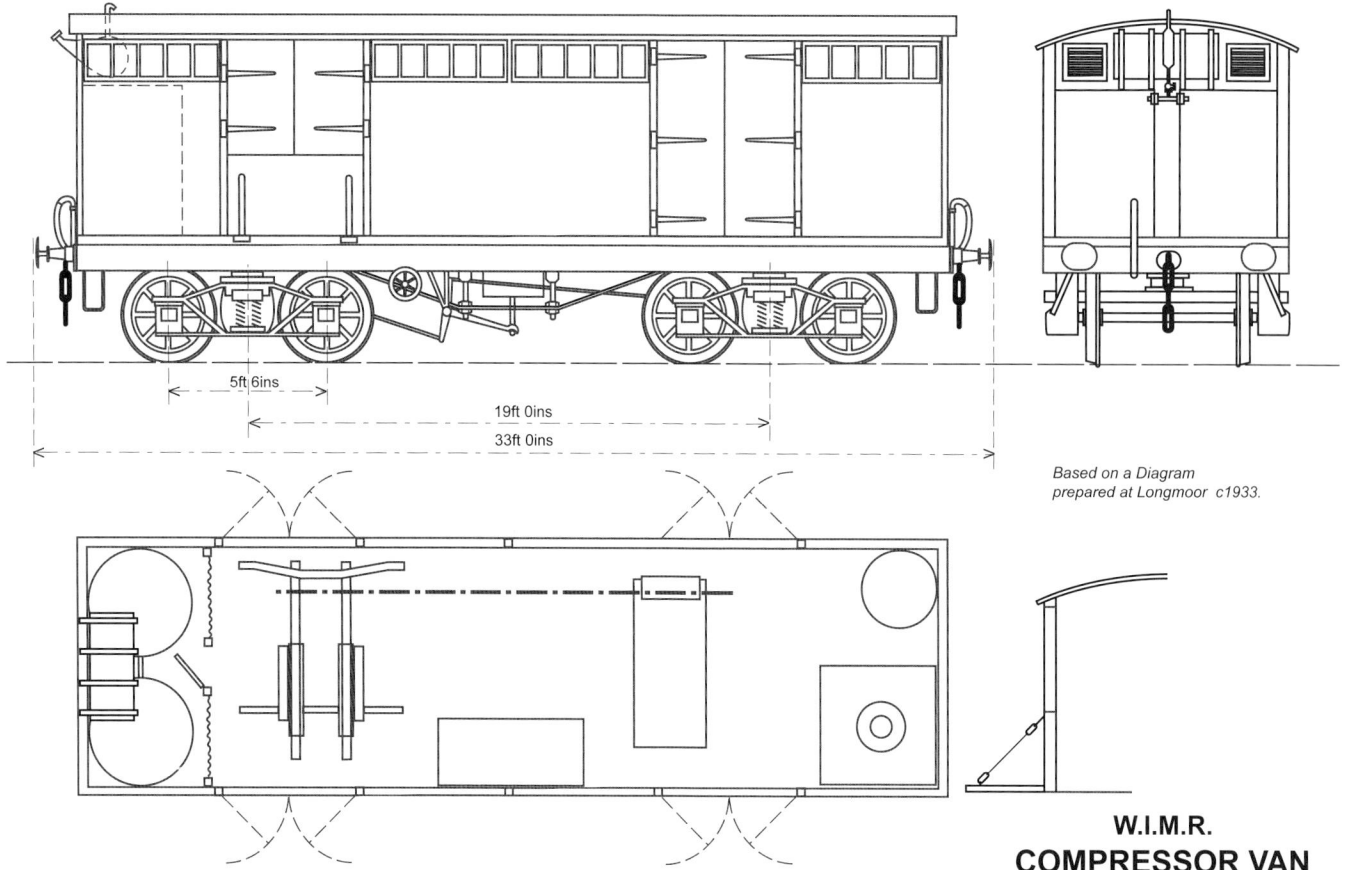

Amongst the 'spoils of war' which ended up at Longmoor after World War One was this 8-wheel bogie compressor van, originally part of a mobile workshop train allocated to the ROD. It was built by Kerr, Stuart & Co. of Stoke-on-Trent and came to Longmoor about 1920. Initially it was an essential piece of construction plant, accompanying the teams building the Liss extension and the Hollywater Loop. In the 1930s its role was partially assumed by more modern lightweight trailer-mounted compressors but (as 120, later WD 13666) it retained a place in the LMR breakdown train until the late 1950s.

Photographer unknown

Though no other complete World War One mobile workshop rolling stock was repatriated to Longmoor, it appears that machine tools and even the original electric generators for the camp had their origins in these ROD mobile workshops. This view shows the electric generator car in one of the trains in France during the war.
LPC 79430

the SE&CR at Ashford in 1900. The second, ex-SRly 7803 and LMR 119 (later 3007) was built by the L&SWR at Eastleigh in 1910. The pair remained in service until closure, the only modifications being the removal of the corridor connections. In 1970 they were presented to the Transport Trust who transferred them to the Severn Valley Railway in 1971. Despite long periods of open storage and deterioration, both have survived and now reside on the K&ESR.

At the Open Day on 3rd September 1949, the ex-SE&CR saloon WD 118 was part of a train waiting to depart from Longmoor Downs. The coach was then in unlined blue livery with the Unit badge (see page 5) at the right-hand end.
D. Cullum

Saloon WD 118 in early post-war condition.   D. J. W. Brough

By 3rd June 1967, 118 had acquired a new number (WD 3006) and had lost the Unit badge. Always stored under cover, the 'Blue Saloons' were in excellent condition when the LMR closed. In the 1990s the K&ESR was able to carry out a full restoration of this beautiful coach in its full original SE&CR livery. Note that the coach still bore a 'WD' number prefix.   *G. Moon*

WD 119, the second saloon delivered to the LMR in 1938, was of L&SWR origins (No. 11, later SRly 7803). This August 1949 Open Day picture shows it paired with 118 and without corridor connections (the corridor connections were removed from both the ex-Southern saloons at Longmoor). This coach has also survived into preservation.   *D. Cullum*

Now running as WD 3007, 119 showed few changes in this picture taken on 3rd June 1967. The two saloons (originally 118 and 119) are unique survivors of a type of carriage which had vanished from the main line railways long before the appearance of the railway preservation movement.
G. Moon

The rolling stock numbering scheme adopted by the WIMR seems to have been quite pragmatic and designed only for the use of the railway staff. By 1930 the railway held:

Locomotives (steam)	6
Passenger coaches	11
Goods vehicles	76
Internal combustion rail cars	1
Ruston steam digger (mounted on Caterpillar tracks)	1
Steam cranes	3
Hand cranes	1

The first record of individual vehicle numbering is in a list dated 1934 (See Appendix Six). It is interesting to note that between 1930 and 1934 the holding of 'goods vehicles' had increased from 76 to 125. It was to further increase dramatically during the World War Two period.

Section VII : Passenger and Goods Stock 1940-1945

The development of Longmoor during World War Two as a major storage area – as well as the greatly increased training commitment – clearly called for more rolling stock. How much of this was initially purchased, requisitioned or borrowed it is now hard to tell. To add to the confusion, there is the problem

continued on page 733

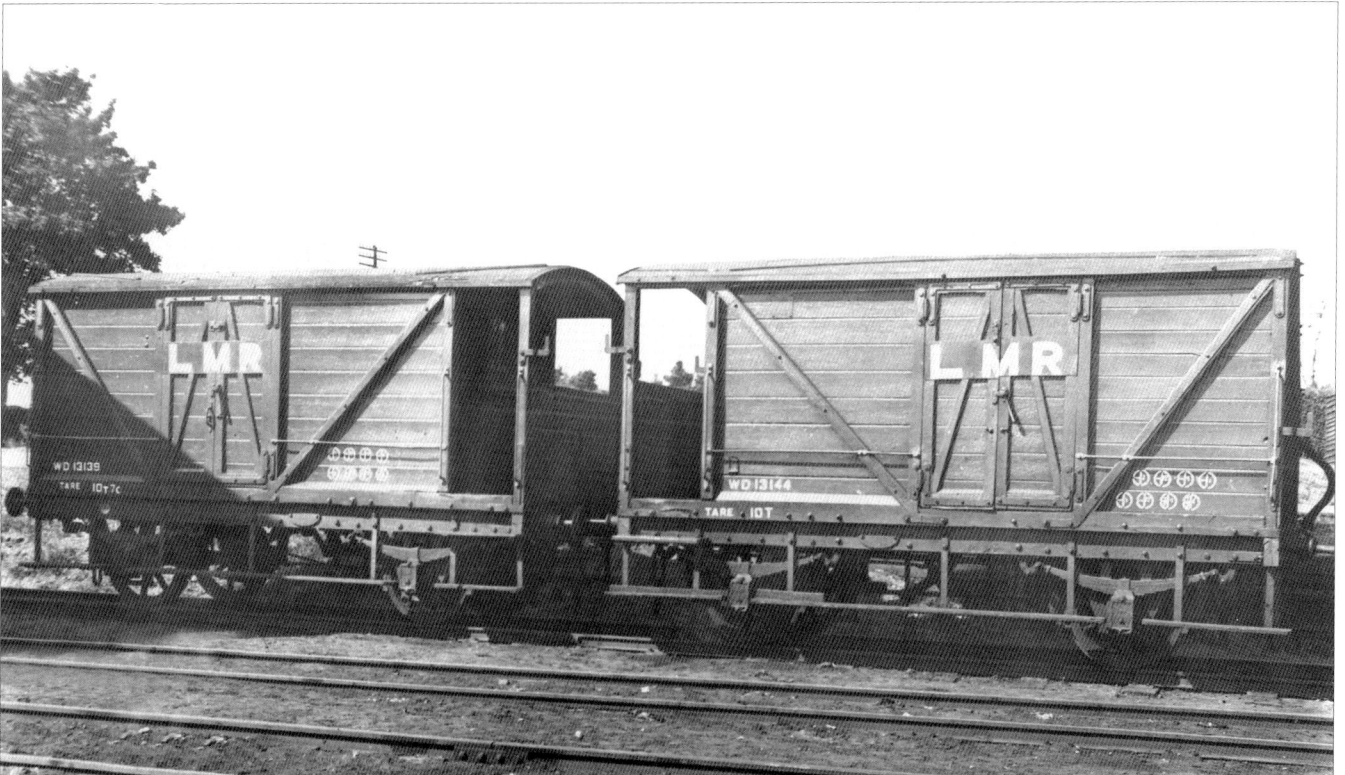

From the mid 1930s, the majority of goods brake vans were purchased from the Southern Railway. WD 13139 (LMR 101) and 13144 (LMR 106) were purchased in 1938. WD 13139 was written off after the Palmers Ball collision in October 1956.
P. Coutanche

Left: WD 13140 (WIMR 102), photographed on 3rd September 1947, was another example of the L&SWR design Road Van, also written off after the Palmers Ball collision. *D. Cullum*

Below: Further vans were required after the loss of two at Palmers Ball in October 1956. British Railways supplied a pair of 20-ton ex-L&NWR 'Crystal Palace' brake vans to the LMR in 1957. Seen here on 3rd June 1967, both were sold for preservation when the LMR closed: WD 49025 (right) went to the K&ESR in 1970, whilst WD 49026 was sold to the East Somerset Railway. Happily 49025 survived but 49026 has not. The van on the extreme left is ex-L&SWR van 82621, now preserved by the Somerset & Dorset Railway Trust. *G. Moon*

Below: Another view of 49025, one of the ex-L&NWR 20-ton brake vans, showing the end windows. Unusually for a goods brake van, it was fitted with screw couplings (49026 had 'Instanter' couplings) rather than three-link couplings. *Bob Vice*

726

Brake van AD 49026, photographed on 10th May 1970. On the left was one of the original (ex-MR) vans, and on the right an ex-L&SWR van (WD 47773), now marked 'BPPS' to show its use by that society as a mobile store. The white paint on the tyres is believed to have been added after the LMR closed. *G. Moon*

The original (ex-Midland) goods brake vans from the pre World War One era all seem to have been scrapped by the end of World War Two. By then the oldest vans in use on the LMR were a pair of ex-Taff Vale 10-ton brake vans (originally WIMR 103 and 104). This view (taken on 10th August 1946) shows the former 103, renumbered 13141 and forming part of the LMR breakdown train. It had been bought from the GWR in 1927 to meet the need for extra vans for the building of the Liss extension.

H. C. Casserley

Officially the number painted on this brake van (WD 49021) was allocated to one of the MoS (Southern Railway) 25-ton brake vans. But by the end of the war in 1945, the numbering of goods rolling stock at Longmoor was in some confusion! This van looks like WIMR 104, later WD 13142, one of the ex-Taff Vale 10-ton brake vans purchased from the GWR in 1927.

Photographer unknown

WD 13174 was a very elderly ex-NER 9-ton Road Van, acquired from the L&NER in 1943 when already more than 40 years old. It retained the topcote (bircage) lookout windows. It was built to the NER Diag. V1 with the vertical planking adopted in 1896.
P. Coutanche

An ex-NER 9-ton Road Van also to Diag. V1, acquired by the WIMR in 1932. Originally WIMR 105, it is seen here – now with the topcote removed – numbered WD13143. Both of the ex-NER Road Vans still had the 'hanging buffers' – downward extensions of the end stanchions for coupling up to the North East of England's large fleet of chaldron wagons. The L&NER had started cutting these off from c1925. *P. Coutanche*

It is very likely that this ex-L&SWR 22ft passenger luggage van came to Longmoor at the end of World War One. The main line company transferred one such van to the Dinton-Fovant line of the Military Camp Railways in April 1916. It was never returned. By 1934 it had been converted to carry electric welding plant on the WIMR, numbered 122. It later became WD 13129 and finally WD 47782. Its origins were hardly recognisable in its final form but it survived until closure in 1969, to be sold to enthusiasts.
D. M Rouse

Pre-war additions to WIMR/LMR freight rolling stock can sometimes be identified because the Railway Office at Longmoor registered them with the main line railway companies as 'private owner' vehicles. Not so WD 47763, an ex-L&SWR 10-ton van which probably reached the LMR around 1940. It survived, still with wooden wheel centres and un-numbered, as the 'Construction Troop Tool Van' until the LMR closed. Note that the steel tyres had been bonded to the axles, so that the vehicle would operate track circuits despite having wooden wheel centres. *Bryan Stone*

Covered vans of many shapes, ages and sizes were operated on the LMR. The very first were two 10-ton ex-Midland Railway vans which formed part of the original WIMR 'train set' in 1905. WD 13124, shown here, joined the WIMR as No. 12 in c1906 (the year of its first registration by the L&SWR as No. 1601). It survived both World Wars but is not recorded with a '1956' series number. *P. Coutanche*

Another ex-L&SWR veteran was WD 47754, a 10-ton van. Probably hired and later purchased from the Southern Railway, this van and 47753 had their identities 'stolen' by a pair of ex-Midland Railway vans which received identical numbers in the 1956 renumbering. 10th May 1970. *G. Moon*

Two more typical survivors of the LMR covered van fleet, photographed on 8th June 1968. AD 47757 was part of a batch of ten ex-L&SWR vans purchased from the Southern in 1940 whilst behind it was AD 47764.

G. Moon

AD 47764 was another early arrival from the Midland Railway, first registered by the L&SWR in 1906. At one time it was used in the LMR breakdown train. By 1969 it had been sealed and was used to make up trains for training purposes. It passed to the East Somerset Railway after the LMR closed, but unfortunately it has since been scrapped.

G. Moon

At the time of Henry Casserley's visit on 10th August 1946, this ex-Midland Railway 10-ton van had been relegated to duties in the LMR breakdown train. It was first registered with the L&SWR in 1906 so was probably a survivor of the original WIMR rolling stock purchase of 1905.

H. C. Casserley

By December 1964, this veteran (WD 47763) formed part of the XEN Construction Train. It was lettered (left) 'Construction Troop Tool Van' and (right) 'Set 5'. *D. W. Ronald*

Another of the ex-Midland Railway vans at Longmoor was AD 47759 (a vacuum fitted van), seen here in use for 'shunting practice' at Woolmer Yard. This van arrived amongst a consignment of twenty assorted vans from the LMS around 1948. *D. W. Ronald*

One van which survived because of its special role was WD 13132 which was assigned to the construction troops (hence the 'XEN' designation). When photographed in the late 1950s, it was additionally labelled 'PLATELAYERS'. It was one of a group of Southern Railway 12-ton vans transferred to the LMR in 1940. Originally built by the L&SWR, its later Southern number was recorded as 43955.
Photographer unknown

Fresh from a complete rebuild in the Longmoor Workshops on 5th July 1969 and probably the last such vehicle to be overhauled there, Army 45064 was built for the North British Railway, possibly in the 1890s. It was part of a consignment of eighteen 8-ton, low dropside wagons transferred to the LMR in 1941. It had probably already been in WD service elsewhere prior to transfer as it carried a number '7' on arrival.

G. Moon

This open low-sided wagon (AD 46270) was probably also acquired during World War Two. Other than the fact that it was originally from the Midland Railway in 1911 (No. 67439) nothing was ever recorded of its history in military service. On 10th May 1970 it awaited the auction sale of redundant rolling stock.

G. Moon

AD 42117 was recorded at closure as 'Wagon, Misc, 4-wheeled'. It was built for the Ministry of Munitions in 1916, arriving at Longmoor after the end of World War One. What numbers it may have carried during the ensuing fifty years have not been recorded. It was unsold at the rolling stock auction in 1970 – photograph taken on 10th May.

G. Moon

continued from page 725

of periodic renumbering schemes. Whilst on paper these would please the tidy military mind, in fact they generated more confusion as application of pen to paper was invariably completed long before that of painted numbers to vehicles. Indeed the only reason any wartime stock list now exists is that one of the storekeepers kept a copy with old and new numbers on a crib-sheet. In 1943 there is a heartfelt plea in the wartime house journal of the Tn Training Centre (*The Rocket*) from the clearly overworked sign-writer on the Melbourne Military Railway "no more wagon renumbering please – we can't keep up with all the changes!"

In 1940 a batch of ferry vans (ordered originally for the support of the BEF but rendered surplus after Dunkirk) were delivered to Longmoor. Being fitted with French pattern Westinghouse brakes, they were used extensively for instructional purposes until later in the war, when they were dispersed as section tool vans to various RE railway construction companies working on projects elsewhere in the UK. The stock thus acquired appears to have consisted of thirty fitted vans, twenty-eight piped vans and five 'old fitted vans'.

Some indication of the chaos of renumbering can be gathered from the fact that all standard RCH 10 and 12-ton open wagons were accidentally omitted from the 1940 list (there were at least twenty held). By 1942, under the generic heading 'Wagons, open, four-wheel, high side' the list had grown to fifty-nine, all apparently numbered at random, though presumably retaining their former owners' numbers. Before looking at the 1943 renumbering (a vain attempt to control the confusion), let us look at the other new items of rolling stock that were acquired between 1940 and 1943.

To cope with the increased demand for the internal passenger service, extra coaches were required. Longmoor's request was passed to the War Office who in turn sought the assistance of the Railway Executive Committee (REC). Resulting from the need to train soldiers for future deployments to Europe, it was essential that any new coaches were Westinghouse braked. By 1941 this limited the available pool of vehicles substantially. Due to the increased wartime demands for their own steam-hauled suburban services, the main line companies had no spare air-braked passenger rolling stock in England. However, the LMS was able to find appropriate vehicles from the stock of the former Caledonian Railway and offered what were probably the largest Westinghouse-fitted carriages in the UK. After the 1923 grouping the LMS had continued to operate the majority of the former CR passenger services with air-braked stock. However by the 1940s post-grouping (vacuum-braked) stock was in the ascendency and the pre-war peak holiday traffic on the Clyde coast lines had declined. The surplus vehicles offered were four ex-Caledonian Railway twelve-wheel bogie compartment carriages with seating for 132 passengers in the eleven compartment coaches (six a side), 96 in an eight compartment coach. In May 1940 the following coaches were delivered:

CR No.	LMSR No.	CR Diag.	Configuration
1281	17337/24316	D 065	8 compt. Bk-3rd
125	16198/15552	D 068	11 compt. All-3rd
1315	17371/15551	D 068	11 compt. All-3rd
1328	17384/24311	D 070	9 compt. Bk-3rd
			(converted to 8 compt. by the LMS)

To meet the extra demand from the huge increase in personnel stationed at Longmoor, 'Bullet' services were progressively intensified during 1940. In May 1940 the overcrowding on the (by then) half hourly interval service was eased by the arrival of four high capacity 12-wheel compartment coaches from Scotland. Here is a typical 'Bullet' formation of that era with a 'Caley' compartment coach 'top and tailed' by two of the ex-GWR ambulance coaches. Motive power was provided by WD 2400 *Earl Roberts* [2]. *H. N. James*

12ft 3ins

12ft 0ins

44ft 0ins

6ft 0ins

6ft 0ins

9ft 0ins

65ft 0¾ins

68ft 6ins

6ft 2ins

6ft 2ins

14ft 7⅞ins

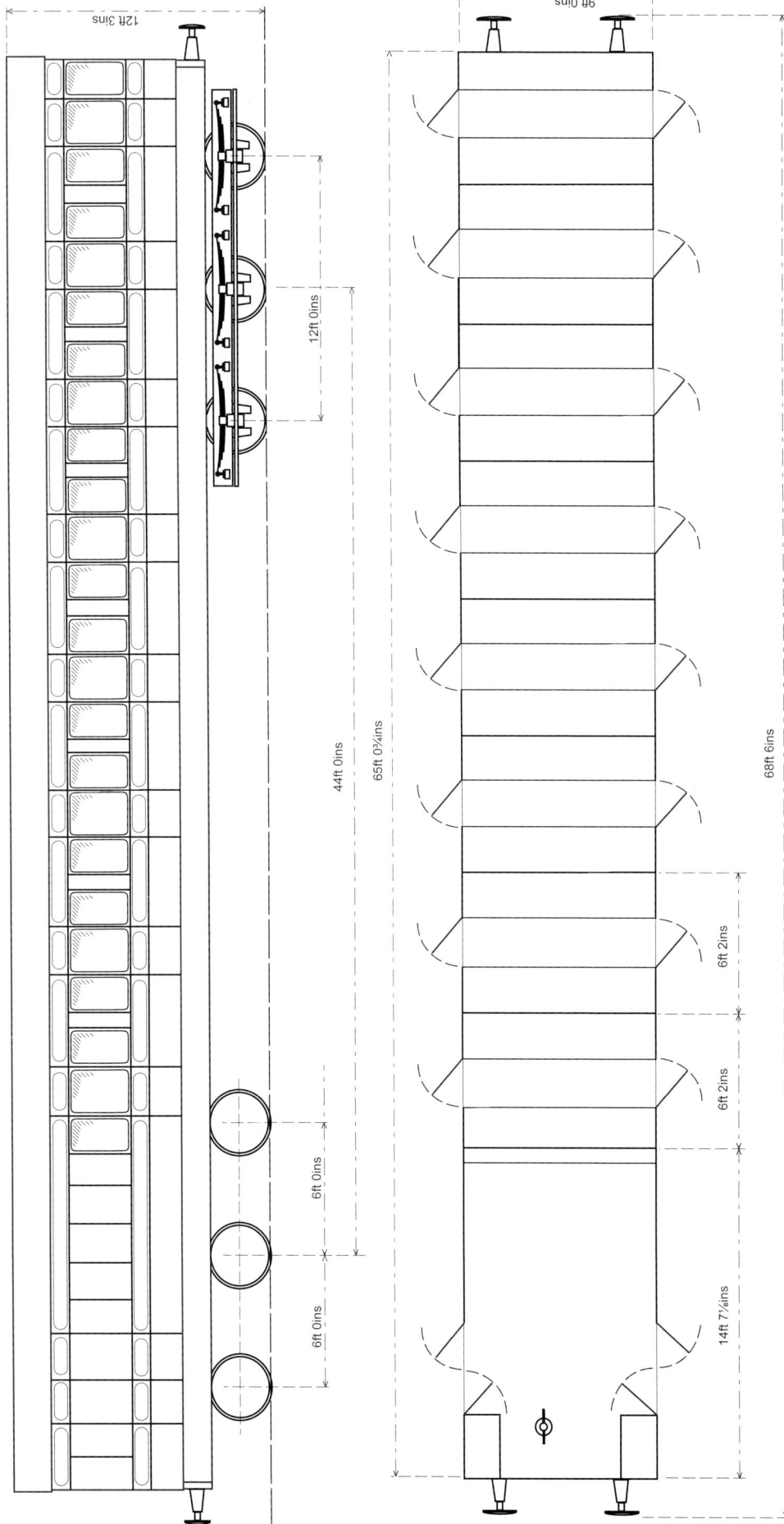

Makers: Caledonian Railway Coy, to Diagram 65
Total weight 34 tons 16 cwts.

Note: due to constraints of the size of the page, this diagram is drawn to
a slightly smaller scale than the other rolling stock diagrams.

12 WHEEL, 65 Ft BRAKE/THIRD

This view of the ex-Caley compartment 3rd carriage taken on 10th August 1946 shows the wartime LMR livery with two compartments nearest the photographer labelled 'O' for the use of officers, and two lettered 'L' for ladies only.

H. C. Casserley

In 1940 four ex-Caledonian 12-wheel compartment coaches were sent to Longmoor by the LMS. After problems with buffer-locking when run as a set, they were divided between the four existing two-coach 'Bullet' sets as the centre coach in 3-coach formations. This was the arrangement in which this example (120 or 121) waited at Longmoor Downs on an Open Day in the 1950s.   *P. Coutanche*

Later, due to the continuing increase in passenger traffic on the LMR, additional coaches were again sought. In August 1943 the LMS offered a further six ex-CR twelve wheelers. That this offer was not taken up is probably a reflection of the operating difficulties which the LMR staff had already experienced with the 'Caley' coaches.

Soon after the coaches were delivered, it was found that there was a problem with buffer-locking on sharp radius curves at

Bordon. A note prepared by the late Ian McNaughton who was present when the coaches first arrived recorded that the coach buffer locked on Free Piece curve and that the somewhat entangled coaches had to be left at Oakhanger until workshops could attend to 'unlock' the buffers. It does however seem unlikely that the coaches would have buffer locked on a curve on the main line, however tight the radius. A more likely cause of the buffer locking problem is suggested in the instructions which were

The Caley 12-wheelers attracted more than their fair share of trouble at Longmoor. In 1943 Lt Barnard (i/c rolling stock repair in the LMR Workshop) had the task of removing the complete body of one of the coaches using jacks and packing to allow repairs to the underframe. Note the USATC 'utility' wagons on the siding behind.   *D. B. Barnard*

From the early years of World War Two, a fine photograph of ex-L&SWR 'A12' Class No. 638 with a three-coach 'Bullet' set climbing towards Weavers Down on the approach to the Top Crossing, with an ex-Caledonian coach in the centre of the set.   *H. N. James*

None of the Caley coaches had a particularly glorious end at Longmoor. WD 120 just disappeared at the end of the war, 121 was damaged in a runaway incident at Liss Forest Road and 122 had been grounded by 1956. 123, by then 'surplus to requirements', was sacrificed as the leading vehicle in the train deliberately derailed for the BBC-TV 'Saturday Night Out' programme in February 1956. Stuart Sellar photographed the coach in April 1956, awaiting disposal.   *W. S. Sellar*

issued that "ex-Caledonian six-wheel bogie stock Nos 120, 121, 122 and 123 are prohibited from using the scissors crossover (Points No. 4 or 7) when coupled together" (see the diagram on page 206). They were thereafter used to strengthen the existing sets by placing one 'Caley' coach between two GWR vehicles. Despite these shortcomings, the 'Caley' coaches gave valuable service at Longmoor. One was written-off after a derailment in the runaway siding at Liss Forest Road whilst the last survivor (WD 123 – its '1934 series' LMR number still being carried in 1956) was also written-off after the deliberate derailment staged in 1955 for the 'Saturday Night Out' TV programme.

It has not been possible to locate any evidence to connect the former main line numbers of these coaches with their later LMR numbers. Minor bodywork differences on WD 123 suggest that it was formerly CR 1328/LMS 24311 and hence that WD 120 was CR 1281/LMS 24311. The two all-third coaches were therefore WD 121 and WD 122, but which was which will probably never be discovered.

Having declined further twelve-wheelers from the LMS, the WD was able to meet the urgent needs of the LMR with vacuum-braked stock from the Southern Railway. The first to arrive was a three-coach 'Birdcage' set (ex-SE&CR) originally numbered 13582-13584. In 1944, three (or possibly four) WD registered ex-L&SWR ambulance coaches were transferred to Longmoor when no longer needed by the American forces based in the UK. Additionally, examples of the standard MOS/MOT goods vehicles were used at Longmoor, some for trials and others (e.g. the brake vans) retained permanently.

By 1943 still more coaches were needed to operate the 'Bullet' services on the LMR. The Southern Railway sold a three-coach ex-SE&CR 'Birdcage' set to the WD. The complete set was seen at the 1949 Open Day. It provided the first vacuum braked passenger stock at Longmoor since 1920. Being newly out of main line service the seats were upholstered in the Southern's latest art deco fabrics which became, for a short period, the target for drunken soldiers' clasp knives. *D. Cullum*

Another view of the Lav/Brake/3rd WD 13583 (ex-SE&CR: 1101, SRly: 3388) from 1949 showing the RE (Tn) unit badge above the running number. *D. Cullum*

Above: This was the centre coach of the ex-SE&CR 'Birdcage' set on 2nd September 1949.   *D. Cullum*

Left: Detail of the brake end of AD 5312 (1956 renumbering) previously 13583, photographed on 30th April 1966, showing dual brake connections and a 'Ladies Only' compartment next to the guard's brake compartment.
A. E. Bennett, Transport Treasury Collection B7164

The centre coach of the ex-SE&CR set (WD 13584) came to a sad end following a mistake whilst under repair in Longmoor Yard. Whilst propped up to remove the bogies, one of the truss rods was disconnected. As a result the underframe twisted. Lacking manpower and resources, the workshop decided to withdraw the coach which was then broken up, still bearing its '1943' number.   *P. Coutanche*

This ex-LMS ambulance conversion (AD 3322, formerly WD 301), shown here at the Ash Dock Siding in use as a temporary mobile classroom on 3rd June 1967, had quite an adventurous war. Converted in 1939 from LMS Open 3rd saloon 2926, it went to the BEF in France, was captured by the Germans in 1940 and, remarkably, survived to the end of the war when it was recaptured by the Allies in 1945. *G. Moon*

Another view of Army 3322, showing the safety side-chains fitted to all UK stock deployed to France in both World Wars. By the time this photo was taken in May 1970, it had been sold to David Shepherd. *G. Moon*

Appendix Twenty shows the rolling stock situation in 1943 with the unified 13xxx series numbers and (where known) the earlier numbers. This was an Army-wide and world-wide attempt to produce a single common numbering scheme to include every item of WD owned and operated rolling stock. Longmoor was issued with a series of numbers commencing with 13101 and, as far as we know, ending at 13693. The intended scheme is outlined in the Appendix but it is not known how fully it was implemented. It is reproduced from a very well-thumbed copy to which its owner had added notes of previous numbers carried. This was to help him relate the numbers 'as painted' with the officially allocated numbers in the new series.

There were clearly many anomalies, particularly amongst the passenger coaches which never seemed to have carried '1943 series' numbers. Some vehicles were never renumbered, retaining their '1934' identification. Newly arrived rolling stock would, in the final years of the war, be shoe-horned into any vacant spaces remaining on the list. The list does not give any details of the origins of the ex-main line vehicles. It is possible to deduce the arrival dates of pre-war acquisitions by the dates of their registration with the Southern Railway as 'private owner wagons'. This practice appears to have lapsed on the outbreak of war, all LMR owned or hired rolling stock then being treated as 'internal users'.

THE ORIGINAL NETLEY AMBULANCE COACHES OF 1900

Almost concurrent with the establishment of the new Railway Training Centre at Longmoor, the Army Medical Department was pioneering the employment of dedicated ambulance coaches for the movement of battle casualties by rail. Railways had been used for this task, but on an ad hoc basis, since the Crimean War when the injured were evacuated from Sebastopol using the empty wagons of the military railway returning to the port at Balaklava. For the Anglo-Boer War, the first dedicated ambulance trains were assembled and operated in South Africa.

In the United Kingdom there was, by the time of the Anglo-Boer War, a well-established military hospital system for the reception and treatment of casualties from overseas. From all corners of the Empire, returning troop ships would make their way to the Port of Southampton. On board every such ship would be a number of injured or sick soldiers. From the early 1860s these men had been conveyed to the nearby Royal Victoria Hospital Netley, newly built for their treatment and convalescence. To assist this transport, the Army Medical Department together with the L&SWR designed and built what was probably the world's first dedicated ambulance carriage. It was converted from 'an old Post Office van' and appears to have remained in use until the new vehicles (described below) were introduced.

This solitary vehicle, plying between Portsmouth, Gosport and Southampton brought the sick and injured to Netley (L&SWR) Station. It was quickly felt that the final road link into the hospital was an unnecessary discomfort and that a direct rail line to the hospital was required. Opened in 1900 and operated by the L&SWR, the Netley Hospital Branch gave direct main line access to a covered platform linked directly to the main hospital.

Its opening was timely as within a week the first casualties from the relief of Ladysmith were arriving by sea at Southampton to be conveyed direct to RVH Netley by special train. Thereafter the Netley Hospital Branch continued to be employed for such traffic until shortly before the closure of the hospital itself. The last train is recorded as leaving the Hospital Station on 30th August 1955, to convey the remaining WD ambulance carriages to Longmoor.

During the early months of 1900, the L&SWR undertook the conversion of five 48ft bogie fruit vans into self-contained ambulance carriages. The work was paid for by the War Department. Each carriage had folding stretchers to accommodate twelve lying patients, with fixed seats for twelve sitting patients and two 'first class seats' for officers. These carriages were kept at the Hospital Station where a special carriage shed was built to house them. Their normal use was to convey sick and injured from Southampton where they had disembarked, to RVH Netley, or other Army hospitals. During World War One they were regularly used as single vehicles attached to express passenger trains to convey casualties to London for specialist treatment. In the 1920s they were also used to convey sick soldiers from BAOR for treatment at Woolwich. They remained at Netley and continued to be employed from there until the entire hospital complex was handed over to the American Forces in 1942.

Their employment during the later years of World War Two is not recorded. It seems likely that the US Army used them to move their own casualties from time to time. Some time in late 1944 or early 1945, they were no longer required by the Americans and three were sent to Longmoor (WD 2, 3 and 4). The fate of carriages 1 and 5 is not recorded.

At Longmoor these coaches were pressed into service as passenger carriages, having 'tram seats' installed along the sides. Two had hand-brakes fitted which allowed the three vehicles to operate together as a set. They do not appear to have lasted very long in their new role, being withdrawn by 1948 and scrapped soon after. No account was taken at the time of their historic significance as the first purpose-built ambulance carriages in Britain.

There is one final chapter to this tale. Someone at Longmoor had done their homework and realised in 1955 that the removal of the second generation of ambulance carriages from Netley following the closure of the hospital left a perfectly good carriage shed 'surplus to requirements'. In due course the building was acquired for the LMR, being dismantled by a party from 8 Rly Sqn in 1957, conveyed to Longmoor and re-erected in Longmoor Yard. Thereafter it was used to house the three 'Blue Saloons'.

The first passenger stock arrivals after World War Two were L&SWR dining saloons converted by the SRly into ambulance coaches which had continued in occasional use from the base at the Royal Victoria Hospital Netley. By 1954, with the closure of the hospital, this traffic ceased and eight surplus ward coaches were transferred to Longmoor. Four were distributed to other Army railways and four kept at Longmoor. WD 3019 shown here was quickly earmarked for the LMR breakdown train, being converted into an equipment van. On closure of the LMR it moved to Bicester, being sold from there into preservation in 1996. It survives in 2014, out of use in a deteriorated condition, on the Pontypool and Blaenavon Railway.   *R. C. Riley*

WD 3019 was an ex-L&SWR dining car (No. 76) converted by the SRly as an ambulance ward car for US Forces in World War Two. After the war it was retained until the closure of RVH Netley, and in 1957 it was transferred to the LMR. It was converted into a new equipment vehicle for the LMR breakdown train. 5th March 1966. *G. Moon*

A 1960s view showing the conversion of one end of WD 3019 to facilitate the transport and unloading of the Deutschland rerailing equipment. The cadets were about to start a rerailing exercise. *J. D. P. Poyntz*

Ex-Ministry of Munitions cistern wagon WD 41001 was first registered with the Midland Railway in 1916. Its arrival at Longmoor is not recorded but by the time it was photographed in 1963, it had been relegated to rerailing exercises. Around the cylinder of the tank can be seen the special securing strops used with the Deutschland hydraulic jacking system to rotate such vehicles if overturned. *D. W. Ronald*

To further relieve the carriage shortage in 1944, three of the five original WD ambulance carriages that had been converted from L&SWR 48ft fruit vans in 1900, were sent to Longmoor when no longer required by the American forces. They had passed to American control when the Royal Victoria Hospital (RVH) at Netley was handed over for US Army use in 1943. At Longmoor they were stripped of their ambulance fittings and wooden seating substituted. Their previous numbers (WD 2, 3 and 4) were retained. They did not last long in this new role and all were scrapped at Longmoor soon after this view taken on 15th September 1948.

D. P. Callender, the G. R. Weddell Collection

One item which was never listed as LMR stock was the train of nine twelve-wheeled gun limber wagons. These were acquired as surplus from the rail-mounted super-heavy batteries when these were disbanded in 1944 and were used to make up a heavy train for driver instruction in continuous long distance running.

The final wartime arrival was a very unusual vehicle. To provide a VIP vehicle for the Melbourne Military Railway in 1940, Colonel Manton had 'pulled a few strings' to obtain a redundant LMS inspection saloon. It had been built at the Wolverton carriage works of the L&NWR in 1890. A six-wheeled

When the ambulance conversions were withdrawn from Netley, their occasional use by BR (SR) for excursion traffic in connection with pilgrimages to Lourdes also ceased. BR then converted four 'nondescript' brake coaches as replacements, one of which was later sold to the Army – becoming AD 777. As a single ward car it was used to prepare Royal Army Medical Corps reservist ambulance train staff for their war duties in BAOR and was seen here at the Open Day on 28th September 1968.

G. Moon

This photograph, although of somewhat indifferent quality, is included because it shows a USA Class S160 locomotive at Longmoor Downs with a train including one of the Gun Trucks and one of the ex-Train Ferry vans first loaned to the WD in 1940. *courtesy Neil Howard*

underframe carried a body with open balconies at both ends and two saloons separated by a central lavatory compartment. It had previously lived a quiet life as the District Engineer's inspection saloon at Northampton. On the closure of the Melbourne Military Railway at the end of 1944, this vehicle was transferred to Longmoor (still carrying its former LMS number 45021) where it was used for inspections and as transport for visiting VIPs. After closure in 1969, the Transport Trust arranged for it to be transferred to the Severn Valley Railway. Here it remained in open storage until 1984 when, along with the two other ex-LMR saloons, it was moved to the K&ESR at Tenterden. At first restored in its original L&NWR livery, this unique survivor was later turned out in early LMS crimson livery and is currently stored awaiting further restoration.

By the end of World War Two, driver training at Longmoor included practice in handling long and heavy freight trains powered by the (then new) WD 2-10-0 locomotives. One source of heavy wagons to make up train weight was the redeployment of surplus 9.2-inch Gun Trucks. This photograph shows *Gordon* [2] preparing to leave the sidings at Liss Junction with such a load. The make-up of the train included at least four Gun Trucks (47.35 tons tare weight each before the addition of any load).

Allan Garraway

L.M.R.
GENERAL ARRANGEMENT OF GUN TRUCK

8ft 11ins over brake handwheels
8ft 5ins maximum width of body
8ft 0ins

10ins
3ft 3ins
3ft 11ins
8ft 0ins

End elevation
Showing superstructure
after Gun and outriggers
removed for travelling.
Load Gauge of L&NWR shown.
Maximum gauge height 13ft 6ins
Maximum gauge width
above platform level 9ft 0ins.
Maximum width of Truck 8ft 11 ins

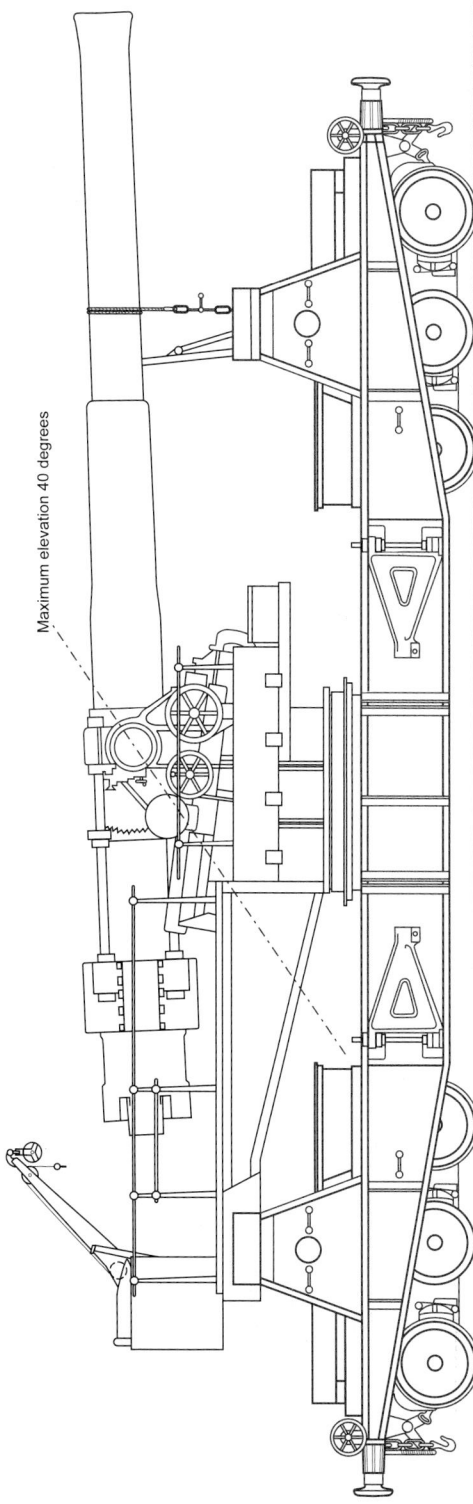

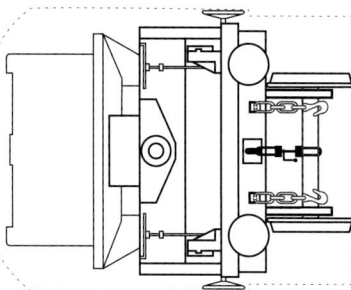

4ft 0ins
4ft 0ins
4ft 0ins

33ft 0ins centre of bogies
43ft 3ins over headstocks
47ft 0ins overall

Maximum elevation 40 degrees

Gun Truck as used on the LMR
Based on Diagram D/66/U4a
prepared at No. 1 Railway Training Centre, Longmoor
by L/CPL Perry on 27 August 1942.
Referenced to LNER Drawing No. 16305S.

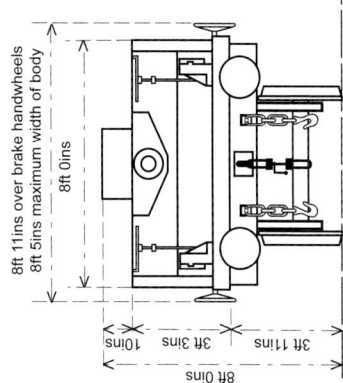

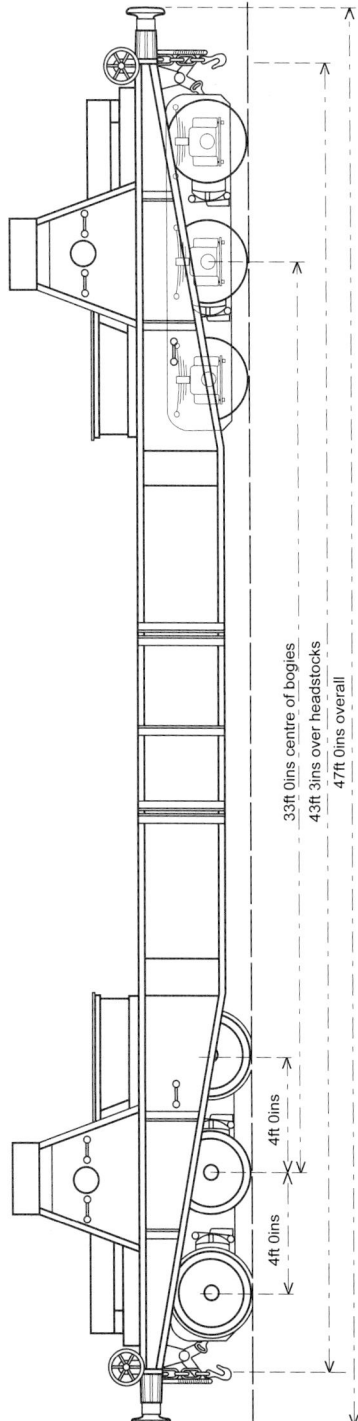

Equivalent B.S.S Loading (2 Gun Trucks, empty, coupled together) – 8 B.S.S units
Tare weight: 47 Tons 7 cwt
Minimum curves; 100ft 0 ins
Brakes: Screw brakes on all wheels, Westinghouse piped
Note: none of the drawings show brakes fitted to the inner axles.

Wheels: 2ft 9ins diameter
Buffers: 1ft 6ins diameter
Couplings: 2ft 10ins screw coupling, with safety chain
Flat tyres on centre axles

Original configuration as a 'Mounting Railway Truck, B.L.9.2 Inch Gun, Mark IV'.

Drawing based on an original (probably prepared by the Elswick Ordnance Company), received at the Office of the Inspector of Guns and Carriages at Woolwich on 2 May 1925. Details of the gun structure have been added from the work of Ian Hogg and John Batchelor, published as 'Rail Gun' ISBN 0 85242 28 4, which book contains additional scale drawing elevations of this gun and of many others. For travel on railways in the UK, the gun and outriggers were removed and the crane for handling shells was lowered. The remaining superstructure was then just within the UK loading gauge, as shown in the end elevation. In the configuration shown the vehicle with gun weighed 87 tons. The Woolwich drawing shows the minimum radius curve that could be traversed as 200 feet. The principal figures for the 9.2 inch Breech Loading gun were: Traverse 360 degrees. Maximum elevation 40 degrees. Shell weight 380lbs. Muzzle velocity 2,100 feet per second. Maximum range 22,600 yards (12.84 miles). Barrel length 335.025 inches.

744

A photograph of the ex-L&NWR saloon, showing that there were no glazed upper side panels in the vestibule/balcony at one end. In its earliest years of Army service, when purchased for the Melbourne Military Railway, it continued to carry its former LMS number (45021), and indeed at the 1945 Longmoor Public Day it appeared still carrying its 'M.M.R.' lettering.   *D. Cullum*

In this view the ex-L&NWR saloon had been given its post-1956 number (WD 3005). The lower steps at each corner were extended for the benefit of Lt-Col G. C. Alexander during his time in command of 16 Railway Training Regiment.
A. E. Bennett, Transport Treasury Collection B7166

WD 62600 remains an enigma. It belonged to the second batch of 'Mobile Workshop Trains' converted by the Southern Railway at Ashford between 1940 and 1943 for the use of the RE railway operating companies. Its origin was a standard SRly Utility Van, converted to form a machine-tool wagon. The presence on the solebar of cleats for tie-down chains suggests that it may have been one of the vehicles shipped to north -west Europe in 1944/45. How and when it made its way to Longmoor after the war is not recorded. The use of the number '62600' (not in the LMR sequence) suggests that it was elsewhere at the time of the first unified WD renumbering scheme.   *Photographer unknown*

W.I.M.R.
WATER TANK

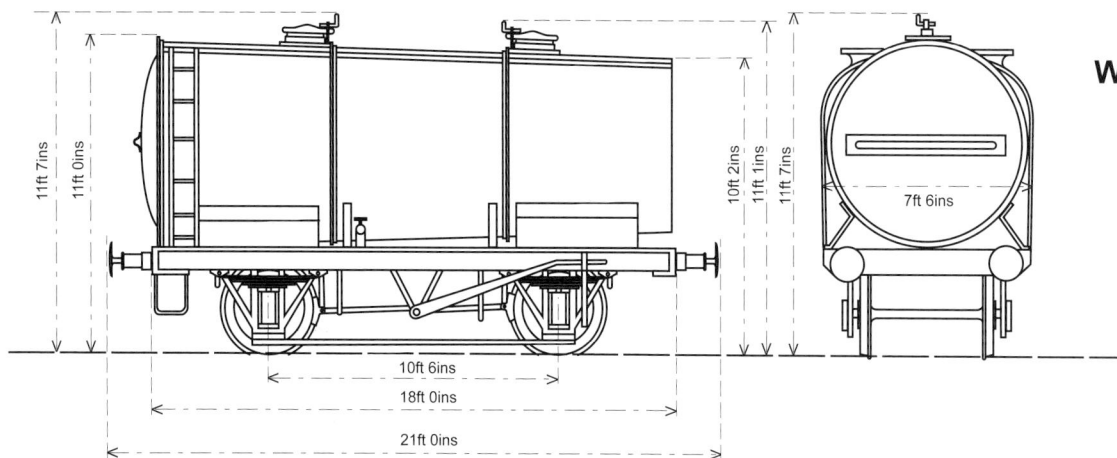

11ft 7ins
11ft 0ins

10ft 2ins
11ft 1ins
11ft 7ins

7ft 6ins

10ft 6ins
18ft 0ins
21ft 0ins

Water Tank wagons, numbered 201 - 206
Tare 9 tons 7cwts
Load 10 tons (2,200 gallons)

*Based on W.I.M.R. rolling stock drawing No. 37
prepared at Longmoor 3 July 1933.*

AD 42118 was one of a trio of 'cistern' wagons purchased in 1940 from the British Molasses Co. Ltd. On 5th July 1969 it stood next to AD 45066, originally a GNR 10-ton wagon, rebuilt at Longmoor in November 1954.　　　　　*G. Moon*

Cistern wagon AD 82620 at Longmoor on 10th May 1970.　　　　　*G. Moon*

746

Above: The weed killing train (WD Weed Killing Unit) in its original formation in August 1946. The demountable tanks on the two RECTANK wagons were later replaced by two of the less leaky 4-wheel cistern wagons. WD 13147 was one of the L&SWR design of Road Vans purchased from the Southern Railway and later renumbered 82621.

WD photograph

Below: The spray unit mounted on the buffer beam of the converted brake van.

WD photograph

747

Section VIII - Passenger and Goods Stock 1945-1970

From the end of the war to closure, the characteristic feature of the LMR stock lists is a steady and continuous rundown in numbers of vehicles. This directly reflected the reduction in training commitments during this period. Generally, as old rolling stock became worn out it was scrapped. A very small number of goods vehicles were rebuilt as workshops training projects. The results of this work were to all intents replicas of the originals. Apart from the ironwork, the entire structure of some vehicles was replaced, testing the skills of the trainee carpenters and joiners. Apart from the machine marks on the wood, it would have been difficult to distinguish these vehicles from the genuine item.

Such 'new' rolling stock as was introduced consisted of ex-main line vehicles often forming part of a larger purchase for 1 Rly Gp RE. Examples of the latter were the Palvans which BR had found to be unsuitable for fast main line fitted freight traffic but which were entirely suitable for internal depot traffic. One exception to this pattern was the purchase specifically for LMR use of new BR covered vans in 1959.

The World War Two WARWELLS and WARFLATS were particularly useful for training purposes. As heavy vehicles, they provided useful train weight when locomotive crews were under instruction. They could also be employed from time to time to assemble improvised armoured trains for demonstrations, and they were used for the instruction of Movement Control trainees in the skills of loading and securing armoured vehicles on trains.

In the mid 1960s there was a general programme of improvements to Army Department internal passenger carriages, initiated by 1 Rly Gp RE. By this time the remaining passenger stock on the LMR was (with the notable exception of the 'Blue Saloons', which were housed under cover and kept immaculately clean) becoming worn out. Due to a lack of carriage-building skills amongst the National Servicemen only limited maintenance was ever carried out at Longmoor. Any significant damage inevitably led to the vehicle being withdrawn. Mindful that there was rapidly growing interest in the railway from enthusiasts of all kinds, 1 Rly Gp offered a number of their newly-acquired coaches to the LMR to enable higher capacity passenger trains to be run on Open Days and other special events. Thus in its last years Longmoor received a number of surplus BR standard non-corridor compartment coaches which had been made redundant by dieselisation or electrification on the main lines. These went into regular service leaving the 'Birdcage' set (by now reduced to the two brake/thirds as the centre coach had been damaged and withdrawn) for special occasions. As a result this set was repainted in the blue livery hitherto reserved for the saloons and restored to something of its former dignity. The story has a happy ending because the importance of these two vintage coaches had been recognised before the LMR closed. As a result they were purchased at auction by the K&ESR. One of the pair has been fully restored for use on that railway whilst the second remains in long-term storage. It is perhaps appropriate that the last two passenger coaches of the LMR should have gone to the K&ESR, the railway that had provided the WIMR with its first passenger carriages over sixty years earlier.

The stock remaining at the closure of the line is listed in Appendix Twenty-one. Stock which was cleared for main line running or had a useful internal role was transferred to other Army depot railways. The remainder was sold, the majority finding its way into the hands of the railway preservation societies.

WD WARWELL and WARFLAT wagons were used at Longmoor for various training exercises and to add weight to freight trains. Two WARWELLS and one of the ex-L&NWR brake vans were standing in Woolmer Yard in December 1964.
                                                                                                    D. W. Ronald

Three standard Southern Railway goods brake vans were part of a wartime Ministry of Supply purchase. AD 49020 of 1941 was seen here in Woolmer Yard in 1965. This particular van survived after the LMR closed. It was moved by 1 Rly Gp RCT to Bicester where it was still in use in 2010.
D. W. Ronald

A brake van line-up in Longmoor Yard on 2nd August 1963 showing (right to left) WD 49022; WD 49027; WD 49025. 49027 was one of the pair of brake vans built for the LMR by the Standard Wagon Co. Ltd in 1959, to the then current BR standard design. Both of these vans passed into preservation in 1970.
G. Moon

AD 46182 was one of a collection of ex-LB&SCR open wagons variously acquired during World War Two, with characteristic rounded end boards (and in this case also retaining the sheet rail). Though rebuilt at Longmoor (and therefore already a 'replica'), it did not survive until closure of the LMR. *Photographer unknown*

By 5th July 1969, these two ex-LMS hopper wagons (AD 82692 and 82691) were largely redundant on the LMR. 1 Rly Gp RCT must have found a use for them elsewhere in its empire as they were removed before the LMR finally closed. *G. Moon*

The WD Ramp Wagon was a unique military 'special'. By means of its built-in screw-jacking system, one end could be raised to allow a (detachable) wheel set to be run out. With the buffers folded back and the jacks lowered, the wagon formed an 'instant' loading ramp for all types of tracked and wheeled military vehicles.
Photographer unknown

Contemporary with the WARWELLS were the World War Two build WD WARFLAT wagons designed to carry the tanks of the BEF in Europe. Long after the tanks themselves became museum exhibits, these robust heavy duty wagons (somewhat modified) were still being employed in BAOR into the 1980s to carry Chieftain tanks. The pair shown in this March 1966 photograph (AD 80113 and 80107) were loaded with the three-axle narrow gauge bogies for the Tank Carrying Rail Wagon (TCRW) which was intended to replace the WARFLATS in Army service. *G. Moon*

When tanks were being loaded it was normal for them to traverse the length of the train, stopping when in place on a WARFLAT or WARWELL to be chained down. In this Open Day demonstration a Comet tank (with turret reversed – probably on loan from SEME Bordon) had moved from a WARFLAT and was being guided onto an empty WARWELL. *Photographer unknown*

Two examples of the TCRW were brought to Longmoor for extended trials in 1966. This view shows them in the standard gauge configuration. *Photographer unknown*

The exchange of bogies was also trialled and a short section of mixed gauge track laid in the siding to allow loading trials of the TCRW in the narrow gauge mode. In this context 'narrow gauge' embraced both metre and 3ft 6in. gauges. Note that this version of mixed gauge track using three rails moved the centre line of the wagon to one side.

Photographer unknown

This photograph is a cruel enlargement, but is included because it shows the four-rail version of the mixed gauge track installed for the trials with the TCRW. The use of two extra rails to produce the narrow gauge track brought the centre line of the wagon into the centre of the structure gauge, which allowed gauging tests using the frames erected above the siding. The various structure gauge templates remained in place after the trials ended, to the bafflement of many later visitors.

G. Moon

Recognised for its historical importance when *Gazelle* was saved was this ex-L&SWR 'royal coach'. Another of H. F. Stephens' 'bargains' it had been moved to the S&MLR before World War Two, so it fell into the hands of the Army when that line was leased for war work. It arrived at Longmoor with the intention that it be restored but due to its poor condition on arrival it proved to be beyond the resources and talents of the LMR's workshop staff. 3rd September 1955.
Hugh Ballantyne

Army 5301, photographed on 10th May 1970, was a typical example of the ex-BR Mk I non-corridor stock purchased by 1 Rly Gp RCT in the late 1960s. This example came to the LMR in early 1968, was repainted in an Army olive drab livery and later in blue as seen here. In 1970 was returned to 1 Rly Gp for further employment. One of this group, the former Army 5304, is now preserved on the North Staffordshire Railway. The coach to the right of Army 5301 was an example of the privately owned preserved rolling stock which accumulated at Longmoor in the 'Shepherd' era. It was a 56ft ex-L&SWR brake third which eventually (in 1977) reached the Bluebell Railway where it has since been restored to its original condition.
G. Moon

Army 3302 was another import from 1 ly Gp RCT, repainted in LMR blue livery in 1968. Although purchased at the closing auction it was scrapped at Liss in 1970.
Photographer unknown

WD 70271 was later named *Bari* [1] and was used on the LMR until 13th October 1956 when it was written off in the Palmers Ball collision. In this 2nd September 1950 view it was seen coupled to the ex-GNR/ECJS corridor 3rd coach, probably converted during World War Two as the equipment van for the LMR breakdown train. Exactly when and how this coach arrived on the LMR is not recorded. There was a need for such a vehicle in the summer of 1940 because the previous 'mobile workshop and stores van' (WIMR 110, converted thus in 1934) had been destroyed in an air raid.

J. J. Smith

Latterly the ex-ECJS converted 3rd class coach was looking rather battered. It is possible that it was first acquired by one of the railway construction companies which were deployed after Dunkirk as 'stand-by' damage repair units around major civilian railway centres in the UK.   *D. M. Rouse*

Above: This was the rail-wrecker, captured during World War Two in Italy where it had been used to good effect by the retreating German army. Eventually repatriated from Venice at the end of the war, it was placed on display at Longmoor. After the Army School of Transport at Longmoor closed a new home was found for it in the Museum of Army Transport at Beverley. When that museum in turn closed the rail-wrecker was stored for a period by the National Army Museum before being loaned to 17 Port & Maritime Regiment RLC at Marchwood where it is now (2014) displayed.   *G. Moon*

Section IX - Railway Construction Equipment

From its inception, one of the main tasks of the WIMR was instruction in the techniques of military railway construction. Indeed it would be fair to say that up to about 1930 the emphasis was more on construction techniques than on railway operating methods.

The first item of rail-mounted plant to be acquired was a four-wheel 5-ton Stothert & Pitt steam crane with pile driver head and bucket attachments. This was delivered in 1906 and in regular use until at least 1914. Its presence is not recorded after World War One so it may be assumed to have been disposed of in the general 'clear-out' of the early 1920s. There was no particular need to retain it because as far as construction plant was concerned, World War One yielded generous spoils.

In 1930, the *Locomotive* magazine noted the following plant in use, of which the first three (or possibly even four) items were 'war surplus' in origin:

Right: The Stothert & Pitt crane could be fitted with a long (seen here) and short jib (for use with an excavator bucket) and it could also be configured as a pile-driver. This picture must date from very soon after delivery in 1906 as the task in hand was the construction of the first water tank, beside the end of the loop line at the Bordon end of Free Piece curve. The dumb buffered wagon numbered '12' was part of the original WIMR 'train set'. There being no technical reason for lifting the wagon, this display was purely for the benefit of the photographer. A view of this crane in the pile driving mode is in Chapter 4 page 61.

WD photograph

This view from 1905 showed the WIMR's first Stothert & Pitt 5-ton crane, rigged in pile driving configuration. To the left of the crane boiler was an improvised wooden shear-legs, used to move the piles into position before driving commenced. *WD photograph*

Brownhoist Steam Crane (1)
Mounted on two cast steel bogies. Spencer Hopwood vertical boiler. Weight 54 tons 14cwt. Total wheelbase 19ft 2in. Lifting capacity: (maximum) 9-tons 12cwt at 17ft radius, (minimum) 1-ton 16cwt at 52ft radius. Returned to Longmoor from France by BEF 1918. It does not appear to have carried a number at Longmoor in 1930. It was manufactured by the Brown Hoisting Machinery Co. of Cleveland, Ohio.

Wilson Steam Crane (WD 4506)
A small four-wheeled crane built by J. M. Wilson & Co. Birkenhead 1918. 35ft jib capable of lifting 5-tons at 17ft radius.

Cowans, Sheldon Crane
Built by Cowans, Sheldon & Co. Ltd (3828/17), it was intended for use on military railways in Egypt or Macedonia. This was a most versatile machine, having piling heads for use with a Lacour 30cwt steam monkey and a digger attachment with ½cu yd capacity. The normal jib was 51ft 3in. long and the short jib (for use with the digger) 34ft long. The crane had four axles, two rigidly fixed under the crane base with the other two on a bogie. The lifting capacity of this crane ranged from 13 tons at 15ft radius to 7-tons at 30ft radius. This crane continued in

Part of the Staff College Demonstration on 21st June 1938 was the loading of military vehicles by various means. Here the first LMR 30-ton crane built by the Brown Hoisting Machinery Co. – from 1931 the Industrial Brownhoist Corporation (Brownhoist) was lifting a 3-ton 6x4 GS truck by means of a cargo net. It seems that this was not the 'live' demonstration as no one was very troubled by the presence of the two small children who had wandered across the road to watch the operation. They would not come to any harm under the watchful eye of the QMSI. What a fascinating place for them to grow up! *WD photograph*

This 1943 view of a 30-ton Brownhoist crane is probably of the first LMR version. It had answered a call-out to remove the wreckage of the derailment of the 'long distance run' train featured on page 364, Volume Two.
H. N. James

This group photograph, taken at the end of a construction project in 1930, shows the Cowans, Sheldon & Co. crane (3828/17). At the time this was the most powerful crane on the WIMR, capable of lifting 13 tons at 15ft radius. The assembled soldiery display a wide range of different forms of working dress of the period.
WD photograph

L.M.R.
COWANS, SHELDON 15 TON CRANE
WITH
EXCAVATOR ATTACHMENT

Crane not to be slued more than 22½ degrees on either side of track when Piledriver is connected to crane.

The digger must only be connected up and worked with the jib fixed at 25 ft radius.

Additional details from drawing LT (ii) 3808 [W.I.M.R. drawing No. 28] dated 12 June 1933
When in use as a crane instead of an excavator.
The operating radius of the main hook is a minimum of 15ft 0ins and a maximum of 36ft 0ins
Maximum height above the rail is 60ft.
Load, using Long Jib, 10 tons at 15ft 6ins radius.
Load, using Short (Main) Jib, 11 tons at 15ft 6ins radius.
When propped and clipped to lift and slew, 16½ tons at 15ft radius, on either Jib.

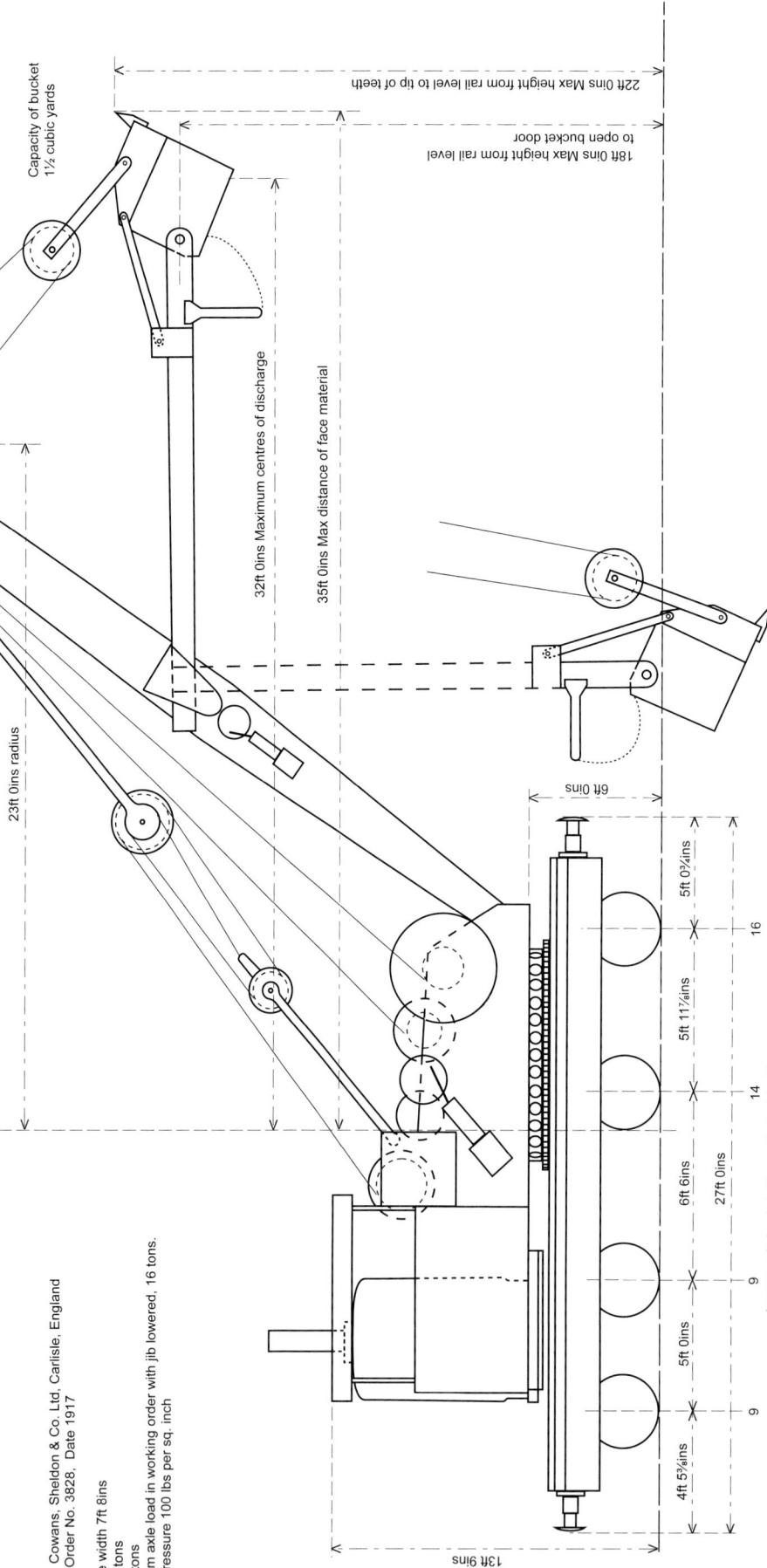

Makers: Cowans, Sheldon & Co. Ltd. Carlisle, England
Makers Order No. 3828, Date 1917

Extreme width 7ft 8ins
Tare 48 tons
Load 9 tons
Maximum axle load in working order with jib lowered, 16 tons.
Boiler pressure 100 lbs per sq. inch

Capacity of bucket 1½ cubic yards

22ft 0ins Max height from rail level to tip of teeth

18ft 0ins Max height from rail level to open bucket door

32ft 0ins Maximum centres of discharge

35ft 0ins Max distance of face material

23ft 0ins radius

6ft 0ins

5ft 0¾ins

5ft 11⅞ins

6ft 6ins

27ft 0ins

5ft 0ins

4ft 5⅜ins

13ft 9ins

Approx axle loads in Tons   9.   9.   14.   16.

16   14   9   9

The Cowans, Sheldon crane in action at the No Road Bridge near Woolmer in June 1936. The longer (lattice) jib was in use. In the distance can be seen one of the signals for Woolmer blockpost. This was on the then-existing main line which swung in a wide arc to the left of this photograph.

WD photograph

Left: This May 1930 photograph shows the versatile Cowans, Sheldon crane rigged by 8 Rly Coy RE as a digger with a short lattice jib and $^7/_8$ cubic yd bucket. It was at work near Liss Forest Road, having negotiated the temporary track seen in the background to access the cutting at the Liss end.

WD photograph

In the days when all heavy construction plant was steam powered, ready access to water and coal on site was essential. The simplest way to provide these was by means of a spare locomotive tender. WIMR 200 filled this role during the twenties and thirties, being paired with the tracked excavator or one of the steam cranes as required. At Longmoor it had been modified by fitting conventional buffers and coupling at the leading end. It originally belonged to the GNR but is alleged to have been acquired from the M&GNJR. By the outbreak of World War Two it was little used and was scrapped during the war years. Of interest is the wagon on the right, one of a large fleet of low-sided wagons used for spoil clearance. Note the protection over the axle-box. It was lettered 'WD' rather than 'WIMR' suggesting that it may only recently have arrived at Longmoor when photographed. *Photographer unknown*

Above: With the cessation of specialist heavy railway bridge construction training at Longmoor during the 1950s, there was little use for the 1917 Cowans, Sheldon crane which was scrapped shortly after this photo of it was taken in November 1956. This view shows it fitted with its short jib. *W. S. Sellar*

Right: Occasionally a derailment would require the use of a crane as shown here as WD 186 (*Manipur Road*) was righted after a spectacular upset at Oakhanger in 1956 (see page 514, Volume Two). *Photographer unknown*

This view shows one of the special displays organised for Open Days. For the LMR breakdown crane the lifting of *Caen* was a simple task but it was quite an impressive way to display the crane's power to the public. *R. K. Blencowe Negative Archive number 23119.*

service at Longmoor until at least the mid-1950s. By 1956 the run-down of RE construction trades training reduced the need for two heavy cranes so the Cowans Sheldon was scrapped.

Hand Crane
There are no details of this machine except that it was rated at 2-tons capacity.

Tracked Steam Digger
A standard Ruston ¾cu. yd steam digger on caterpillar tracks was obtained for use in the construction of the Liss extension. Despite its being considerably out of gauge, it was on occasions moved to and from worksites by rail. When deployed to a work site it was usually accompanied by an old locomotive tender which served as a mobile water tank. Both items disappeared either shortly before, or after, the outbreak of World War Two in 1939. Thereafter diesel-powered excavators were used for any earth moving necessary for railway construction at Longmoor.

Pile Driver
This was an experimental Longmoor design in which all parts were light enough to be carried in a 30cwt truck except for the boiler. On arrival at the worksite it was assembled on its pontoon and floated into position.

Ruston tracked steam shovel at work with 8 Rly Coy RE in May 1930 on the first cut of the excavation east of Liss Forest Road, part of the Liss extension works. Standard gauge low-sided wagons were being used to remove the spoil to fill the ground later used to build Woolmer Yard. Some (but not all) wagons had dirt covers over the axleboxes. *WD photograph*

'The Contraption'

Without doubt the finest piece of Longmoor construction plant was the unique home-grown end-on track laying machine. Its design was derived from earlier machines assembled in France during World War One by soldiers of the Canadian Railway Construction Corps. It was constructed (and continuously modified) in the Longmoor workshops using a variety of components including marine winches and a Yorkshire Patent Steam Wagon Co. boiler. It had to be finally assembled on site as it was well outside the British loading gauge when operating. In use it was described as "distinctly Heath Robinson, swaying and clattering in an alarming manner", the nautical flavour added to by an NCO atop the derrick mast as a kind of lookout, controlling operations below.

Although it might have worked well in a desert or the open expanses of North America (and indeed on trackbed beside the Liphook Road it is alleged, on brief occasions, to have achieved a rate of construction equivalent to one mile of track laid in an hour) it was much too cumbersome for European use. For training purposes at Longmoor, the 'Contraption' was formed into a train with the 'pioneer wagon' (WIMR 40) leading, followed by two of the 40-ton MACAW wagons loaded with rails and three or four RECTANK wagons loaded with sleepers. Such a train had the ability to lay around half a mile of track before requiring replenishment. Clearly such replenishment would cause significant delays and it now seems unlikely that it was carried out during training exercises at Longmoor.

The photographs on pages 101 to 109 give a good idea of the evolution of this remarkable machine. The upper view on page 108 probably shows its final appearance on a training exercise in May 1934. Thereafter it appears to have fallen out of favour and had completely disappeared by the outbreak of war in 1939.

Small cranes for depot work

During World War Two, the various Transportation Stores Depots and sub-Depots required cranes for materials handling. A number of steam cranes rated between 2 and 5-tons were obtained secondhand for use in these areas. Identified machines include:

- Taylor & Hubbard 2-ton No. 869
- Taylor & Hubbard 3-ton No. 1035
- Taylor & Hubbard 3-ton No. 1014
- Cowans & Sheldon 5-ton Nos 6997, 6998, 6999

Brownhoist Steam Crane [2]

A second Industrial Brownhoist Corporation crane of 1943 vintage acquired from the American army was also in use. This was a No. 4 Special Steam Crane similar to the 1918 model (which was scrapped in 1945) having a lifting capacity (blocked) of 20 short-tons at 12ft radius (maximum) falling to 3.9 short-tons at 50ft radius. It was numbered 8416 on acquisition and renumbered 62201 in 1956. [The short or American ton is 2,000lbs, as distinct from the long or UK ton of 2,240lbs and the metric tonne of 1,000 kilograms or 2,205lbs].

A view of the end-on track laying 'contraption' developed at Longmoor during the 1920s from earlier versions used by the Canadian railway construction troops in France during World War One. It underwent many modifications and improvements until around 1935 when it was no longer deemed to be an essential part of the training of railway construction troops. Further illustrations of the 'contraption' are in Chapter 6 page 101. *WD photograph*

45-ton Ransomes & Rapier Ltd Steam Crane
During and after World War Two, for all tasks except specialist railway bridging, the RE railway construction troops used standard items of military construction plant. This, coupled with the closure of the Transportation Stores Depots with their large stocks of heavy railway bridging, much reduced the need for rail mounted cranes. By the mid-1950s, the fleet of cranes had been reduced to two, the second Brownhoist and a 45-ton Ransomes & Rapier Ltd steam breakdown crane (5739/49) numbered 214. Primarily for railway breakdown use, this crane was supplied (with a single jib) new to the LMR in 1949. This crane remained at Longmoor till about 1967 when it was transferred to Marchwood where all heavy crane operators were then being trained. This transfer effectively ended the use of cranes for rerailing rolling stock, reliance now being placed on the Deutschland hydraulic jacking equipment.

20-ton Thos Smith & Sons Ltd (Rodley) Crane
The final crane at Longmoor was a modern Smith's 20-ton diesel crane which was numbered 63049 and replaced the second Brownhoist steam crane.

This review of construction plant concludes the survey of rolling stock. The almost total lack of records has inevitably made the lists less than complete. Nevertheless they serve to show the range of equipment and its extremely complex origins.

Ransomes & Rapier Ltd 45-ton crane (5739) was built new for the LMR in 1949 and worked there until 1967 as WD 62006. Latterly it was little used. The majority of derailments could be dealt with using the Deutschland hydraulic jacking system and there was no longer any training requirement for railway bridging construction. Anyway, unlike earlier cranes this one had no 'multi role' capacity – it was permenantly fitted with the swan neck jib. The syllabus for the 'Heavy Crane Operator' trade continued to include familiarisation with this type of crane after the closure of the LMR. 62006 was therefore transferred to Marchwood. Note the hallmark 'Rapier' name on the outer end of the jib and also on the rear of the cab.
Photographer unknown

The Ransomes & Rapier Ltd 45-ton crane in use on the LMR, lifting a prefabricated bridge component with track panels attached. This view clearly shows the arrangement of spreader beams used to stabilise the crane when working. *WD photograph*

The final rail-mounted crane to be used on the LMR was this 20-ton diesel crane (WD 62169) from Thomas Smith & Sons Ltd, Rodley, Leeds which replaced the second 30-ton Brownhoist crane. It is seen here in travelling mode, in which configuration a converted bogie carriage underframe was used to provide a 'runner' wagon.
Dr I. Allen, Transport Treasury Misc 338

In May 1965 it was removing redundant sidings in Woolmer Yard.
Photographer unknown

Left: Conventional cranes from the RE plant inventory could be adapted for rail use. This view shows a tracked RB 19 diesel crane on a WARFLAT demonstrating prefabricated tracklaying at an Open Day.
Photographer unknown

Below: But care needs to be taken that the crane is within the structure gauge before setting off! Note also, in the foreground, the end of a siding from the 75cm gauge Weaversdown Light Railway.
Photographer unknown

A publicity photograph for the making of 'The Magnificent Two' showing Eric Morecambe and Ernie Wise larking about on the footplate to AD 118 *Brussels*.

Photographer unknown

CHAPTER TWENTY

LONGMOOR ON FILM

With some justification, it can be claimed that the LMR was probably the most filmed secondary railway in Britain. Thanks to the work of John Huntley and researchers at the British Film Institute, much more is known about these films today than in the early 1970s when we first attempted to list them. It is now only necessary to gather the film titles and refer readers to Horton's Guide to Britain's Railways in Feature Films *in which details of the individual titles will be found.*

It is stressed that the filming work was always fitted-in between the normal training activities (though at times it absorbed significant manpower). For the very first film recorded ('The Sappers' Hour' instalment of the silent film 'Mons', filmed at Larkhill c. 1923), the Sappers were paid 7s 6d (37.5p) for their work with £1 for the detachment commander. This is one film which has not yet been re-released.

The first director to exploit Longmoor's potential as a location was Alfred Hitchcock. Two of his thrillers ('The Secret Agent'; 1936 and 'The Lady Vanishes'; 1938) included footage shot at Longmoor. Unfortunately most of this footage seems to have been 'cut' during later editing.

During World War Two several instructional films were shot at Longmoor for use in training RE (Tn) tradesmen. Though photographs exist of the filming taking place, few complete versions of these films have yet been discovered – partly due to the efficient distribution (and later destruction) systems used by the Army Kinema Corporation who were responsible for such productions. Some that are known to have survived are the series 'Tanks by Train', which were released on VHS video tape

The largest film set built on the Longmoor Military Railway was that for 'Bhowani Junction'. Built on the Hollywater line adjacent to Linchborough Bridge (just visible on the right), construction of the set did not interfere with the working of the main line. Surplus old Southern Region coaches were used in making the set, but the accurate depiction of a locomotive and tender of the North Western Railway of India was made in wood by the film studios. On the embankment behind could be seen the Ransome & Rapier 45-ton crane together with an Austerity locomotive and one of the ex-Caledonian coaches. Beside the smokebox of the NWR loco could be seen one of the stars of the film, a grim-faced Stewart Granger. Men from the Camp were enrolled as 'extras' – laid out as 'bodies' in the foreground (you can tell they are soldiers by their boots!).

Photographer unknown

in 2000 by Beulah as product MT8. The making of theses films is shown on pages 344 and 393, and includes clips of *Marlborough* and the ex-LSWR 'A12' Class locos.

Post-war films included cameo appearances of the LMR with locomotives, trains and stations in a variety of disguises. A whole new format was developed for 'Bhowani Junction', filmed at Longmoor in 1955. A spectacular train crash scene was required, built up from a combination of redundant rolling stock (suitably disguised) and a complete and highly realistic wooden mock-up of an Indian State Railways locomotive. The scene was painstakingly assembled by studio technicians over a period of several weeks on the embankment near Linchborough Bridge on the Hollywater Loop. The 45-ton breakdown crane assisted in placing the rolling stock (and later appeared in the background of the filmed sequences). One happy sapper had the enviable task of running round the scene breaking carriage windows! 'Bhowani Junction' was shot over several weeks, during which time some of the stars and production team were accommodated in the officers' mess. The impact of Ava Gardner's presence on the mess Saturday night parties was never to be forgotten. There were plenty of authentic 'extras' available in the camp as 10 Rly Sqn had just returned from the Canal Zone to the UK prior to being re-roled as a port squadron. Not only did the sappers retain a realistic sub-tropical tan and 'brown knees', they still held their ex-MELF khaki drill uniforms, authentic for the period of the film.

By the 1960s filming techniques were becoming more sophisticated, allowing directors to use more imaginative locations. Longmoor became increasingly favoured at this time. Two films stand out for their military railway content; 'Runaway Railway', (1965) and 'The Great St. Trinian's Train Robbery', (1966). In 'Runaway Railway' (essentially a children's film) there is a sequence with two trains making use of Longmoor's signalling system so that they appear to be in the same block section simultaneously. This idea was exploited more fully in 'The Great St. Trinian's Train Robbery'.

Whilst the photograph on page 767 is a 'studio still', the remainder of the 'Bhowani Junction' images are from the camera of one of the many bystanders who just came along to watch the filming in progress.

Chris Shepheard/Rural Life Centre

'St. Trinian's' required up to three trains 'in section' together and a switching sequence with a gap of only 10 yards between the villains' train and the pursuing locomotive. However, if the Operating Superintendent was satisfied that the action could be carried out safely, he was able to over-ride the LMR Technical Instructions. After many delays due to bad weather, in early October 1965 the whole film company assembled at Woolmer to film the critical switching sequence.

First *Gordon* hauling two coaches left Two Range Halt, followed at a discreet interval by '68961', gathering speed as they neared Woolmer Blockpost. Unfortunately, after the first train had passed, the blockman did not change the road quickly enough and caught '68961' in the points at 'half-cock'. Right in front of the entire company the locomotive subsided into the ballast with a series of dull thuds and crashes. All were aghast – but none more so than Frankie Howerd (a world expert in that sort of thing!) for, had it been a live shot, he would have been on the footplate in the midst of all this mayhem. The LMR crew reassured him that all would be back to normal ready for his ride, to be greeted with mutterings of "not on your Nellie". But he did go on to make this and many other hair-raising sequences in this splendid film. The twenty minute long chase sequence is a classic of its genre; probably the best ever made (and without any computer generated footage!).

The final film ('Young Winston', 1972) was also the final activity on the already-closed LMR and has been described in Chapter Sixteen. Since closure there have been several DVDs assembled which include LMR footage. One of these still stands out, Nick Lera's nine-minute documentary of the closure ceremony in October 1969, a beautifully crafted tribute to mark the end of the LMR.

Summary of Films which Include Longmoor Footage

Date of Release	Film Title	Starring	Director
1936	The Secret Agent	John Gielgud, Peter Lorre	Alfred Hitchcock
1938	The Lady Vanishes	Margaret Lockwood, Michael Redgrave	Alfred Hitchcock
1949	The Interrupted Journey	Valerie Hobson, Richard Todd	Daniel Birt
1950	The Happiest Days of Your Life	Alastair Sim, Margaret Rutherford	Frank Launder
1952	Top Secret	George Cole, Oscar Homolka, Nadia Grey	Mario Zampa
1953	Melba	Patrice Munsel, Robert Morley	Lewis Milestone
1956	Bhowani Junction	Stewart Granger, Ava Gardner	George Cukor
1958	The Inn of the Sixth Happiness	Ingrid Bergman, Curt Jurgens	Mark Robson
1960	The Challenge	Jayne Mansfield, Anthony Quayle	John Gilling
1960	Sons and Lovers	Dean Stockwell, Trevor Howard	Jack Cardiff
1960	Weekend with Lulu	Bob Monkhouse, Leslie Phillips	John Paddy Carstairs
1964	Runaway Railway	Ronnie Barker, Graham Stark	Jan Darnley Smith
1964	Invasion Quartet	Bill Travers, Spike Milligan	Jay Lewis
1966	The Wrong Box	Michael Caine, Ralph Richardson	Bryan Forbes
1966	The Great St. Trinian's Train Robbery	Frankie Howerd, Dora Bryan, George Cole	Frank Launder & Sidney Gilliat
1967	The Magnificent Two	Eric Morecambe, Ernie Wise	Cliff Owen
1968	Chitty Chitty Bang Bang	Dick Van Dyke, Sally-Ann Howes	Ken Hughes
1972	Young Winston	Simon Ward, Robert Shaw	Richard Attenborough

A high level view (taken from the west end of Linchborough Bridge) shows the extent of the 'crash' location. Note the very rudimentary (and coal-free) 'tender' with just enough detail to be convincing in the background.

Chris Shepheard/Rural Life Centre

Above: Filming continued even in adverse weather, so whilst the minor actors were being filmed rescuing 'survivors' with powerful lights to simulate the Indian sun, the many spectators (and the lighting technician) dressed for a rainy afternoon in Hampshire.
Chris Shepheard/Rural Life Centre

Right & Below: The impressive pile of derailed coaches was carefully created by the LMR breakdown crew, directed by the film makers. The track was retained in working order to allow the breakdown crane to appear in the background during filming.
Chris Shepheard/Rural Life Centre

A scene for the film 'The Inn of the Sixth Happiness' depicted the arrival of the heroine (Ingrid Bergman) at a country railway junction in China. Whilst other railway scenes in the film could be created on main line stations in London, the requirement for a 'basic' station meant filming on a 'private' railway. Suitable preserved standard gauge railways did not then exist in the UK, so the film-makers came to Longmoor. This film set was built in the locomotive yard at Longmoor. The litter on the track was supposed to enhance the 'Chinese' ambiance. A lot of effort was put into creating the scene, which lasts for under fifty seconds in the film.

Tony Edwards

The train for the 'The Inn of the Sixth Happiness' scene consisted of one of the USA 0-6-0 tank locomotives (which looked sufficiently 'foreign' to most film goers), two open wagons and a couple of coaches. The film director wanted the appearance of a busy junction, so it was arranged that a passenger train of two coaches would pass across No. 6 Bridge in the background (though this is barely visible in the final version of the film) and a locomotive would shunt wagons in the yard (which does not appear in the film at all).

Tony Edwards

With the lighting in place, the camera crew got ready for a 'take'. The event naturally attracted a gathering of men whose duties did not require them to be elsewhere, including a couple of Regimental Police (distinguishable by their white webbing), but they seldom had much to do at Longmoor anyway.   *Tony Edwards*

Right: For the purposes of filming, plates carrying 'Chinese' script were attached to the locomotive, wagons and carriages. Note the train appearing as an 'extra' on No. 6 Bridge in the background.   *Tony Edwards*

Below Left: Not perhaps the best of photographs, but included to show that the 'chinese script' plates were attached only on the side of the train that the cameras could see. On the other side there was no need to cover up the locomotive nameplate nor the LMR markings on the wagons and coaches.
Tim Edwards

Below Right: During a break in filming, a press cameraman took this photograph of Ingrid Bergman.   *Photographer unknown*

For a 'live' television outside broadcast event (which was still a novelty at the time) it was arranged the BR loco 30740 *Merlin* would be deliberately derailed. It would be running at a speed as great as could be arranged and hauling three coaches. The result was something of an anti-climax, with the engine simply rolling to one side. If anything, the exercise showed how difficult it can be to disable a railway. This view of *Merlin* in the shed yard at Longmoor after the event shows that the engine had sustained relatively little damage. 11th February 1956.　　　　*W. S. Sellar*

The filming of a BBC TV programme 'Detective' shown on 13th July 1964 required a train running on the Great Eastern Railway. The LMR duly obliged by providing coaches with plates lettered 'G.E.R.' covering the LMR lettering. The nearest coach, by now renumbered WD 5308, in this view on 2nd September 1964 shows how remarkably well the ex-GWR coaches had survived. The coach behind was ex-LMS ambulance coach WD 5310. This was a brake third corridor coach that had been converted into an ambulance ward car.　　　　*G. Moon*

For the making of the children's film 'Runaway Railway' one of the 0-6-0STs was given elaborate lining and the name *Matilda*. During filming extensions to the chimney and dome, simple dummy outside cylinders and a large nameplate were added.
Photographer unknown

The film which arguably made most advantage of the LMR's 'operational flexibility' was 'The Great St. Trinian's Train Robbery'. Locomotives were painted in British Railways livery, wagons were given BR markings, and BR rolling stock was brought on to the line for filming purposes. This scene, photographed alongside No Road during a break in filming, typifies the use that was made of 'operational flexibility' – three trains closely following one another (there was one behind the photographer) and vehicles being propelled. The nearer locomotive (WD 196) had been disguised as BR 68011. *courtesy Neil Howard*

One of the Austerity tank locos 157 *Constantine* was fitted with dummy side tanks to alter its appearance, and given the fictitious BR number 68961 together with the crest then in use on BR. Waiting for the next 'take' the actors relaxed in the cab – Frankie Howerd wearing the tabard with a portcullis motif befitting his role as a jester. *courtesy Neil Howard*

It could take a while for the lighting crew to get ready, and there is an air of boredom on the faces of the young actresses on the footplate of '68011'. Beyond the camera was the third train required for the next scene – a BR diesel-electric 'Hampshire Unit' No. 1102.

courtesy Neil Howard

For the filming, Longmoor Downs Station became 'Nutcombe'. This view shows the Hampshire Unit in the platform, with young actresses trooping off at the end of yet another filming session.
courtesy Neil Howard
Inset: The presence of unusual rolling stock on the line gave the LMR men the opportunity to gain experience with new equipment. Ssgt John Poyntz was pictured in the cab of the Hampshire Unit. The black triangle on the yellow 'hazard warning panel' indicated to platform staff that this end of the train was the location of the guard's accommodation.
R. Bagnall

For the opening sequence of 'The Great St. Trinian's Train Robbery' the Director required a large locomotive, so one of the 2 10 0s was a natural choice. The Director also wanted the engine painted green, even though the scene was to be set at night-time. The LMR agreed, when assured that the type of paint to be used would wash off afterwards. It did not wash off, and thereafter *Kitchener* ran in a mixture of green and blue patches. It did not remain in service for long after the filming. It suffered a firebox fusible plug failure which resulted in further damage to the firebox (this was an oil burning locomotive) that meant that the locomotive was sidelined, never to be steamed again. For filming the locomotive was numbered 90152 and fitted with an 'AD 4' shed plate.
R. C. Riley

The storyline of 'The Great St. Trinian's Train Robbery' required that points were moved between closely following trains. It was perhaps inevitable that this would not always go to plan and that there would be a derailment. This happened during a practice run at Woolmer. '68961' became derailed all wheels and turned to block both running lines. *Hassan* brought up the breakdown train – a crane would not be needed, rerailing could be done using jacks. Whilst it looked scary to the actors, it was all quite routine for LMR men. Note the fictitious shed numberplate on the smokebox door 'AD 2' (Army Department). *courtesy Neil Howard*

Preparations for rerailing being made – packing, jacks and beams on which to slide the engine sideways. Frank Collinson (with arms folded) was the fireman of the derailed locomotive – Tom Hughes (in front of Frank) was the driver. *courtesy Neil Howard*

The jacks used were the latest equipment available to the LMR, hydraulic jacks made by Maschinenfabrik Deutschland (MFD). The men were photographed while setting up the jacks and the hydraulic control panel. Meanwhile, the other trains involved in filming waited in the distance, on the curve towards Longmoor. *courtesy Neil Howard*

ARMY FORM A. 3129

Longmoor M.R.   No. 882921

SPECIAL CAUTION TICKET*
~~ORDER~~

To the Driver of No. Spl 4 (Description) Pass Train

You are authorized to proceed*

From   L M D   to   W H L

Exercise SPECIAL CAUTION because† 1st TRAIN IN SECTION
ENGINE LINE Line 133 his STARTER AT DANGER
ACC 355 WRONG LINE WORKING

Time   0935   Sgd.   N Murray
                                    Blockman

Date   16-10-65   at   L M D

†Insert reason for SPECIAL CAUTION. *Strike out when used as an Order.
M.1754/1660. 4,000 bks. 3/44. C.P.S.Ltd., 52-6354.

Special Caution forms were regularly made out as **orders** used to warn the driver of the first train to proceed at caution and examine the line, in case it had become obstructed (by fallen trees or the like) since the previous day. Such an order did not constitute an authority to enter the single line. The driver had in addition to be in possession of some form of staff or token – which for the first train would usually be an O. E. S. Key. On this occasion the form had been made out as a **ticket** not an order, because it dealt with an unusual working. Spl 4 would be the first train in section that day, so the driver was to examine the line and could pass the starting signal at danger. This ticket contained an additional note that (because the train involved in filming was blocking the Up line – the line that was normally used for single line working from Longmoor Downs to Whitehill) the train was exceptionally to proceed to Whitehill on the Down line (which the O. E. S. Key did not authorise).

courtesy Tim Edwards

With Whitehill Blockpost open and double line working thus in operation between Longmoor Downs and Whitehill, it was then possible to open Two Range Halt and Woolmer blockposts. If the trains involved in filming were occupying the Up line between Longmoor Downs, Woolmer and Two Range Halt, it was necessary to use the Down line for all ordinary LMR traffic. There was no staff or O. E. S. Key for this form of working, so a caution form was made out as a **ticket**, both authorising the movement and in addition advising the locomotive crew that caution was needed.

courtesy Tim Edwards

ARMY FORM A. 3128

Longmoor M.R.   A 772331

CAUTION TICKET*
~~ORDER~~

To the Driver of No. Spl 2 (Description) L E Train

You are authorised to proceed*

From   L M D   to   T R H

Exercise CAUTION because† SINGLE LINE
WORKING OVER DOWN LINE

Time   1305   Sgd.   N Murray
                                    Blockman

Date   15-10-65   at   L M D

†Insert reason for CAUTION.   *Strike out when used as an Order.
Wt. 24233/6698 8,000 bks 11/45 KJL/947/18 Gp. 38/3

The filming of 'Young Winston' took place after most of the army railwaymen had departed from Longmoor (see page 610). So it fell to volunteers to run the trains. This photograph, taken at Liss Forest Road, showed David Shepherd sitting in front of the smokebox of his engine. On the ground were (from left to right) Ron Druce (Locomotive Driver), Richard Attenborough (Actor & Director), Arthur Young (Locomotive Driver), and Barry Buckfield (Locomotive Driver). The modifications to David Shepherd's 2-10-0 locomotive 92203 included partial blanking off of the numberplate, removal of the smoke deflectors, and the addition of an oversize chimney and dome (made in fibreglass), a headlight and 'cowcatcher'. As always when running steam locomotives at Longmoor, the provision of coal and water needed planning. Coaling was done by using the grab hoist in the background. Water was catered for by having one of the LMR's cistern wagons (capacity 2,200 gallons) as the first vehicle in the train behind the locomotive's tender.

The Dick Weisham Photographic Archive Collection, Photographic Restoration John William Rees.

The soldiers from 127 Construction Regiment RE (TA) also undertook some much-needed repairs to the viaduct at Dolgoch on the Talyllyn Railway during their summer camp in July 1953.

courtesy Soldier *magazine*

CHAPTER TWENTY-ONE

THE LEGACY OF LONGMOOR

Forty years after its closure, what is the legacy of the military railway at Longmoor? Surprisingly its influence, particularly within the railway preservation movement, is far more important than is generally realised. When the LMR was active, it certainly influenced the main line railways in specific areas, two of which are outlined below as examples. From 1951 – when the first pioneers of the railway preservation movement took control of the Talyllyn Railway in mid-Wales – elements of Longmoor methods, training and equipment were adopted to restore and operate the preserved railways. Indeed at that time Longmoor was probably the only source of up-to-date information on 'how to run a minor railway'.

Post-World War Two Influences on British Railways

After the end of World War Two, large numbers of RE (Tn) footplate crew returned to their previous employment with the British main line railways. Following training at Longmoor these men had gained experience on a wide variety of railways, often in the most trying conditions. Many of the techniques they used were not well known in the UK at that time. Adoption of locomotive oil-firing in the UK in the austerity years of the late 1940s succeeded in no small part due to the presence of ex-RE (Tn) drivers and firemen who had learned how to operate oil-fired locomotives in the Middle East during the recent war. In addition, a number of key Longmoor-trained instructors were in the employment of British Railways and able to assist in developing the necessary training programmes.

A second example may be found in the introduction of the 'Deutschland' hydraulic jacking systems for rerailing of rolling stock. Members of RE (Tn) units deployed to NW Europe in the closing years of the war had quickly discovered the advantages of the 'Deutschland' hydraulic jacking system. This system was widely used by the former Deutsche Reichsbahn. It incorporated a centralised control panel operating a number of powerful hydraulic jacks coupled to a portable pump driven by a locomotive's air-brake pump. The sappers themselves quickly adopted the equipment and its success on later exercises at Longmoor led the AER soldiers to press for its introduction at work when they returned to their civilian jobs with BR.

Longmoor and the Railways Inspectorate

Whilst these examples were important at the time, the world moves on. Today there would be very little from Longmoor to inspire or inform the managers of Britain's sophisticated 21st century main line rail network. However in the realm of the preserved railways, Longmoor's influence was critical from the earliest years of the movement and remains significant today. The first such preserved line, the Talyllyn Railway (TR), was indeed fortunate when it discovered that it had attracted the attention of the Ministry of Transport in 1951. The executive authority within the Ministry at that time was HM Inspectorate of Railways, founded as part of the Board of Trade under the Railway Regulation Act of 1842. Since that date every Inspector appointed had been an officer of the Corps of Royal Engineers. The great majority of 20th century Inspectors had trained at Longmoor. Here they had learned a pragmatic approach to the construction, repair and operation of railways, broad in scope but sometimes at variance with the techniques which the UK main line railways had developed. Provided the essential safety of the line was assured, they were invariably open to new ideas.

This background was probably unfamiliar to the late L. T. C. Rolt when in 1952, as manager of the TR, he received notification that an official inspection of the newly reopened line would take place. He describes awaiting the arrival of the Inspector (Colonel Dennis McMullen) "with considerable trepidation". The previous inspection had taken place on the opening of the line in 1866 so such a visit was thought to be long overdue. The inspection set a pattern that was to be followed with numerous other railway preservation schemes in years to come. Utterly un-bureaucratic, Colonel McMullen made a thorough examination of the line and then handed down a series of recommendations which were "entirely constructive and helpful". Rolt sums up the inspection thus: "From his long practical experience, Colonel McMullen could and did appreciate our difficulties, so his attitude could not have been less like that of the popular idea of 'the man from the Ministry' with a briefcase stuffed with arbitrary Rules and Orders."

The Practicalities of Railway Preservation

Thus began a most fruitful relationship between HM Inspectorate of Railways and the preserved railway movement. Such was the growth of this movement that eventually one Inspector (the late Major Peter Olver) was employed full-time in the sector. It was another Longmoor-trained officer, applying the same pragmatic and common-sense approach to railway operating, who was responsible for the widespread introduction to the railway preservation movement of the train control system developed originally on the LMR. Allan Garraway had been brought up in a professional 'railway' family. In 1947, having trained for a commission in the Royal Engineers, he was posted from Longmoor to 348 Rly Optg Sqn RE (the post-war successor to 153 Rly Optg Coy, one of the original Supplementary Reserve units raised at Longmoor in the 1920s). At the time the unit was employed running what had become the Detmold Military Railway. This section of German secondary main line railway had been taken over in 1945 to provide an 'in-theatre' training facility for RE (Tn) railway tradesmen posted for duty with BAOR.

Allan's full-time service ended in December 1948, by which time the DMR was being handed over to a civil/military unit. He wanted to maintain his military railway connections so continued to serve in the newly formed Army Emergency Reserve. He attended the annual camps at Longmoor, serving with R. H. N. (Dick) Hardy under Major Gordon Nicholson. It was another ex-LNER officer (Bill Harvey), then the shedmaster at Norwich, who first introduced Allan Garraway to the narrow gauge railways of Wales in 1951. Allan's subsequent involvement, first with the Talyllyn, then with the Festiniog as its general manager need not be recounted here. Whilst working at Porthmadog he was instrumental in reviving the Association of Minor Railways and successfully guiding it as the organisation's chairman for several years. He went on to give much practical assistance to the Association of Railway Preservation Societies (ARPS), eventually leading to the amalgamation of these two bodies to form the Heritage Railways Association. Throughout this period he used his Longmoor background to good effect devising simple and achievable solutions to the many problems of restoring old railways, predominantly using volunteers.

Two aspects of military railway operating in particular have, under Allan's guidance, been absorbed into the preserved sector. The first is the adoption of variants of the military system of improvised flag signalling as laid down in the Military Railway Rule Book (MRRB) and the second is the use of the simple graphical train control system as taught and used at Longmoor. From his very first inspection of the Talyllyn in 1952, Colonel McMullen was always most emphatic not to allow main line signalling enthusiasts to indulge in over-complicated methods and he encouraged the adoption of the MRRB as the basis of a simple but safe operating system on preserved lines.

Military Signalling Methods Adapted by the Talyllyn Railway

The line that arguably demonstrates MRRB principles most clearly is the Talyllyn Railway. The line is supervised by a Traffic Controller, who maintains a daily graph of all movements on the line as they happen and are reported to him by telephone. The form of the Train Graph is based directly on the Army Form W3021 (Revised) and includes details of the locomotives used together with the opening and closing times of blockposts. Except on the final section of the line from Abergynolwyn to Nant Gwernol (which is operated by train staff and metal ticket), the TR uses Electric Key Tokens. The Key Token instruments can be worked with 'automatic operators' in circuit when a blockman is not present at any blockpost so that the train crew can release a token (after obtaining permission from Control) to proceed into the next section. This allows the line to be 'opened by train' with the blockmen travelling out on the first train of the day – another military railway practice. 'STOP' boards are used to act as home signals although here there is a divergence from WD practice. On the TR the 'STOP' board is put in place by the blockman when opening the blockpost – if there is no blockman on duty the train crew will approach a 'U' board (which is covered by

Under guidance from Longmoor, soldiers from 127 Construction Regiment RE (TA) – based at Smethwick – went for their annual camp on exercise on the Talyllyn Railway (TR) in July 1953. Uncovering the sleepers to find out whether any were still capable of holding the rails to gauge (2ft 3ins) was the first task. The result was always that the sleepers would have to be totally replaced. *courtesy* Soldier *magazine*

Sappers shovelling stone at Brynglas during the relaying exercise. The stone – from the local Bird Rock scree quarry – was far from the constant size required for successful packing under the sleepers. *courtesy* Soldier *magazine*

The sappers at least had some power tools to aid in the trackwork – more than the TR possessed. On the right was Isaac 'Pop' Davies a Talyllyn Railway employee 1952-55.
courtesy Soldier *magazine*

The Talyllyn Railway provided two steam locos to move wagons as required by the railway troops. Unfortunately during the work No. 4 *Edward Thomas* (previously on the Corris Railway) had an accident which damaged the motion so that it was not able to move under its own steam. The locomotive was seen here shunted into the loop at Brynglas with the valve gear was partly dismantled – hence the 'u/s' ('unserviceable', sometimes interpreted as useless) chalked on the smokebox.
courtesy Soldier *magazine*

the 'STOP' board when that is in use) informing them that the blockpost is unmanned and that they may pass the board with appropriate caution. With the 'STOP' board in place, the driver is authorised to pass the board by a flag displayed by the blockman at a flagboard beside the blockpost. Here again there is a minor departure from MRRB practice. Instead of red and green flags to indicate to the driver what action should be taken, the TR uses red, yellow and green. A yellow flag to a driver at the 'STOP' board indicates that he may proceed up to a stopping marker at the fouling point in the loop line whilst a green flag indicates that the driver may proceed through in to the next block section once he has obtained the necessary Train Token from the blockman.

Use on other Preserved Railways

Elements of military railway working can be found on other 'preserved' railways too. On the Ravenglass & Eskdale, the line is operated through a controller, who gives permission to drivers to proceed into the block sections by radio. He maintains a full train graph in the same way as the Talyllyn. The Festiniog Railway used a version of military flagboard signalling for a time at some of its passing loops (for example at Penrhyn). However, it is on the Festiniog that graphical train control has been most fully developed. A single controller located in an office at the Harbour Station at Porthmadog controls, by telephone, all traffic on both the Festiniog and Welsh Highland Railways (amounting to over 40 miles). The developing Corris Railway uses MRRB pattern Station Limit boards in lieu of any other form of fixed signals.

Military Assistance with Construction Projects

Physical assistance with construction and permanent way projects has brought the Army to the preserved railways since 1953. AER units based at Longmoor went to Towyn in that year to assist the Talyllyn Railway to overcome seventy or more years of neglect to its permanent way. This was not an entirely satisfactory arrangement as these units only ever came together for their annual camp and it was difficult to carry out all their other essential military training at such a distance from Longmoor. Though undoubtedly of assistance to the Talyllyn, the military value of such a deployment was questionable and the exercise was not repeated for some years.

We move now to December 1964 when disaster struck the newly reopened Welshpool & Llanfair Light Railway (WLLR). This 2ft 6ins gauge railway had earlier been closed by BR as an 'uneconomic branch line'. After a heroic struggle, a group of enthusiasts had leased part of the line, setting up their operating base at the line's western terminus, Llanfair Caereinion. A short distance from there towards Welshpool the line crosses the Afon Banwy by a three-span viaduct. One stormy December night the Banwy effectively demolished one pier, scouring below it to the extent that the bridge girders dropped several feet. At that time the WLLR had little by way of financial reserves and the cost of repairs might have been beyond the company's resources. The Chairman of the WLLR, Lt-Col Sir Thomas Salt, arranged that the Royal Engineers would undertake repairs as training. Reconnaissance was carried out as an exercise for the Officers' Transportation Course (at that time based at Longmoor) and the work was executed by 8 Rly Sqn RE – one of its last tasks before being incorporated into the new Royal Corps of Transport. The two sagging girders were jacked up, the stonework of the leaning pier was removed, foundations for a new steel trestle pier were drilled into the bed of the river and the girders were lowered on to the new pier. To finish the job the sappers re-laid the track from Heniarth Station that had been removed to allow access to the bridge

The fledgling Welshpool & Llanfair Light Railway Preservation Company (WLLR) did not have the resources to repair the flood damage to the Banwy Bridge that happened on the night of 13th/14th December 1964. There was a real risk that the efforts to preserve this 2ft 6ins gauge line might founder. A team from Longmoor surveyed what was required to put temporary supports under the girders and remove the failed stone pier. The work was begun in April 1965.
Ralph T. Russell, courtesy of Ralph Cartwright

WLLR volunteers prepared the base for the new pier but would have struggled to build the replacement pier, so in June 1965 troops from Longmoor came back to complete the rebuilding. The girders were lowered on to the new pier on 24th July. The sappers also reinstated the track from the end of the bridge to Heniarth Station. The light trestle pier built by the sappers seen in this view has since been encased in stone, with a more robust concrete footing, to more closely match the remaining original pier and to reduce the risk of damage caused by debris carried by the river when in flood.

M. Christensen

The rebuilding of the Banwy Bridge was done just at the time when the railwaymen of the Royal Engineers were being reorganised into the Royal Corps of Transport (effective 15th July 1965). This was not to the universal liking of the men, who made sure that their old Corps was not forgotten by placing the badges of both organisations in the commemorative memorial for a formal ceremony on 9th July 1966 (the bridge was re-opened to passenger traffic on 14th August 1965).   *M. Christensen*

The names of both the Royal Engineers and the Royal Corps of Transport were also recorded on the commemorative plaque, cast at Longmoor.   *M. Christensen*

PIER RECONSTRUCTED BY
SPECIALIST TEAM
RAILWAY CONSTRUCTION R.E.
AND
8 RAILWAY SQUADRON R.C.T.
1965

site. In many ways 8 Rly Sqn (a regular army unit) was better placed to carry out such tasks than the reservists of the AER. Indeed there was an Army-wide scheme – 'Military Aid to the Civil Community' (MACC) which specifically laid down the conditions under which such work could be carried out at no cost to the recipients. Of these conditions the key elements were that the work must have good military training value, that the recipients should not be a 'for profit' organisation and that the work should not take employment opportunities from civilian workmen.

Following the success of the Welshpool project, MACC was used to good effect to help the Festiniog Railway in the autumn of the same year when Major 'Rush' Dray, then the OC of 8 Rly Sqn RCT, took his unit to North Wales for a month's training. Camping in a field at Minffordd, the squadron was able to deploy teams to technical tasks at Boston Lodge, to a major permanent way task above Tan-y-Bwlch and still have time for several imaginative 'adventure training' exercises in the mountains of Snowdonia. In the final period before the camp ended, the squadron took over the entire operation of the FR. In addition to the timetabled service, the military railwaymen ran their own special train to Dduallt, the first to travel over the new track which they had laid as the initial portion of the upper line to be restored.

The advantage for the soldiers of such training was the opportunity to take over and operate a completely unfamiliar railway at relatively short notice. This was one of the strengths of the RE(Tn) service, where units contained a complete cross-section of skilled tradesmen. They were able to offer valuable construction skills with all the necessary plant and to do jobs which were beyond the capacity of the small groups of enthusiastic volunteers who were restoring the railways.

In many ways this unexpected legacy of an almost forgotten military railway in Hampshire continues to this day, a further tribute to the thousands of men who passed through Longmoor Camp and trained on the LMR. Though these veterans may not have enjoyed all their days at Longmoor, they generally remember their time there with affection. An event on one of the preserved railways relating to Longmoor is certain to bring them out in force. This is especially true of the Severn Valley Railway which is now home to the preserved Stanier 8F (ex-LMR/WD 500) and *Gordon* (ex-LMR/WD 600). Both these fine locomotives are now (2014) displayed in the 'Engine House' at Highley along with the Roll of Honour recording the names of the men of the RE (Transportation) Service who lost their lives on service during World War Two and since then.

In September 1965 men from 16 Railway Regiment RCT Longmoor undertook a lengthy exercise on the Festiniog Railway (FR), which at that time was open as far as Tan-y-Bwlch. The sappers re-laid a section of track between Tan-y-Bwlch and Garnedd tunnel (visible in the background) and undertook other work such as replacing a ground frame at Minffordd.   *J. D. P. Poyntz*

Above: Part of the agreement with FR was that the men on exercise should get the experience of taking over the running of the railway for a few days. This view shows the Army crew on *Prince* at Tan-y-Bwlch: Spr John Turnpenny on the footplate and Spr George McGee on the right in the tender.

Roger Bagnall

Right: Sapper drivers gained useful experience in the management of small boilers, with very different reserves of steam and water from their usual locomotives at Longmoor. Cpl Tony Kelly at the regulator. *Roger Bagnall*

The men also gained experience on the unique Double Fairlie *Merddin Emrys*. In discussion with FR regular driver Bill Hoole was Ssgt John Poyntz.

Roger Bagnall

On 9th May 1945 a small celebration was held at Dover to mark the departure of the 1,000th British locomotive to be shipped from England to Europe. The locomotive was given the name *Longmoor* and fitted with nameplates that commemorated the event. The wording beneath the RE crest and above the name reads 'The 1000th British built freight locomotive ferried to Europe since 'D' Day Locomotive No 73755 Wed 9th May 1945'.

WD photograph

Longmoor was taken into service with the Dutch railways as NS number 5085. After its service in Europe was finished the engine was preserved, and it is now on display at Spoorwegmuseum Utrecht (the Dutch National Railway Museum).

Photographer unknown

In a time when not every man would have a personal watch, and if he did it might not be a reliable timekeeper, operating staff on the LMR were issued with pocket watches. These naturally had to be signed for, so they were numbered. *Mike Saxton courtesy Jayne Long*

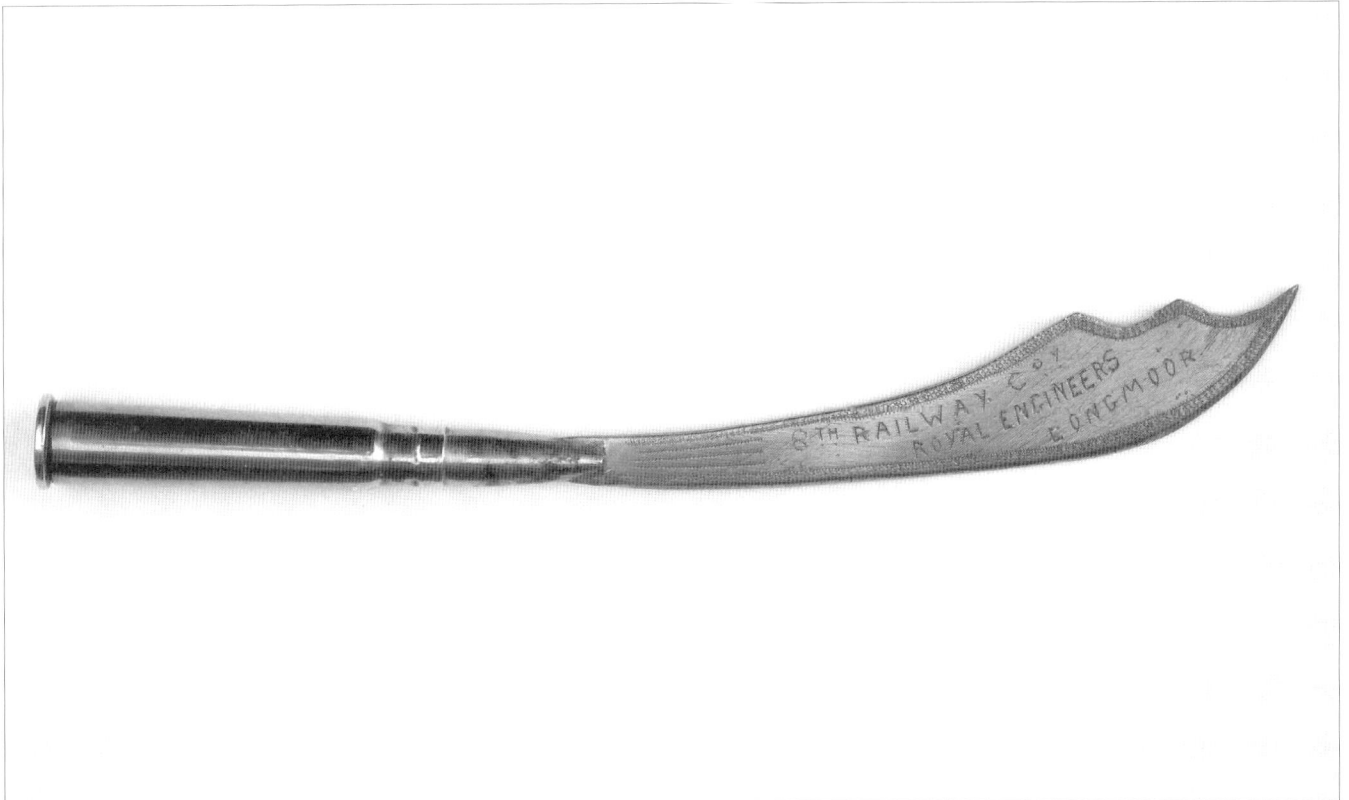

The men who served at Longmoor made all manner of small items for themselves or as presents, a number of which have survived as mute tribute to the skills of the men who trained on the LMR. This small scimitar with a copper blade, made from a used .303 cartridge case, was one of a pair crafted by Sapper H. Parker as a wedding present for a friend. The patterning was made by repeated hammering. *M. Christensen*

WD 181 crossing the road to Liphook as it arrived at Longmooor Downs from Liss. Note the lifting barrier beside the second coach which, when lowered, would prevent road vehicles from using No. 6 Bridge as a 'short cut'.

Trevor Owen (Photos/Fifties reference W104)

CHAPTER TWENTY-TWO
LONGMOOR IN COLOUR

WD 400 *Sir Guy Williams* at Bordon on 4th October 1958 hauling the RCTS tour of that year. The wheels and frames were painted black.

Colour Rail

WD 876 *Bari*, photographed on 12th September 1959, in the darker 'Prussian Blue' livery with the footplate framing and details below (except the springs) painted in red. Note the short destination board on the coach side.

Photographer unknown

The crew of WD 400 *Sir Guy Williams* preparing its train in Longmoor Yard on 1st May 1965. The ex-BR Mark 1 suburban rolling stock had arrived earlier that year, to be in time for the Open Day. As events were to turn out, *Sir Guy Williams* would be taken out of use, as a result of boiler damage, in March 1966. In 1962 WD 400 had received the unique livery of red frames with blue wheels and motion.

Photographer unknown

WD 400 *Sir Guy Williams* arriving at Longmoor Downs with a train from Liss on 1st May 1965. The locomotive was still painted in the darker version of blue, unlined except on the cylinders, cab side and tender, with red frames and polished motion. The leading coach had recently been purchased from British Railways and was still in BR colours, complete with the white X symbol indicating that BR had condemned the vehicle. The reason why the station nameboard had been painted in the colours of the RE is not known – this colour scheme did not last long. *N. L. Browne*

WD 700 *Major General Carl. R. Gray Jr.*, out of use beside the carriage shed in Longmoor Yard in September 1957. The blue paintwork had faded but the faded red lining was still evident. The engine was cut up the following month. *Colour Rail reference WD XXX*

With Cpl Tony Edwards (driver) in the cab, WD 300 *Major General Frank. S. Ross.* was pictured at Longmoor Shed in September 1957.
Colour Rail reference WD10

LMR locomotive No. 890 *Tobruk* in Longmoor Yard on 12th September 1957. To the left were a pair of 'spare' bogies from sister locomotive WD 891 *Algiers*. On the right of this photograph can be seen the rusting remains of *Bari* [1], damaged in the collision at Palmers Ball twelve months before.
W. S. Sellar

N. L. Browne

WD 195 photographed on the Wood Siding at Longmoor Downs during shunting in May 1965.

WD 195, previously named *Sapper* at Bicester, arrived on the LMR in 1964. This view of the locomotive – which did not carry a name at Longmoor – is believed to have been taken on 1st May 1965.
Photographer unknown

AD 195, standing on the Wood Siding at Longmoor Downs between duties, on 30th April 1966.
Photographer unknown

Brussels standing outside the shed at Longmoor on 1st May 1965, running fitted with the vacuum brake (not air brake) on the train. The cut-out section in the saddle tank had been covered over with plating bolted on. In the background (left), painted silver, was the old locomotive boiler retained for instruction on boiler construction. *Photographer unknown*

Brussels photographed just under a year later (on 16th April 1966) showing the air brake pump which had been re-fitted so that the engine now had dual air and vacuum brake for working the train (in addition to the steam brake on the loco itself). The locomotive had been left stabled beside the steam supply pipe stand in readiness for lighting-up for its next duty. Note that the rails either side of the pit were bull-head rail in chairs, with a transition to the usual 75lb flat bottomed rail under the rear wheels of the loco (where the rail head sloped down to effect the join). *Hugh Ballantyne*

157 on shed in September 1964, devoid of its *Constantine* nameplates. Withdrawn from traffic in 1962, 157 was used for display purposes until restored to traffic in 1964 because one of the 350hp diesels (876) was out of use. The engine featured, with additional dummy side tanks, as 68961 in folmint 'The Great St. Trinians Train Robbery' in 1965 for which the frames were painted black. *Photographer unknown*

AD 102 (previously WD 75035 *Caen* [2] but by now bereft of nameplates) at Longmoor shed on 30th April 1966.   *Photographer unknown*

The big engines side by side on 30th April 1966. On the left was AD 600 *Gordon* [2], on shed for watering during a break in hauling the second RCTS rail tour. On the right, sadly out of use, was WD 601 *Kitchener* [3]. This locomotive had been painted in green, with its motion blackened down, in connection with filming work in October 1965. Unfortunately the green paint did not wash off after filming as had been expected. In addition, the locomotive had suffered damage after a failed firebox fusible plug, requiring that the boiler cladding be removed for access, so that overall the engine presented a rather neglected appearance.
Geoff Plumb

A general view of the running shed at Longmoor on 3rd June 1967. The locos in view (from left to right) were WD 890 *General Lord Robertson* and 195, with 600 *Gordon* [2] under repair and its cab removed.
Hugh Ballantyne

Rail car WD 9110 arriving at Bordon on 4th October 1958, painted blue overall with the bumper and radiator cap picked out in deep red.
Trevor Owen (Photos/Fifties reference W46)

ARMY 440 (previously WD 8227) *Hassan* at Longmoor Downs in the summer of 1966, in the charge of Driver 'Ginger' Cashman. The non-matching side covers to the engine housing were the result of local 'repairs'. The story was that one of the panels had been accidentally run over in the workshops.
Photographer unknown

A line-up of diesels on 28th September 1968. The nearest, 8227 *Hassan*, was the only one of the Ruston & Hornsby locomotivess to be fitted with vacuum brake apparatus for working passenger trains – AD 8219 beyond was not. Behind the diesels was the preserved double-chimney locomotive BR 75029.
Hugh Ballantyne

On the morning of 28th September 1968, 8219 (AD 425) waited at Liss Forest Road to depart for Longmoor with the single coach of the 1144hrs from Liss to Longmoor while AD 600 *Gordon* [2] departed into the distance with the 1126hrs from Oakhanger to Liss.
Hugh Ballantyne

Recently repainted in LMR blue with red frames but polished side rods, although not yet carrying its number 8200, photographed in Longmoor Yard. The locomotive was still fitted with an exhaust scrubber (spark eliminator). *Colour Rail*

Although the North British diesel saw little use on the day, ARMY 412 was available for display and 'back-up' (hauling the breakdown train) at the Open Day on 5th July 1969. *Photographer unknown*

ARMY 412 in olive green livery (as used by 1 Rly Gp RCT) with frames painted in black and side rods in red.
W. Potter/Kidderminster Railway Museum reference C006726

Right: ARMY 425, which was transferred to the LMR in 1967 and carried an Army identity rather than an LMR one, photographed while standing on the Hollywater line at Whitehill on 5th July 1969.
Hugh Ballantyne

Whitehill Station on the afternoon of 5th July 1969, with the new blockpost building prominent in the centre of the view and the Hollywater Loop curving away behind. The 1639hrs train for Longmoor Downs was about to depart, with AD 440 *Hassan* leading and AD 425 at the rear of coach 5310.   *Hugh Ballantyne*

WD 890 *General Lord Robertson* in its original colour scheme on shed at Longmoor in June 1967. The short wheelbase, long distance between the outer wheels and the very large buffers (provided to avoid buffer-lock) are apparent.
                                                                          Photographer unknown

General Lord Robertson, now as ARMY 610, on a Duty 'A' passenger train near Liss Forest Road on 5th July 1969.   *Photographer unknown*

The six-wheel saloon was often used for tours around the LMR system by visiting officers and guests and was kept well cleaned in readiness. 30th April 1966.
Photographer unknown

The 'Blue Saloons' in the Ash Platform at Longmoor Downs in June 1967.

N. L. Browne

The interior of the passenger saloon of the ex-SE&CR coach WD 118 (3006), with the servant's compartment beyond. The LMR retained the original light fittings (adapted for electricity) and ventilators, and had added a system map so that visiting guests would understand the layout of the railway and the locations of the Sub-Depots. The map was coloured to show the original WIMR line (blue), the 1930s Liss Extension (red), and the 1940s Hollywater Loop (yellow). 12th May 1959. The name of the photographer is unknown but he is visible in the mirror.

The formation badge of the HQ Transportation Centre RE, displayed on a coach side. This badge was first seen in the late 1940s – a winged locomotive wheel over some blue and white waves. It appeared on a few locomotives and coaches but it was not widely used, except on posh notepaper.
Trevor Owen (Photos/Fifties reference W107)

AD 196 *Errol Lonsdale* shunting in Longmoor Yard during the Open Day on 28th September 1968. These ex-BR steel sided coaches had by this date been painted into 'standard' LMR blue.
Photographer unknown

Gordon [2] at Woking on the morning of 30th April 1966, waiting to take over the RCTS rail tour.   *Hugh Ballantyne*

195 was photographed in the exchange sidings at Liss Junction, waiting to proceed on to the BR line and attach to the rear of the first RCTS rail tour (after it arrived on the main line) on 16th April 1966. The building in the left background was the BR electric sub-station. *Hugh Ballantyne*

AD 600 *Gordon* [2] running round the RCTS special at Liss (LMR) Station on 30th April 1966. Note the Lcpl acting as blockman, in his No. 2 Dress and No. 1 Cap.
Geoff Plumb

When the RCTS rail tour arrived at Liss (BR) Station, 195 went on to the rear of the train to draw it on to the LMR main line. 600 then drew the train into Liss (LMR) Station – with 195 at the rear – after which 600 ran round and attached to the front of the train. This view shows 600 being coupled on prior to departure for Longmoor.
Geoff Plumb

In comparison with the smart appearance of 195, locomotive 196 (still carrying the fictitious BR number 68011 on the smokebox door after filming work) looked rather shabby. Photographed in the goods yard at Bordon. *Photographer unknown*

196 approaching Woolmer Halt from Two Range Halt Blockpost (just visible in the background) with the first of the two special trips around the Hollywater line on 30th April 1966. 196 started so many fires on the dry heathland during this journey that it was decided that the second trip had to be hauled by diesel power.
Geoff Plumb

AD 199 approaching Longmoor Downs in June 1967 during its short time of working on the LMR. Some of the coaches received from BR in 1965 had yet to be repainted in LMR livery. The adjacent roadway had for a long time been known as No Road, because for many years it did not lead to Longmoor Camp and there were 'No Road' signs at the Woolmer end to indicate that this was not a through route. When a through road was made this route was renamed as 'Greatham Road late No Road'.
Hugh Ballantyne

ARMY 196 at Longmoor Downs on 12th September 1967, after it had been transferred from Bicester but before the allocation of the name *Errol Lonsdale*. The reason for the gold paint on the dome and chimney cap is not known. This did not last long – the engine was 'properly' painted for its naming ceremony on 8th January the following year.

Chris Tanous

A view of the bunker of AD 196 *Errol Lonsdale* during preparation of the engine on 5th July 1969. During the repainting of the engine the maker's plate had been painted in overall blue, with the lettering picked out in red. *Photographer unknown*

196 *Errol Lonsdale* arriving at Longmoor Downs from Liss with a short train consisting of just one of the 'Blue Saloons' (No. 119, by now WD 3007). 196 was back in use on ordinary service trains in the spring and summer of 1969 because so many of the diesels were out of use. Extra coal had to be purchased for the purpose – in the run up to closure coal stocks had been reduced to the bare minimum. *Photographer unknown*

A photograph which captures the easy atmosphere (for the visitors anyway) of one of the Open Days on the LMR – September 1968. Rail car 9034, standing beside a temporary Stop Board adjacent to the locomotive shed whilst working trips round the Hollywater Loop, together with a lady and her pram.

Photographer unknown

Gordon [2] arriving at Longmoor Downs with the last train (1830hrs departure from Liss) on the last Open Day - 5th July 1969. *Hugh Ballantyne*

Woolmer proudly displayed outside the HQ building at Longmoor on 30th April 1966, painted out in blue with red lining and side rods, with the dome polished. This livery became difficult to replicate as the skills drained away from the LMR, and later repainting had to be done in a simpler style.
Photographer unknown

Outside the HQ building in July 1969, the elderly *Gazelle* stood in an honourable position facing the parade ground. Beyond the flag pole was a WIMR veteran *Woolmer*, by now painted in unlined green.
Photographer unknown

L.M.R. TRAIN GRAPH - LONGMOOR CONTROL

L.M.R FORM F/6

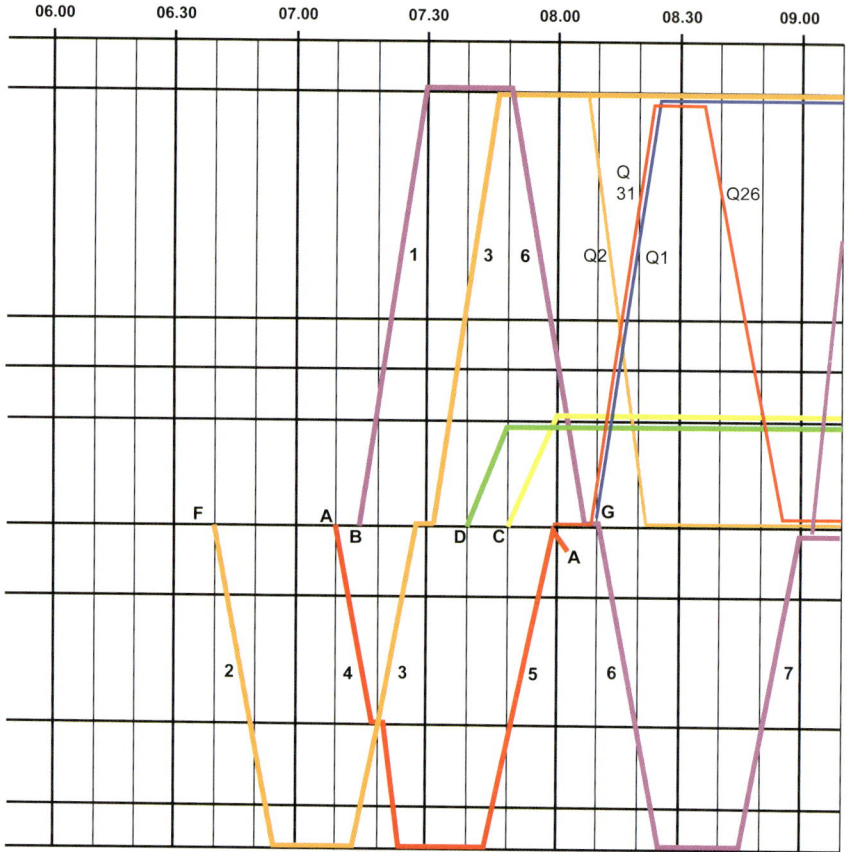

L.M.R. TRAIN GRAPH - LONGMOOR CONTROL

L.M.R FORM F/6

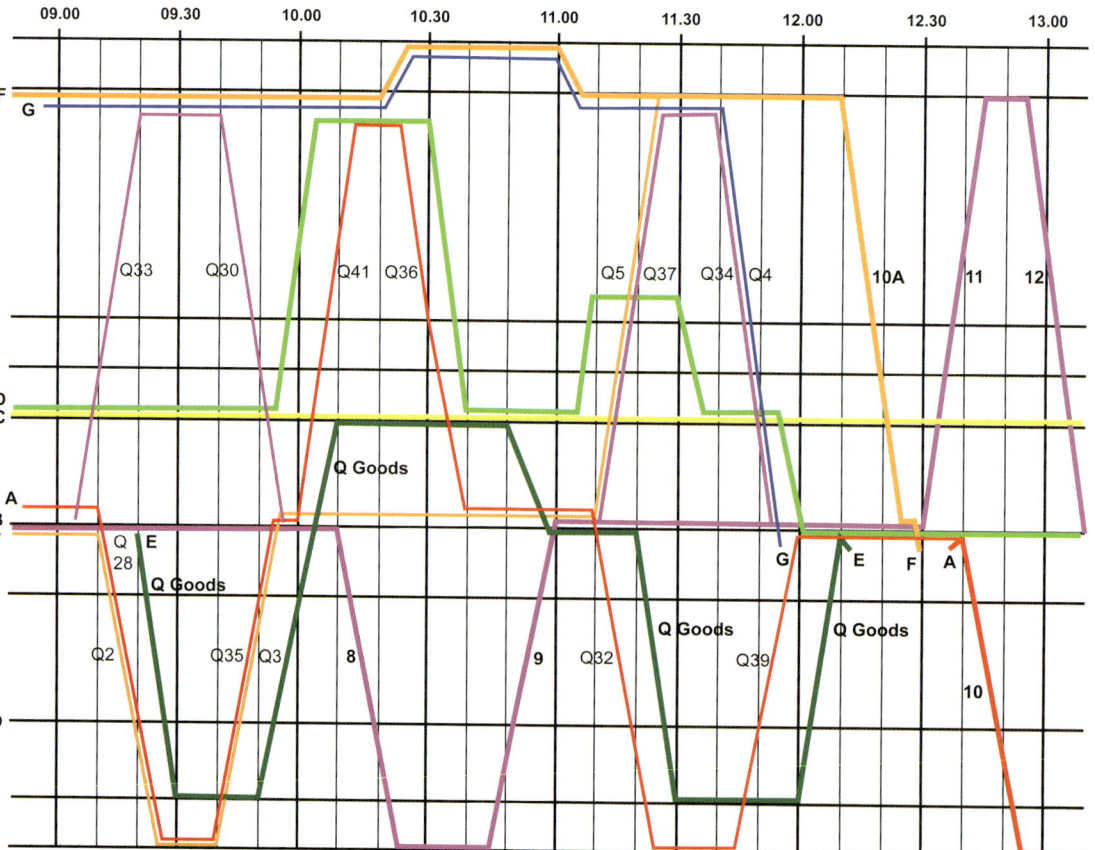

L.M.R. TRAIN GRAPH - LONGMOOR CONTROL

L.M.R FORM F/6

DATE

STATIONS

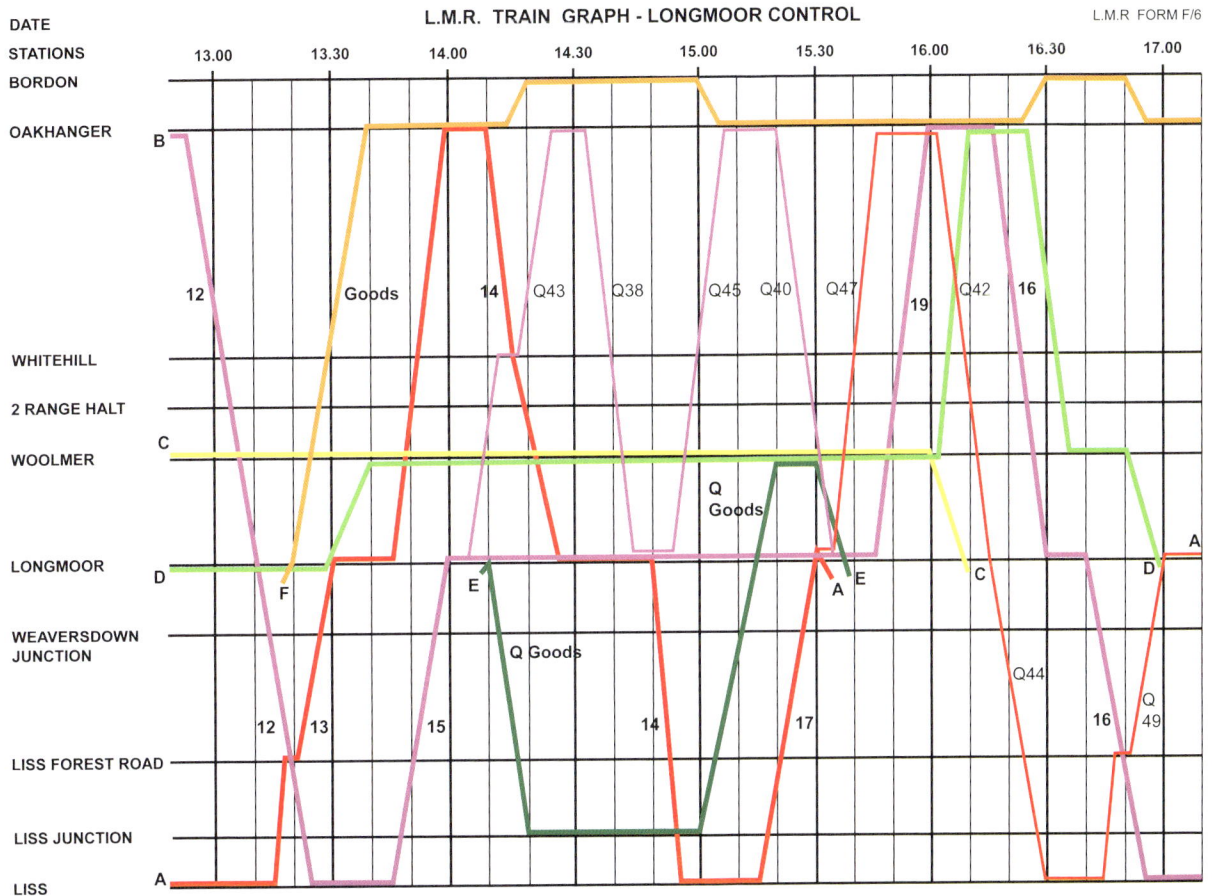

L.M.R. TRAIN GRAPH - LONGMOOR CONTROL

L.M.R FORM F/6

DATE

STATIONS

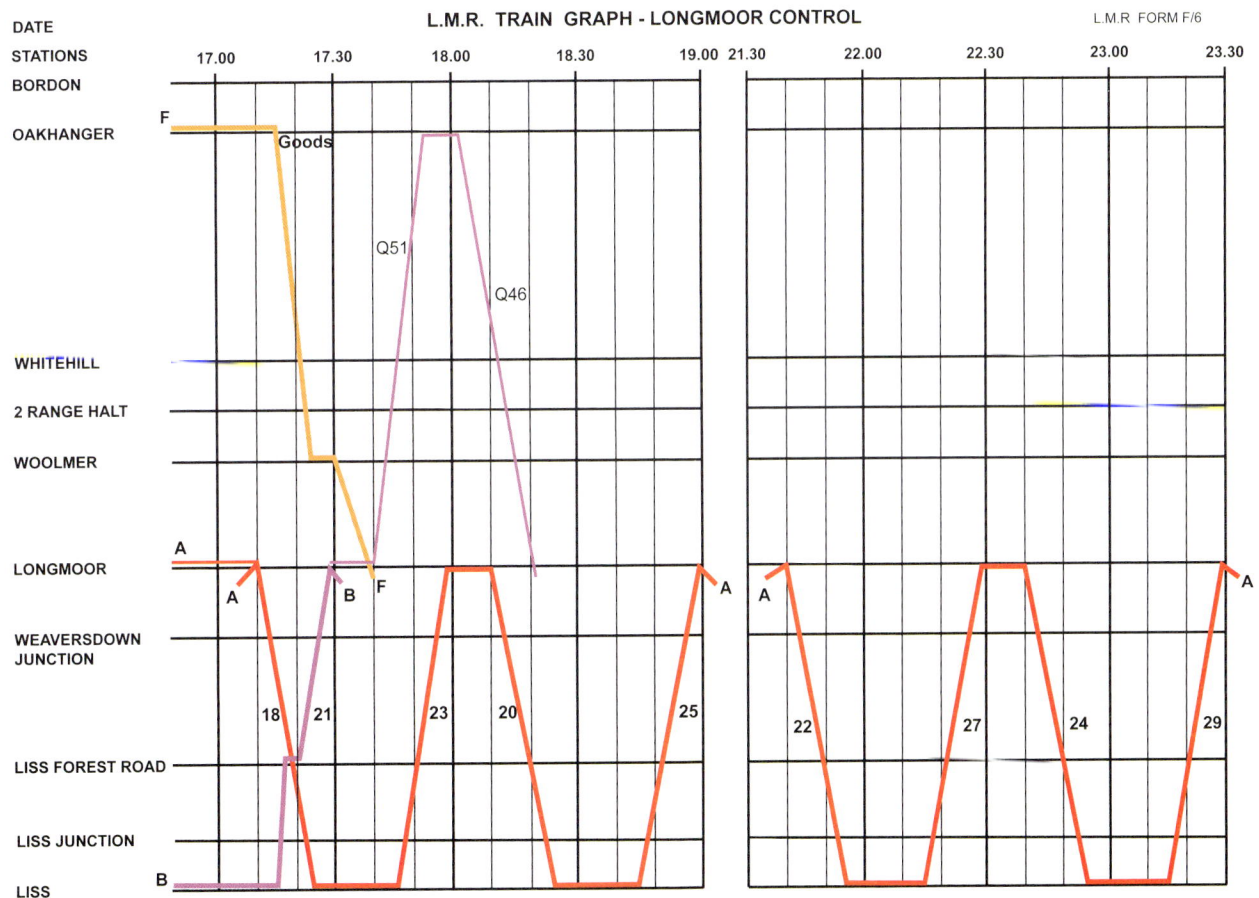

APPENDIX SIXTEEN
LMR TRAIN GRAPH – OCTOBER 1949

The Train Graph for Mondays, Tuesdays, Thursdays and Fridays in October 1949
(Wednesdays traditionally had a different level of service, because the afternoons were given over to sporting activities).

The Train Graph was the document on which the Duty Controller recorded the events of the day. The passage of the trains was recorded by means of coloured lines drawn on the graph. The times of opening and closing of the blockposts was also noted. From this information it was possible to prepare the operating statistics, such as mileage run by each locomotive.

A typical military graph is a large document, each sheet some 15 x 35 inches. The blank graph sheet was available as military stationery (Order as: Army Form W 3021 [Revised]). Pre-printed variants were sometimes prepared locally through Ordnance channels with station details, mileages etc. printed as appropriate. Its completion requires the use of different coloured inks to represent each locomotive. Because of these constraints, an original would not reproduce well in a book. As an illustration, the drawings here show the booked service for weekdays in mid-1949. Passenger trains were numbered sequentially throughout the day. Up direction trains (from the Liss direction) were allocated odd numbers and Down trains the even numbers. Some trains ran only 'as required' (RR) – the time slots (known as 'paths') for these trains being designated as Q. For clarity, the customary 'hrs' description has been omitted in this account.

Duty A commenced with the locomotive coming off shed at Longmoor in time to work Train 4, the 0710 passenger train to Liss (arrive 0725). This train was timed to be at Liss Forest Road from 0719 to 0721, to pass Duty F working Train 3. After running round at Liss, the loco worked Train 5, the 0745 from Liss arriving at Longmoor at 0759. The engine was then not required until after mid-day. It came off shed again to work Train 10, the 1240 to Liss (arrive 1254). The return train, No. 13, ran through from Liss (depart 1315) to Oakhanger (arrive 1400), passing Train 12 at Liss Forest Road and pausing at Longmoor from 1331 to 1345. After 10 minutes at Oakhanger, Duty A departed with Train 14 at 1410, arriving at Longmoor at 1425 and then going forward at 1440 to Liss, arriving there at 1454. After returning with Train 17, departing Liss at 1515 and arriving at Longmoor at 1529, the locomotive was again not required for a while and went on shed. It was off shed again in time to work Train 18, the 1710 to Liss, arriving at 1725. The return journey Train 23 left Liss at 1745 and arrived back at Longmoor at 1759. This trip was repeated in the following hour – Train 20 down – Longmoor 1810, Liss 1824 until 1845 and as Train 25 back at Longmoor at 1859. The locomotive was then again 'not required' until 2140, when it began two round trips to Liss to bring back soldiers returning to the camp. Train 27 left Liss at 2215, and the last train of the day, Train 29, at 2315. After finally returning to Longmoor at 2329, the engine went on to shed for the last time that day. This duty would be worked by two sets of men, changing over during the mid afternoon layover at Longmoor locomotive shed.

Duty B commenced at much the same time as Duty A, and similarly was involved solely with the working of passenger trains. The locomotive was off shed in time to work Train 1, the 0715 service to Oakhanger (arriving there at 0730). Train 6 left Oakhanger at 0750, was at Longmoor from 0805 to 0810 and arrived at Liss at 0824. The return journey, as Train 7, left Liss at 0845 and arrived at Longmoor at 0859. The morning trains to get workmen to their places of work having ended, the locomotive was then not required for just over an hour. At 1010 it worked Train 8 from Longmoor to Liss (there from 1024 until 1045) and Train 9 back to Longmoor, arriving at 1059. There was then a long lay-over until the train worked forward at 1230 as Train 11 to Oakhanger, arriving at 1245. After running round quite smartly, the loco departed on Train

12 at 1253, through to Liss (arrive 1324), en route passing Train 13 (Duty A) at Liss Forest Road. Train 15 left Liss at 1345 and arrived at Longmoor at 1359. The loco then lay over until 1545, when it departed for Oakhanger (shortly after the arrival at Longmoor of Train 17 hauled by Duty A) as Train 19, arriving at Oakhanger at 1600. Departure as Train 16 was at 1615, through to Liss (arrive 1654) after a wait at Longmoor from 1630 to 1640. The final journey of the day was as Train 21 from Liss at 1715, arriving at Longmoor at 1729, after which the locomotive was finished for the day.

Duty C was a purely shunting engine turn. The locomotive left Longmoor Shed at 0750 and arrived at Woolmer at 0800. It worked at Woolmer Yard until 1600 when it returned to Longmoor Shed (1609).

Duty D worked trip goods journeys on the northern end of the line. The locomotive came off shed at 0740 with any goods traffic for Woolmer, where it arrived at 0750. It then went forward at 0955 working to Oakhanger (arrive 1005). Any traffic for Bordon was exchanged with Duty F, after which Duty D worked back from Oakhanger (1030) to Woolmer (1040). Next came an 'if required' trip from Woolmer (1105) through Whitehill to the Hopkins Bridge site (arrive 1109) and returning at 1130, arriving back at Woolmer at 1135. The locomotive then worked back from Woolmer (depart 1155) to Longmoor Yard, arriving at 1205. After an hour and a half break, the loco left Longmoor Yard at 1330, arriving again at Woolmer at 1340. It then worked as required at Woolmer until 1600, when it left on another trip to Oakhanger, arriving at 1610. Again any traffic for Bordon was transferred to Duty F. Duty D then departed back to Woolmer at 1625, arriving at Woolmer at 1635. After a short while for disposing of any traffic brought in, the locomotive left Woolmer at 1650, arriving at Longmoor Yard at 1659 and then finishing.

Duty E worked only if required. Its three trips were all 'Q paths' to Liss Junction, for exchange of goods traffic with the BR Southern Region. The first trip, if required, left Longmoor at 0920 and arrived at Liss Junction at 0930. This trip left Liss Junction at 0950 (following the train Q3 hauled by Duty F, if it was running) and ran through to Woolmer, arriving at 1010. This trip finished with a return from Woolmer (1050) to Longmoor Yard (arrive 1058). If there was traffic, the next trip left Longmoor at 1120, arriving at Liss Junction at 1130. The return was at 1200, arriving at Longmoor at 1210. The third and last trip was timed to leave Longmoor at 1410 and arrive at Liss Junction at 1420. It departed from Liss Junction at 1500 and worked through to Woolmer (arrive 1520). After leaving its load, the locomotive returned light engine from Woolmer at 1530 and arrived back at Longmoor Yard at 1539, to finish.

Duty F was basically the shunting locomotive for Oakhanger, but the duty included some passenger train working, and varied depending on which Q trains were run. The locomotive was the first off shed at Longmoor, to work Train 2, the 0640 to Liss (arrive 0654). It then worked Train 3, the first workmen's train from Liss (depart 0715) through to Oakhanger (0747), passing Duty A at Liss Forest Road and pausing at Longmoor from 0729 to 0732. What happened next depended on the choice of Q trains. Normally the locomotive would stable the coaches at Oakhanger and commence duty shunting the Oakhanger/Martinique station area and working three short trips to Bordon with traffic to be exchanged with the Southern Region there. The first was Oakhanger 1020, Bordon 1025 until 1100 then Oakhanger 1105 (this trip took forward any wagons brought by Duty D which arrived at 1005). The locomotive then brought the coaches from stabling and worked a passenger train, the 1210 from Oakhanger to Longmoor, arriving at 1225. There was then an opportunity to change crew to the second shift and take coal if necessary. Duty F worked north again on a goods trip, leaving Longmoor Yard at 1320, and arriving at Oakhanger at 1338. Next it worked the trip – Oakhanger 1415, Bordon 1420 to 1500, Oakhanger 1505. The loco then shunted at Oakhanger until its final trip to Bordon – Oakhanger 1625, Bordon 1630 to 1650, Oakhanger 1655 (this trip took forward any wagons brought by Duty D which arrived at 1610). Duty F then finished the shunting at Oakhanger until 1715, when it departed, calling at Woolmer Yard from 1725 to 1730 thence finally to Longmoor Yard at 1740.

That was the 'basic service', necessary for the running of the camp, getting the men to their place of work, moving freight traffic and the 'recreational' trains in the evening. There were also additional Q trains that could be run for the purpose of training the men. Supplement No. 1 dated 24 November 1949 set out the detail. For clarity, these trains have been superimposed on the Train Graph drawings in thinner lines.

The first variation of the basic service provided for an extra passenger train from Oakhanger in the morning. Duty F after working Train 3, did not stable the coaches. Instead it worked passenger duty Q2. This train departed from Oakhanger at 0806 to Longmoor, arriving there at 0821. After waiting for just under an hour, the train went forward at 0910 to Liss, arriving there at 0924. It waited at Liss until 0940 (during which time Duty E followed with a goods trip to Liss Junction, if required). Duty F continued with Q3, the 0940 passenger to Longmoor, arriving at 0954. The engine was then not required until 1110, when it worked Q5 passenger train to Oakhanger. It arrived there at 1125 and resumed the remainder of its normal duty, running round the coaches for a departure at 1210.

Duty G The absence of Duty F from Oakhanger between 0806 and 1125 was covered by an extra locomotive. This worked Q1 passenger RR (Runs as Required, and using a third set of coaches)

train from Longmoor (depart 0810) to Oakhanger, arriving at 0825. En route, it passed Duty F working RR train Q2 at Whitehill. Duty G then shunted at Oakhanger (effectively deputising for Duty F) until 1140. By this time Duty F had returned on Q5, so Duty G was available to work another RR passenger train Q4, which departed from Oakhanger at 1140 and arrived at Longmoor at 1155, after which the engine was finished.

There was a second variation to the basic service, in which a significant number of extra trains were operated, for training purposes only, by Duty A and Duty B.
The following trains did NOT run
Q2, Q3 and Q5 in Duty F
Q1 and Q4 in Duty G
Third Q Goods path in Duty E

Duty A:
After working No. 5, instead of going on shed,
Work Q31, 0810 Longmoor to Oakhanger (arrive 0825) [this would have been the path of Q1]
Q26 0836 Oakhanger to Longmoor (0851) going forward as
    Q28 Longmoor 0910 to Liss (0924).
Q35 0940 Liss to Longmoor (0954) going forward as Q41
    Longmoor 1000 to Oakhanger (1015)
Q36 1025 Oakhanger to Longmoor (1038) going forward as
    Q32 1110 Longmoor to Liss (1124)
Q39 1145 Liss to Longmoor (1159)
Then resume normal timetable by working No. 10 at 1240.

After working No. 17, instead of going on shed
Work Q47, 1534 from Longmoor to Oakhanger (1547)
Q42 1602 Oakhanger to Longmoor (1615) going forward as
Q44 1616 Longmoor to Liss (1630)
Q49 1643 Liss to Longmoor (arrive 1659) passing 16 at Liss
    Forest Road
Then resume normal timetable by working No. 18 at 1710.

Duty B:
After working No. 7,
Work Q33, 0905 Longmoor to Oakhanger (arrive 0920)
Q30 0940 Oakhanger to Longmoor (0955)
Then resume normal timetable by working No. 8

After working No. 9
Work Q37, 1110 Longmoor to Oakhanger (1125)
Q34 1140 Oakhanger to Longmoor (1155)
Then resume normal timetable by working No. 11

After working No. 15
Work Q43, 1406 Longmoor to Oakhanger (1423)
Q38 1431 Oakhanger to Longmoor (1445)
Q45 1455 Longmoor to Oakhanger (1508)
Q40 1520 Oakhanger to Longmoor (1533)
Then resume normal timetable by working No. 19

After working No. 21
Work Q51, 1740 Longmoor to Oakhanger (1753)
Q46 1804 Oakhanger to Longmoor (1819)
Then to Longmoor Yard and finish.

APPENDIX SEVENTEEN
SUMMARY OF ESTABLISHMENT STEAM LOCOMOTIVES

Name	MCR/WD Number	Builder	At Longmoor From	At Longmoor To	Wheel Arr'gt	Cylinders[1] Dia (ins)	Cylinders[1] Stroke (ins)	Coupled Wheels	Wheel-base	Capacity Water (gals)	Capacity Bunker (tons)	Weight in working order	Heating Surfaces Tubes	Heating Surfaces Firebox	Heating Surfaces Total	Grate Area (ft²)	Boiler pressure (psi)	Tractive Effort (lbs)	Brake	NOTES
Mars [1]	-	VF/1160/86	1905	1924/5	0-4-2T	7½	12 (O)	1ft 8¼in.	n/k	200	1/4	7T 14C	202.9	22.3	225.2	4.0	100	3,000	H	18-inch gauge
Venus [1]	-	VF/1161/86	1905	c1919	0-4-2T	7½	12 (O)	1ft 8¼in.	n/k	200	1/4	7T 14C	202.9	22.3	225.2	4.0	100	3,000	H	18-inch gauge
Flamingo	-	JF/5062/85	1905	1919	0-4-2T	7½	12 (O)	1ft 8¼in.	n/k	n/k	n/k	n/k	n/k	n/k	n/k	n/k	n/k	n/k	n/k	18-inch gauge
Bordon	-	AE/1505/06	1906	1910	0-6-0ST	14	20 (O)	3ft 3in.	n/k	750	1	30T	446.0	52.0	498.0	8.0	160	13,300	V/S	sg
Woolmer	70074/010	AE/1572/10	1910	1919[2]	0-6-0ST	14	20 (O)	3ft 3in.	n/k	750	1	30T	446.0	52.0	498.0	8.0	160	13,300	V/S	sg
Hampshire	–	AE/1520/06	1906	c1924	0-6-0ST	15	20 (O)	3ft 4in.	9ft 8½in.	750	1	33T	n/k	n/k	722.0	12.2	160	14,400	V/S	sg
Longmoor	–	Sdn/1179/90	1908	1921	0-4-4T[3]	16	24 (I)	4ft 1½in.	20ft 2in.	n/k	n/k	40T 6C	1142.2	93.0	1235.2	14.8	150	16,765	V/S	sg
Sir John French	70203/110	HL/3088/14	1914	1946	0-6-2T	16	24 (O)	4ft 0in.	17ft 0in.	1,330	2½	56T 10C	927.9	88.8	1016.7	17.0	170	18,500	W/V/S	sg
Kingsley [1]	(70202)	HC/224/80	1917	1952[4]	4-4-0T	15	20 (O)	4ft 6in.	17ft 7in.	600	1½	37T 15C	754.52	67.25	821.75	11.3	140	8,000	V/S	sg
Thisbe	MCR 84	HL/2878/11	1916	1930/3	0-6-2T	14	22 (O)	3ft 6in.	15ft 6in.	720	3	43T 10C	n/k	n/k	723.5	11.3	170	14,800	V/S	sg
Salisbury	MCR3	HC/1069/14	1918	c1926	0-6-0T	16	20 (O)	3ft 6in.	10ft 3in.	n/k	n/k	33T	n/k	n/k	n/k	n/k	160	12,672	V/S	sg
Selborne	70204	HL/3531/22	1922	1946	0-6-0T	16	24 (O)	4ft 0in.	11ft 0in.	1,100	1½	42T 14C	n/k	n/k	800	14.5	170	18,496	W/V/S	sg
Kitchener [1]	–	K/2977/86	1927	c1941	0-6-2T	17½	26 (I)	4ft 6½in.	19ft 3in.	1,400	1¾	58T	n/k	n/k	1,022.0	18.25	140	17,400	V/S	sg
Gordon [1]	70205	Cdf/306/97	1927	1947	0-6-2T	17½	26 (I)	4ft 6½in.	19ft 3in.	1,400	1¾	60T	n/k	n/k	1,148.5	19.14	170	21,110	V/S	sg
Earl Haig	(70282)	Crw/3160/91	1930	1940	2-4-2T	17	24 (I)	5ft 6in.	22ft 5in.	1,350	2½	50T 10C	n/k	n/k	1,074.6	17.1	150	12,910	W/V/S	sg
Earl Roberts [1]	70206	Crw/3165/91	1931	1945	2-4-2T	17	24 (I)	5ft 0in.	22ft 5in.	1,350	2½	50T 10C	n/k	n/k	1,074.6	17.1	150	12,910	W/V/S	sg
Marlborough	70207	Stoke/158/13	1936	1946	0-6-2T	18½	26 (I)	5ft 0in.	23ft 0in.	1,700	3½	64T 10C	1,085	113	1,198	17.7	175	22,600	V/S	sg
Kitchener [2]	70208	WB/2587/38	1938	1946	0-6-2T	18	24 (O)	4ft 3in.	17ft 0in.	1,500	100 Cu.ft	55T 5C	975	99	1,074	18.0	180	23,328	W/V/S	sg
Earl Roberts [2]	72400	Brtn/08	1941	1946	4-4-2T	17½	26 (I)	5ft 6in.	30ft 10in.	n/k	n/k	68T 10C	1,003.14	96.89	1,100.33	n/k	170	17,443	W/S	sg
Kingsley [2]	72401	Brtn/08	1941	1946	4-4-2T	17½	26 (I)	5ft 6in.	30ft 10in.	n/k	n/k	68T 10C	1,003.14	96.89	1,100.33	n/k	170	17,443	W/S	sg

Notes:
1 (O) Outside Cylinders;
(I) Inside Cylinders
2 Returned to LMR for display 1953
3 Built by GWR as 0-4-2ST
4 Out of use by 1940, retained for re-railing exercises

Name	MCR/WD Number	Builder	At Longmoor From	At Longmoor To	Wheel Arr'gt	Cyl Dia	Cyl Stroke	Coupled Wheels (diam.)	Wheel-base (ft ins)	Water (gals)	Bunker (tons)	Weight in working order	Tubes	Firebox	S'htr	Total	Grate Area (ft²)	Boiler pressure (psi)	Tractive Effort (lbs)	Brake	NOTES
Stanier '8F'	Various See Chapter 17, page 665				2-8-0	18½	28 (O)	4ft 8½in.	57ft 7¾in.	4,000	9T	Loco: 72T 5C; Tender: 55T 10C; Total: 127T 15C	1,479.0	171.0	245.0	1,895.0	28.75	225	32,438	W/V/S	sg
Gordon (2)	73651	NBL/25437/43	1943	1971	2-10-0	19	28 (O)	4ft 8½in.	29ft 8in.	5,000	9T	Loco: 78T 6C; Tender: 55T 10C; Total: 133T 16C	1,759.0	192.0	423.0	2374.0	40.0	225	34,125	W/V/S	sg
Kitchener (3)	73757	NBL/25643/45	1946	1967								as Gordon (2)									
Sir Guy Williams	77337	NBL/25205/43	1944/5	1967	2-8-0	19	28 (O)	4ft 8½in.	24ft 10in.	5,000	9T	Loco: 70T 5C; Tender: 55T 10C; Total: 125T 15C	1,512.0	168.0	310.0	1,990.0	28.6	225	34,125	W/V/S	sg
Major General McMullen	79250	VF/5193/45	1945	1958								as Sir Guy Williams									
Major General Carl R. Gray Jr.	93257	ALCO/ 71512/44	1945	1957	2-8-0	19	26 (O)	4ft 9in.	23ft 3in.	6,500	9T	Loco: 72T 10C; Tender: 58T 0C; Total: 130T 10C	1,773.0		480.0	2,253.0	41.0	225	31,490	W/V/S	sg
Major General Frank. S. Ross.	94382	Dav/2531/43	1945	1958	0-6-0PT	16½	24 (O)	4ft 6in.	10ft 0in.	999.0	0.9T	Loco: 47T 1C	790	86.0	–	876.0	19.4	210	21,600	S	sg
WD Standard 0-6-0 'Austerity'	Various See Chapters 17 and 18		1943 on	1970	0-6-0ST	18	26 (I)	4ft 3in.	11ft 0in.	1,200	2.5T	Loco: 48T 4C	872.5	87.5	–	960.0	16.8	170	23,870	as fitted	sg

BUILDERS' DETAILS

AE	Avonside Engine Co. Bristol
ALCO	American Locomotive Co. Schenectady, NY (USA)
Brtn	LB&SCR, Brighton Works
Cdf	Taff Vale Railway, Cardiff Works
Crw	L&NWR, Crewe Works
DAV	Davenport Locomotive Works, (USA)
HC	Hudswell, Clarke & Co. Ltd, Leeds
HE	Hunsle: Engine Co. Ltd, Leeds
HL	R. & W. Hawthorn, Leslie & Co. Ltd, Newcastle-upon-Tyne
JF	John Fowler (Leeds) Ltd, Leeds
K	Kitson & Co. Ltd, Leeds
NBL	North British Locomotive Co. Ltd, Glasgow
RSH	Rober: Stephenson & Hawthorns Ltd, Newcastle-upon-Tyne
SDN	GWR, Swindon Works
Stoke	North Staffordshire Rly, Stoke-on-Trent Works
VF	Vulcan Foundry Ltd, Newton-le-Willows
WB	W. G. Bagnall Ltd, Stafford

APPENDIX EIGHTEEN
SUMMARY OF STANDARD GAUGE INTERNAL COMBUSTION LOCOMOTIVES

Name	WD Running Numbers[1] Pre-1952	52 - 68	68 on	Builder[3]	At Longmoor From	To	Wheel Arr'ment & Drive[2]	Class	Engine Maker	Engine Type etc	Trans. Maker	Trans. type etc	Weight in working order	Remarks
–	WD1	–	–	MW/1867/15	1915	1916	0-4-0 M	–	Thorneycroft	S6 180hp	Keyser-Ellison	3-speed	26T 0C	Reversible marine petrol engine, air start
–	(700)29	–	–	DC/2159/41	1941	1944	0-4-0 M	–	Gardner	6L3 153hp	Wilson-Drewry	4-speed air-actuated	21T 6C	Prototype WD 153hp shunter
–	(7000)2	810	–	JF/22500/38	1941	1943	0-4-0 M	–	Sanders	150hp	n/k	n/k		No details
–	70215	–	–	AW/D57/35	1940	1957	0-6-0 E	–	Armstrong-Sulzer	6LTD22 400hp	Crompton Parkinson	Electric to jackshaft final drive	40T 10C	To BAOR
–	70216	883	–	AW/D58/35	1940	1952	0-6-0 E	–	Armstrong-Sulzer	6LTD22 400hp	Crompton Parkinson	Electric to jackshaft final drive	40T 10C	Returned to LMS 11/42 - 11/44 To Cairnryan in 1952
Bari (2)	70270	876	–	Derby/1945	1957	1969	0-6-0 E	D1	English Electric	350hp	English Electric	Electric to spur gear drive	47T 5C	Standard LMS design
Bari (1)	70271	(877)	–	ditto	1945	1956	0-6-0 E	D1	English Electric	350hp	English Electric	Electric to spur gear drive	47T 5C	Written off in Palmers Ball accident
Chittagong (1) then Basra (2)	70272	878	601	ditto	1945	1969	0-6-0 E	D1	English Electric	350hp	English Electric	Electric to spur gear drive	47T 5C	Standard LMS design
–	70273	879	–	ditto	1945	1948	0-6-0 E	D1	English Electric	350hp	English Electric	Electric to spur gear drive	47T 5C	Standard LMS design
–	70238	853	–	JF/22796/42	1945	1947	0-4-0 M	–	McLaren	150hp	?	Mechanical	n/k	no details
Tobruk (1)	71232	890	–	Wh/60174/41	1945	1957	Bo-Bo E	–	Buda-Lanova	2 x 6DHS (ea 325hp)	Westinghouse	Electrical 4-motor spur drive	65T 0C	65 'Short Tons' of 2,000lbs
Algiers	71233	891	–	Wh/60175/41	1945	1958	Bo-Bo E	–	Buda-Lanova	ditto	Westinghouse	ditto	65T 0C	65 'Short Tons' of 2,000lbs
Basra (1) then Chittagong (2)	72220	829	–	DC/2175/45	1945	1966	0-4-0 M	A7	Gardner	6L3 153 hp	Wilson-Drewry	4-speed air-actuated	23T 12C	
Caen (1)	72214	807	–	RH/224345/45	1945	1959	ditto	A1	Ruston	48 hp	Ruston	Chain drive	7T 6C	
–	–	8200	400	NBL/27421/55	1956	1960	0-4-0 H	C1/2	National	275 hp	Voith	L/24/V	32T 0C	
Matruh (2)	–	8205	405	NBL/27426/55	1957	1962	0-4-0 H	C1/2	National	275 hp	Voith	L/24/V	32T 0C	
–	–	8212	412	NBL/27647/59	1969	1970	0-4-0 H	C2	Paxman	275 hp	Voith	L/24/V	32T 0C	
General Lord Robertson	–	890	610	RR/10143/63	1964	1970	0-8-0 H	D2	Rolls Royce	2 x 310 hp	2 x Twin Disc	3-stage torque converter	54T 0C	
–	17	–	–	JF/22912/40	1963	1969	0-4-0 M	–	McLaren		150 hp			non-runner used in Diesel Fitters' School for instruction
–	–	8219	425	RH/459519/61	1966	1970	0-6-0 H	C3	Paxman	275 hp (V6)	Twin Disc	Torque converter	36T 0C	
Hassan	–	8227	440	RH/468041/62	1962	1969	0-6-0 H	C4	Paxman	275 hp (V6)	Twin Disc	Torque converter	36T 0C	

NOTES:
1. Numbers in plain type are those carried by locomotives when in service on the LMR, italic numbers are others used whilst in WD/AD service at other locations.
2. Drive code: M = Mechanical transmission; E = Electrical transmission; H = Hydraulic transmission.
3. Locomotive builders:

AW — Armstrong Whitworth, Newcastle-upon-Tyne
DC — Drewry Car Co. Ltd (Drewry-Baguley)
Derby — LMS Works, Derby
RH — Ruston & Hornsby Ltd, Lincoln
RR — Rolls Royce (Sentinel Works), Shrewsbury
Wh — Whitcomb Locomotive Corporation (USA)
Other builders' abbreviations as listed in Notes to Appendix 17, page 819

APPENDIX NINETEEN
TABLE OF RAIL CARS

WD Numbers			Building	At Longmoor		Engine		Transmission		Bodywork		Brakes	Remarks
Pre-1944	44-52	52 on	Details †	From	To	Make	Type	Make	Type	Type	Seats	§	
–	–	–	DC/1023/18	1918	c1946	Baguley	2-cyl 10 hp	Baguley	3-speed	Semi-open	6	H	Rebuilt 1929; new engine 1940. No details of scrapping
–	–	–	DW/1000/33	1933	c1946	JAP	1232cc Air cooled	Wickham	–	'Motor Gang Trolley'	8-10	H	Wickham Type 17
–	–	–	DW/2204/37	1937									Delivered with a No. 17 Lightweight trailer
(2)	941	(9111)	DC/1820/36	1936	1959	Gardner	4LW 62 hp	Wilson-Drewry s.c.g. with Voigt-Sinclair coupling		All enclosed	20	H, SA	Scrapped at Longmoor
3	930	9109	DW/2877/40	1940	1967	Ford	V8 Petrol	Ford	4-speed	Semi-open Car	30	H, SA	Scrapped at Longmoor 1967
4	931	9110	DW/2878/40	1940	1961								Sold to E. L. Pitt (Coventry) Ltd 1961
–	11966 to 11972	–	DW/3374/43 to DW/3380/43	1945	1945	JAP	1323cc Air cooled	Wickham	–	'Motor Gang Trolleys'	8-10	H	With windscreens & fixed canvas canopies. Delivered new to 1 Tn Stores Depot. Available for use on LMR as needed. Post-war disposal not known
–	–	–	DW/3812/45 - DW/3815/45	1945	1945	–	–	Wickham	–	Trailers	14	H	Delivery and use as for trolleys above
–	–	9033	DW/6857/54	1954	1970	Ford	13 hp Petrol	Morris	3-speed	'Motor Gang Trolley'	8-10	H	Wickham Type 27A Mk II canopy pattern trolley
–	–	–	DW/6858/54	1954	nk	–	–	–	–	Trailer	–	U	No. 17 steel trailer. Supplied new with 9033 and probably accompanied it to Bicester
–	–	9034	DW/7397/57	1960	1969	Perkins	P4 40 hp	Ford	3-speed	'Motor Inspection Car'	8-10	H	Wickham Type 40 Mk IIA with slatted wooden cross-benches. New to 1 Rly Gp RE in 1957 and transferred to LMR in 1960.

NOTES:

† Builders' Details: DC Drewry Car Co. Ltd
DW D. Wickham & Co. Ltd

§ Braking Systems: H Hand brake
SA Straight Air-brake
U Unbraked

APPENDIX TWENTY
LMR GOODS AND PASSENGER ROLLING STOCK – 1943 to c1956

Showing unified WD renumbering where known

This table shows the LMR rolling stock holdings at their maximum. The first Longmoor numbering scheme was devised and executed by the WIMR staff. A 1934 version of this list was reproduced in Appendix Six to Volume One (page 321). In 1943 the War Office issued a single block series of rolling stock numbers to the LMR. These were grouped by vehicle type but there was no attempt to record previous owners' numbers etc. To accommodate the ever-growing needs of the LMR in wartime, at least one additional allocation was given. On the ground there were many inconsistencies and it has become clear during our researches that the 1943 renumbering was never fully applied. Where possible, the post-1956 numbers (based on designations promulgated in ACI 21/56) are shown in Column (c). Those vehicles which survived to undergo renumbering in the 1956 series are described in more detail in Appendix Twenty-one. The original version of this list was essentially a 'quartermaster's list' with no technical details or notes as to origins etc.

1934 WIMR Numbering	1943 WD Numbering	1956 WD Numbering	Quantity (in 1943)	Remarks
Wagon, flat 8-wheel			1	
31/279	12078	80011		Regd by L&SWR 1/1906
Wagon, semi-well, 8-wheel, RECTANK, 35-ton			19	
	12023	84003		Built MR 1918, Regd by SRly 146/34
	12084	84008		Built L&YR (no date)
	12093	84011		Built L&YR 1918
	12096	84012		Built L&YR 1918
	12099	84014		Built L&YR 1918
178	12102	84016		Built L&YR 1918
	212107*	84029		Built L&YR 1918
	212115*	(84032)		No details, scrapped after Palmers Ball collision, October 1956
	212120*	84034		Built L&YR 1918
	13101	84019		Built L&YR 1918
	13102	84020		Built L&YR 1918
	13103	84021		Built L&YR 1918
172	12008	84000		Built MR (Derby) 1918, Regd by SRly 147/34, Regd by BR --/56
* These 2xxxx numbers arose because these three vehicles were hired by the GWR in 1940 whilst the wagons were located at COD Didcot and were renumbered thus while in GWR service. The 'GWR' numbers were retained when the wagons were returned to the WD and transferred to Longmoor.				
Wagon, semi-well, 8-wheel, RECTANK, 35-ton			6	
174	174**	–		Regd with SRly in 1934
175	175**	84002		Regd with SRly in 1934
180	180**	–		No details, transferred away or scrapped by 1956
181	181**	–		No details, transferred away or scrapped by 1956
184	184**	–		No details, transferred away or scrapped by 1956
194	194**	–		No details, transferred away or scrapped by 1956
** These serials appear to have retained their former WIMR numbers.				
Wagon, 3-plank, open low-sided, 4-wheel			1	
	13000	46278		Fitted 'LNE-E' axle-box covers; later written 'LOCO USE ONLY'
Wagon, low-sided, 8-wheel			4	
30	13104	–		No details, transferred away or scrapped by 1956. Built 1906, Leeds Forge Co. Ltd, vacuum piped when new
31	13105	–		Built 1906, Leeds Forge Co. Ltd
32	13106	80013		Built 1906, Leeds Forge Co. Ltd, Regd by L&SWR 4/1907
33	13107	80012		Built 1906, Leeds Forge Co. Ltd, Regd by L&SWR 3/1906, converted to flat wagon 2/55
Wagons, flat, assorted, 8-wheel (for PWay use)			8	
40	13108	–		Ex-GWR built 1910, MACAW, load 40-tons, registered with SRly No. 152
41	13109	–		ditto, GWR No. 53981, load 40-tons, registered with SRly No. 153
42	(13110)	–		No details
43	(13111)	–		No details
(46)	13112	80016		35-ton RECTANK, built Leeds Forge Co. Ltd 1917, Regd by SRly --/34
13113	80017			Carriage underframe (no additional details), used as a crane runner truck
(48)	13114	–		? Similar to 13113? No details; transferred away or scrapped by 1956
Covered 4-wheel vans of various capacities			14	
2	13116	47758		Built L&YR 1915, 12-ton, Regd by SRly No. 143, fitted with side chains
3(?)	13117	–		Built L&YR 1915, 12-ton, Regd by SRly No. 144, fitted with side chains

1934 WIMR Numbering	1943 WD Numbering	1956 WD Numbering	Quantity (in 1943)	Remarks
Covered 4-wheel vans of various capacities (cont.)				
4	13118	–		Built L&YR 1915, 12-ton; Regd by SRly No. 145, fitted with side chains
7	13119	47753		ex-L&SWR 12-ton
8	13120	47763		ex-L&SWR, Diag. 1410, 10-ton
9	13121	–		ex-L&SWR 12-ton; no details; transferred away or scrapped by 1956
10	13122	47764		ex-MR; Regd by L&SWR 1406/06, 'Breakdown Train Van', 10-ton, grease axle-boxes. Built by S. J. Claye (?)
11	13123	47768		ex-MR, Regd by MR 44134/04, 10-ton, grease axle-boxes. Built by S. J. Claye
12	13124	–		Built by T. Moy, Regd with L&SWR 160/1908, wooden underframe
13	–	–		Scrapped before 1943
14	–	–		Scrapped before 1943
15	13125	47751		ex-L&SWR 'long van', load 10-tons, no details
16	13126	–		ex-L&SWR 'long van', load 10-tons, no details
17	–	–		Scrapped before 1943
18	13127	47769		ex-L&SWR, 'XEN Platelayers', load 8-tons
19	13128	–		ex-L&SWR 8/10-ton(?), written 'XEN ON CALL VAN'
122	13129	47782		To WD in 1915, ex-L&SWR passenger brake van. On MCR (Dinton to Fovant Rly), to WIMR 1920; fitted on WIMR as electric welders' van
12-ton 4-wheel covered vans ex-SRly 1940			8	
-	13130	47761		Former L&SWR, ex-SRly No. 43093
-	13131	nk		Former L&SWR, ex-SRly No. 43085, scrapped by 1956
-	13132	nk		Former L&SWR, ex-SRly No. 43955; written: 'XEN PLATELAYERS'
-	13133	47774		Former L&SWR, ex-SRly No. 44425
-	13134	47755		Former L&SWR, ex-SRly No. 44066
-	13135	nk		Former L&SWR, ex-SRly No. 43694, probably scrapped by 1956
-	13136	nk		Former L&SWR, ex-SRly No. 44020, probably scrapped by 1956
-	13137	47757		Former L&SWR, ex-SRly No. 44040
10- / 12-ton 4-wheel covered vans ex-MR			20	
-	-	47780		Built Derby 1916
-	-	47759		Built Derby, (no date) 'Gen Rep LMS Derby 3-1947'
-	-	47762		Built Derby, (no date)
-	-	47756		Built Derby, (no date) . 'Gen Rep M Bromsgrove 12-1948'
-	-	47766		Built Derby 1914
-	-	47776		Built Derby 1914, LMS 114207 'Gen Rep Derby 7-1948'. 'XEN Platelayers On Call'
-	-	47778		Built Derby, (no date)
-	-	47750		Built Derby, (no date)
-	-	47767		Built Derby, 1915
-	-	nk		Scrapped by 1956, no details
-	-	47781		Built Derby, 1916
-	-	47752		Built Derby, 1915
-	-	47771		Built Derby, 1915, 'Breakdown Van - Packing'
-	-	47760		Built Derby, (no date)
-	-	47779		Built Derby, (no date)
-	-	47773		Built Derby, (no date), the LMR number 47773 appears to have been issued twice
-	-	47754		Built Derby, (no date), the LMR number 47754 appears to have been issued twice
-	-	47770		Built Derby, 1913
-	-	47775		Built Derby, (no date)
-	-	47772		Built Derby, (no date) , BR No. M76071; 'Gen Rep M Bromsgrove 1-1949', 'Breakdown Van – Slings & Chains'
Goods Brake Vans			11	
100	13138	–		20-ton van, Ex-ROD to MCR Catterick then to WIMR c.1922.
101	13139	–		Ex-L&SWR 10-ton 'Road Van', to LMR 1938, replaced original WIMR (ex-MR) van. Scr after collision damage 10/56
102	13140	–		Ex-L&SWR 10-ton 'Road Van', (SRly No. 54936)
103	13141	–		Ex-Taff Vale Rly 10-ton van, ex-GWR 1927, by 1946 in breakdown train
104	13142	–		Ex-Taff Vale Rly 10-ton van, ex-GWR 1927. Scr by 1956
105	13143	–		Ex-NER 9-ton van; Built R. Y. Pickering, ex-L&NER 1932
106	13144	49023		Ex-L&SWR 12-ton van (Diag. D1541); ex-SRly between 1938 and 1943
-	13145	–		Ex-L&SWR 12-ton van (Diag. D1541). To LMR 1943; (SRly No. 54618). Scrapped by 1956
-	13146	–		Ex-L&SWR 12-ton van (Diag. D1541), (SRly No. 54668), Scrapped by 1956
-	13147	82621		Ex-L&SWR 12-ton van (Diag. D1541), (SRly No. 54885); later WD 82621 in weed-killing train
-	13148	-		Ex-L&SWR 10-ton van, (SRly No. 54897), to LMR 1938-1943

1934 WIMR Numbering	1943 WD Numbering	1956 WD Numbering	Quantity (in 1943)	Remarks
Goods Brake Vans (War Increment)			5	
-	13174	-		Ex-NER 9-ton van, (b. 1901), Road Van with top lookout. To LMR 1943
-	13175			No details, 20-ton van, scrapped by 1957
-	13176	-		Ex-L&NWR van, to LMR 1944 (?). No details
-	11004	49020		SRly 25-ton design purchased for WD. Vacuum fitted, Regd by SRly 1011/41
-	11003	49022		SRly 25-ton design purchased for WD. Vacuum fitted, Regd by SRly 1010/41. Initially allocated LMR No. 13176 (in error)
Wagon 4-wheel Flat, Single Bolster			1	
21	13149	-		Original WIMR stock?
Wagons, 4-wheel, Open; High-side				
-	13150 - 13169		20	

The 1943 numbering here is confused. This batch was originally completely omitted from the 1940 stock list. Origins of the wagons are unknown. The entire series with the exception of 13163 had disappeared by 1956.

1934 WIMR Numbering	1943 WD Numbering	1956 WD Numbering	Quantity (in 1943)	Remarks
Wagons, 4-wheel, Flat, Double Bolster			8	
??	13179	-		Ex-WIMR, original number not recorded
??	13180	-		Ex-WIMR, original number not recorded
??	13181	-		Ex-WIMR, original number not recorded
-	13182			MoS No. 602889
-	13183	-		MoS No. 661048
-	13184	-		MoS No. 606758
-	13185	-		MoS No. 605639, written-off after collision in 1943
-	13186	-		MoS No. 610951
-	13187 to 13190			NUMBERS NOT ALLOCATED
Wagons, 4-wheel, Open, Low Drop-side, 8-ton			18	
(1)***	13191	-		
(5)***	13192	-		Ex-GER, rebuilt as drop-side wagon by LMR, tare 5tons. Scrapped by 1956
(6)***	13193	-		No details, scrapped by 1956
(7)***	13194	45064		Ex-NBR
(8)***	13195	-		No details, scrapped by 1956
(116)***	13196	-		Ex-NBR No. 18893, scrapped by 1956
(257)***	13197	-		No details, scrapped by 1956
-	13198	-		MoS No. 634137, scrapped by 1956
-	13199	-		MoS No. 634179, scrapped by 1956
-	13200	-		MoS No. 634029, scrapped by 1956
-	13201	-		MoS No. 634153, scrapped by 1956
-	13202	-		MoS No. 535468, scrapped by 1956
-	13203	45063		MoS No. 706692
-	13204	-		MoS No. 725353 , scrapped by 1956
-	13205	-		MoS No. 714574 , scrapped by 1956
-	13206	'45047'/45067		MoS No. 534926, LMR number written as '45047', number allocated was 45067. Load 10-tons, tare 5ton 10cwt
-	13207			MoS No. 748923, scrapped by 1956.
-	13208	-		MoS No. 764 964, scrapped by 1956

*** These were alleged to be 'old WIMR numbers' but do not match earlier records. It is possible that the numbers were acquired in another WD depot prior to transfer to the LMR.

1934 WIMR Numbering	1943 WD Numbering	1956 WD Numbering	Quantity (in 1943)	Remarks
Wagons, 4-wheel, open, low drop-sided 8-ton			5	

(Probably similar to 13191-13208 above) On delivery this group was incorrectly numbered 13119-13123 in the van series. Amended numbers shown here.

1934 WIMR Numbering	1943 WD Numbering	1956 WD Numbering	Quantity (in 1943)	Remarks
-	13209	-		-
-	13210	45065		To LMR 1943, ex-NBR, no other details.
-	13211	-		To LMR 1943, no details, scrapped by 1956
-	13212	-		To LMR 1943, no details, scrapped by 1956
-	13213	-		To LMR 1943, no details, scrapped by 1956
	13214-13299			NUMBERS NOT ALLOCATED
Wagon, 4-wheel, open, drop-side			1	
-	13300	-		ex-GER, no further information.
	13301-13304			NUMBERS NOT ALLOCATED
Wagons, 4-wheel, open, high-sided			1	
-	13305	-		See 13585-13617 (below)

1934 WIMR Numbering	1943 WD Numbering	1956 WD Numbering	Quantity (in 1943)	Remarks
-	13306-13308			NUMBERS NOT ALLOCATED
Wagons, 4-wheel, open, high-sided			1	
	13309			See 13585-13617 (below)
-	13310-13580			NUMBERS NOT ALLOCATED
Van, 4-wheel, 10-ton			1	
-	13581	47765		Ex-L&NER, no delivery date information. Scrapped by 1963
Coach, 8-wheel, Lav/Brake/3rd			3	
-	13582	5311		Ex-SE&CR No. 1100, SRly No. 3368, part of 3-car set 113 (later SRly Set 552), to LMR Oct 1943
-	13583	5312		Ex-SE&CR No. 1101, SRly No. 3388, part of set 113 (later SRly Set 552), other details as for 13582
Coach, 8-wheel; Lav/Compo				
-	13584	(5205)?		Ex-SE&CR 1093, SRly 5398, part of set 113. Acquired as part of the set in 1943, scrapped in 1956
Wagons, 4-wheel, open, high-sided			38	
151-170	13585			No details, scrapped by 1956
	13586	-		No details, scrapped by 1956
	13587	-		No details, scrapped by 1956
	13588	-		ex-NER, load 10-tons, tare 6ton 10cwt
	13589 to 600	-		No details, scrapped by 1956
	13601	46274		Ex-LB&SCR
-	13602	-		No details, scrapped by 1956
-	13603	46266		
-	13604	-		No details, scrapped by 1956
-	13605	-		No details, scrapped by 1956
-	13606	46275		Ex-LB&SCR?
-	13607 to 12	-		No details, scrapped by 1956
-	13613	46267		
-	13614	-		No details, scrapped by 1956
-	13615	-		No details, scrapped by 1956
-	13616	46269		Ex-LB&SCR No. 3346, SRly No. 22568; load 8-tons, tare 6ton 10cwt
-	13617	-		No details, scrapped by 1956
-	13618	-		No details, scrapped by 1956
-	13619	46270		Ex-MR, 4-plank dropside wagon Regd by MR 67439/11
-	13620	-		No details, scrapped by 1956
-	13621	46268		Ex-MR built by Gittus & Sons, 1911 No. 67235; 12-ton open, low-sided. Numbered incorrectly?
	13622	-		No details, scrapped by 1956
-	13623	46272		Ex-MR 1912 No. 67737; 12-ton open, low-side. Numbered incorrectly?
	13624 to 26	-		No details, scrapped by 1956
-	13627	46276		Ex-MR, no details, built Gittus & Sons
-	13628	-		No details, scrapped by 1956
-	13629	46273		
-	13630	-		No details, scrapped by 1956
-	13631	46277		4-plank dropside 10-ton wagon, Regd by MR 67434/1911, grease axle-boxes, reduced to frame only by 10/5/1970
-	13632	-		No details, scrapped by 1956
-	13633	46279		
-	13634 -37	-		No details, scrapped by 1956
Miscellaneous Vehicles			16	
50 to 64	13638/9	-		No details, but 50, 61, and 62 were 3-plank low-sided wagons, see page 721
	13640	-		8-ton open, low drop-sided
	13641	-		SHUNTERS TRUCK NUMBER 2
	13642	-		SHUNTERS TRUCK NUMBER 1
	13643/4			
-	13645	45066		Ex-GNR, load 10-tons, tare 5ton 6cwt
Nk	13646	45068		Ex-? load 8-tons, tare?; plated 'Rebuilt Longmoor 1925'
-	13647 to 51	-		No details, scrapped by 1956
Nk	13652	-		Ex-? open, low drop-sided. Written-off 10/56, never re-numbered
	13653 to 56	-		No details
66 to 73	13657	45069		Ex-? 10-ton open, low-sided. Plated: 'Rebuilt LMR 1953'. Grease axle- boxes
	13658	46265		No details
	13659/60	-		No details, scrapped by 1956

1934 WIMR Numbering	1943 WD Numbering	1956 WD Numbering	Quantity (in 1943)	Remarks
Miscellaneous Vehicles (cont.)				
75	13661	-		No details, scrapped by 1956
76	13662	-		No details, scrapped by 1956
Wagons, 4-wheel, Cistern (for water)			3	
201	13663	41001		Ex-British Molasses Co. Ltd (PO tank wagon No. 23). Regd by MR 78619/1916. Built by Leeds Forge Co. Ltd. To WIMR by 1930 for use with steam diggers etc.
to	13664	(41002)		As above (No. 25). This may have replaced an earlier (wood framed) cistern
206	13665	41003		As above (No. 26), Regd by MR 78648/1916. Later renumbered 82620 as part of the weed-killing train
Van, 8-wheel, Mobile Workshop			1	
120	13666	-		Ex-ROD mobile workshop c1920, built by Kerr, Stuart & Co. Converted in WIMR Workshop as mobile compressor. Later in Breakdown Train. Out of use by end of World War Two.
	13667 to 89			NUMBERS NOT ALLOCATED
Wagon, 4-wheel, Cistern			1	
Nk	13690	(42117)		Similar to 41002; timber framed.
Coaches, 8-wheel, Ambulance conversion			3 or 4	
-	13691 to 13693 + (?) 13694	-		Ex-L&SWR, converted from 48ft Fruit Van for WD use, based at RVH, Netley. Transferred to US Army when Netley Hospital transferred to their control in 1942. Four vehicles transferred 'from store' to LMR in Feb 1944. Converted for passenger use by LMR and in use until late 1940s. Original L&SWR vehicle numbers: 234, 242, 245, 247 and 274. Former WD No's 2, 3 and 4 definitely transferred to LMR. Possibly one more.
Coaches, 8-wheel (Various configurations)			11	
107	-	5307		Ex-GWR Ambulance conversion; to WIMR ex-BAOR 1930. No brake compartment.
108	-	§		Origin as 107, originally Bk/3rd configuration.
109	-	§		ditto; originally Bk/3rd configuration. Scrapped by 1956.
110	-	-		Ex-K&ESR coach; to WIMR 1909, converted to mobile workshop, destroyed in air raid in 1940.
111	-	-		Ex-K&ESR coach; to WIMR 1909, converted to Inspection Saloon, transferred to 1 (Home) Rly Gp RE at Bicester, 1946.
112	-	§		Ex-GWR Ambulance Coach, to WIMR ex-BAOR 1930. Originally Bk/3rd Corridor.
113	-	5308		Ex-GWR Ambulance Coach
114	-	§		Ex-GWR Ambulance Coach, scrapped by 1956 or very soon after
115	-	-		Ex-GWR Ambulance Coach, gone by 1956, probably not renumbered
116	-	§		Ex-GWR Ambulance Coach, left LMR after 4/56
117	-	5309		Ex-GWR Ambulance Coach; Bk/Compo Corridor

Note § : These coaches were renumbered in 1956 but the individual allocation of numbers was not recorded. For further details see Volume One (p 184).

1934 WIMR Numbering	1943 WD Numbering	1956 WD Numbering	Quantity (in 1943)	Remarks
Coach, 6-wheel, Saloon			1	
-		3005		Ex-L&NWR, LMS No. 45021 (aka ED 33). To Melbourne Mil Rly 1940, transferred to LMR 1945 but not initially numbered in LMR stock.
Coaches, 8-wheel, Saloon			2	
118	-	3006		Ex-SE&CR No. 177, SRly 7913. To LMR 1938
119	-	3007		Ex-L&SWR No. 11, SRly 7803. Movements as for 118 above
Coaches 12-wheel, Compartment			4	
120	-	-		Ex-Caledonian Rly No. 1281, LMS Nos 17337/24316. Bk/3rd; to LMR 1940
121	-	-		Ex-CR No. 125, LMS Nos 16198/15552. All 3rd. To LMR 1940
122	-	-		Ex-CR No. 1315, LMS Nos 17371/15551. All 3rd. To LMR 1940. Grounded as hut (5/56)
123	-	-		Ex-CR No. 1328, LMS Nos 17384/24311. Bk/3rd. To LMR 1940. Scr 7/56
Wagons, 12-wheel Gun Truck			9	
-	-	-		These vehicles (surplus to requirements) were allocated to the LMR in 1944, stripped of their 9.2-inch Breech Loading Guns and intended to form heavy trains for long-distance training for loco crews prior to deployment to NW Europe. No LMR numbers were allocated and all were withdrawn by 1949.
Van, 8-wheel, Miscellaneous			1	
-	PB1	-		Ex-GNR (originally ECJS) 3rd Class coach to Diag. 19). Arrived at LMR during WW2, possibly after previous departmental use by L&NER and transfer to a UK-based Rly Const Coy RE. Formed part of the LMR Breakdown Train.

APPENDIX TWENTY-ONE
LMR ROLLING STOCK – 1956 NUMBERING SERIES

This Appendix lists all LMR rolling stock known to have been included in the 1956 WD-wide renumbering scheme. At no time was any official attempt made to record the origins or provenance of individual vehicles. Individual attempts to record such information were made by dedicated enthusiasts from the late 1950s, culminating in a brave effort by members of the RCTS to complete a comprehensive survey during their two visits to the LMR in 1966. Thereafter, as the run-down of the LMR gained pace, many vehicles 'disappeared', some locally for scrap, others for further use on other UK military railways. The symbol '†' beside a number indicates that the vehicle was no longer present at Longmoor during the 1966 survey. Where known, an outline of such vehicles later history is given.

| 41001 | Cistern | Leeds Forge Co. Ltd | 1916 |

Built for Ministry of Munitions (MoM). Regd MR 78619/1916. To British Molasses Co. Ltd, became No. 23. To LMR, 1940, number unknown, became WD 13663 in 1943 series and AD 41001 in 1956 series. Renumbered, sold or scrapped by 1968, as number reallocated to new 24-ton PALVAN built by Gloucester RC&WCo. (TOPS PVB, 6800).

| 41002† | Cistern | Leeds Forge Co. Ltd | 1916 |

Ex-British Molasses Co. Ltd, No. 25. To LMR, 1940, number unknown, became WD 13664 in 1943 series, allocated AD 41002 in 1956 series. Timber framed wagon. Renumbered, sold or scrapped by 1968, as number reallocated to new 24-ton PALVAN built by Gloucester RC&WCo. (TOPS PVB, 6801).

| 41003 | Cistern | Leeds Forge Co. Ltd | 1916 |

Ex-British Molasses Co. Ltd, No. 26. Regd by MR 78618/16. To LMR, 1940, number unknown, became WD 13665 in 1943 series and AD 41003 in 1956 series. Renumbered c1968 as 82620. Old number reallocated to new 24-ton PALVAN built by Gloucester RC&WCo. (TOPS PVB, 6802).

| 42047 | Ramp | SRly Ashford | 1941 |

New as WD-FVR-47. Regd SRly 933/1941. To LMR, date unknown but possibly 27/04/1956, became AD 42047 in 1956 series; to CVD Ludgershall, prior to 16/10/1985; allocated TOPS 95000, date unknown. For sale from CVD Ludgershall, 10/07/1997. Fate unknown.

| 42117 | Cistern | Leeds Forge Co. Ltd | 1916 |

Built for Ministry of Munitions (MoM). To LMR, date unknown. Timber framed wagon. Sold as part of Lot 6. Fate unknown.

| 42118 | Cistern | Leeds Forge Co. Ltd | 1916 |

Built for Ministry of Munitions (MoM). To LMR, date unknown. Unsold as part of Lot 6. Still on site in 1970. Fate unknown

| '45047' | 10-ton 3-plank open dropside | Not known | Not known |

Number wrongly applied to AD 45067, (qv).

| 45063† | 8-ton 3-plank open dropside | Not known | ?1940? |

MoS No 706692. To LMR, -/1941; became WD 13203, became AD 45063 in 1956 series. Fate unknown.

| 45064 | 8-ton 3-plank open dropside | NBR | Not known |

To LMR, 1940-43; became WD 13203 and then AD 45064 in 1956 series. GCR or GER buffers, sources vary. Fate unknown.

| 45065 | 8-ton 3-plank open dropside | NBR | Not known |

To LMR, 02/1943, as WD 13210, became AD 45065 in 1956 series. Fate unknown.

| 45066 | 10-ton 3-plank open dropside | GNR | Not known |

Ex-GNR. To WIMR, date unknown, WIMR number not known (but was between 50 and 64), became WD 13645 in 1943 series, became AD 45066 in 1956 series; rebuilt by LMR, 11/1954. Fate unknown.

| 45067† | 10-ton 3-plank open dropside | NBR | Not known |

MoS No 534926. To LMR, 1940-43, as WD 13206, became AD 45067 in 1956 series but 'AD 45047' incorrectly applied. Fate unknown.

| 45068† | Open high sided | Not known | Not known |

Origin unknown. To WIMR, date unknown, WIMR No. not known (but was between 66 and 73), became WD 13646 in 1943 series and AD 45068 in 1956 series; plated 'Rebuilt Longmoor 1925'. Fate unknown.

| 45069 | Open high sided | Not known | Not known |

Origin unknown. To WIMR, date unknown, WIMR No. not known (but was between 50 and 64), became WD 13657 in 1943 series and AD 45069 in 1956 series; rebuilt LMR -/1953. Grease axle boxes. Fate unknown.

| 46265† | 10-ton open low sided | Not known | Not known |

Origin unknown. To LMR, date unknown, as WD 13658, became AD 46265 in 1956 series; to OESD Yardley Chase prior to 24/08/1978. Fate unknown.

| 46266† | Open high sided | Not known | Not known |

Origin unknown. To LMR, date unknown, as WD 13603, became AD 46266 in 1956 series. Fate unknown.

| 46267† | Open high sided | Not known | Not known |

Origin unknown. To LMR, date unknown, as WD 13613, became AD 46267 in 1956 series. Fate unknown.

| 46268† | 8-ton open high sided | Not known | Not known |

Ex-Private Owner. Regd. MR 67235/1911 for Luke Nichols of Ibstock Colliery, Leicestershire but as a 10-tonner. Built by Thomas Hunter of Rugby. To LMR, date unknown, as WD 13621, became AD 46268 in 1956 series; grease axle-boxes. Fate unknown.

| 46269 | 10-ton open 'Hi-Bar' | LB&SCR | 1914 |

Ex-LB&SCR 3346, SRly 22568. LB&SCR Diag. 29, SRly Diag. 1366. To LMR, date unknown (1940-43), as WD 13616, became AD 46269 in 1956 series; original rounded ends squared by LMR Workshops, sold as part of Lot 5. To Bluebell Railway, date unknown. Preserved with rounded ends restored.

| 42670 | Open high sided | MR | Not known |

Origin unknown. Regd. MR 67439/1911. To WIMR, date unknown, later as WD 13619, became AD 46270 in 1956 series; sold as part of Lot 5. Fate unknown.

| 46271 | Open (no other details) | Not known | Not known |

Origin unknown. To LMR, date unknown; sold as part of Lot 5. Reduced to frame only by 1971. Fate unknown.

| 46272 | 10-ton Open high sided | North Central Wagon Co. Ltd, Rotherham | Not known |

Ex-Private Owner. Regd, MR 67737/1912 for the Buxton Lime Firms, shown in register as being built by William Gittus of Penistone, Yorkshire. Probably financed by North Central Wagon Co. To LMR, date unknown, as WD 13623, became AD 46272 in 1956 series. Fate unknown.

46273 Open high sided — Not known — Not known
Origin unknown. To LMR, date unknown, as WD 13629, became AD 46273 in 1956 series. Fate unknown.

46274 12-ton Open high sided — LB&SCR — 1914
Ex-LB&SCR/SRly as per 46269 (above). To LMR, date unknown (1940-43), as WD 13601, became AD 46274 in 1956 series. To Bluebell Railway following closure but no longer recorded there.

46275† 8-ton Open high sided — Not known — Not known
Ex-LB&CSR. To LMR, date unknown, as WD 13606, became AD 46275 in 1956 series. Fate unknown.

46276† Open high sided — Not known — Not known
Origin unknown. To LMR, date unknown (1940-43), as WD 13627, became AD 46276 in 1956 series. Fate unknown.

46277 Open high sided — Not known — Not known
Origin unknown. To LMR, date unknown (1940-43), as WD 13631, became AD 46277 in 1956 series. Fate unknown.

46278 3-plank open — Not known — Not known
Origin unknown. To LMR, date unknown (1940-43), as WD 13000, became AD 46278 in 1956 series; fitted with 'LNE-E' oil axle boxes; repainted in 1961 and lettered as 'LOCO USE ONLY'; sold as part of Lot 5. Fate unknown.

46279 Open — Not known — Not known
Ex-Private Owner. Regd. MR 67436/1911 for the Buxton Lime Firms, shown in register as being built by William Gittus of Penistone, Yorkshire. To LMR, date unknown, as WD 13633, became AD 46279 in 1956 series. Fate unknown.

47075† 12-ton van (Diag. 1/208) — Chas. Roberts & Co., Wakefield — 1959
New to LMR as AD 47075, to CVD Ludgershall date unknown (but before 1966), to COD Bicester, date unknown; became WGB 4067, date unknown. Noted at Bicester, 22/06/1992. Fate unknown.

47076 12-ton van (Diag. 1/208) — Chas. Roberts & Co., Wakefield — 08/1959
New to LMR as AD 47076, to COD Bicester, date unknown, became WGB 4068, date unknown, noted at Bicester 11/06/1996. Fate unknown.

47077 12-ton van (Diag. 1/208) — Chas. Roberts & Co., Wakefield — 08/1959
New to LMR as AD 47077, to COD Bicester, date unknown, became WGB 4069, date unknown, noted at Bicester 22/06/1992. Now preserved as WGB 4069 by Somerset & Dorset Rly Heritage Trust, Midsomer Norton.

47078 12-ton van (Diag. 1/208) — Chas. Roberts & Co., Wakefield — 08/1959
New to LMR as AD 47078, to COD Bicester, date unknown, became WGB 4070, date unknown, noted at Bicester 22/06/1992. Fate unknown.

47079 12-ton van (Diag. 1/208) — Chas. Roberts & Co., Wakefield — 1959
New to LMR as AD 47079, fate unknown.

47080† 12-ton van (Diag. 1/208) — Chas. Roberts & Co., Wakefield — 1959
New to LMR as AD 47080, moved before 1966, fate unknown.

47081 12-ton van (Diag. 1/208) — Chas. Roberts & Co., Wakefield — 1959
New to LMR as AD 47081, fate unknown.

47082 12-ton van (Diag. 1/208) — Chas. Roberts & Co., Wakefield — 1959
New to LMR as AD 47082, fate unknown.

47083 12-ton van (Diag. 1/208) — Chas. Roberts & Co., Wakefield — 1959
New to LMR as AD 47083, fate unknown.

47084 12-ton van (Diag. 1/208) — Chas. Roberts & Co., Wakefield — 1959
New to LMR as AD 47084, fate unknown.

47750† Van — MR Derby — Not known
To LMR, date unknown, converted to flat by 17/10/1966. Fate unknown.

47751 10-ton van — L&SWR — Not known
To LMR, date unknown. Numbered WD 13125 in 1943. Fate unknown.

47752† Van — MR Derby — 1915
To LMR, date unknown. Fate unknown.

47753† 12-ton (?) van — L&SWR — Not known
Origin unknown, to LMR, date unknown. Fate unknown.

47754 10-ton van — L&SWR — Not known
Diag. 1410. To LMR, date unknown. Sold as part of Lot 7 to East Somerset Railway, 1970, to Somerset & Dorset Heritage Trust; ESR website states 'Due to poor condition, it was deemed beyond economical repair and so was scrapped in May 2005'.

47755† 10-ton van — L&SWR — Not known
L&SWR number unknown, SRly 44066. To LMR, date unknown. Fate unknown.

47756† Van — MR Derby — Not known
To LMR, date unknown, to CAD Longtown, before 1969, for sale Tender No. 5399, date due 10/12/1981, reference D/Sales(S) 6/29/1/40. Fate unknown.

47757 10-ton Van — L&SWR — Not known
L&SWR number unknown, SRly 44040. To LMR, date unknown. Fate unknown.

47758† 12-ton Insulated van — L&YR Newton Heath — 1915
L&YR Diag. 97. Built for War Office for overseas service, fitted with side chains. Regd. SRly 143/1915(?). To WIMR, date unknown (c1920), became WIMR 2, then WD 13116 in 1943 series and AD 47758 in 1956 series. Renumbered, sold or scrapped prior to 06/1963 when number applied to new PALVAN built by Standard Railway Wagon Co. Fate unknown.

47759 Van VANFIT — MR Derby — Not known
To LMR, date unknown. To Diag. D633; Fitted with 3ft 7in. dia. wheels for passenger traffic. Fate unknown.

47760 10-ton Van — MR Derby — Not known
Diag. D664. To LMR, date unknown. Sold as part of Lot 7 to East Somerset Railway, date unknown. Status unknown.

47761†   Van   L&SWR   Not known

L&SWR number unknown, SRly No. 43093; to LMR, date unknown, became AD 47761 in 1956 series. Retained for re-railing use only by 5/3/66. Number applied to new PALVAN built by Standard Railway Wagon Co. in 6/1963. Fate unknown.

47762†   Van   MR Derby   Not known

Origin unknown. To LMR, date unknown. Fate unknown.

47763   10-ton van   L&SWR   Not known

Diag. 1410. To LMR, date unknown, converted to flat wagon, by 27/10/1966, but not renumbered. Sold as part of Lot 7 to East Somerset Railway, 1970, arriving 12/1973. Since scrapped.

47764   Van   S. J. Claye, Long Eaton, Derbyshire   Not known

Ex-MR. Regd. L&SWR 1406/1906 (probably part of original WIMR purchase), grease axle-boxes. To WIMR, c1906 date unknown. Sold as part of Lot 7, purchased by Bulleid Pacific Pres. Society (BPPS), date unknown, to East Somerset Railway, date unknown, later scrapped.

47765†   10-ton van   Not known   Not known

Ex-L&NER. To LMR, date unknown (1940-43), as WD 13581, became AD 47765 in 1956 series. Renumbered, sold or scrapped prior to 06/1963 when number applied to new PALVAN built by Standard Railway Wagon Co. Fate unknown.

47766†   Van   MR Derby   Not known

To LMR, date unknown. Renumbered, sold or scrapped prior to 06/1963 when number applied to new PALVAN built by Standard Railway Wagon Co. Fate unknown.

47767   10-ton van   MR Derby   1915

MR Diag. D664. To LMR, date unknown. Fate unknown.

47768†   10-ton van   S. J. Claye, Long Eaton, Derbyshire   Not known

Ex-Private Owner. Regd. MR 44134/1904 for Wallace & Son, London. Grease axle-boxes. To WIMR, date unknown. Fate unknown.

47769†   8-ton van   L&SWR   Not known

To LMR, date unknown, lettered 'XEN PLATELAYERS VAN'. Fate unknown.

47770   10-ton van   MR Derby   1913

MR Diag. D664. To LMR, date unknown, to OESD Yardley Chase, prior to 24/08/1978. To Colne Valley Railway, date unknown. Fate unknown.

47771†   Van   MR Derby   1913

To LMR, date unknown, lettered 'BREAKDOWN VAN-PACKING'. Fate unknown.

47772†   Van   LMS Derby   Not known

Ex-BR M76071? To LMR, date unknown, moved to CAD Kineton before 1966, on disposal list dated 05/10/1981, for disposal from CAD Kineton to Bird's Commercial Motors Ltd, Long Marston, Worcestershire, as per Army Form G 3658 dated 02/04/1982.

47773   10-ton van   L&SWR   Not known

L&SWR Diag. 1410. To LMR, date unknown, for sale as part of Lot 7, 1970, purchased by BPPS, 1970, used at Liss, resold to Bluebell Railway, repainted as L&SWR 2773, preserved.

47774   10-ton meat van   SRly Eastleigh   1924

L&SWR Diag. 1408. Allocated No. 9128, but not built until after the Grouping, became SRly 44425. To LMR, date unknown. Sold to Longmoor Steam Railway, 05/1970, to East Somerset Railway, 11/1973, preserved in L&SWR livery as No. 9128. Transferred to S&DHT, Midsomer Norton, on static display.

47775(?)†   Van   MR Derby   Not known

Origin unknown. To LMR, date unknown. When photographed on 16/04/1966, by H. C. Casserley, it was incorrectly numbered AD 47763, the 'genuine' 47763 was nearby. Fate unknown.

47776   10-ton van   MR Derby   1914

MR Diag. D664. MR number unknown, LMS No. 14207. To LMR, date unknown; lettered 'XEN PLATELAYERS-ON CALL'. Fate unknown.

47777   12-ton van   SRly   1940

SRly Diag. 1458. SRly No. 49471. Paired plank body. Regd. SRly 1170/1942. To LMR, date unknown, in use as Tool Van, 04/1967, lettered 'XEN PLATELAYERS', to Marchwood, prior to closure of LMR. Sold to Mid-Hants Railway, date unknown, restored as SRly No. 49471. Originally formed part of 'Mobile Workshop Train 10(S)', preserved.

47778†   Van   MR Derby   Not known

Origin unknown. To LMR, date unknown. Fate unknown.

47779†   12-ton van   MR or LMS Derby   Not known

To LMR, date unknown. Sold or scrapped prior to 06/1963 when number applied to new PALVAN built by Standard Railway Wagon Co.

47780†   10 or 12-ton van   MR Derby   1916

To LMR, date unknown. Fate unknown

47781   8-ton van   MR Derby   1916

MR Diag. D664. To LMR, date unknown. Fate unknown.

47782   22ft Passenger Brake Van   L&SWR   1883

Diag. DB97. L&SWR number believed to be 5047. Sold to WD, 1915 (after initial loan) for use on Fovant Military Railway, to WIMR c1920, renumbered 122, became WD 13129 in 1943 series and AD 47782 in 1956 series. Fate unknown.

47783   12-ton van   SRly   1940

SRly No. 49754, Diag. 1458. Regd. SRly 1043/1942. To LMR, 30/08/1957, to COD Morton-on-Lugg, 08/07/1970, to ROF Glascoed, 26/04/1971, to COD Bicester, 13/11/1974, to Marchwood, date unknown, became WGB 4272, date unknown. Believed to be awaiting restoration.

47784   12-ton van   SRly   1940

SRly No. 49917, Diag. 1458. Regd. SRly 1050/1942. To LMR, date unknown c1957, redeployed by 1 Rly Gp RCT following closure of LMR, to COD Bicester, from unknown location, 19/9/1984. Fate unknown.

47785   12-ton van   SRly   1940

SRly No. 49572, Diag. 1458. Regd. SRly 1047/1942. To LMR, date unknown c1957, to COD Bicester, for sale Tender No. 5940, Lot 32, date due 14/03/1985, reference D/Sales Support 6/29/1/52. Fate unknown.

47786   12-ton van   SRly   1940

SRly No. 47086, Diag. 1458. Regd. SRly 1133/1943. To LMR, date unknown c1957. Fate unknown.

47794   12-ton van   SRly   1940

SRly No. 49676, Diag. 1458. Regd. SRly 1044/1942. To LMR, date unknown c1957. Re-deployed after closure of LMR by 1 Rly Gp RCT, later to Cambrian Heritage Railways, date unknown. Preserved on static display.

47795   12-ton Ventilated Van   SRly Ashford   1940

SRly No. 49703, Diag. 1458. Regd. SRly 1044/1942. To LMR date unknown c1957. To Shackerstone Railway, date unknown. Preserved.

49010†   25-ton Goods Brake Van   SRly Ashford   1942

New as WD 11035, SRly Diag. 1579, Lot No. 1852. Regd. SRly 1021/1942. To LMR, date unknown (1942?), to RNAD Bedenham, -/1969. Sold to J. J. Smith and delivered to SVR, 10/07/1990. Parts from SRly 55577 used in its restoration, renumbered and restored as 55577.

49020   25-ton Goods Brake Van   SRly Ashford   1941

New as WD 11004, SRly Diag. 1579, Lot No. 1852. Regd. SRly 1011/1941. On closure of LMR to COD Bicester 08/09/1969, became WGM 4802, date unknown, still in use in 2012 (according to WW2RSG Bulletin Vol. 22, No. 3).

49021†   25-ton Goods Brake Van   SRly   Not known

New to WD. SRly Diag. 1458. To LMR, date unknown. Redeployed prior to 1966.

49022   25-ton Goods Brake Van   SRly Ashford   1941

New as WD 11003, SRly Diag. 1579, Lot No. 1852. Regd. SRly 1010/1941. To LMR by 1956. Sold to Ivatt Loco Trust, 1969, on K&ESR restored and painted as fictional SRly 56495 in 1982, overhauled and re-entered service in 2006 in BR livery as fictional M320327.

49023†   Goods Brake Van   L&SWR   Not known

SRly Diag. 1541. To LMR, date unknown. May have been re-designated as a maintenance vehicle – see 82621

49025   20-ton Goods Brake Van   L&NWR Earlestown   1921

L&NWR Diag. 17B. Delivered to L&YR in anticipation of 1923 Grouping, became L&YR No. 5945, then LMS No. 135945. To LMR, 1957. Sold as part of Lot 9 to K&ESR and stored at Bodiam, into traffic in 1979, deteriorated badly whilst out of use, undergoing extensive overhaul.

49026   20-ton Goods Brake Van   L&NWR Earlestown   Not known

L&NWR Diag.17B. Date of construction, together with the L&NWR and LMS Nos, unknown. To LMR, 1957. Sold as part of Lot 8 to East Somerset Railway, 1970, withdrawn in 1986 for major repairs, declared to be beyond economical repair (BER) in 2005 and scrapped.

49027   20-ton Goods Brake Van   Standard Railway Wagon Co., Stockport   1959

New to LMR. To BR Diag. 1/506, sold as part of Lot 8 to East Somerset Railway, 1970, to Bluebell Railway then c1996 to East Kent Rly and awaiting restoration.

49028   20-ton Goods Brake Van   Standard Railway Wagon Co., Stockport   1959

New to LMR. To BR Diag. 1/506, sold as part of Lot 8 to East Somerset Railway, 1970, preserved as 'B49028'.

62006   45-ton Steam Crane   Ransome & Rapier F5937/49   1942

New, WD 214. To LMR, date unknown during World War Two; transferred to Marchwood c1967 for trade training of Heavy Crane Operators; later to COD Bicester, date unknown, converted to diesel, date unknown, sold to Gloucestershire & Warwickshire Railway, c1992. Preserved.

62201†   Steam Crane   Brownhoist   1943

Ex-USATC, No. 4 Special Steam Crane with 20 (short) ton capacity. To LMR, c1945 as 8416, became AD 62201 in 1956 series, to Marchwood by 1966. Fate unknown.

62600   Breakdown Van   SRly   1934

SRly No. 2198, Regd SRly 1053/1942. Formed part of Mobile Railway Workshop No. 11. To LMR, date unknown. Fate unknown.

62601   Breakdown Van   SE&CR   1922

SE&CR No. 2008, Regd. SRly 1131/1943. Formed part of Mobile Railway Workshop No. 10. To LMR, date unknown. Fate unknown.

63049   25-ton Crane   Thomas Smith & Sons (Rodley) Ltd (25512 No. 15)   c1962

To LMR new, to Bicester Workshops on closure of LMR to Marchwood, 23/05/1970, to COD Hilsea, date unknown, to REME Aldershot, date unknown, to P&EE Eskmeals, date unknown, to COD Bicester, 26/05/1988, sold to Gloucestershire & Warwickshire Railway after 15/05/1990. Preserved.

80011   30-ton flat   Leeds Forge Co. Ltd   1906

New to WIMR (No. 30 or 31). Fox's Patent bogies. Regd. L&SWR No. 1/1906. Became WIMR 279 in 1934, WD 12076 in 1943 and AD 80011 in 1956. Fate unknown.

80012   30-ton flat   Leeds Forge Co. Ltd   1906

New to WIMR (No. 33), Regd. L&SWR 4/1907. Renumbered WD 13107 in 1943 series and AD 80012 in 1956 series. Fate unknown.

80013†   30-Ton flat   Leeds Forge Co. Ltd   1906

New to WIMR (No. 32); Regd. L&SWR 3/1906. Renumbered WD 13106 in 1943 series and AD 80013 in 1956 series; converted from drop-side to 30-Ton Flat, 02/1955 (by permanently removing the drop-sides). Fate unknown.

80016   40-ton flat   Leeds Forge Co. Ltd   1917

Regd. SRly 156/1934. To LMR, c1935-39, allocated No. 46 (but believed not carried), became WD 13112 in 1943 series and AD 80016 in 1956 series. At LMR until closure, then moved to Marchwood. Declared 'BER' there after 08/1984. Fate unknown.

80017†   Crane Runner   Not known   Not known

Coach underframe of unknown origin, converted to crane runner at Longmoor. To LMR before World War Two, allocated 47 (but believed not carried), became WD 13113 in 1943 series and AD 80017 in 1956 series. Fate unknown.

80018   Flat   GER?   Not known

Match Truck to Brownhoist Crane and later to 63049. To WIMR, (No. 121) date unknown, became WD 13115 in 1943 series and AD 80018 in 1956 series, to Bicester, date unknown, to Marchwood, 23/05/1970, to COD Hilsea, date unknown, to REME Aldershot, date unknown, to P&EE Eskmeals, date unknown; to Bicester, 26/05/1988. Sold to Gloucestershire & Warwickshire Railway after 15/05/1990. Preserved.

80106   WARFLAT   Metropolitan Cammell   1940

To LMR 1957, (formerly WD FVF 11) as AD 80106, to Bicester on closure of LMR, 28/11/1969, to CAD Kineton, 31/10/1972, became WGF 8110, 18/08/1987. In 1997 noted still carrying plate AD 80106. Fate unknown.

80107   WARFLAT   Metropolitan Cammell   1940

To LMR (formerly WD FVF12) 13/11/1957, as AD 80107, as for 80106 above, became WGF 8109. Fate unknown.

80112   WARFLAT   Metropolitan Cammell   1940

To LMR 1957, (formerly WD FVF 19), as AD 80112, as for 80106/7 above, became WGF 8106. Fate unknown.

| 80113 | WARFLAT | Metropolitan Cammell | 1940 |

To LMR 1957, (formerly WD FVF 20), as AD 80113, as for 80106/7/12 above, became WGF 8080. Later purchased by West Somerset Rly and preserved.

| 80275 | WARFLAT | Metropolitan Cammell | 1940 |

To LMR 1957, (formerly WD 300, not an LMR number), as AD 80275, as for 80106/7/12/13 above, became WGF 8108. This vehicle had been widened and strengthened as for AD WARFLATS used in BAOR. Fate unknown.

| 82620 | Cistern | Leeds Forge Co. Ltd | 1916 |

At LMR, date unknown, used in weed-killing train. Similar to Nos 41001/3 and may indeed have been 41003 re-classified. Sold to East Somerset Railway as part of Lot 6 in 1970, tank removed and underframe converted to shunters' runner and match truck for Dubs crane tank No. 4101. Later was converted into a rolling chassis to store jib of Grafton crane No. 1540. Preserved.

| 82621 | Goods Brake Van | L&SWR | 1900 |

L&SWR No. 12424, SRly Diag. 1541; SRly No. 54885. To LMR date unknown, used in weed-killing train. Sold to East Somerset Railway as part of Lot 6 in 1970, to Somerset & Dorset Railway Trust, 1988, rebuilt, late 1990s. Preserved.

| 82691 | Hopper | Metropolitan Cammell | 1936 |

LMS Diag. D1941, LMS Lot No. 967, 1936. LMS No. not known. To LMR, date unknown. Fate unknown.

| 82692 | Hopper | Metropolitan Cammell | 1934 |

To LMR, date unknown. Fate unknown.

| 83063 | WARWELL | Gloucester RC&WCo. | 1944 |

New as WD 14067. Regd. LMS 1119/1944. To LMR, date unknown but after 04/1956. Became AD 83063 in 1956 series, date unknown, TOPS 95539, date unknown. Fate unknown.

| 83077 | WARWELL | Gloucester RC&WCo. | 1944 |

New as WD 14100. Regd. LMS 1152/1944. To LMR, date unknown but after 04/1956. Became AD 83077 in 1956 series, date unknown, TOPS 95549, date unknown. Fate unknown.

| 83100 | WARWELL | Head Wrightson | 1944 |

New as WD 14154. Regd. LMS 1031/1944. To LMR, date unknown but after 04/1956. Became AD 83100 in 1956 series, date unknown, TOPS 95564, date unknown. Fate unknown.

| 83109 | WARWELL | Head Wrightson | 1944 |

New as WD 14168. Regd. LMS 1045/1944. To LMR, date unknown but after 04/1956. Became AD 83109 in 1956 series, date unknown, TOPS 95572, date unknown. Fate unknown.

| 84000† | 35-ton RECTANK | MR Derby | 1918 |

Regd. SRly 147/1934. To WIMR, date unknown, became 172, WD 12008 in 1943 series and AD 84000 in 1956 series. Departed LMR before 1966, to Bicester, date unknown, to P&EE Eskmeals prior to 1981. For sale in 1981 and later moved to Brechin Railway, Brechin, Angus. Preserved.

| 84002† | 35-ton RECTANK | L&YR Newton Heath | 1918 |

Regd. SRly in 1934. To WIMR date unknown, departed from LMR before 1966. Later to P&EE Eskmeals, date unknown. For sale in 1981. Fate unknown.

| 84003† | 35-ton RECTANK | MR Derby | 1918 |

Diag. D1095, Lot No. 931. WD/GB No. 12023. To WIMR, probably before 1934, to Marchwood by 1956, became AD 84003 in 1956 series, to Long Marston prior to 22/06/1981, for sale in 1981. Purchased by Gloucestershire & Warwickshire Railway, 1981, moved to West Somerset Railway, 1986. Preserved.

| 84008† | 35-ton RECTANK | L&YR Newton Heath | 1918 |

(Formerly WD/GB 12084, not an LMR number). To WIMR, probably before 1934, to MMR, by 1956, became AD 84008 in 1956 series, for sale in 1981. Fate unknown.

| 84011 | 35-ton RECTANK | L&YR Newton Heath | 1918 |

(Formerly WD/GB 12093, not an LMR number). To LMR, after 1943, probably loaned. AD 84011 in 1956 series, redeployed by 1 Rly Gp RCT on closure of LMR and moved to Marchwood, prior to 23/07/1977, for sale in 1981. Fate unknown.

| 84012 | 35-ton RECTANK | L&YR Newton Heath | 1918 |

(Formerly WD/GB 12096, not an LMR number). To LMR, after 1943, probably loaned. Became AD 84012 in 1956 series, redeployed on closure of LMR by 1 Rly Gp RCT to Marchwood. For sale in 1981. Fate unknown.

| 84014 | 35-ton RECTANK | L&YR Newton Heath | 1918 |

(Formerly WD/GB 12099, not an LMR number). To LMR, after 1943, probably loaned. Became AD 84014 in 1956 series. Redeployed on closure of LMR by 1 Rly Gp RCT to Marchwood. Then to Bicester, prior to 10/12/1981 and for sale. Fate unknown.

| 84016 | 35-ton RECTANK | L&YR Newton Heath | 1918 |

(Formerly WD/GB 12102, not an LMR number). To LMR, after 1943, probably loaned, became AD 84016 in 1956 series, redeployed on closure of LMR by 1 Rly Gp RCT to Marchwood. Remained lettered 'LMR' and fitted with plate stating 'RETURN TO BORDON LMR', (plate removed by 22/07/1978), for sale in 1981. Fate unknown.

| 84019 | 35-ton RECTANK | L&YR Newton Heath | 1918 |

(Formerly WD/GB 13101, not an LMR number). To LMR, after 1943, probably loaned. Became WD 13101 in 1943 series. Became AD 84019 in 1956 series, redeployed on closure of LMR by 1 Rly Gp RCT to Marchwood. To Bicester, prior to 10/12/1981 for sale. Fate unknown.

| 84020† | 35-ton RECTANK | L&YR Newton Heath | 1918 |

(Formerly WD/GB 13102, not an LMR number). To LMR, running as WD 13102, from date unknown, became AD 84020 in 1956 series. Departed Longmoor before 1966. Fate unknown.

| 84021 | 35-ton RECTANK | L&YR Newton Heath | 1918 |

(Formerly WD/GB 13103, not an LMR number). To LMR, running as WD 13103, from date unknown, became AD 84021 in 1956 series, redeployed on closure of LMR by 1 Rly Gp RCT to Marchwood. To Bicester, prior to 1981 when offered for sale. Fate unknown.

| 84029 | 35-ton RECTANK | L&YR Newton Heath | 1918 |

Original WD/GB No. 12107, however, was hired to GWR from COD Didcot in 1940 and was renumbered 212107 by GWR, it continued to carry this number until renumbered AD 84029 in the 1956 series. To LMR, date unknown but prior to 1966, redeployed on closure of LMR by 1 Rly Gp RCT to Marchwood by 1978, for sale in 1981. Fate unknown.

| (84032)† | 35-ton RECTANK | L&YR Newton Heath | 1918 |

Original WD/GB No. 12115, however, was hired to GWR from COD Didcot in 1940 and was renumbered 212115 by GWR, it continued to carry this number until renumbered in the 1956 series to AD 84032. To LMR, date unknown, scrapped after collision in 1956.

| 84034 | 35-Ton RECTANK | L&YR Newton Heath | 1918 |

Original WD/GB No. 12120; however, was hired to GWR from COD Didcot in 1940 and was renumbered 212120 by GWR, it continued to carry this number until renumbered AD 84034 in the 1956 series. To LMR, date unknown, redeployed on closure of LMR by 1 Rly Gp RCT to CAD Kineton, date unknown, for disposal from CAD Kineton to Bird's Commercial Motors Ltd, Long Marston, Worcestershire, in 1982.

| 107 | (Corridor) Brake Third* | GWR | Not known |

Ex-GWR Ambulance Coach, converted at Swindon in 1915 for BEF 'Continental Ambulance Trains', adapted for use in BAOR leave trains, to WIMR as 107, 1929, became AD 3321 in 1956 series. Fate unknown.

| 108 | (Corridor) Third* | GWR | Not known |

Ex-GWR Ambulance Coach, converted at Swindon in 1915 for BEF 'Continental Ambulance Trains', adapted for use in BAOR leave trains in 1919, to WIMR as 108, 1929, retained old WIMR number until it became AD 5307 in 1956 series, to Marchwood, date unknown, fate unknown.

| 109 | (Corridor) Brake Third* | GWR | Not known |

Ex-GWR Ambulance Coach, converted at Swindon in 1915 for BEF 'Continental Ambulance Trains', adapted for use in BAOR leave trains, to WIMR as 107, 1929; retained old WIMR number. 1956 series number unknown. Fate unknown.

| 112 | (Corridor) Brake Third* | GWR | Not known |

Ex-GWR Ambulance Coach, converted at Swindon in 1915 for BEF 'Continental Ambulance Trains', adapted for use in BAOR leave trains in 1919, to WIMR as 112, 1929; retained old WIMR number. 1956 series number unknown. Fate unknown.

| 113 | (Corridor) Brake Third* | GWR | Not known |

Ex-GWR Ambulance Coach, converted at Swindon in 1915 for BEF 'Continental Ambulance Trains', adapted for use in BAOR leave trains in 1919, to WIMR as 113, 1929, retained old WIMR number until becoming AD 5308 in 1956 series. To Marchwood (as office), 1969. Fate unknown.

| 116 | (Corridor) Brake Composite* | GWR | Not known |

Ex-GWR Ambulance Coach, converted at Swindon in 1915 for BEF 'Continental Ambulance Trains', adapted for use in BAOR leave trains in 1919, to WIMR as 116, in 1929, retained old WIMR number. 1956 series number unknown. Fate unknown.

| 117 | (Corridor) Brake Composite* | GWR | Not known |

Ex-GWR Ambulance Coach, converted at Swindon in 1915 for BEF 'Continental Ambulance Trains', adapted for use in BAOR leave trains, to WIMR as 107, 1929, retained old WIMR number until it became AD 5309 in 1956 series. Condemned by 28/9/1968.

* Corridor connections removed after delivery to WIMR and before 1939. Connections also removed from L&SWR dining saloons and the blue saloons (3006 and 3007) after delivery to LMR.

| 777 | Ambulance Coach | SRly Eastleigh | 1933 |

Built as a Non-descript Brake Open to Drawing.2654, SRly 4444, became S4444S on nationalisation. Converted to Ambulance Car by BR in 1959 and renumbered S7921S, withdrawn in 1968, sold to MoD, becoming AD 777 and based at CAD Bramley. Sent to LMR for ambulance crew training in 1968 (?) and 1969. For sale in 1980. Acquired by the Bluebell Railway, for preservation, despite conservation work, it may eventually be preserved by donating its underframe to the identical coach, S4441S, the body of which was a much better condition. Status unknown.

| 3005 | 6-wheel Inspection Saloon | L&NWR | 1889 |

L&NWR number not recorded, LMS ED33, later 45021. To Melbourne Military Railway, 1940 then to LMR, 1945. On closure of LMR donated to Transport Trust. Moved to Severn Valley Railway, 1971, then to Kent & East Sussex Railway, 1985 became K&ESR No. 82. Preserved.

| 3006 | Invalid Saloon | SE&CR Ashford | 1900 |

SE&CR No. 177, SRly No. 7913. To LMR, 1938, as No. 118, became AD 3006 in 1956 series. To Severn Valley Railway, 1970, to Kent & East Sussex Railway, 1985, became K&ESR No. 84. Preserved.

| 3007 | Invalid Saloon | L&SWR | 1910 |

L&SWR Drawing 1906, SRly Diag. 581. L&SWR No. 11, later No. 4105, became SRly No. 7803. To LMR 1938, became No. 119, then AD 3007 in 1956 series. To Severn Valley Railway, 1970, to K&ESR, 1985 became K&ESR No. 83. Preserved.

| 3016† | Dining Saloon | L&SWR | 1905 |

L&SWR built 3/1905 to Drawing 1601, SRly Diag. 590. L&SWR No. 61, then 4123, became SRly No. 7823, converted to Ambulance Coach 11/1943, to USATC as US 204, regd by SRly 1217/43, later by BR as WD RXC/000753. To RVH Netley, c1945, to LMR, 1954 on closure of Netley stabling facility. Transferred to COD Bicester, date unknown. Allocated AD 3016 in 1956 series, but probably not applied. Fate unknown.

| 3017† | Dining Saloon | L&SWR | 1905 |

L&SWR built 4/1905 to Drawing 1601, SRly Diag. 590. L&SWR No. 62, then 4124, became SRly No. 7824, converted to Ambulance Coach, 11/1943, to USATC as US 205, regd by SRly 1218/43, later by BR as WD RXC/000754. To RVH Netley, c1945, to LMR, 1954 on closure of Netley stabling facility, to COD Bicester, date unknown. Allocated AD 3017 in 1956 series, but probably not applied. Fate unknown.

| 3018 | Dining Saloon | L&SWR | 1907 |

L&SWR built 5/1907 to Drawing 1601, SRly Diag. 590, L&SWR No. 72, later 4134, became SRly No. 7834, to USATC as Ambulance Coach 201, 09/1943, regd by SRly 1214/43, later by BR as WD RXC/000758. To RVH Netley, c1945, to LMR, 05/1955, became AD 3018 in 1956 series, to Bicester, 1963, where converted to Inspection Saloon. To NRM collection, date unknown. Survives but (2014) in deteriorated condition.

| 3019 | Dining Saloon | L&SWR | 1908 |

L&SWR built 8/1908 to Drawing 1601, SRly Diag. 590, built 08/1908 as L&SWR 76, later 4138, became SRly No. 7838, to USATC as Ambulance Coach 202, 10/1943, regd by SRly 1215/43, later by BR as WD RXC/000759. To RVH Netley, c1945 as WD 13691, to LMR, 1954, became AD 3019 in 1956 series, converted to breakdown train equipment coach at Longmoor, date unknown, on closure of LMR re-deployed to Bicester. To Mid-Hants Railway, 1978, to Pontypool & Blaenavon Railway, c1996. Preserved.

| -----† | Compartment Second (S) | BR Doncaster | 1954 |

Diag. 371, Lot 30093, BR (M) M43233. To LMR, date unknown, never renumbered or repainted, condemned by mid-1967. Scr by 1969.

| ----- | Compartment Second (S) | BR Doncaster | 1954 |

Diag. 371, Lot 30093, BR (M) M43234. To LMR, date unknown, never renumbered or repainted, condemned by mid-1967. Scr by 1969.

| AD 03029 | Compartment Second (S) | BR Doncaster | 1954 |

Diag. 371, Lot 30093, BR (M) M43235. To LMR, 22/2/1965, never repainted, condemned by mid-1967. Scr by 1969.

| AD 03030 | Compartment Second (S) | BR Doncaster | 1954 |

Diag. 371, Lot 30093, BR (M) M43245. To LMR, 22/2/1965; renumbered AD 03030 (1966), then AD3030 (1967) and finally ARMY 5300; (1968) although it had been condemned by June 1967, scrapped at Longmoor in Jan 1970.

AD 03031   Compartment Second (S)   BR Doncaster   1954

Diag. 371, Lot 30093, BR (M) M43231. To LMR, 22/2/1965, renumbered AD 3031 (1966), then AD 3031 (1967) and finally ARMY 5301 in 1968, olive drab in 1966, repainted blue in 1967, on closure passed to East Somerset Rly then to K&WVR where cut-up in 1982.

AD 03032   Compartment Second (S)   BR Doncaster   1954

Diag. 371, Lot 30093, BR (M) M43258. To LMR, 22/2/1965, renumbered AD 03032 (1966), then AD 3032 (1967) and finally ARMY 5302 in 1969. Painted blue in 1968. Fate unknown.

AD 03033   Compartment Second (S)   BR Doncaster   1954

Diag. 371, Lot 30093, BR (M) M43239. To LMR, 22/2/1965, renumbered AD 03033, (1967) then AD 3033, (1968) and finally ARMY 5303, painted LMR blue from 1968. Fate unknown.

AD 03034   Compartment Second (S)   BR York   1955

Diag. 371, Lot 30087, BR (M) M43275. To LMR, 22/2/1965, renumbered AD 03034, (1966), then AD 3034 (1967) and finally ARMY 5304, in 1968. Painted LMR blue in 1968. On closure of LMR re-deployed to MOD Radway Green then sold in 1982 to North Staffordshire Rly.

ARMY 3301   Compartment Second (S)   BR Derby   1951?

Diag. 371, Lot 30051, BR (M) M46069. To LMR, early 1968, renumbered ARMY 3301, repainted in olive drab at LMR. After closure of LMR in 1969, redeployed to Marchwood for MMR and there converted into an observation saloon. Sold to Mid Hants Rly in 1978 and there scrapped in 1983.

ARMY 3302   Compartment Second (S)   BR Derby   1951?

Diag. 371, Lot 30051, BR (M) M46070, built between 6/1951 and 01/1955. To LMR, early 1968, renumbered ARMY 3302, repainted in blue in 1968. After closure sold to East Somerset Rly but scrapped in 1970 at Liss.

ARMY 5305   Brake Second (BS)   BR York   1955

Diag 326, Lot 30087, BR(M) 43269, To LMR in 1968, renumbered ARMY 5305, repainted in olive drab in 1969. Fate unknown.

ARMY 5310   Brake Second (BS)   BR York   1955

Diag 326, Lot 30087, BR (M) 43286, to LMR in 1968, renumbered ARMY 5310, repainted in olive drab in 1969. Purchased by ESRly for preservation.

ARMY 5313   Brake Second (BS)   BR Derby?   1951?

Diag 326, Lot nk, BR (M) 43296, to LMR in 1968, renumbered ARMY 5313, repainted in olive drab in 1969. On closure of LMR transferred to Marchwood. Fate unknown.

3321[†]   Dining Saloon   L&SWR   1907

L&SWR Drawing 1601, SRly Diag. 590, L&SWR No. 70, later 4132, became SRly 7832, converted to Ambulance Coach, became WD 1641, regd by SRly 1187/43. To RVH Netley for stabling 1945-55. Transferred to LMR 1955, became WD 3321 in 1956 series, to Marchwood, by 1958. To Mid Hants Rly in 1978, then transferred to Pontypool & Blaenavon Rly c1996. Preserved.

3322   Coach, Open Third   LMS   1929

Ex-LMS, probably No. 2924. Diag 1692, converted 1939 for BEF Ambulance Trains, captured by German forces in France in 1940, recaptured in 1944, repatriated 1945 to LMR, date unknown, as WD 301, became WD 3322 in 1956 series. Sold to East Somerset Railway, date unknown, transferred to MAT Beverley, c2003 moved to Long Marston for restoration. However, it was by then in very poor condition.

3323[†]   Dining Saloon   L&SWR   1905

L&SWR built 5/1905 to Drawing 1319, SRly Diag. 590, L&SWR No. 65, later 4127, became SRly No. 7827, converted to Ambulance Coach, 10/1943, became WD 1642, regd by SRly 1188/43, BR Reg not recorded. Stabled at RVH Netley 1945-55, until facilities closed, then to LMR, 02/1955, became WD 3323 or 3324 in 1956 series. Fate unknown.

3324[†]   Dining Saloon   L&SWR   1907

L&SWR built 5/1907 to Drawing 1601, SRLY Diag. 590, L&SWR No. 69, later 4131, became SRly No. 7831, converted to Ambulance Coach, became WD 1640, regd SRly 1186/43. To RVH Netley, date unknown, to LMR, 02/1955(?), possibly became WD 3324 or 3323 in 1956 series. Fate unknown.

3009†   Dining Saloon   L&SWR   1913

L&SWR Drawing 2158, SRly Diag. 591. L&SWR No. 4147, became SRly No. 7847, converted to Ambulance Coach 6/1944, to USATC as US 207. To LMR, possibly in transit only (date unknown) because the vehicle was recorded at CAD Kineton, in 1954. It became WD 3009 in the 1956 series, damaged by fire prior to 1960. Fate unknown.

5307   (Corridor) Brake Composite*   GWR   Not known

History as for WIMR 107-109 etc. Ex-BAOR Leave Trains to WIMR 1930. It is possible that this is the former 116. To PSD West Moors, date unknown, stripped down to make an internal user flat wagon, possibly for use as a barrier wagon. Fate unknown.

5308   Brake (Third) Coach   GWR   Not known

Ex-GWR Ambulance Coach. To WIMR, ex-BAOR, 1930, as 113, became WD 5308 in 1956 series. Originally (Corridor)* Brake Third. Redeployed to Marchwood on closure of LMR in 1970. Fate unknown.

5309   Brake (Third) Coach   GWR   Not known

Ex-GWR Ambulance Coach. To WIMR, ex-BAOR, 1930, as 117, became WD 5309 in 1956 series. Originally (Corridor)* Brake Composite. Scrapped at Longmoor, 1968.

5310(1st)†   Brake Third Coach   LMS   Not known

Ex-LMS Diag. 1693, converted to Ambulance Coach, 1939/40. To LMR, date unknown became 302. Fitted with old bus seats and used to form 'Set 2' with 3322. Scrapped at Longmoor 1967.

5311   Brake Third Lavatory ('Birdcage')   SE&CR   Not known

Ex-SE&CR No. 1100, SRly No. 3368; part of 3-car set 113 (later SRly Set 552). Purchased from SRly 1943 and transferred to LMR; numbered WD 13582; became WD 5311 in 1956 series; LMR blue livery from c.1967. Sold to K&ESR, 1970 became K&ESR No. 61. Lavatory compartment sealed on delivery to Longmoor. Preserved.

5312   Brake Third ('Birdcage')   SE&CR   Not known

Ex-SE&CR No. 1101, SRly No. 3388; part of 3-car set 113 (later SRly Set 552). Purchased from SRly, 1943 and transferred to LMR, date unknown; numbered WD 13583; became WD 5312 in 1956 series. Sold to K&ESR, 1970 became K&ESR No. 60. Preserved.

Certain cranes (for example WD 7149) appear to have been treated as Engineer Construction Plant and numbered accordingly.

APPENDIX TWENTY-TWO
WIMR/LMR - ROLLING STOCK STATISTICS

The data below has been compiled from official returns and details published from time to time in the technical press. Where appropriate, the figures have been tempered by information gathered in the preparation of this book. The aim of the table is to show general trends in rolling stock holdings at Longmoor. Due to the changes in the designations of vehicle types between lists and the known omission of entire sections in the World War Two censuses, the table cannot be guaranteed to be either totally consistent or completely accurate.

Serial	Type	1906	1930	1940	1943	1950	1956	1969
1	Locomotive Steam	2	6	21[1]	33[2]	19	22[3]	2
2	Locomotives (i/c)	-	-	-	3	9	7	6
3	Rail Cars	-	2	3	4	4	3	2
4	Carriages 6-wheel	-	-	-	-	1	1	1
5	Carriages 8-wheel	-	11	10	18	14	11	12
6	Carriages 12-wheel	-	-	4	4	3	2	-
7	Wagons 8-wheel RECTANK	-	6	10	10	16	11	-
8	Wagons 8-wheel WARFLAT	-	-	-	-	-	9	5
9	Wagons 8-wheel WARWELL	-	-	-	-	4	4	-
10	Wagons 8-wheel Low Side	2	9	10	12	12	8	2
11	Wagons 4-wheel Flat	-	-	2	-	1	1	-
12	Wagons 4-wheel Single Bolster	-	-	1	1	-	-	-
13	Wagons 4-wheel Double Bolster	-	-	7[4]	7	4	-	-
14	Wagons 4-wheel Open Low Side	25	23	23	48	34	12	2
15	Wagons 4-wheel Open High Side	-	20	20[5]	55	31		
16	Wagons 4-wheel Open High Drop Side	-	-	20	20	14		
17	Wagons 4-wheel Cistern	-	-	3	3	7	5	3
18	Wagons 4-wheel AFV Ramp	-	-	-	-	1	2	1
19	Vans 4-wheel Covered	2	7	15	23	25	41	13
20	Vans 8-wheel Covered	-	1	1	1	3	1	-
21	Vans Goods Brake	1	4	7	15	16	9	6
22	Service Vehicles (Not Specified)	-	6	3	nk	2	2	3

Notes:
1 Includes 12 loan stock
2 Includes 22 loan stock
3 Includes ex-MELF locomotives
4 Omitted from official list but known to be present
5 Omitted from official list but known to be present

APPENDIX TWENTY-THREE
NOTES ON ROLLING STOCK LIVERIES

Early Days

Records of the various liveries adopted are incomplete. There was no such thing as a 'house style' and individual vehicles were often painted according to the whim of the Commandant, Commanding Officer or Officer i/c Workshops. But even their decision could be varied by the individual painter (whose skills, particularly in the era of National Service, could vary widely). Very little written evidence has been found to endorse the personal recollections of former staff.

The makers' specification for *Bordon* quotes the original painting scheme as 'Prussian Blue lined out and varnished' with a marginal note 'Inside Cab to be painted buff and lined with red same as L&NW Rly'. How long this livery survived after 1905 is not known but subsequent new locomotives were delivered painted black and lined in red. One source states that by 1915 all the locomotives were in this livery. *Bordon's* original paint scheme may be a pointer to the later adoption of the blue livery after World War Two.

Carriage and wagon liveries for the earliest period have not been recorded. The contemporary photographs appear to show the freight stock in a light colour which we assume to be grey and similar to the colour used by their previous owners, the Midland Railway. The ex-K&ESR carriages appear to have been delivered in a two colour scheme – presumably that of their former owner. The upper panels were cream or white and the lower panels olive green – assumed to be similar to the 'Colonel Stephens Green' which has been reproduced on contemporary rolling stock as restored on the Festiniog Railway.

The colour of lettering used prior to 1920 is conjectural. The locomotives were unlettered until the MCR era when some received running numbers. The use of gold leaf on the carriages is quite possible as its application was a skill taught to the higher grades of the 'Painter and Decorator' trade at SME. It was certainly used on the rolling stock of the Military Camp Railways which passed through the Longmoor Workshops for overhaul.

1930 – 1940

By 1930 the locomotives were all painted black with simple red lining. Contemporary photographs suggest that they were kept well cleaned with polished brass-work. Carriages and wagons are described in the *Locomotive* magazine feature in 1930 as being painted "in service colour (grey-green), without lining and lettered in gold or yellow (Passenger vehicles) and white (freight stock)". The 'service colour' was a less intensely green variant of the 'olive-drab' colour used after World War Two, sometimes loosely described as 'khaki' though it was quite different from the khaki colour of uniform clothing. For modelling purposes, it would be reasonable to assume that the shade was the same as that used on contemporary British Army road vehicles (MT, motorised transport), examples of which can be found in many military museums.

Photographs of Military Camp Railways' carriages show the class distinctions 'Officers' and 'NCOs' painted on the door waist panels. Later 'Officers' appears to have been abbreviated to 'O' and the additional marking 'L' (for 'Ladies') used. This was certainly the practice during World War Two.

One distinctive feature probably brought back from France after World War One was the painting of brake handles, grab irons and hand-rails on freight stock in bright yellow. This was intended to make them more visible at night or in bad light, especially under black-out conditions.

In 1936 *Sir John French* was given a full overhaul at Eastleigh Works and returned to Longmoor painted in the contemporary Southern Railway green with panel borders separated from the main colour by a thin yellow line. This livery appealed to the staff at Longmoor and was adopted for further repaints in the period immediately prior to the outbreak of war. As a result, *Gordon*, *Marlborough* and possibly *Wellington* were repainted in this livery. When the new locomotive (*Kitchener*) arrived from the makers in 1938, it too was finished in Southern green. Early wartime photographs of *Lord Roberts* and *Selborne* suggest that they too had received this livery by 1940.

World War Two and After

During World War Two the locomotives on Longmoor's establishment were repainted black (generally unlined) after repairs and/or overhaul. Most of the loaned locomotives arrived at Longmoor in their parent company's black livery. An exception was SR 625 (one of the ex-L&SWR Adams 'Jubilee' 0-4-2 locomotives). It had already been withdrawn from main line service before the outbreak of war and in its declining years had retained its earlier green livery. This was kept at Longmoor and the locomotive was suitably 'bulled-up' to haul the Commandant's saloon. It was known affectionately by the staff as 'The Emerald Queen' but, based on photographic evidence, did not carry this as a nameplate.

The Austerity locomotives were delivered from the makers in WD 'Khaki', assumed to be the same as that used on contemporary MT vehicles. Initially 7015 carried its WD number in very small lettering but all seem to have received larger numbers (6-inches high was specified in 1952, but 12-inch or 14-inch examples can be found on contemporary photographs) whilst at Longmoor. Once more the style and grouping of numbers and lettering seem to have been an individual decision by the sign-writer at the time. The American Austerity locomotives arrived at Longmoor in a dark 'battle-ship grey' scheme. Those which were taken on to the Longmoor establishment were subsequently repainted black

At the end of the war, there was a period of transition but by 1946 decisions had been made on the livery and style to be used on the LMR's permanent locomotives. The first to be so treated was 75079 which emerged from the workshops in 1946 as *Sir John French*, carrying the nameplate previously fitted to 70203. The blue livery with red lining (specified as ¾ins wide, 3ins from the panel edge) proved popular and was adopted for all steam locomotives thereafter. Initially this was a dark shade, more akin to the original 'Prussian Blue' of 1905. 75079 quickly became *Lisieux* in accordance with the naming scheme set out in the table on page 671. The panels were normally finished with 90 degree 'scalloped' corners. This is not to say that the livery was in any way standardised – the details continued to be varied on the whim of the painter and his skills. It was probably quite unusual for two locomotives to be painted and lined by the same soldier in the National Service era. Some of the variants were quite distinctive and indeed have helped to identify individual locomotives.

When the Stanier 8Fs were first received from the makers, they were painted black with plain 14-inch lettering ('W^D') on cab-side and tender. Those which returned to the LMR in the mid 1950s were similarly painted with the exception of 501 which received the full treatment of lined blue livery, red frames and white tyres. It also received its nameplates *Lt. W.O. Lennox. V.C.* which it had previously carried with 10 Rly Sqn in the Middle East.

Additions to the livery in the form of various embellishments appeared from time to time and were later removed again. These included the cast badges of the Transportation Training Centre, 16 Rly Trg Regt and, after 1965, the cap badge of the RCT. Running numbers in large cast characters were fitted to the buffer beams of several locomotives during the 1950s. Latterly the tyres of selected engines were picked out in white.

Post-war, the carriage fleet was finished in unlined olive drab with yellow lettering. Various cast badges were removed during the 1950s. The three saloons were painted in the same blue as the locomotives with yellow lettering but unlined. At a late stage the remaining two coaches of the 3-coach SE&CR 'Birdcage' set were upgraded to blue livery as were some of the ex-BR compartment coaches and even goods brake-vans in the final years.

Some interesting background information was unearthed by George Moon at a Longmoor reunion in 2000. Speaking to Major A. L. ('Chalky') White (one-time OC Longmoor Workshops) he discovered that from c1962 this officer instituted a repainting programme for the locomotives using 'Dulux' Oxford Blue for the upper-works and Signal Red for wheels and frames. This treatment was applied to 400 (*Sir Guy Williams*), both the 2-10-0s, the two 'Derby' 350hp diesels (867 and 868) and to the Austerity 0-6-0STs numbers 203 and 157, the latter kept for display purposes. After Major White left, the red external frames were not perpetuated, so numbers 195, 196 and 199 had black exterior frames though the insides of the frames, motion and coupling rods continued to be painted red. Oxford Blue was the colour specified for the new diesel locomotives *General Lord Robertson* and *Hassan* prior to delivery. Apart from the cast replica cap-badges fixed to the cab sides, there were no other livery changes after the formation of the RCT, and the RE cap-badges on individual locomotive nameplates were not changed.

It has become ever more obvious that there were many variations of livery, both between locomotives and indeed on individual locomotives down the years. In the search for authenticity, we strongly recommend the use of contemporary photographs for guidance.

A 'posed' view taken during the winter of 1965, showing a trainee blockman at Longmoor Downs handing a key (in a leather carrying hoop) to the driver of *General Lord Robertson*. This view shows the lining on the locomotive as delivered from the makers – a black band edged in white.
WD photograph

APPENDIX TWENTY-FOUR
WHERE ARE THEY NOW?

A SUMMARY OF THE POST-1969 LOCATIONS OF THE KNOWN SURVIVING
FORMER LONGMOOR MILITARY RAILWAY LOCOMOTIVES

Woolmer (AE/1572/1919); Avonside Class B3. WD 74/70074 MOD 010 (not carried). Formerly displayed outside HQ TnC RE from 1953 to 1977. After display and cosmetic restoration at 'Locomotion', Shildon, Co. Durham, transferred by NAM to NRM. Now displayed (2014) at the Milestone Museum, Basingstoke.

Westminster (P/1378/1914) (MCR 13); Sold c1921 to Cohens thence to Dunstable Portland Cement Co. Successors (APCM) sold it to K&ESR Association in 1970. Restoration incomplete, loco plinthed at former East Tisted Station until 1998 when purchased by supporters of Northampton & Lamport Railway with a view to eventual restoration.

Gordon [1] (TVR/306/1897); WD 205/70205; Sold as WD 70205 to Jas N. Connell Ltd of Coatbridge in 1947 then re-sold to NCB. Ran at NCB South Hetton Colliery until 1960 when presented by NCB to BRB for preservation (as the last surviving Welsh-built standard gauge locomotive). Transferred to National Museum of Wales and placed in the care of South Wales Switchgear Ltd as the successor occupiers of the former GWR works at Caerphilly. Currently (2014) in the care of the Gwili Railway.

Gordon [2] (NBL/25437/1943); WD 3651/73651/600. Left LMR as AD 600; moved to SVR on loan (initially, but later donated) and in service 1972-1995; wdn awaiting heavy boiler overhaul. Superficial restoration (with incorrect lining) carried out at Bridgnorth in 1975 for Shildon (S&D 150 Anniversary) and again, (still with incorrect lining) in 2007 for display in the 'Engine House' at Highley.

LMS 8233 (NBL/24670/1940); WD 307/70307/500; At LMR 1955-57. Sold as WD 500. One of three Stanier 8F locomotives sold to BR in 1957, renumbered as 48773. In 1968 purchased by the Stanier 8F Locomotive Society and transferred by them to the SVR. In revenue service until 2008 when withdrawn pending heavy overhaul. Subject of cosmetic restoration in BR livery and placed on display in the 'Engine House' at Highley.

Chittagong [1], *Basra* [2] (EE/LMS Derby/1945); WD 70272/878/601; Overhauled at BR Swindon 1965/66; To 1 Rly Gp RCT Bicester 7/69; Various locations between 1970/73; Stored at Bicester 1973/80 when disposed of to Lakeside & Haverthwaite Railway, Cumbria.

AD 400 (NBL/27421/1955); WD 8200; Army 400; New to West Moors 22/4/55; to LMR 15/6/56 then returned to Bicester wksps 29/4/60; to Sudbury Staffs 7/4/61; to CAD Kineton 2/11/61; to Bicester wksps 27/4/65; to Long Marston 6/10/65. To Andrew Barclay, Kilmarnock 12/73; Long Marston, Bicester and Ruddington 1974-75; stored at Ashchurch 10/83-1/84; to RAF Leuchars where named *River Eden* [1]; Sold to Lochty Private Railway Co., Fife 6/89. On closure of LPR in 1992 moved to Kingdom of Fife Railway Preservation Soc. and restored as *River Eden* with RAF markings. Serviceable 2014.

Matruh (NBL/27426/1955); WD 8205; Army 405; Left LMR as WD 8205 15/6/62; to Marchwood until June 69 then to Andrew Barclay, Kilmarnock, June-Aug 73; at Bicester until July 75 then to Marchwood and Bicester and CAD Longtown until Dec 75; Moved to RAF Leuchars July 76 and named *River Tay*; Given to Lochty Private Railway Co., Fife in 1989; Later moved to Shropshire Locomotive Collection; Purchased by S. A. Pyle of Bamford; Undergoing restoration.

General Lord Robertson (RR/Sentinel/10143/1963); WD890; Army 610; left LMR at end of 1969; to P&EE Shoeburyness where renumbered AD 890; rebuilt at Thos Hill, Kilnhurst 1977/78; returned to Shoeburyness 1/78; Sold to Mid Hants Railway 7/5/85; To Avon Valley Railway, Bristol 1987, allegedly because of damage to track on Mid Hants Railway. Transferred to Long Marston to undergo overhaul in 2010 it is now (2014) back at the Avon Valley Railway, stored unserviceable and partially dismantled (minus engines & torque converters) awaiting replacement engines etc to be fitted and a full overhaul.

Hassan (R&H/4688041/1962); WD 8227; Army 440; left LMR after closure as AD 440; To Long Marston 8/12/69; To Bicester wksps 21/7/75 and returned to Kineton; In traffic Bicester 25/3/82; To Thos Hill, Rotherham 14/3/86 (Name removed); To CAD Longtown 31/01/87; To RAF Leuchars 30/3/89 where renamed *River Eden* [2]; To Bicester 6/7/95; on hire to Spieenertrans, Heathrow Extension Railway contract 8/8/95.

WD 8219 (R&H/459519/1961); WD 8219; AD 425; From 1 Rly Gp RCT at Ludgershall to LMR 11/67; left LMR as AD 425 c8/69; Transferred to 1 Rly Gp RCT at Long Marston. To store at Bicester 25/5/72; To Marchwood 14/7/73; To Thos Hill, Rotherham 10/3/86; To CAD Longtown 24/10/86; To RAF Leuchars 28/8/87 (where named *River Tay* [2]; To CAD Longtown 10/3/94; To Shoeburyness 4/5/95. In 2010, located at Shipley (Crossley Evans) and named *Venom*, still there in 2014.

Gazelle (Dodman –/1893); On extended loan from BTC from 1950 and displayed outside HQ Tn C RE; transferred to ASMT Leconfield in 1972; later displayed at MAT Beverley. Returned to NRM collection after closure of the MAT in 2003 and now on loan to Col Stephens Museum at K&ESR Tenterden for display.

WD 0-6-0ST Standard Austerity locomotives. Note: The locomotives listed below were all at some time in regular use on the LMR. Many others were simply assembled and/or test run there before shipment overseas for war service or they were stored in one of the sub-depots of the Tn Stores Depot Longmoor after delivery from the manufacturers.

Foggia (HE 2890/1943); WD 75041/107; On LMR -/45; To Hunslet Engine Co. 1/51-8/51; returned to LMR; Sold to Hunslet 12/60 and there rebuilt as HE 3882/1962. Sold to NCB and transferred to Maesteg in 2/62; Sold to Bristol Suburban Railway, Bitton 3/77; Sold to Dart Valley Railway 3/78 and there named *Barbara*; to Mid Hants Railway in 2000. Rebuilt as 0-6-0 tender loco *Douglas* (as a 'Thomas the Tank Engine' character).

Brussels (HC/1782/1945); WD 71505/WD 118; Left the LMR as AD 118 in early 1969; sold to the Brussels Preservation Society; operated on the K&WVR in early 1970s; Now on static display.

Rennes (RSH/7139/1944); WD 75189/WD 152; Sold in 1960 to Hunslet Engine Co. and there rebuilt as HE/3880/1962; Sold to NCB Mountain Ash; eventually transferred to the Big Pit Mining Museum Trust in 1982 for static display.

Insein (VF/5272/1945); WD 75282/181; Sold as AD 181 to Hunslet Engine Co., Leeds; rebuilt there becoming HE/3879/1961 and sold in 1961 to NCB South West Division. Transferred to the Caerphilly Railway Society in 1981. Moved with CRS to Gwili Railway in 1996 and restoration commenced in 2002. Now carries the name *Haulwen*.

Errol Lonsdale (HE/3796/1953); WD 196/AD 96; stored after delivery at 1 TnSD, Longmoor 7/53 to 6/55. Transferred to 1 Rly Gp RE at Bicester then various locations until 11/64 when transferred to LMR until 10/69. Sold in 1969 to the K&ESR Association. Transferred to the Mid Hants Railway in 1976. Now carrying builders' plate 'HE/3799' formerly carried by AD 199 (plate transferred at Longmoor before sale). Offered for sale by South Devon Railway in 2010 and purchased by private owner for restoration in Belgium.

Sapper [2] (HE/3797/1953); WD 197 stored after delivery at 1 TnSD, Longmoor 7/53 to 9/55; in service at Bicester 1955-77 where named *Sapper* after AD 195 was transferred to LMR. Loaned as AD 197 to K&ESR in 1977, then purchased by K&ESR in 1979, renumbered No. 25 and renamed *Northiam*.

In addition to these locomotives, rail car 9033 – famous for its appearance in 'The Great St. Trinians Train Robbery' is now (2014) preserved privately.

During its sojourn on the South Devon Railway, *Errol Lonsdale* was painted up in a black livery carrying the 68011 number that it gained for the filming of 'The Great St. Trinian's Train Robbery'. The locomotive also carried *Errol Lonsdale* nameplates and RTC crests on the nameplate and cabside. Note the extra step added on the footplate after the engine left Longmoor, to make it easier to climb up on the tank to reach the water tank filler lid.

M. Christensen

APPENDIX TWENTY-FIVE
COMMANDANTS AND COMMANDING OFFICERS AT LONGMOOR

(Later ranks, orders and decorations in brackets)

Officers Commanding Railway Troops

Major (Brigadier-General) F. G. Fuller (CB CMG)	1905-06
Captain (Major-General) C. G. Fuller (CMG DSO)	1906-07
Major (Major-General Sir Dudley) H. Ridout (KBE CB CMG)	1907-09
Major (Brigadier-General) C. G. W. Hunter (CMG DSO)	1910-11
Lieutenant-Colonel (Brigadier-General) J. H. Twiss (CB CBE)	1911-14

Commandants Railway Training Centre RE

Colonel H. M. Sinclair CB (CMG)	1914-19
Colonel (Major-General) A. G. Stevenson DSO (CB CMG)	1919-20
Lieutenant-Colonel C. E. G. Vesey	1920-23
Lieutenant-Colonel (Major-General) A. Brough DSO (CB CMG CBE)	1923-25
Lieutenant-Colonel (Colonel) J. Day DSO	1925-29
Lieutenant-Colonel E. Woodhouse OBE	1929-30
Lieutenant-Colonel (Brigadier) L. Manton OBE DSO	1930-35
Lieutenant-Colonel (Brigadier) J. P. S. Greig (CBE)	1935-37
Lieutenant-Colonel (Major-General Sir Donald) J. McMullen DSO (KBE CB)	1937-39
Lieutenant-Colonel R. D. Waghorn	1939
Brigadier W. G. Tyrrell DSO	1939-41
Brigadier R. D. Waghorn (CBE)	1941-42

Commandants Transportation Training Centre RE

Brigadier H. A. Joly de Lotbiniere MC	1942-46
Brigadier C. A. Langley (CB) CBE MC	1946
Brigadier R. Gardiner CBE	1946-48

Directors of Transportation and Commandants Transportation Centre RE

Brigadier R. Gardiner (CB) CBE	1948-50
Brigadier C. E. M. Herbert CBE	1950-53

Commandants Transportation Centre RE

Brigadier C. H. Barnett	1953-56
Brigadier P. D. G. Buchanan	1956-59
Brigadier A. G. P. Leahy (CBE) OBE	1959-61
Brigadier F. H. Lowman MBE DSO	1961-64
Brigadier (Major-General) J. C. Woollett CBE MC	1964-65

Commandants, School of Transport RCT

Brigadier (Major-General) J. C. Woollett CBE MC	1965-66
Brigadier (Major-General) P. F. Claxton OBE ADC	1966-68
Brigadier R. A. Nightingale MBE	1968-69

Commandant, Army School of Transport

Brigadier R. A. Nightingale MBE	1969-73

In 1973 the Army School of Transport moved from Longmoor to form the (then) new Army School of Mechanical Transport at Leconfield, East Yorkshire.

Following the adoption by the Corps of Royal Engineers of a regimental system in March 1947 and the abolition of the wartime 'wings' within the Transportation Training Centre RE, railway training within the Corps was undertaken by a railway training regiment, responsible for all railway trades training and the operation of the LMR.

Commanding Officer, 5 Railway Training Regiment RE

Lieutenant-Colonel H. G. Pottle OBE MC	1947-48
Lieutenant Colonel (Colonel) G. H. B. Moss	1948

Commanding Officer, 16 Railway Training Regiment RE

Lieutenant-Colonel (Colonel) G. H. B. Moss	1948-50
Lieutenant-Colonel (Colonel) W. H. Bond	1950-53
Lieutenant-Colonel (Colonel) G. C. L. Alexander OBE TD	1953-56
Lieutenant-Colonel D. C. Merry	1956-58
Lieutenant-Colonel E. R. Paterson MBE	1959-61
Lieutenant-Colonel D. R. Hildick-Smith MBE	1961-63
Lieutenant-Colonel A. H. Gye MBE	1963-65

Commanding Officer, 16 Railway Training Regiment RCT

Lieutenant-Colonel A. H. Gye MBE	1965-66
Lieutenant-Colonel H. A. Ablett MBE	1966-67

16 Railway Training Regiment RCT was disbanded in January 1967. The LMR was placed under the control of the Railway Wing AST until final closure in 1969. During the post-closure period, the LMR was controlled by the Army Railway Organisation (ARO) until the completion of dismantling the line.

BIBLIOGRAPHY

We have attempted to write these three volumes for the benefit of general readers, without footnotes and detailed references. In the absence of many official files, much material has come from records now owned by private individuals (many of whom served at Longmoor and, being interested in what they did, kept notes and retained papers that were issued to them). One such is the notebook of the late R. C. Riley. However, references to sources not available to the public would be complicated and would serve to obscure the story we have been telling.

The principal primary sources are the local railway working instructions, of which three versions are known to exist:

Woolmer Instructional Military Railway Service Book (Nov 1934)
Technical Orders for the LMR (War Period)
Technical Orders and Working Instructions for the LMR, (Oct 1959)

For a railway on which the War Department made many changes, there are very few official files that have survived. We were able to examine a number of files that were once in the library at the Museum of Army Transport, but have been unable to refer to these files since that museum was disbanded in great haste. These files may have been destroyed, or may be (currently – 2014 – not indexed) at the RE Museum at Gillingham, Kent.

There are surprisingly few files in The National Archives at Kew. The following have been used in our research:

MT6/1736/3   The Bordon and Longmoor Military Tramway
MT6/1847/5   Light Railway Order Bordon to Bentley
RAIL411/805   Agreement between the WD and the L&SWR regarding Bordon to Bentley
T161/650   Working agreements re Bordon to Bentley
MT114/2   Level crossings 1955-1960
HO199/119   Damage to military targets
WO32/21711   Closure of the LMR 1969-70
TS 54/42   Lease to the Longmoor Trust

The following list includes published sources which we feel readers might wish to consult in furthering their knowledge of military railways.

We remain wedded to E. A. Pratt's *The Rise of Rail-Power in War and Conquest* (King and Sons, 1915) as the most authoritative work on the 19th century development of military railways. There are two more recent works which readers may find more readily available: John Westwood's *Railways at War* (Osprey Publishing, 1980) – written by an ex-Longmoor man, is a good general history – whilst the more recent *Engines of War* by Christian Wolmar (Atlantic Books, 2010) brings the story up to date.

Specific to the Crimean War, there is now Brian Cooke's *The Grand Crimea Central Railway* (Cavalier House, 1997) in addition to Michael Robbins' earlier monograph, reprinted in *Points and Signals – a Railway Historian at Work* (G. Allen & Unwin, 1967). The railway aspects of the 1867 Abyssinian campaign do not feature in contemporary sources (for example the *Graphic* magazine contains not one word!) – P. A. L. Vine's article 'By Train to War' (*Railway Magazine*, February 1973) remains the most accessible account.

Turning to the ill-fated Suakin venture, contemporary magazines carried a few details of the railway operations. One is left with the impression that the government in London would rather the whole episode was forgotten as quickly as possible. We are better served by Winston Churchill writing about the Sudan campaign leading up to the battle of Omdurman in 1899. Chapter Eight of *Frontiers and Wars* is entitled 'The Desert Railway' and gives a good (but non technical) account of the campaign. More details of a technical nature are to be found in Richard Hill's *Sudan Transport* (OUP, 1965).

The operation of the railways in South Africa, a key element of Kitchener's successful strategy in the Anglo-Boer War, does not appear in any depth in the standard histories of that war. All the essentials are covered by Wolmar in *Engines of War* (see above). Following the end of hostilities, Girouard prepared two reports which were widely circulated: *History of the Railways during the War in South Africa 1899 - 1902* was a single volume published by HMSO in 1903 whilst a larger (two volume) report *Detailed History of the Railways during the South African War 1899 - 1902* followed in 1904.

The construction of the camps at Bordon and Longmoor passed unrecorded apart from brief notes in the local press. Lts Mount and Ling wrote a report on the hut shifting operation which appeared in the RE *Journal* as 'Works at Longmoor and Borden (sic) Camps III - Moving Huts by Rail from Longmoor to Borden' (RE *Journal*, December 1904).

The only surviving original source of information on Longmoor's contribution to World War One is Colonel Sinclair's article (probably based on an official report) which appeared in the July 1919 edition of the RE *Journal* entitled; 'History of the Railways and Roads Training Centre RE Longmoor', a shortened version of which appeared later in a *Railway Gazette* supplement. E. A. Pratt's *British Railways and the Great War, Organisation, Efforts, Difficulties and Achievements*, Selwyn & Blount 1921, (2 Vols) lists the Military Camp Railways but ignores (as do the official histories) the contribution of Longmoor.

Railway operations and construction in France and Belgium during World War One are covered in the official history *Transportation on the Western Front* (Colonel A. M. Henniker) re-published (without the supporting maps) by the Imperial War Museum c1990. However the loss of maps has been magnificently overcome in William Aves' recent volume *The ROD on the Western Front* Shaun Tyas, (2009) wherein they are reproduced along with an outstanding collection of contemporary images.

By 1930, the use of the UK railway technical press to publicise the Supplementary Reserve railway units was a deliberate recruiting strategy. The three-part article in *The Locomotive* in July, August and September 1930 was probably the first such effort but it was followed by a (more technical) article in *The Railway Gazette* in November 1932 and a general article in *The Railway Magazine* in August 1933. Thereafter annual progress reports, detailing the training carried out by the Supplementary Reserve unit appeared each autumn in *The Railway Gazette* following the summer camp season.

Following the outbreak of World War Two there begins a series of autobiographical books and articles which mention training at Longmoor in varying depth. These are generally 'my life with locomotives' biographies written by main-line drivers following retirement. As a general history, our own book *The Longmoor Military Railway,* David & Charles (1974) was a 'first' in its field and was followed by Vic Middleton and Keith Smith's *Branch Lines to Longmoor*, Middleton Press (1987), excellently illustrated and including extracts of contemporary Ordnance Surveys of parts of the line. A most useful book is Peter Bancroft's *Railways Around Alton*, (1995), Nebulous Books, Alton. Modestly described as "an illustrated bibliography", it includes a full and detailed listing of both books and magazine articles about Longmoor.

Finally, presenting an outsider's view of the final days of the LMR, there are two books by David Shepherd which describe his struggles to acquire, house and maintain his two ex-BR locomotives. His autobiography *The Man Who Loves Giants*, David & Charles (1975) puts his railway preservation activities into the context of his busy life as a professional artist and successful wild-life conservator. His second book *A Brush With Steam*, David & Charles (1983) is a more personal and detailed account of triumphs and disasters of his life with two steam locomotives.

For the rolling stock of the LMR we will make no specific recommendations, as specialist monographs cover virtually every aspect. From the ex-L&SWR converted dining cars (detailed in Gordon Weddell's books and many articles on the rolling stock of the L&SWR) to the 'Austerity' 0-6-0ST locomotives – each of whose CV is detailed in *Continent, Coalfield and Conservation* (by A. P. Lambert and J. C. Woods, published by the Industrial Railway Society in 1991) – pieces of true railway detective work abound.

ERRATA

The following corrections should be made to Volume One:

p.11 (right column), line 36: For '1826' read '1830'.

p.76 (lower illustration): for 'at Bordon' read 'in Longmoor Yard, with the Mobilisation Store in the Background. This image must date from 1914/15 because the Carriage Shed has not yet been built.'

p.88 (lower illustration): for 'that had originated with the North London Railway' read 'loaned by the LB&SCR. The coach on the extreme left is probably the same ex-Metropolitan Railway rigid 8-wheeler shown on p.61 (upper illustration).'

p.89, (table), line 4: for 'Ditton' read 'Dinton'. Line 8; for 'Rippon' read 'Ripon'.

p.100 (caption), line 6: for 'Simpson' read 'Simson'.

p.196 (centre illustration): for '122' read '120'. This vehicle was 120 in the wagons numbering series. There was also a coach 120.

p. 210 (left column), line 6: for 'practice' read 'practise'.

p.219 (caption): for 'Selborne' read *'Selborne'*.

p. 247 (upper illustration): for 'Class 01 locomotive' read 'Class 'O1' locomotive'.

p. 252 (upper illustration): in connection with the filming of 'The Great St. Trinian's Train Robbery' for '1966' read 'October 1965'.

p.287 (caption): for '195' read '196'.

The following corrections should be made to Volume Two

p.341 (lower caption): for 'C' read 'O1'

p.344 (centre caption): for 'A1' read 'A12'

p.336 (right column): for 'Appendix 13' read 'Appendix 14'.

p.401 (upper illustration): for '72979' read '73979'.

p.407 (centre illustration), last line: for '152 *Rennes*' read '181 *Lisieux*' and add 'Locomotive on extreme right is WD 152 *Rennes*'.

p.434 (left column), last line: for '13.906' read '13.905' – also on page 435. The locomotives were 13.905 *Mars* and 13.915 *Venus*, but the number 906 was incorrectly painted on one of the locomotives.

p.435 (lower illustration): for 'WARWELL' read 'WARFLAT'.

p.436 (right column): for 'then Chairman of the Railway Executive' read 'then Deputy Chairman of the Railway Executive'.

p.492 (diagram), Note C, 1st line; for 'beyound' read 'beyond'.

p.493 (right column), line 21: for '(123)' read '(121)'.

p.499 (attribution of lower illustration): for 'Photographer unknown' read 'Gordon Marshall'.

p.515 (upper illustration): for '*Folognio*' read '*Foligno*'™.

p.561 (attribution): for 'Photographer unknown' read 'David Kelso via Stanier 8F Locomotive Society

---

A little story...

I was once out as brakesman/shunter with 'Barney' Barnes and 118 *Brussels* in the Gypsy Hollow sidings along the Liphook Road. We were pushing up some old flat wagons to be stabled. 118 slipped – not unusual because the fuel oil dripped. In an entirely unselfish wish to help, and intending to help by putting ash ballast under the loco wheels, I asked for the firing shovel to be passed down. 'Don't bi so bluddy daft' was the immediate answer. Now I knew of course that oil burners don't have firing shovels. 'Barncy' was always very cheerful and friendly – I just had to live it down. But then one of my colleagues kept being asked about matches and offered candles. He had committed the 'crime', during a break, of letting his fire out.

Bryan Stone

INDEX

A

Abbreviations
general & military 322-327
for LMR blockposts pre-1939 322
LMR locations post-1939 535
Abyssinia (1867) 16
Alexander G. C. L. (Lt-Col) 455-6, 459
'Anthony Armstrong' ('AA') 97
Andrew Barclay 0-6-0 DH locos on trial 1966 **704**
Apple Pie (APE)
air photo (1939) **262**
construction of camp **98**
conversion to stores depot 332
refurbishment as ESD 448
TSD/ESD track plans (c1945) 261
Army Emergency Reserve
creation, 1946-48 403
mobilisation (1956) 519
recruiting **487**
reorganisation 1959/60, 1965 420, 584
Army School of Mechanical Transport (ASMT) (Leconfield) 116, 611
Army Service Corps
13th Coy, 59th Coy 43, **45**
Army Works Corps 12, 16
Association of Railway Preservation Societies (ARPS) 584, 780
'Austerity' 0-6-0ST locomotives 385
class historical outline 660
class naming schemes 677
in store post-World War Two **394-5, 401**
loans to PLA **403-4**
on trial 1943 395
Peace Establishment locomotives 395, 667-9
War Reserve 1952 673, **674**
WD 5001 **347**
WD 75028 (100)(Ahwaz [1]) **230, 418, 670**
WD 75041 (107)(Foggia) **303, 402, 447**
WD 75079 (114)(Sir John French)(Lisieux) **258, 311, 427, 477, 667-8, 669**
WD 75275 (Matruh) **672**
WD 75282 (181)(Insein) **284, 669, 788**
WD 75290 (186)(Manipur Road) **231, 468-9, 474, 514, 670**
WD 75291 **676**
WD 102 (Caen [2]) **450-1, 538, 675, 796**
WD 106 (Spyck) **337, 404, 682, 685**
WD 75042 (108)(Jullundur) **403, 425-6, 580, 683, 685**
WD 71515 (118)(Brussels) **266, 314, 407-8, 428, 440-1, 449-50, 661, 666, 766, 795**
WD 152 Rennes **475, 672**
WD 156 Tobruk/McMurdo **283, 684**
WD 157 Constantine **244, 267, 315, 447, 485, 677, 683, 796**
WD 178 Foligno **468, 515, 685**
WD/AD 195 **266, 269, 306, 311, 676, 806-7**
WD/AD 196 Errol Lonsdale **259, 269, 287, 676, 685, 805, 809-11,**
WD/AD 199 **238, 273, 684, 809, 838**
WD 203 Ahwaz [2] **475, 583, 674-5, 685**

'Austerity' 2-10-0 Locomotives 652
WD 73651 (600) Gordon [2] **250, 263, 266, 273, 284, 285, 298, 306, 458, 651-3, 797, 806-7, 812**
WD 73979 (601) Kitchener [3] **281, 286, 401, 405-6, 436, 443, 461-3, 553-4, 654-5, 775**
WD73755 **786**
'Austerity' 2-8-0 Locomotives 655
WD 77337 (400) Sir Guy Williams **269, 271, 274, 297, 302, 304-5, 312-3, 423, 427, 461, 655-6, 789-91**
WD 79250 (401) Major General McMullen **402, 437, 441-2, 459, 657**

B

Barnard (Lt D. B.) 370
Baro – Kano Railway (Nigeria) 32, 72
Barrington-Ward M. (Lt/Lt-Col) 97
Bassett-Lowke (W.J & Co) 71, 121, **122**
Battle of Bull Run (1861) 13
Battle of Chickamauga (1863) 15
Battle of Magdala (1867) 16
Blackmoor Sheds 250, 419
Blackout Hazards 365-6
'Blue Saloons'
first use (1938) **197**
details see 'L&NWR', 'L&SWR' and 'SE&CR'
Bombing
German raids 331
RAF trials on LMR 1938 197
Bond W. H. (Lt/Lt-Col) **100**
Bordon (0-6-0ST) 60, 73, **77, 615-6**
Bordon & Longmoor Military Tramway
Draft Provisional Order 60, 62, 70
Bordon (BDN) 222-231
3-position signals 205, **226**
proposed 'cut-off' (World War Two) 366
shunting in yard **472-3**
signal cabin 204
signalling diagrams (1924, 1941, 1955) 203, 206, 510
signalling reduced 1955 510
stations (c1935), air photo **221**
wagon exchanges (WW2) 340, **341**
WD station track plans 222-4, 228
WD station views **222-231**
Bowman-Manifold M. G. E. (Capt) 36
Brimstone Sidings (BSS) track plan (1959) 287-8
British Army of the Black Sea 95
Brough A. (Lt-Col/Maj-Gen) 97
'Bullet' train services
origins in 1916 84
working in early 1950s 536
World War Two 340, 370
'Butterflies' see Economic Facing Point Lock

C

Cadet camp special train (1966) **589-592**
Caen [1] Ruston & Hornsby 4w D/M **697, 761**
Ex-Caledonian Railway coaches 340, **390, 392, 470, 735-6**

Canadian Forestry Corps (CFC) — 91, **92**
'Chanak Affair' (1922) — 95
Chantler F. C. (WO2) — 96
Charlton class locos (RAR) — **27**
Chattanooga (USA) — 13, 15
Chattenden & Upnor Lt Rly *see* Upnor & Chattenden
Chinaman siding — 288, **467**
Churcher A. (Sgt/QMSI) — 96
Collision at Palmers Ball (1956) — 519-527, **520-4**
   Coroner's Inquest — 525-6
   Court of Inquiry — 526-7
   lessons learned — 528
Colour light signalling — 508
Conference on Communications & Transit — 95
Continental Ambulance Train No. 38 (CAT 38) — 87-8, 716-7
'Contraption' *see* Tracklaying Machine
Cranes (Rail-mounted) — 755-765
   Brownhoist 20-ton — **445-6, 597**
   Brownhoist 30-ton — **139-40, 144, 756-7**
   Cowans Sheldon 15-ton — **171, 757, 758, 759, 760**
   Ransomes & Rapier 45-ton — **439, 460, 760-1, 763**
   RB 19 crane on WARFLAT — **765**
   Smith (Rodley) 20-ton — 763, **764**
   Stothert & Pitt 5-ton — **61, 64-6, 68, 70, 755-6**
Cranmer Pond (CMR) — **127-8, 192, 252,** 253, 257
Crimean War (1854-56) — 12

D

Daisy (WD 70228) (0-6-0ST) — 396, **397**
Day J. (Lt/Lt-Col) — **44-5,** 99, **100**
Director of Movements and Quartering (DMQ) — 75
Displays
   Aldershot Tattoo — **485-6**
Docks Groups RE (SR) — 190
Double line block instruments
   GWR pattern — **122-3, 483**
   Sykes Type TS — **512-3**
   SGE Indian pattern — **482**
Drawing Office — **383**
Dray H.R. (Maj/Brig) — 116, 784
Drewry rail cars
   10hp (1917) — 704
   62hp (1936) (WD 941/9111) — **190, 229, 448, 705-6**

E

Earl Haig see also L&NWR — **183, 633,** 634
Earl Roberts [1] *see also* L&NWR — **168, 185, 344,** 633
Economic Facing Point Lock (EFPL) ('Butterfly') — 202, **359**
Elliot Wood Committee — 35-7
Elliot Wood (Maj-Gen Sir) — 35
Engineer & Railway (Volunteer) Staff Corps — 37, 78
Engineer Stores Depot (Liphook), (2ESD) — 337
Esher (Viscount Lord) (War Office reforms) — 35
Everall (Lt-Col) W. T. — 197, 409
Everall Sectional Truss Bridge — 409, **410-11**
Excavators (steam) — **64-66, 70, 146, 156-8, 162, 761**

F

Farthing A. (Spr) — 156
Festiniog Railway Co.
   8 Rly Sqn camp (1965) — **784-5**

train control system — 782
Fieldworks
   annual training — 443, **471**
   demolitions — **57**
   improvised lifting — **79, 176**
   training — 182
   water supply — **179**
Films
   summary of commercial films made at Longmoor — 769
   'Bhowani Junction' — **767-9, 770**
   silent film 'Mons' — 767
   training films — 767
   'The Great St. Trinian's Train Robbery' — 768, **774-6,** 777
   'The Inn of the Sixth Happiness' — **771-2**
   'The Runaway Railway' — **773**
   'Young Winston' — 610, **777**
Flagboard Signalling
   employment on military railways — 215-6
   Warning Board — **531**
Flamingo (0-4-2T) — 49, **55,** 613
Forbes (Lt-Col Sir William) — 78,80
Fort Darland (Chatham) — 613
Fortification railways (RE) — 49
Frame release keys — **512**
Free Piece Curve — 222
'Future of Railways' –1967 Study — 575

G

Gaines, Edmund P. (Maj-Gen) — 13
Garraway A.G.W. — 779-80
Garraway R. — 92
Gazelle (0-4-2T) — **438,** 708, **710, 813**
Geddes (Sir Eric) — 83-4
Girouard E. P. C. (Brig-Gen) — **8,** 25, 29, 30, 32-3, 35, 72
Gordon [1] (0-6-2T) — **99, 134, 168, 169, 187, 295-6, 339, 343, 388, 429,** 630, **632,** 837
Gordon [2] *see* 'Austerity' above.
Gordon, Charles (General) — 18, 632
Grand Crimean Central Railway — 12
Great Western Railway
   ambulance coaches — 97, **183,** 184, **225, 242, 361-3, 392, 718-9**
   'Dean Goods' 0-6-0 locomotives — 640
      WD 70177 — **372**
      WD 70195 — **468, 642**
      WD 70198 — **641**
      WD 70179 — **371**
Grieg (Lt-Col/Brig) J. P. S. — 186
'Grieg's Patent' narrow gauge track — 41, **50**
Griggs Green (GGN) — 288, **289, 396, 518**
Guard Room — 116, **119,** 538
Gun Trucks (9.2-inch) World War Two — **743, 744**
Gypsy Hollow (GHW) — 287-8, 516

H

Hampshire (0-6-0ST) — **71,** 73, 617, **618-9**
'Hassan', play by James Elroy Flecker — 397, 702
HM Inspectorate of Railways — 13, 779
Heifers Down (HFD) — 287-8, **353**
Hogmoor Pond (HGM) — **128-30,** 240, **241**
   track layout (1934) — 213

Hollywater Loop 287-91, 385
    Brimstone sand siding (BSS) 287-8
    'Chinaman Siding' 287
    completion in 1942 492
    Griggs Green (GGN) **289, 518**
    Gypsy Hollow Siding (GHW) 287-8
    Hollywater (HWR) **289-90**
    Hopkins Bridge and Sidings 291
    No. 1 Circle 287-8
    operating arrangements 536, 538
    Waterloo Bridge sidings 287-8
Hopkins (Col late RE) (bridge designer) 71
Hopkins Bridge (location) (HBG) 71, **131**, 291, **359**
Hopkins Bridge (structures) **133, 135-7, 152, 356-7, 359**
Hut-shifting (Longmoor to Bordon etc) 41, 42, **43-7**

I

Infantry Battalions
    1st Bn Argyll & Sutherland Highlanders 38, **39**
    2nd Bn Wiltshire Regt 38
    8th (City of London) Bn Rifle Brigade **72**
Inland Water Transport Service (IWT) 80
    formation of SR units 180
    move to Marchwood 403
    World War Two development 336
Inspector General of Fortifications (IGF) 75
Instructional Model Railway 71, **121-6, 482-3**
Internal combustion locos
    Manning, Wardle (World War One) 688
    Drewry/Baguley 0-4-0 DM 688-9
    WD 29 **689**
    WD 72220 (Victory parade) **690**
International Peace Conference, Versailles (1919) 95

J

Johnson R. M. (Capt RA) 78
Joly de Lotbinière, (Lt-Col/Brig) H. A. 336, 340, **354**

K

Kay J. A.(*Railway Gazette*) 116, 432
Kelbus re-railing equipment **378**
Kingsley (4-4-0T) **156, 191, 625-6**
Kingsley viaduct 366, **368-9**
Kirke E. St. G. (Capt/Maj) 100, **156**
Kitchener [1] (0-6-2T) **130**, 630, **631**
Kitchener [2] (0-6-2T) **150, 341, 343-4, 389-90, 429, 637-8**
Kitchener [3] *see* 'Austerity' above
'Kitchener Coach' (ex-S&BR) **22, 23**
Kitchener H. H. (FM Lord) 29, 83, 632

L

Land Ship
    s.s. Apple Pie **180-1**
Land Transport Corps (1855) 12
Langley C. A. (Capt/Brig) **100, 156**, 432
Lawson H. M. (Brig-Gen) 75
Level crossing review (1955) 514
Linchborough Bridge **358**
Liphook
    2 ESD **337**
Liphook Road, Longmoor **34**

Liss Exchange Sidings (LSJ)
    alterations to connections **367**, 495, 532-3
    exchange traffic **306, 308, 586-7**
    signalling diagrams (1943, 1966) 495
    track plans 307
Liss Extension 292-315
    Bridges No's 1 to 6 **159, 160-2, 164-5**
    construction 126, 217
    excavating cuttings **162**
    improvements (World War Two) 493-6
    operating methods 217-8
Liss Forest Road (LFR) **299-305, 530-1**
    construction (1930-32) **158-9**
    derailments **361-3, 591-2**
    improvements (1941) **360**, 493, **494**
    signal box **300, 302-3, 530**
    signalling diagrams (1941, 1949, 1968) 493-4, 531
    track plans (1933, 1940) 217, 299
Liss Station (LSS) **309-15**
    collapse of embankment **167**
    connection to SRly 496, 532
    construction **166**
    platform (extended) **312, 527, 533-4**
    signalling diagram (c.1943) 496
    track plan (1941) 217
    water column **314**
Liss Historic Transport Centre 608
Liss Station (SRly)
    general views **585-6**
    LMR ground frame diagram 532-3
Liverpool & Manchester Railway (L&MR) 11
Lloyd George (David) 83
Loading ramps (for AFVs etc.) **174, 379**
Locomotive and wagon load table (LMR) 517
Locomotive Magazine (1930) 113
London & North Eastern Railway
    Loaned locomotives (WW2) **639**
    7054 **373**
    7056 **361-4, 640**
    7088 **333-4, 373**
    7167 ('A.B.F. 7167' – A Poem) 367
    7344 **392**
    7362 **372, 639**
    WD 83 **390**
    WD 89 **639**
    WD 91 **342, 639**
London & North Western Railway
    locomotive *Earl Haig* (2-4-2T) **183, 633-4**
    locomotive *Earl Roberts* (2-4-2T) **168, 185, 633-4**
    officers' saloon (ex-MMR) **568, 745, 803**
London & South Western Railway
    0-4-2 Class 'A12' 644
    638 **245, 374-5, 644**
    625 **273, 392, 644**
    614 **300**
    618 **391, 644**
    0-4-4T Class 'O2' (SRly 213) **245, 365, 374, 387, 646**
    4-4-2T Adams Radial Tank (ex-L&SWR 424) **86, 622, 623**
    Bentley to Bordon branch 222
    Boer War ambulance coaches (for RVH Netley) 740, **742**
    Bordon Station views **231**

family saloon (WD 119) **724-5, 804**
World War Two ambulance coaches **315, 447, 740-1**
'Queen Adelaide' coach **753**
London Brighton & South Coast Railway
  4-4-2T Class 'I'
    WD 2401 **226, 296, 374, 377, 642-4**
    WD 2400 (*Earl Roberts* [2]) **301, 333, 375**, 642-4
  0-4-2T Class 'D1'
    2233 **248, 645**
    2240 **334, 385-7**
    2286 **364, 645**
  0-6-0T 'Terrier' Class (on loan) 623
  Sir William Forbes (General Manager) 78,80
London Midland & Scottish Railway
  Loaned steam locos (WW2) 642
  School (Derby) 114, 331
  Stanier 8F 2-8-0 locos 662-5, **456-7**
    WD 500 **662**
    WD 501 **663, 665**
    WD 508 **663**
    WD 511 **662**
    WD 512 **456-7, 520-1, 524, 663**
    at work 456, **457**, 459
    on bridging trials **412**
  350hp diesel electric locos 691-3
    LMS 7058 (on loan) **691**
    LMS 7098 (on loan) **692**
    WD 876 (*Bari* [2]) **576-7, 686, 693, 789**
    WD 878 (*Basra* [2]) **230, 454, 576, 693-4**
    WD 883 **691**
Longmoor (0-4-4T) **73, 85, 619, 620**
Longmoor Camp
  achievements during World War Two 353
  Army Elementary School 99
  entertainment during war years 396-7
  guardroom 116, **119**
  headquarters building 116-7, **118**
  officers' messes 116, **119, 120**
  panoramic views (1910) **58-9**
  St. Martin's Church **115**, 116
  sergeants' mess 116, **120**
  Seymour Hall 115
  Signalling School 121, **121-6**
  site plans (1908 and 1930) 52, 117
  Transportation Museum **118**, 584, 593, **755**
Longmoor Downs (LMD) 260-74
  block post **370, 501-7**
  double wire signalling (1930) 209-10, **501-2**
  general air photos **260, 263**
  level crossings **273-4**
  new lever frame (1951) 501, **504-6, 539**
  signals 210, **270-2**
  signalling plan (1941) 492
  signalling plan (1968) 501
  station views **269-74**
  track plan (1945) 261
  West platform **84**, 85, 200
Longmoor Military Railway (LMR)
  1956 Re-numbering 827-33
  additional facilities (World War Two) 489
  alignments WHL to LMD 81

closure ceremony 603, **607-9**
creation (1935) 182
demolition of railway 610-1
duty roster (1958) 542
engine diagram 1944 338
location map 9
Longmoor WETC 611
mile posts **231**
new signals (1930) 210
operating exercises 186
Peace Establishment (1945) 652
route map & gradient profile 220
single line tokens & staffs **499, 500, 529, 530, 539**
structure and loading gauge 544
summary of Steam Locos 818-9
summary of I/C Locos 820
summary of Rail Cars 821
summary of Stock 1943-1956 822-6
timetables
  passenger timetable (1946) 540
    (1965) 541
trackside signage **230-1, 256**
traffic control office **525**
traffic statistics World War Two 337
traffic summary (LMR to ports) 1944 545-53
train graph **814-5, 816-7**
token working diagram (1940) 496
  (1959) 528
Longmoor West
  block post 212, 260
Longmoor Workshops
  trainees etc. at work **79, 381-2, 477-80**
Longmoor Yard 275-86
  air photographs **275, 277**
  coaling stage (old) **280**
    (new) **285, 465**
  diagram of signals (1922) 200
  Diesel Fitters' School **282-3, 583**
  Locomotive sheds **283, 464, 477**
  Mobilisation Store **281**
  No. 6 Bridge **153-5, 284, 417, 455**
  track plan (as at closure) 276
Louisburg (LBG) **232-3**
  track plan (1933) 232
Low, Gavin (Lt/Lt-Col) 96
Lucas & Aird (contractors for S&BR) 18

M

Mance (Lt/Brig-Gen) Sir Osbert 75, 95, 96
Manning, Wardle – 'K' Class locomotives 19, **21**
Manton L. (Lt-Col/Brig) 113-4, 331,
Marching Allowance 11
Marlborough (0-6-2T) **155, 189, 334, 342, 393, 634, 635-6**
Mars (0-4-2T) 49, **53, 55, 98, 612**, 613, **708**
McCallum D. C. (Col) 15, 16
McLeod Committee 421
McMullen (2-8-0) see 'Austerity' above.
McMullen (Colonel) Dennis 779-80
McMullen (Lt-Col/Maj-Gen) Sir Donald 186, 657
Mediterranean Lines of Communication (MEDLOC) 88
Meyrick T. (WO2, QMSI) 123

Military Aid to the Civil Community (MACC) 784
Military Camp Railways (MCR) 83,89,96
named locos listed individually
MCR 94/95 **627**
MCR 100–102 (ex- Rhymney Rly) **628**
Military Forwarding Directorate (MFD) 80
Military Railways Rule Book (MRRB)
origins 215
flagboard signalling 216
use in training 376
Military Tramways Acts (1871, 1887) 60
Military Works Acts (1897 & 1899) 38
Ministry of Munitions 33, 83-4
Mobile Refrigeration Unit **349-50**, 351-2
Mobilisation
1914 75-77
1939 197
Monmouth (MCR 86) (0-6-0T) **624**
Movement Control
BEF deployment 1914 78
exercises at Longmoor **170-3**
Manton proposals 113
origins 78
Technical Training & Depot Bn 339

N

Napier (FM Lord) of Magdala 16
Narrow-gauge locomotives
steam (18-inch gauge) 49, 613
Mars [1] **53, 55, 612**
Venus [1] **614**
Flamingo **55**, 613
WD 3239/4530 Hunslet 4-6-0T **384, 708-9**
internal combustion World War One 687, **687-8**
75cm gauge (ex-Wehrmacht) 698, 432-4
Venus[2] 699
National Service 403, 420, 423, 443
Neale's electric tablet 536
Nicholson (Gen Sir William) 38
No Road
construction of trestle bridge **194-6**
failure of **380-1**
location views **258-9**
TSD track plan 259
No. 1 Railway Training Centre 335
Establishment Inspection (1942) 339
No. 1 Transportation Stores Depot (RE) 336, 395-6
No. 2 Military Port (Cairnryan) 336, 664
No. 2 Railway Training Centre 114, 331, 336
North British Locomotive Co. Ltd
275hp diesel locomotives 409, 700
WD 8200 **700-1, 800**
WD 8205 (*Matruh*) **579, 581, 701**
AD 412 **701, 800-1**

O

Oakhanger (OKR) 232-40
level crossing 60, **77, 234, 236, 239**, 488, 513-4
station plans and sidings 213, 232 ,240, 491, 513
platform **232, 235-7**

signal box **232, 235-6**
World War Two developments 491
Martinique Sidings 491
further alterations 514, 534
Oil-fuel apparatus for WD locomotives 555-64, **554, 560-4**
'One Engine in Steam' keys
system in 1938 218-9
Open Days
1947 Public Day 432
Final Open Day 598, 602-3, 607, **599-606**

P

Palmer's Ball Sidings (PBS) **298**, 497
Collision 13 Oct 1956 519-25, **520-4**
Pasley C. W. (Lt-Col) 13
Permanent Way Exhibit 414, **415-6**
Peto, Brassey & Betts (contractors) 12
Public Days *see* Open Days
Pyramus (MCR 85) (0-6-2T) 623, 624

Q

'Queen Anne's Oak' 255

R

Radio Control (of rail traffic) **169**
Rail cars
Drewry No. 1 704
Drewry No. 2 (WD 9111) **190, 229, 448, 570, 705-6**
Wickham Car WD 9110 **228-9, 570-1, 798**
Wickham Car AD 9033 **571, 707**
Wickham Car WD 9034 **262, 572, 707, 812**
Rail Wreckers
ex-German World War One 87
'Gordon Anstey' pattern (1917) **88**
ex-German World War Two **755**
Railway Bridging School 432, **481**
Railway Companies RE (Regular Army)
8th **17, 31**, 75, 77, 100, **127**, 182, 519, 567
10th 19, 100, 101, **128-30**, 417, 768
53rd 41
Railway Construction Corps (RCC) 78
Railway Construction Troops Depot (RCTD[RE]) 83
Railway Correspondence & Travel Society (RCTS) 1966 tours
584, **585-8**
Railway Executive Committee 37
Railway Troops Sub-committee 80
RECTANK wagons **720**
Railway Operating Division (ROD) 78, 95
Railway Squadrons RE (Regular Army)
Coys re-designated as squadrons 416
Railway Staff Officers (RSO) 75
Railway Transport Establishment (RTE) 78
Railway Traffic Officers (RTO) 75
Railway Training Centres
No. 1 RTC (RE) (Longmoor)
World War Two statistics 353
technical training (officers) 355-6, 543-4
(soldiers) 371
technical projects **356-9**
No. 2 RTC (RE) (Derby and Melbourne) 331

Ramp Wagons
    redesign (1938) — 197
    in use at — **484, 750**
Ratledge W. (Spr/Maj) — 96
Rawlinson (General Sir Henry) — 96
Redman A.S. (Lt/Lt-Col) — 96, 97
Roads & Railways Technical Training Centre (RRTTC) — 84
Robins J. A. (Capt/Maj) — 124, 455
Rolling stock
    pre-1940, passenger and freight stock — 711-25
    30-ton Leeds Forge wagons — **711-2**
    ex-K&ESR Pickering coaches (110 and 111) — 72, **85-6, 110,**
    168, 185-6, 290, 310, 713-4, **715**
      World War One hired coaches — **716,** 717
      ex-NLR ambulance train — 716, **717**
      ex-GWR MACAW — **717**
      low-side wagons for spoil — **721, 732**
      ex-ROD compressor van — **722**
      ex-SE&CR saloon (118) — **723-4**
      ex-L&SWR saloon (119) — **724-5**
      goods brake vans (various) — **725-8**
      ex-L&SWR van (welders') — **728**
      covered vans (various) — **729-31**
      cistern (tank) wagons — 732, 741, 746
    1940–45 passenger and freight stock — 725, 733-47
      ex-Caley coaches — 733-4, **734-6**
      ex-SE&CR birdcage set — **737-8**
      ex-LMS ambulance coaches — **739**
      weed-killing train — **747**
    1945-70 Rolling stock — 748
      brake vans — **748-9**
      ballast hoppers — **750**
      WD ramp wagon — **750**
      WARFLATS — **750-1**
      WARWELL — **751**
      TCRW — **413, 751-2**
      ex-BR non-corridor coaches — **753**
Rolls Royce/Sentinel 0-8-0 DH — 703
    AD 890/610 *General Lord Robertson* — **236, 241, 269, 315,**
    578, 703, 797, 802-3
Royal Artillery
    Medium Brigade at Longmoor — 170
Royal Engineers' Board — 96
Royal Corps of Transport
    formation of (1965) — 567
    unit titles etc. — 569
    411 Rly Optg Tp — 569
Royal Monmouthshire RE (Militia) — 37, 38, 63, 99
Royal Visit to Longmoor (1928) — **110**
Russell W. H. (war correspondent) — 12
Ruston & Hornsby 0-6-0 D/H
    WD 8227 (*Hassan*) — **251, 702, 798-9, 802**
    AD 8219/425 — **702, 799, 801**
Ruston tracked 'steam navvy' — **146, 156-8, 162, 761**

S

Salisbury (0-6-0T) — **100,** 626-7
'Scenic Railway' (1916) — 91, **262**
School of Military Engineering (SME) — 13, 17
School of Transport (RCT) — 569
Scott D. A. (Maj/Maj-Gen) — 18, 37

Selborne (0-6-0T) — 97, **132, 159, 186, 191, 242, 310,**
388, 398-9, 400, 628, **629-30**
Sentinel D/H 0-4-0 on trial — **699**
Shepherd, David (Artist) — 584, 593, 598, **777**
Siege Park — 41, 49, 613
Signalling methods 1905-20 — 199
    enhancements from 1922 — 199-201
Simmons (FM) Sir Linthorn — 37
Simson I. (Capt) — **100,** 101, 156
Sinclair H. M. (Colonel) — 80, **93**
Single line token instruments
    Electric Train Staff/METS — **211**
    No. 5 Tablet instrument — **122, 214**
    frame release keys — **500, 512**
    train staffs & tokens — **499, 500, 529, 530**
Sir John French (0-6-2T) — 76, **86, 140, 188-9, 268, 389, 620,** 621-2
South Eastern & Chatham Railway
    0-6-0 Class 'O1' WD 1046 — **247, 298, 341,** 645
    'Birdcage' 3-coach set — 371, **408, 419, 427-8, 737-8**
Southern Railway
    Armoured Fighting Vehicle Train — **295-6, 344**
    loaned locos (World War Two) *see* entries under pre-group
    constituent railways
Staff College, Camberley
    military railway instruction — 170
    demonstrations — **176-8**
Stevenson A. G. (Capt/Maj-Gen) — 36, 93, 96
Stokes Bay (RE) Light Railway
    ex-WDLR loco WD 3239 — **182, 708-9**
Strikes (General)
    1921 — 96
    1926 — 101
Suakin campaign (1884/5) — 18, **19-23**
    dump (at Woolwich) — 19
    signal equipment re-used — 198
Sudan
    River Nile routes map — 18
    military railways (North Sudan) — 29
Supplementary Reserve
    formation of — 97, 99
    programme for 1935 — 141
    publicity — 169
    IWT units formed — 180
    further expansion — 190
    mobilisation (1939) — 197

T

Taff Vale Railway
    ex-TVR Brake vans — **163, 537, 727**
    ex-TVR Locomotives *see* entries by name.
Talyllyn Railway
    restoration — 779, **780-1**
    method of signalling — 780, 782
Tank Carrying Rail Wagon (TCRW) — 413-4, **413,** 751-2
Technical Policy Wing
    creation — 404
    projects — 409, 413-4, 416
Telephone and Ticket working — 497-8, **498-9**
Telephones Troop (R Signals) — 121
Territorial & Volunteer Reserve (TAVR) — 584
Thisbe (0-6-2T) — **90,** 623, **624**

Thomas Heywood & Sons Ltd lever frame **237**, 514
Track Laying Machine 101, **102-9, 762**
Transportation Training Centre (RE), TnTC
  new title 399
  technical training 403
  re-organisation 416, 418-9
  badge **805**
  'Transportation Centre Charter' (1960) 419, 420
Trades training
  19th century origins 13
  first training of military railwaymen 17
  trainees on civilian railways 72
  introduction of new techniques 97
  during World War Two 371, 376, 379
  post-war re-start 403
  training in the National Service era 443
  changes in 1965 575
Travers Martin (designer) 116
Twiss J. H. (Maj/Brig-Gen) 36, 77, 83
Two Range Halt (2RG later TRH) and Woolmer (WMR)
  192-3, 251-8, **252-7**
  signalling diagrams (1941, 1943, 1963) 490, 511
Tyrrell W. G. (Lt/Brig) **48, 100**, 145, 219
  as Commandant 335

U
Union Internationale des Chemins de Fer (UIC) 95
Upnor & Chattenden Railway
  transfer to Admiralty control (1906) 36, **198**
US Army Transportation Corps
  755th Railway Shops Bn 116, 353
  763rd Railway Shops Bn 116
USATC locomotives 385, 648, 657, 659
  0-6-0T
    WD 1255 **255, 345, 650**
    WD 1286 **330, 650**
    WD 1417 & 1419 **346**
    WD 1954 **651**
    WD 94382 (*Major General Frank. S. Ross.*) 431, 537, 659, 792
  2-8-0 Class 'S160'
    WD 94382 (*Major General Carl. R. Gray Jr.*) **422, 424, 430, 437, 458, 658, 791**
    WD 2292 **348, 651**
  650HP Whitcomb DE Bo-Bo
    WD 71232/890 (*Tobruk*) **436, 452-3, 695-6, 792**
    WD 71233 (*Algiers*) **696**

V
Vesey C.E.G. (Lt-Col) 96
Victory Parade (1945) 423
Volunteers
  2nd Cheshire (Engineer) 37-8
  Royal Monmouthshire RE (V) 38, 63, 73, 615

W
Wakeford J. C. B. (Maj) 124
Walker (Col Sir Herbert) 169
War Department Light Railways (WDLR) 91
War Department Standard Locomotives (1941-45) 646, 648-9
War surplus equipment (1945) 399
Waterloo Bridge Sidings 287, 288, 448

Weavers Down Junction (WDJ) 293-7
  track layout (1934, 1945, 1949) 218, 294-5, 493, 508
  air photograph **293**
  signal box **295-6**
  mortar range 492
'Weaversdown Light Railway' 432-435
Westminster (MCR) (0-6-0ST) 626
White, Gilbert (of Selborne) 6
Whitehill (WHL) 242-50
  level crossing **46, 50**, 62
  crossroads (diagram) 63
  excavation for road bridge 64-9
  police station 43, 70
  proposed passing loop (1914) 199
  signal cabins 201, **248-9**
  cuttings and bridge 63, **241-2**
  signal diagrams (1941, 1949, 1953) 508-9
  track plans (1923, 1934, 1933) 201, 213, 243
  station views **243-9**
  Sub-Depot (TSD West) (1945) 250
  re-signalled (1965/6) 538
Wickham rail cars 705-7
  WD 931/9110 **228-9, 236, 706, 798**
  trollies (WW2) 701, 707
  WD 9033 **707**
  AD 9034 **262, 707, 812**
Willis A. A. (Lt) *see* 'A. A.'
Woodhouse E. (Lt/Lt-Col)
  section comd and O i/c Workshops 71, 77, 96-7, 113, 116
  appointed Commandant RTC(RE) 111
  report on WIMR (1930) 207-8
Woolmer (0-6-0ST) 73, **438**, 615, **616-7, 813**
Woolmer (WMR) 251-257
  Advanced Transportation Stores Depot **193**
  development of yard 207
  platform 251,253
  signal cabin **255**
  signalling diagrams (1941, 1952) 491, 511
  track plans (1930, 1935, 1945, 1943, 1965) 207, 250, 253, 491, 257
  doubling main line 207, 257
  marshalling yard 489, 491, **574**
Woolmer Instructional Military Railway
  locomotives – *see* individual names
  naming of the line 72
  track plan, WHL to LMD (1914-38) 81
  operating methods 1922/25 201/203
  Improvements at Bordon 203/206
  method of working (1930) 208
  alternative systems of token working 212
  Working Timetable - Summer 1932 317
  ditto - from WIMR Service Book 1934 318/9
  Passenger Timetable - 1932 317
  rolling stock list - 1934 321
  standing orders 1913 316
  'Service Book', publication 215
    extracts from 320
  'Telephone and Line Clear Message' working 214

X, Y, Z
Young Officer (YO) Training 448
'Young Winston' – film 610, 769, **777**